BARRON'S

HOW TO PREPARE FOR THE

AP®

COMPUTER SCIENCE
ADVANCED PLACEMENT EXAMINATION

Roselyn Teukolsky
Ithaca High School

BARRON'S

AP and Advanced Placement Program are registered trademarks of the College Entrance Examination Board,
which was not involved with the production of and does not endorse this book.

© Copyright 2001 by Barron's Educational Series, Inc.

All rights reserved.

No part of this book may be reproduced in
any form, by photostat, microfilm, xerography,
or any other means, or incorporated into any
information retrieval system, electronic or
mechanical, without the written permission
of the copyright owner.

All inquiries should be addressed to:
Barron's Educational Series, Inc.
250 Wireless Boulevard
Hauppauge, New York 11788
http://www.barronseduc.com

International Standard Book No.: 0-7641-0546-9

Library of Congress Catalog Card No.: 00-049816

Library of Congress Cataloging-in-Publication Data
Teukolsky, Roselyn.
    How to prepare for the AP computer science examination : advanced placement
    examination / by Roselyn Teukolsky.
        p. cm.
    Includes index.
    ISBN 0-7641-0546-9
        1. Computer science–Examinations, questions, etc.
    [1.Computer science–Exminations–Study guides.
    2. Advanced placement programs (Education)]
    I. Title

    QA76.28 .T48 2001
    004'.076–dc21   00-049816

PRINTED IN THE UNITED STATES OF AMERICA
9 8 7 6 5 4

Contents

Preface

This book is aimed at students reviewing for the AP Computer Science Exam. It would normally be used at the completion of an AP course. However, it contains a complete summary of all topics for both Level A and AB exams, and it can be used for self-study if accompanied by a suitable textbook.

The book provides a review of programming, algorithm analysis, and data structures. It can therefore be used as a supplement to first-year college courses where C++ is the programming language, and as a resource for teachers of high school and introductory college courses.

Each review chapter is followed by AP exam-style multiple-choice questions with detailed explanations of the answers.

There is a similarly thorough review of the Marine Biology Case Study.

There are four complete practice exams, two Level A and two Level AB. The exams follow the format of the AP exam, with multiple-choice and free-response sections. Detailed solutions with explanations are provided. There is no overlap of questions between the exams.

Acknowledgments

I owe thanks to many people who helped in the creation of this book.

My 1999–2000 AP Computer Science class at Ithaca High School, who used the first draft of the book to review for the AP exam, will be remembered with fondness. Not only were they unflagging in their quest for finding errors, they were unstinting in offering advice and helpful suggestions.

I have much love and gratitude for my students Matthew Concia, Kevin Egan, and Matthew Wachs, who painstakingly combed through the manuscript looking for errors. They all made wise and wonderful suggestions for improvement. A special thank-you to Mark Stehlik for the care he took in reading the manuscript. His comments were invaluable. Thanks to Sarah Fix and Reg Hahne for feedback on both the text and accompanying questions. And thanks to Ari Rabkin for help in checking the practice exams.

I am grateful to my project editor, Wendy Sleppin of Barron's, for her friendly guidance and moral support throughout this project. I also thank Melody Covington, who did a great job typesetting the book; Sara Black for her painstaking copy editing; Dave Bock for the recommendation to Barron's, and Grace Freedson for encouraging me at the start.

I am grateful to Steven Andrianoff and David Levine of St. Bonaventure University, New York, for their excellent workshop on the Marine Biology Case Study.

The following people contributed (some without their knowledge!) with their advice, materials, textbooks, and expertise: Owen Astrachan, Alyce Brady, Severin Drix, Richard Kick, Joe Kmoch, Ken Lambert, Chris Nevison, and Mark Weiss.

My husband, Saul, has been my partner in this project—typing the manuscript, producing the figures, and giving advice and moral support every step of the way. Without his help I could not—at the very least—have made the deadline!

Roselyn Teukolsky
Ithaca, NY
September 2000

Introduction

Computer Science: The boring art
of coping with a large number of trivialities.
—*Stan Kelly-Bootle,* The Devil's DP Dictionary *(1981)*

General Information about the Exam

The AP Computer Science Exam is a three-hour written exam. No books, calculators, or computers are allowed! The exam consists of two parts that have equal weight:

- Section I: 40 multiple-choice questions in 1 hour and 15 minutes.

- Section II: 4 free-response questions in 1 hour and 45 minutes.

Section I is scored by machine—you will blip your answers with a pencil on a mark-sense sheet. Each question correctly answered is worth 1 point, while incorrect answers get $\frac{1}{4}$ of a point deducted; a question left blank is ignored.

Section II is scored by human readers—you will write your answers in a booklet provided. Free response questions typically involve writing functions in C++ to solve a given problem. Sometimes there are questions analyzing algorithms or designing and modifying data structures. To ensure consistency in the grading, each grader follows the same rubric, and each of your four answers may be examined by more than one reader. Each question is worth 9 points, with partial credit awarded where applicable. Your name and school are hidden from the readers.

Your raw score for both sections is converted to an integer score from 1 to 5, where 1 represents "Not at all qualified" and 5 represents "Extremely well qualified." Be aware that the awarding of AP credit varies enormously from college to college.

The exam can be taken at two levels: Level A covers roughly a one-semester introductory college course, while Level AB covers roughly a two-semester course, including data structures. In terms of getting credit at colleges, it makes more sense to get a 4 or 5 on the Level A exam than a 2 or 3 on the Level AB exam.

The language of the AP exam is currently C++. Only a subset of C++ will be tested on the exam. For a complete description of this subset, see the College Board web site at *http://www.collegeboard.org/ap/computer-science/*. **Every language topic in this review book is part of the C++ subset unless explicitly stated otherwise. Note that the entire subset is covered in the book.**

At least one free-response and five multiple-choice questions will be based on the Marine Biology Case Study. The full text of the case study can be found at the College Board web site.

At the exam, you will be given copies of the case study code. You will also be provided with copies of the AP class header files `apstring.h`, `apvector.h`, `apmatrix.h`, `apstack.h`, and `apqueue.h`. All these files are available at the College Board web site.

Hints for Taking the Exam

The Multiple-Choice Section

- Since $\frac{1}{4}$ of a point is deducted for each wrong answer, don't guess unless you can eliminate at least two choices.

- You have a little less than two minutes per question, so don't waste time on any given question. You can always come back to it if you have time at the end.

- Seemingly complicated array questions can often be solved by hand tracing the code with a small array, two or three elements. The same is true for other data structures such as matrices, stacks, queues, or linked lists.

- Many questions ask you to compare two pieces of code that supposedly implement the same algorithm. Often one program segment will fail because it doesn't handle endpoint conditions properly (e.g., `num == 0` or `list == NULL`). *Be aware of endpoint conditions throughout the exam.*

- Since the mark-sense sheet is scanned by machine, make sure that you erase completely if you change an answer.

The Free-Response Section

- Each free-response question is worth 9 points. Take a minute to read through the whole exam so that you can start with a question that you feel confident about. It gives you a psychological leg up to have a solid question in the bag.

- Don't omit a question just because you can't come up with a complete solution. Remember, partial credit is awarded. Also, if you can't do part (a) of a question, don't omit part (b)—they are graded independently.

- Often part (b) of a question says, "You may want to use function `Blurf`" (the function that was written in part a). Use it! Chances are it's the route to the best solution.

- If an algorithm is suggested to solve a problem, just follow it. Don't reinvent the wheel.

- Don't waste time writing comments: the graders generally ignore them. The occasional brief comment that clarifies a segment of code is OK.

- Points are not deducted for inefficient code unless efficiency is an issue in the question. So remember, brute-force code that works is preferable to elegant code that does not.

- Most of the standard C and C++ library functions are not included in the AP subset. They are accepted on the exam if you use them correctly. However, there is always an alternative solution, and you should try to find it.

- Don't cross out an answer until you have written a replacement. Graders are instructed not to mark anything crossed out, even if it would have gotten credit.

- Have some awareness that this section is graded by humans. It is in your interest to have the graders understand your solutions. With this in mind,

  - Use a sharp pencil, write legibly, space your answers, and indent correctly.
  - Use self-documenting names for variables, functions, etc.
  - Use the identifiers that are given in a question. You will lose a usage point if you persist in using the wrong names.
  - Write clear readable code. This is your goal. Don't write one obscure convoluted statement when you can write two short clear statements. The APCS exam is not the place to demonstrate that you're a genius.

How to Use This Book

Each chapter in the book contains a comprehensive review of a topic, multiple-choice questions that focus on the topic, and detailed explanations of answers.

In both the text and questions/explanations, a special code font is used for parts of the text that are C++ code.

```
//This is an example of code font
```

A different font is used for pseudo-code.

```
<Here is pseudo-code font>
```

Sections in the text and multiple-choice questions that are directed at Level AB only are clearly marked as such. Unmarked text and questions are suitable for both Levels A and AB. Chapters 8–10 are for level AB only. This is stated on the first page of each of these chapters.

Following the review chapters are four practice exams with complete solutions, two for each level. There is no overlap in the questions, so Level AB students can use the Level A exams for additional practice. Some questions in the Level AB exams are also fair game for Level A students. These are clearly marked as such.

Each practice exam contains five multiple-choice questions and one free-response question on the Marine Biology Case Study.

There are three appendices at the end of the book:

- Appendix A is a glossary of computer terms that occasionally crop up on the exam.

- Appendix B is the ASCII table.

- Appendix C is a pointer implementation of `apstack` and `apqueue`. This is *not* part of the AP Committee materials. (See Chapter 9.)

A final hint about the book: Try the questions before you peek at the answers. Good luck!

CHAPTER ONE

Introductory C++ Language Features

One of the main causes of the fall of the Roman Empire was that,
lacking zero, they had no way to indicate successful termination
of their C programs.
— Robert Firth

The AP Computer Science course is about algorithm analysis, data structures, and the techniques and methods of modern programming. A high-level programming language is used to explore these concepts. C++ is the language currently in use on the AP exam.

C++, a widely used programming language and superset of C, was developed by Bjarne Stroustrup; it continues to evolve. The AP exam covers a clearly defined subset of C++ language features that are presented throughout this book. (The College Board web site, *http://www.collegeboard.org/ap/computer-science/*, contains a complete listing of this subset.)

C++ has fundamental built-in data types and allows for complex, user-defined types. It provides basic control structures such as the `if-else` statement, `for` loop, `while` loop, and `do...while` loop. C++ supports object-oriented programming. The AP course lays the foundation for object-oriented programming, while leaving the more sophisticated features for a later course.

Modules, Header Files, and Libraries

A cornerstone of C++ philosophy is the use of modularity in programming. A *module* is a set of related functions with the data they manipulate. Each module has its own type declarations, variables, constants, and so on. A C++ user-defined class is an example of a module.

Other modules that a C++ programmer can use are provided by the many standard C++ libraries, such as `iostream` and `fstream`. A *library* is a collection of related functions. Standard C libraries such as `stdlib`, `ctype`, and `math` are also available in C++.

Modules are transportable pieces of code whose interfaces can be included in a program via a header file with a `.h` suffix.

Here is the format of a typical C++ program.

```
#include <iostream.h>        //library for standard stream I/O
#include <fstream.h>         //library for file manipulation
```

```
        . . .
#include "apstring.h"        //interface of the apstring class
#include "apvector.h"        //interface of the apvector class
#include "myclass.h"         //interface of this user-defined class
        . . .
type1 f1(parameter list);       //function declarations (called
type2 f2(parameter list);       //headers) go here
        . . .
int main()
{
    your code
    . . .
    return 0;
}
//Implementations of above functions f1, f2, ... go here
```

NOTE

1. Every C++ program must have a function named main(). The program starts by executing this function. The int value 0 returned by main() indicates successful completion of the program.
2. An alternative to the preceding structure is to omit the function prototypes and instead have complete definitions of the functions before main(). This should only be done in small programs.
3. To prevent header files from being included in a program more than once, *preprocessor directives* #ifndef, #define, and #endif are used for every header file. Typically a header file has this format:

```
#ifndef SOME_FILE
#define SOME_FILE
    function declarations
#endif
```

At compile time, the directive #ifndef instructs the preprocessor to check whether SOME_FILE has already been defined. If it hasn't, the preprocessor defines it and then proceeds to process the file; otherwise, it jumps to the #endif at the end of the file.

Types and Identifiers

An *identifier* is a name for a variable, parameter, constant, user-defined function, or user-defined data type. In C++ an identifier is any sequence of letters, digits, and the underscore character. Identifiers may not begin with a digit. Identifiers are case-sensitive, which means that age and Age are different. Wherever possible identifiers should be concise and self-documenting. A variable called area is more illuminating than one called a.

Reserved Words

Certain words, like const, break, switch, and enum, have special meaning in C++ and may not be used as identifiers. They are called *keywords* or *reserved words*.

Built-in Types

Every identifier in a C++ program has a type associated with it. The fundamental built-in types that are included in the APCS subset are

`int`	Integer. For example 2, –26, 3000
`char`	Character. For example, `'p'`, `'Q'`, `'4'`, `'?'`
`bool`	Boolean. Just two values, `true` or `false`
`double`	Double precision floating-point number. For example, 2.718, –367189.41, 1.6e4

Integer values are stored exactly. Because there's a fixed amount of memory set aside for their storage, however, integers are bounded. If you try to store a value whose magnitude is too big in an `int` variable, you'll get an *overflow error*.

An identifier is introduced into a C++ program with a *declaration* that specifies its type. Some examples follow:

```
int x;
double y,z;
bool found;
int count = 1;           //count initialized to 1
char ch = 'a';           //ch initialized to 'a'
int i=1, j=2, k=3;       //i,j,k initialized to 1, 2, 3
                         //respectively
double p(2.3), q(4.1);   //p and q initialized to 2.3 and 4.1
```

One type can be cast to another compatible type if appropriate. For example,

```
int total, n;
double average;
    ...
average = double(total)/n;  //total cast to double to ensure
                            //real division is used
```

Alternatively,

```
average = total/double(n);
```

typedef

Data types can be renamed using the keyword `typedef`. This is useful, but won't be tested on the AP exam. Typically, `typedef` is used to provide a meaningful name for a built-in type. For example, in a program that deals with amounts of money:

```
typedef double money;
    ...
int main()
{
    money cost, amtPaid, change;
        ...
}
```

Here `money` is synonymous with `double`. The variables `cost`, `amtPaid`, and `change` are declared to be of type `money` (i.e., double).

`typedef` is also used as a shorthand for a type with a long, unwieldy name. For example,

```
typedef apvector <apstring> wordList;
wordList vocab;      //vocab declared to be apvector of
                     // apstrings
```

Note that `typedef` provides a synonym for an existing type, rather than creating a new distinct type.

Scope of Identifiers

The *scope* of an identifier is the part of the program in which the identifier can be used.

An identifier is *local* if it's declared in a function or class. Its scope extends from the point where it is declared to the end of the block in which its declaration occurs. A *block* is a piece of code enclosed in a {} pair.

An identifier is *global* if it is defined outside any function or class. The scope of a global identifier extends from its declaration to the end of the file in which the declaration occurs.

A name in a block takes precedence over the same enclosing global name. Avoid writing code that does this—not only is it bad style, but it also tends to cause errors!

Constants

A *user-defined constant*, identified by the keyword `const`, is used to name a quantity whose value will not change inside its scope. Some examples of `const` declarations follow:

```
const double TAX_RATE = 0.08;
const int CLASS_SIZE = 35;
const char BLANK = ' ';
const apstring REFRAIN = "Whoop de doo!";
```

NOTE
1. `const` identifiers are often, by convention, capitalized.
2. Because constants cannot be assigned to, they must be initialized when they are declared.
3. A common use for a `const` is as an array bound. For example,

   ```
   const int MAX = 200;
   apvector <int> v(MAX);
   ```

4. Using constants makes it easier to revise code. Just a single change in the `const` declaration need be made, rather than having to change every occurrence of a value.

Enumerations

Syntax and Style

An *enumeration* is a user-defined type with a limited number of values. Its intent is to enhance readability of a program. For example,

```
enum Suit {CLUBS, DIAMONDS, HEARTS, SPADES};
```

Here `enum` is a keyword, `Suit` is an identifier, and `CLUBS`, `DIAMONDS`, `HEARTS`, and `SPADES` are integer constants called *enumerators*. An enumeration behaves much like an integer type. By default, the enumerators are assigned values starting at 0. Thus `CLUBS=0`, `DIAMONDS=1`, `HEARTS=2`, and `SPADES=3`. You can override the default by explicit assignment; for example,

```
enum Color {RED=1, WHITE, BLUE=4};
```

assigns RED=1, WHITE=2, and BLUE=4. In general, an omitted value gets the previous value +1.

1. The style of capitalizing enumerators emphasizes that they are constants. They must still, however, follow the rules for identifiers. Thus, the following is illegal:

```
enum Place {1ST, 2ND, 3RD};      //identifier may not start
                                 //with a digit.
```

2. Identifiers in the same scope must be unique. Thus, the following two declarations are separately legal but illegal if defined together:

```
enum Day {SUN, MON, TUES, WED, THUR, FRI, SAT};
enum HeavenlyBody {SUN, MOON, STAR};
//illegal - may not use SUN again
```

Use of Enumeration Types

1. Consider

```
enum Suit {CLUBS, DIAMONDS, HEARTS, SPADES};
Suit s1 = HEARTS, s2 = SPADES;
//assigns the value HEARTS to variable s1 and
//SPADES to s2
    ...
s2 = s1;    //legal, assigns the value HEARTS to s2
```

2. Relational operators can be applied to variables with enumeration type values since these types are ordered:

```
if (s1 < s2)    //legal. If s1 is HEARTS and s2 SPADES,
    ...         // returns true
```

3. Variables of an enumeration type can be used in a switch statement (see discussion of switch statement later in this chapter):

```
void f(Suit s)
{
    switch (s)
    {
        case CLUBS:
            DoSomething();
            break;
        case DIAMONDS:
            DoSomethingElse();
            break;
            ...
    }
}
```

4. Enumerations are not printed symbolically. Thus if s is of type Suit, cout << s; will print out the int value of s, 0, 1, 2, or 3, depending on whether s is CLUBS, DIAMONDS, HEARTS, or SPADES.

5. To increment an enumeration type variable, s++ or ++s or s += 1 are all illegal (unless the ++ or += operators have been explicitly overloaded; see Chapter 2). A cast must be used:

```
Suit s = CLUBS;
s = Suit(s+1);        //s now has the value DIAMONDS
```

Incrementing enumerators will not be tested on the AP exam. Since enumerators have integer values, you can use an enumeration type in a loop as follows:

```
for (int s = CLUBS; s <= SPADES; s++)
        . . .
```

Operators

Arithmetic Operators

Operator	Meaning	Example
+	addition	3+x
−	subtraction	p-q
*	multiplication	6*i
/	division	10/4 //returns 2, not 2.5!
%	mod (remainder)	11%8 //returns 3

NOTE

1. These operators, except mod, can be applied to any of types int, char, bool, or double, even if more than one type occurs in the same expression. Types char and bool are converted to int before the operation is applied. For an operation involving a double and an int, the int is promoted to double, and the result is a double.
2. The mod operator is used only with type int: a%b is the integer remainder when a is divided by b. Thus 10%3 evaluates to 1.
3. Integer division a/b where both a and b are of type int returns the integer quotient only (i.e., the answer is truncated). Thus 22/6 gives 3, and 3/4 gives 0. If at least one of the operands is of type double, then the operation becomes regular floating-point division, and there is no truncation. You can control the kind of division that is carried out by explicitly casting (one or both of) the operands from int to double and vice versa. Thus,

```
3.0/4          →      0.75
3/4.0          →      0.75
int(3.0)/4     →      0
double(3)/4    →      0.75
```

4. The division operator, /, is an example of an *overloaded operator*, one that performs different tasks depending on the types of the operands (see Chapter 2).
5. The arithmetic operators follow the normal precedence rules (order of operations):

    (1)   parentheses, from the inner ones out (highest precedence)
    (2)   *, /, %
    (3)   +, − (lowest precedence)

Here operators on the same line have the same precedence, and, in the absence of parentheses, are invoked from left to right. Thus the expression 19 % 5 * 3 + 14 / 5 evaluates to 4 * 3 + 2 = 14.

Relational Operators

Operator	Meaning	Example
==	equal to	if (x == 100)
!=	not equal to	if (response != "yes")
>	greater than	if (salary > 30000)
<	less than	if (grade < 65)
>=	greater than or equal to	if (age >= 16)
<=	less than or equal to	if (height <= 6)

NOTE

1. Relational operators are used in *boolean expressions* that evaluate to true or false. (false has a value of 0 and true has any nonzero value.)

```
bool x = (a != b);        //initializes x to true if a!=b, false
                          //otherwise
return p == q;            //returns true if p equals q, false
                          //otherwise
cout << (3 > 5);          //outputs 0 (false)
```

2. If the operands are of different types, the same conversions as for arithmetic operators are applied (Note 1 in the section on arithmetic operators).
3. Be careful when comparing floating-point values! Since floating-point numbers cannot always be represented exactly in the computer memory, they should not be compared directly using relational operators.

Comparing Floating-Point Numbers

Since floating-point numbers are manipulated and stored with a fixed number of significant digits, arithmetic operations generally produce results that must be rounded. This causes *round-off error*. One consequence is that you can't rely on using the == or != operators to compare two double values for equality. They may differ in their last significant digit or two because of round-off error. Instead you should test that the magnitude of the difference between the numbers is less than some number about the size of the machine precision. The machine precision is usually denoted ε, and is typically about 10^{-16} for double precision (i.e., about 16 decimal digits). So you would like to test something like $|x - y| < \varepsilon$. But this is no good if x and y are very large. For example, suppose $x = 1234567890.123456$ and $y = 1234567890.123457$. These numbers are essentially equal to machine precision, since they differ only in the 16th significant digit. But $|x - y| = 10^{-6}$, not 10^{-16}. Here you should check the *relative* difference:

$$\frac{|x - y|}{\min(|x|, |y|)} < \varepsilon$$

> But this test will fail for very small numbers, in particular if one of the numbers is zero. So the best general strategy is to test the relative difference unless the numbers are small ($< \varepsilon$ say), in which case you test the absolute difference, $|x - y| < \varepsilon$. Whew!

Logical Operators

Operator	Meaning	Example
!	NOT	if (!found)
&&	AND	if (x < 3 && y > 4)
||	OR	if (age < 2 || height < 4)

NOTE

1. Logical operators are applied to boolean expressions to form *compound boolean expressions* that evaluate to `true` or `false`.
2. Values of `true` or `false` are assigned according to the truth tables for the logical operators.

&&	T	F
T	T	F
F	F	F

||	T	F
T	T	T
F	T	F

!	
T	F
F	T

For example, F && T evaluates to F; T || F evaluates to T; !F evaluates to T.

3. *Short-circuit evaluation.* The subexpressions in a compound boolean expression are evaluated from left to right, and evaluation automatically stops as soon as the value of the entire expression is known. For example, consider a boolean OR expression of the form A || B, where A and B are some boolean expressions. If A is `true`, then the expression is `true` irrespective of the value of B. Similarly, if A is `false` then A && B evaluates to `false` irrespective of the second operand. So in each case the second operand is not evaluated. For example,

```
if (numScores != 0 && scoreTotal/numScores > 0.90)
```

will not cause a run-time division-by-zero error if `numScores` has a value of 0. This is because `numScores != 0` will evaluate to `false`, causing the entire boolean expression to evaluate to `false` without having to evaluate the second expression containing the division.

Assignment Operators

Operator	Example	Meaning
=	x = 2	simple assignment
+=	x += 4	x = x + 4
-=	y -= 6	y = y - 6
*=	p *= 5	p = p * 5
/=	n /= 10	n = n / 10
%=	n %= 10	n = n % 10

NOTE
1. All these operators, with the exception of simple assignment, are called *compound assignment operators.*
2. Left and right sides must be type compatible.
3. The left side of any assignment operator must be an *lvalue*. An lvalue (l stands for left) is an object that has a place in memory. Note that a variable is an lvalue that can be modified, while a constant is an lvalue that cannot be modified.
4. *Chaining* of assignment statements is allowed, with evaluation from right to left:

```
int next, prev, sum;
next = prev = sum = 0;   //initializes sum to 0, then prev to 0
                         //then next to 0
```

Increment and Decrement Operators

Operator	Example	Meaning
++	i++ or ++i	i is incremented by 1
--	k-- or --k	k is decremented by 1

Note that i++ (postfix) and ++i (prefix) both have the net effect of incrementing i by 1, but they are not equivalent. For example, if i currently has the value 5, then cout << i++ will print 5 and then increment i to 6, whereas cout << ++i will first increment i to 6 and then print 6. It's easy to remember: if the ++ is first, you first increment. A similar distinction occurs between k-- and --k.

Input/Output Operators

Operator	Name	Example	Meaning
>>	extraction operator	cin >> x	extract x from input stream
<<	insertion operator	cout << y	insert y onto output stream

NOTE
1. Input and output streams are discussed in more detail in Chapter 6. For now the discussion will be limited to reading in and writing out numerical values.
2. The standard input stream variable, cin, in combination with the extraction operator >>, gets data from the keyboard ("standard input"). Thus, the statement

```
cin >> num1 >> num2 ... ;
```

assumes that

- The user will enter values to be assigned to num1, num2, ... that are consistent with the type declarations for these variables.
- The values will be separated by *whitespace*: blank, tab, or newline are the most common.

3. The standard output stream variable, cout, together with the insertion operator <<, sends data to the screen ("standard output"):

```
cout << expr1 << expr2 << ... ;
```

- Here the expressions are either variable names, character strings, numbers, or numerical expressions.

- Character strings (between double quotes) and numbers are called literals and appear literally as typed. A numerical expression is evaluated, and its result is printed.

- The following escape sequences can be used for output:

\n	newline
\t	tab
\\	backslash
\'	apostrophe
\"	quote
\b	blankspace (not explicitly in the APCS subset)

Example

Suppose the variable radius has a value of 3. Each of the following statements will produce

```
Radius = 3 cm.
```

on the screen, with the cursor going to the next line:

```
cout << "Radius = " << radius << " cm." << endl;
cout << "Radius = " << radius << " cm." << '\n';
cout << "Radius = " << radius << " cm." << "\n";
cout << "Radius = " << radius << " cm.\n";
```

4. Chaining of the << and >> operators evaluates from left to right.
5. Note that output can be formatted using functions from the C++ library iomanip. These are not included in the APCS subset.

Operator Precedence

highest precedence	→	(1)	!, ++, --
		(2)	*, /, %
		(3)	+, -
		(4)	<<, >>
		(5)	<, >, <=, >=
		(6)	==, !=
		(7)	&&
		(8)	||
lowest precedence	→	(9)	=, +=, -=, *=, /=, %=

Here operators on the same line have equal precedence. The evaluation of the operators with equal precedence is from left to right, except for rows (1) and (9) the order is right to left. It is easy to remember: the only "backwards" order is for the unary operators (row 1) and for the various assignment operators (row 9).

Example 1

What will be output by the following statement?

```
cout << 5 + 3 < 6 * 5;
```

The intent is that the truth value of the boolean expression (5 + 3 < 6 * 5) should be printed. Since << has precedence over <, however, the program will try to output the value of 5 + 3 before evaluating the boolean expression. (A typical error message is "illegal operand.") The moral is that you should use parentheses to make the intent clear:

```
cout << (5 + 3 < 6 * 5);
```

will output 1, since the expression is true.

Example 2

Suppose the int variables x, y, and z currently have the values 3, 4, and 5. What will the following statement do?

```
x += y -= z *= 2;
```

It will

assign a value of 10 to z
then assign a value of -6 to y
then assign a value of -3 to x
(This is the kind of unreadable coding style you should avoid!)

Control Structures

Control structures are the mechanism by which you make the statements of a program run in a nonsequential order. There are two general types: decision making and iteration.

Decision-Making Control Structures

These include if, if ... else, and switch statements. They are all selection control structures that introduce a decision-making ability into a program. Based on the truth value of a boolean expression, the computer will decide which path to follow.

The if Statement

```
if (boolean expression)
{
    statements
}
```

Here the *statements* will be executed only if the boolean expression is true. If it is false, control passes immediately to the first statement following the if statement.

The if ... else Statement

```
if (boolean expression)
{
    statements
}
```

```
else
{
    statements
}
```

Here if the boolean expression is `true`, only the statements immediately following the test will be executed. If the boolean expression is `false`, only the statements following the `else` will be executed.

Nested `if` Statement

If the statement part of an `if` statement is itself an `if` statement, the result is a *nested* `if` *statement*.

Example 1

```
if (boolean expr1)
    if (boolean expr2)
        statement;
```

This is equivalent to

```
if (boolean expr1 && boolean expr2)
    statement;
```

Example 2

Beware the dangling `else`! Suppose you want to read in an integer and print it if it's positive and even. Will the following code do the job?

```
cin >> n;
if (n > 0)
    if (n % 2 == 0)
        cout << n << endl;
else
    cout << n << " is not positive" << endl;
```

A user enters 7 and is surprised to see the output

```
7 is not positive
```

The reason is that `else` always gets matched with the *nearest* unpaired `if`, not the first `if` as the indenting would suggest.

There are two ways to fix the preceding code. The first is to use {} delimiters to group the statements correctly.

```
cin >> n;
if (n > 0)
{
    if (n % 2 == 0)
        cout << n << endl;
}
else
    cout << n << " is not positive" << endl;
```

The second way of fixing the code is to rearrange the statements.

```
    cin >> n;
    if (n <= 0)
        cout << n << " is not positive" << endl;
    else
        if (n % 2 == 0)
            cout << n << endl;
```

Extended `if` Statement

For example,

```
char grade;
cin >> grade;
if (grade == 'A')
    cout << "Excellent!";
else if (grade == 'B')
    cout << "Good";
else if (grade == 'C' || grade == 'D')
    cout << "Poor";
else if (grade == 'F')
    cout << "Egregious!";
else
    cout << "Invalid grade";
```

If any of `'A'`, `'B'`, `'C'`, `'D'`, or `'F'` are entered, an appropriate message will be written and control will go to the statement immediately following the extended `if` statement. If any other character is entered, the final `else` is invoked, and the message `Invalid grade` will be written.

The `switch` Statement

The `switch` statement provides an alternative way of performing multiple tests on a single variable in one statement. The following is equivalent to the extended `if` statement in the previous example.

```
char grade;
cin >> grade;
switch (grade)
{
    case 'A':
        cout << "Excellent!";
        break;
    case 'B':
        cout << "Good";
        break;
    case 'C':        //2 cases with the same action
    case 'D':
        cout << "Poor";
        break;
    case 'F':
        cout << "Egregious!";
        break;
    default:
        cout << "Invalid grade";
}
```

NOTE

1. The variable grade is called the *selector* for the switch statement. The selector can be an expression or variable of any ordinal type (i.e., countable type like int or char). It cannot be a real number or a string.
2. The case labels must be literals of type int, char, or bool (i.e., they are constants, not variables).
3. If the value of grade is found among the case options, the statements following that value are executed.
4. break must be included in each case section to exit the switch statement. If break is omitted, execution passes to the next statement in the switch statement. This is not always the desired behavior! For example, if there were no breaks in the preceding example and grade was equal to 'D', all the messages Poor, Egregious!, and Invalid grade would be printed.
5. Sometimes it is convenient to terminate each case section with a return statement instead of a break, if returning from a function is the desired action.
6. If no case value matches the selector, the default part of the switch will be executed. If there is no default, then none of the statements in the switch statement will be executed. A default label is optional.
7. switch, case, break, and default are all reserved words (C++ keywords).

Iteration

C++ has three different control structures that allow the computer to perform iterative tasks: the for loop, while loop, and do...while loop.

The for loop

The general form of the for loop is

```
for (initialization; termination condition; update statement)
{
    statements      //body of loop
}
```

The termination condition is tested at the top of the loop; the update statement is performed at the bottom.

Example 1

```
//outputs 1 2 3 4
for (i=1; i<5; i++)
    cout << i;
```

Here's how it works. The *loop variable* i is initialized to 1, and the termination condition i < 5 is evaluated. If it is true, the body of the loop is executed and then the loop variable i is incremented according to the update statement. As soon as the termination condition is false (i.e., i>=5), control passes to the first statement following the loop.

Example 2

```
//outputs 20 19 18 17 16 15
for (k=20; k>=15; k--)
    cout << k;
```

Example 3

```
//outputs 2 4 6 8 10
for (j=2; j<=10; j += 2)
    cout << j;
```

NOTE

1. The loop variable should not have its value changed inside the loop body.
2. The initializing and update statements can use any valid constants, variables, or expressions.
3. The scope of the loop variable can be restricted to the loop body by combining the loop variable declaration with the initialization. For example,

```
for (int i=0; i<3; i++)
{
    ...
}
```

4. The following loop is syntactically valid:

```
for (i=1; i<=0; i++)
{
    ...
}
```

The loop body will not be executed at all, since the exiting condition is true before the first execution.
5. It is possible to exit a for loop early by using the keyword break. For example,

```
bool found = false;
for (int i=0; i<n; i++)
{
    if (a[i] == key)
    {
        found = true;
        break;      //breaks out of the loop if key
                    //is found in the array
    }
}
```

The while loop

The general form of the while loop is

```
while (boolean test)
{
    statements      //loop body
}
```

The test is performed at the beginning of the loop. If true, the loop body is executed. Otherwise, control passes to the first statement following the loop. After execution of the loop body, the test is performed again. If true, the loop is executed again, and so on.

Example 1

```
int i = 1, mult3 = 3;
while (mult3 < 20)
{
    cout << mult3;
    i++;
    mult3 *= i;
}                       //outputs 3 6 18
```

NOTE

1. It is possible for the body of a while loop never to be executed. This will happen if the boolean test evaluates to false the first time.
2. Disaster will strike in the form of an infinite loop if the boolean expression can never be false. Don't forget to change the loop variable in the body of the loop in a way that leads to termination!

Example 2

```
int power2 = 1;
while (power2 != 20)
{
    cout << power2;
    power2 *= 2;
}
```

Since power2 will never exactly equal 20, the loop will grind merrily along causing an eventual integer overflow.

Example 3

```
//screen out bad data
//The loop won't allow execution to continue until a valid
//integer is entered
cout << "Enter a positive integer from 1 to 100\n";
cin >> num;
while (num < 1 || num > 100)
{
    cout << "Number must be from 1 to 100.\n";
    cout << "Please reenter\n";
    cin >> num;
}
```

Example 4

```
//using a sentinel to terminate data entered at the keyboard
const int SENTINEL = -999;  //a value that cannot be part of
            //the data. Signals the end of the list
cout << "Enter list of positive integers, end list with "
    << SENTINEL << endl;
cin >> value;
while (value != SENTINEL)
{
    Process (value);
    cin >> value;
}
```

The do ... while loop

The general form of the do ... while loop is

```
do
{
    statements       //loop body
} while (boolean test);
```

Here the loop body is executed at least once. The test is done at the end of the loop. If true, the loop body is executed again. If false, control passes to the next statement. Again, you must make sure to avoid an infinite loop situation.

Example 1

```
count = 0;
do
{
    count++;
    cout << count;
} while (count < 5);
//outputs 1 2 3 4 5
```

Example 2

Here is a convenient way to produce multiple runs of a program.

```
//circle area program
    ...
int main()
{
    int radius;
    char response;
    do
    {
        cout << "Enter radius";
        cin >> radius;

        //code to find area and print result goes here

        cout << "Do you want to continue? y/n";
        cin >> response;
    } while (response == 'y' || response == 'Y');
    return 0;
}
```

Nested Loops

You create a *nested loop* when a loop is a statement in the body of another loop.

Example 1

```
for (int k=1; k<=3; k++)
{
    for (int i=1; i<=4; i++)
        cout << '*';
    cout << endl;
}
```

Think:

```
for each of 3 rows
{
    print 4 stars
    go to next line
}
```

Output:

```
****
****
****
```

Example 2

This example has two loops nested in an outer loop.

```cpp
for (int i=1; i<=6; i++)
{
    for (int j=1; j<=i; j++)
        cout << '+';
    for (int j=1; j<=6-i; j++)
        cout << '*';
    cout << endl;
}
```

Output:

```
+*****
++****
+++***
++++**
+++++*
++++++
```

Functions and Parameters

C++ programs are implemented with the help of functions that perform various subtasks of the program.

Every function must have a return type, name, parameter list (which may be empty), and body (implementation between {} brackets). The return type of a function can be any built-in or user-defined type (such as a class or an enumeration type). A return type of void indicates that the function doesn't return a value, it just does something.

Parameters used in the definition of a function are called *formal* or *dummy parameters*. Parameters that are passed to a function in a function call are *actual parameters* or *arguments* of the function. The actual parameters should match the type declarations of the formal parameters.

**Types of
Parameters**

Parameters can be passed to functions in three ways: by value, by reference, or by constant reference (const reference).

Pass by Value

A *value parameter* is passed to a function and used by the function, but it remains unchanged. The actual parameter can be either a value (literal), a variable, or an expression of the appropriate type.

Example 1

```
void PrintLine(int length, char ch)
//Print line consisting of length copies of ch
//Both length and ch are passed by value
{
    for (int i=1; i<=length; i++)
        cout << ch;
    cout << endl;
}
int main()
{
    int len = 10;
    char c = '*';
    PrintLine(len, c);
    PrintLine(2*len, '$');
    PrintLine(6, 'D'-2);
    return 0;
}
```

The program will output a row of 10 stars, followed by a row of 20 dollar signs, followed by 6 uppercase Bs.

Example 2

```
int NumDigits(int n)         //n is passed by value
//Returns number of digits in n, where n ≥ 0
{
    int count = 0;
    do
    {
        n /= 10;
        count++;
    }
    while (n != 0);
    return count;
}
```

It would appear that the parameter n gets destroyed in the process of having its digits counted. Not true! Here is what happens. When the function is invoked, a copy is made in memory of each actual parameter that is passed by value. These copies may be changed in the function. On exiting the function, all local copies are destroyed, leaving the actual parameters unchanged.

Let's trace this for Example 2. Suppose NumDigits is invoked in main() as follows:

```
int num;
cin >> num;
int c = NumDigits(num);
```

and suppose a value of 27 is input for num. Picture the state of the memory slots just before the function call:

num
```
┌────┐
│ 27 │
└────┘
```

When the function is invoked, a copy of the actual parameter, num, is made in the memory slot for n. It is this copy that will be modified during execution of the function.

num   n
```
┌────┐              ┌────┐
│ 27 │              │ 27 │
└────┘              └────┘
```

Just before exiting the function, the algorithm has reduced n to 0.

num   n
```
┌────┐              ┌────┐
│ 27 │              │ 0  │
└────┘              └────┘
```

After exiting the function, num remains unchanged, while n's memory slot has been reclaimed.

num
```
┌────┐
│ 27 │
└────┘
```

Pass by Reference

Parameters are *passed by reference* when the function returns more than one value (see Example 1), or when it is required that the value of the actual parameter be changed (see Example 2). Pass by reference is signaled by the & symbol in front of the parameter name. *The actual parameter must be a variable (lvalue)—no values (literals) or expressions.*

Example 1

```
void GetDimensions(int &l, int &w)
//reads length l and width w from keyboard
{
    cout << "Enter length followed by width" << endl;
    cin >> l >> w;
}
```

Suppose GetDimensions is invoked with the function call

```
GetDimensions(length, width);
```

where length and width have been declared of type int. The reason the values of length and width are not lost on exiting the function is that the parameters passed by reference share the same address in memory with their actual parameters. When the function is exited, the formal parameter labels are erased, but the changes to the actual parameters remain.

Example 2

```
void Swap(double &a, double &b)
{
    double temp;
    temp = a;
    a = b;
    b = temp;
}
int main()
{
    double x=2.7, y=3.1;
    Swap (x,y);
    cout << x << y;
        ...
}
```

Again, picture the memory slots. Just before the Swap(x,y) function is called:

x	y
2.7	3.1

During execution of the function, after the statement temp = a;:

x	y	temp
2.7	3.1	2.7
a	b	

Just before exiting the function:

x	y	temp
3.1	2.7	2.7
a	b	

Just after exiting the function:

x	y
3.1	2.7

Notice what happens if the parameters of the Swap function are passed by value instead of by reference, that is, by mistake you use the header

```
void Swap(int a, int b)
```

Just before the Swap(x,y) function call:

x	y
2.7	3.1

After the function call, just after the statement `temp = a` (copies of x and y are made for a and b):

x	y	a	b	temp
2.7	3.1	2.7	3.1	2.7

Just before exiting the function:

x	y	a	b	temp
2.7	3.1	3.1	2.7	2.7

Just after exiting the function (memory for value parameters and local variables has been erased):

x	y
2.7	3.1

Oops! The swap didn't happen.

Pass by Constant Reference

A parameter should be *passed by* `const` *reference* when one needs to pass a large data object whose member values are to remain unchanged. For example, imagine passing a large array or a user-defined class object such as an `apstring`. Copying the data into duplicate memory slots is expensive and unwieldy. Passing the parameter by `const` reference lets the formal parameter share memory with the actual parameter, but the actual parameter is protected from being altered.

Example

Consider a function that uses an `apstring` parameter as a prompt. The string will not be altered, merely printed out, and is therefore a perfect candidate for `const` reference.

```
int GetValue(const apstring &prompt)
{
    int value;
    cout << prompt;
    cin >> value;
    return value;
}
```

Functions from `<math.h>`

Each of the following functions returns real values (specifically, type `double`). The arguments are typically real, but `int` arguments won't cause an error—the `int` is converted to `double`.

Function	Returns
`fabs(x)`	$|x|$, the absolute value of x
`pow(x,y)`	x^y, the yth power of x
`sqrt(x)`	$\sqrt{x}$, the square root of x
`floor(x)`	$\lfloor x \rfloor$, rounds x down to next lower integer
`ceil(x)`	$\lceil x \rceil$, rounds x up to next higher integer
`sin(x)`	$\sin x$
`cos(x)`	$\cos x$
`tan(x)`	$\tan x$

Note: The functions other than `fabs`, `pow`, and `sqrt` will not be tested on the AP exam, but they are often useful.

Overloaded Functions

Functions that perform the same task on objects of different types can be given the same name. This is called *overloading*. For example,

```
void Print(int n);                //prints an integer
void Print(const apstring &s);  //prints a string
```

Each version must have a separate declaration and implementation. Overloaded functions can differ in the number of parameters and/or the type of each. These two characteristics comprise the function's *signature*. The type of the return value is not included in the signature, however, so you cannot overload that.

When the function `Print` is called, the compiler will figure out which `Print` function to invoke by comparing the types of the actual arguments with the types of the formal parameters. The function with matching parameters is the one that gets called.

Templated Functions

In a templated function, a single piece of code can manipulate any type of object, either built-in or user-defined.

The function header must be preceded with

```
template<class T>
```

where `template` and `class` are reserved words. `T`, which is any identifier of your choice, becomes a placeholder for any type.

Example

Here is a templated `Swap` function that swaps two objects of the same type.

```
template <class T>
void Swap(T &a, T &b)
{
    T temp;
    temp = a;
    a = b;
    b = temp;
}
```

In a program that uses a templated function, the actual types are declared:

```
int main()
{
    double d1 = 2.3;
    double d2 = 4.7;
    char c1 = 'a';
    char c2 = 'h';
    ...
    Swap(d1, d2); //compiler knows T is type double here
    Swap(c1, c2); //compiler knows T is type char here
    ...
}
```

More elaborate functions may use two or more parameterized types. The syntax:

```
template <class T1, class T2, ...>
```

Multiple-Choice Questions on Introductory C++ Language Concepts

1. Which represents a correct declaration of an enumeration type?
   (A) `enum Card {ACE, KING, QUEEN, JACK, 10};`
   (B) `enum Place {1st, 2nd, 3rd};`
   (C) `enum Fruit {Pear, Apple, Grape};`
   (D) `enum Vowel {'A', 'E', 'I', 'O', 'U'};`
   (E) `enum Digit {1, 2, 3, 4, 5};`

2. For the declaration

   ```
   enum Weekend {FRI, SAT, SUN};
   ```

   which of the following is incorrect usage?
   (A) `Weekend day = SAT;`
   (B) `Weekend day1 = FRI, day2 = SAT;`
       `if (day1 < day2)`
       `{`
           `...`
   (C) `for (int d=FRI; d<=SUN; d++)`
           `...`
   (D) `int FRI = 5;`
   (E) `Weekend d1 = FRI, d2 = SUN;`
       `int numDays = d2 - d1;`

3. The following code fragment outputs 13/5 = 2.

   ```
   double answer = 13/5;
   cout << "13/5 = " << answer;
   ```

   The programmer intends that it should print 13/5 = 2.6. Which of the following changes to the first line of code will *not* fix the problem?
   (A) Casting 13 to a double (i.e., `double(13)`)
   (B) Casting 5 to a double (i.e., `double(5)`)
   (C) Writing 13 in floating-point notation (i.e., `13.0`)
   (D) Writing 5 in floating-point notation (i.e., `5.0`)
   (E) Writing `double answer = double(13/5);`

4. What value is stored in ans if

   ```
   int ans = 13 - 3 * 6 / 4 % 3
   ```

   (A) −5
   (B) 0
   (C) 13
   (D) −1
   (E) 12

5. Suppose that addition and subtraction had higher precedence than multiplication and division. Then the expression

$$\left(2 + 3 * 12 / 7 - 4 + 8\right)$$

would evaluate to which of the following?
  (A) 11
  (B) 12
  (C) 5
  (D) −4
  (E) −9

6. Let x be a variable of type double that is positive. A program contains the boolean expression (pow(x,0.5) == sqrt(x)). Which of the following is the most likely reason why this expression can have the value false?

  (A) x was imprecisely calculated in a previous program statement.
  (B) The computer stores floating-point numbers with 32-bit words.
  (C) There is round-off error in calculating the pow and sqrt functions.
  (D) There is overflow error in calculating the pow function.
  (E) The expression will always have the value true since $x^{1/2} = \sqrt{x}$.

7. Consider the following code segment

```
if ((n != 0) && (x/n > 100))
    statement1;
else
    statement2;
```

If n has a value of 0 when the segment is executed, what will happen?
  (A) A run-time error will occur.
  (B) A syntax error will occur.
  (C) statement1, but not statement2, will be executed.
  (D) statement2, but not statement1, will be executed.
  (E) Neither statement1 nor statement2 will be executed; control will pass to the first statement following the if statement.

8. What will the output be for the following poorly formatted program segment, if the input value for num is 22?

```
cin >> num;
if (num > 0)
if (num % 5 == 0)
cout << num << endl;
else cout << num << " is negative";
```

  (A) 22
  (B) 4
  (C) 2 is negative
  (D) 22 is negative
  (E) Nothing will be output.

9. Look at the following poorly formatted program segment. If a = 7 and c = 6 before execution, which of the following represents the correct values of c, d, p, and t after execution? An undetermined value is represented with a question mark.

```
if (a == 6)
if (c == 6)
{
    c = 9;
    d = 9;
}
else
{
    t = 10;
    if (c == 6)
        c = 5;
}
else p = 9;
```

(A) c = 6, d = ?, p = 9, t = ?
(B) c = 5, d = ?, p = ?, t = 10
(C) c = 6, d = ?, p = ?, t = ?
(D) c = 5, d = 9, p = ?, t = 10
(E) c = 9, d = 9, p = ?, t = ?

10. What values are stored in x and y following execution of the following program segment?

```
int x=30, y=40;
if (x >= 0)
{
    if (x <= 100)
    {
        y = x*3;
        if (y < 50)
            x /= 10;
    }
    else
        y = x*2
}
else
    y = -x;
```

(A) x=30 y=90
(B) x=30 y=-30
(C) x=30 y=60
(D) x=3 y=-3
(E) x=30 y=40

11. What will be printed by the following code segment if the input value for `AP_score` is 3?

```
switch(AP_score)
{
    case 1: cout << "You needed a good review book!\n";
    case 2: cout << "Mediocre.\n";
    case 3:
    case 4: cout << "Well done.\n";
    case 5: cout << "Excellent!\n";
}
```

(A) Well done.
     Excellent!
(B) Well done.
(C) Nothing will be printed.
(D) No output—syntax error because no `default` case was supplied
(E) No output—run-time error because no statement was provided for case 3

12. The boolean expression `!A && B || C` is equivalent to
(A) `!A && (B || C)`
(B) `((!A) && B) || C`
(C) `(!A) && (B || C)`
(D) `!(A && B) || C`
(E) `!(A && B || C)`

13. Assume that a and b are integers. The boolean expression

    `!(a <= b) && (a*b > 0)`

will always evaluate to `true` given that
(A) `a = b`
(B) `a > b`
(C) `a < b`
(D) `a > b` and `b > 0`
(E) `a > b` and `b < 0`

14. Given that a, b, and c are integers, consider the boolean expression

    `(a < b) || !((c == a*b) && (c < a))`

Which of the following will *guarantee* that the expression is true?
(A) `c < a` is false.
(B) `c < a` is true.
(C) `a < b` is false.
(D) `c == a*b` is true.
(E) `c == a*b` is true, and `c < a` is true.

15. Consider this program:

```
void Add(int k, int &sum)
{
    int i;
    k *= 2;
    sum = 0;
    for (i=1; i<=k; i++)
        sum += i;
}
int main()
{
    int n=2;
    int total;
    Add(n, total);
    cout << total;
    return 0;
}
```

After execution of the statement Add(n, total), the values of total, n, k, and i are, respectively,

(A) 10, 2, 4, 5
(B) 10, 2, no value, no value
(C) 10, 2, 4, 4
(D) 3, 2, 4, 5
(E) 10, 4 , no value, no value

16. What will the output be after execution of this program?

```
void Foo(int a, int &b)
{
    a += b;
    b *= 2;
    cout << a << b << endl;
}
int main()
{
    int x=5, y=8;
    cout << x << y << endl;
    Foo(x,y);
    cout << x << y << endl;
    return 0;
}
```

(A) 5   8
    13   16
    5   8

(B) 5   8
    13   16
    13   8

(C) 5   8
    13   8
    13   16

(D) 5   8
    13   16
    13   16

(E) 5   8
    13   16
    5   16

17. Which statements about function declarations are true?

> I `void` functions that don't take arguments do not need declarations.
>
> II Declarations of functions invoked in `main()` may be listed before or after the `main()` function.
>
> III Declarations of standard library functions are supplied in header files.

(A) I only
(B) II only
(C) III only
(D) I and III only
(E) I, II, and III

18. Given that n is an integer ≥ 0, and count is of type `int`, which of the following code segments are exactly equivalent?

> I
> ```
> for (count=1; count <= n; count++)
>         cout << count << endl;
> ```
>
> II
> ```
> count = 1;
> while (count <= n)
> {
>         cout << count << endl;
>         count++;
> }
> ```
>
> III
> ```
> count = 1;
> do
> {
>         cout << count << endl;
>         count++;
> } while (count <= n);
> ```

(A) I and II only
(B) I and III only
(C) II and III only
(D) I, II, and III
(E) The three segments are all different.

19. The following fragment intends that a user will enter a list of positive integers at the keyboard and terminate the list with a sentinel:

```
int value;
const int SENTINEL = -999;
do
{
    cin >> value;
    //code to process value
} while (value != SENTINEL);
```

The fragment does not work as intended. What is the problem with it?

(A) The sentinel gets processed.
(B) The last nonsentinel value entered in the list fails to get processed.
(C) Poor choice of SENTINEL value causes the loop to terminate before all values have been processed.
(D) An infinite loop will result if the user fails to enter the SENTINEL value.
(E) Entering the SENTINEL value as the first value will cause a run-time error.

20. Which *best* describes function Mystery?

```
int Mystery(int x, int y)
//precondition: x > y
{
    int m, i=1;
    do
    {
        m = i*x;
        i++;
    } while (m % y != 0);
    return m;
}
```

(A) It returns the smallest common factor of x and y, that is, the smallest positive integer divisor of both x and y.

(B) It returns the greatest common factor of x and y, that is, the largest integer divisor of both x and y.

(C) It returns the least common multiple of x and y, that is, the smallest integer that has both x and y as a factor.

(D) It returns y raised to the xth power, that is, y^x.

(E) It returns x raised to the yth power, that is, x^y.

21. Consider the function AddUp:

```
int AddUp(int n)
//precondition: n > 0
//postcondition: the sum of the integers 1+2+...+n has been
//returned
{
    int i=0, sum=0;
    do
    {
        i++;
        sum += i;
    } while (i <= n);
    return sum;
}
```

This function does not work as intended. Which of the following changes would make it work correctly?

I Change while (i <= n) to while (i < n) and make no other changes.

II Interchange the statements i++ and sum += i and make no other changes.

III Change while (i <= n) to while (i < n) and interchange the statements i++ and sum += i; make no other changes.

(A) I only

(B) II only

(C) III only

(D) I and II only

(E) I, II, and III

22. Consider this code segment:

```
int x=10, y;
while (x > 5)
{
    y = 3;
    while (y < x)
    {
        y *= 2;
        if (y % x == 1)
            break;
    }
    x -= 3;
}
cout << x << y << endl;
```

What will be output after execution of this code segment?

(A) 1   6
(B) 7   12
(C) -3   12
(D) 4   12
(E) -3   6

Questions 23 and 24 refer to the following function CheckNumber, which checks the validity of its four-digit integer parameter.

```
bool CheckNumber(int n)
//precondition: n is a 4-digit int
//postcondition: validity of n has been returned
{
    int d1,d2,d3,checkDigit,nRemaining,rem;
    //strip off digits
    checkDigit = n % 10;
    nRemaining = n/10;
    d3 = nRemaining % 10;
    nRemaining /= 10;
    d2 = nRemaining % 10;
    nRemaining /= 10;
    d1 = nRemaining % 10;
    //check validity
    rem = (d1 + d2 + d3) % 7;
    if (rem == checkDigit)
        return true;
    else
        return false;
}
```

A program invokes function CheckNumber with the statement

```
bool valid = CheckNumber(num);
```

23. Which of the following values of `num` will result in `valid` having a value of `true`?
    - (A) 6143
    - (B) 6144
    - (C) 6145
    - (D) 6146
    - (E) 6147

24. What is the purpose of the local variable `nRemaining`?
    - (A) It is not possible to separate n into digits without the help of a temporary variable.
    - (B) `nRemaining` prevents the parameter `num` from being altered.
    - (C) `nRemaining` enhances the readability of the algorithm.
    - (D) On exiting the function, the value of `nRemaining` may be reused.
    - (E) `nRemaining` is needed as an lvalue for integer division.

25. What output will be produced by this code segment?

```
for (int i=5; i>=1; i--)
{
    for (int j=i; j>=1; j--)
        cout << 2*j-1;
    cout << endl;
}
```

- (A) 9 7 5 3 1
      9 7 5 3
      9 7 5
      9 7
      9

- (B) 9 7 5 3 1
      7 5 3 1
      5 3 1
      3 1
      1

- (C) 9 7 5 3 1
      7 5 3 1 -1
      5 3 1 -1 -3
      3 1 -1 -3 -5
      1 -1 -3 -5 -7

- (D) 1
      1 3
      1 3 5
      1 3 5 7
      1 3 5 7 9

- (E) 1 3 5 7 9
      1 3 5 7
      1 3 5
      1 3
      1

26. Which of the following program fragments will produce this output? (Ignore spacing.)

```
2 - - - - -
- 4 - - - -
- - 6 - - -
- - - 8 - -
- - - - 10 -
- - - - - 12
```

```
 I  for (int i=1; i<=6; i++)
    {
        for (int k=1; k<=6; k++)
            if (k == i)
                cout << 2*k;
            else
                cout << '-';
        cout << endl;
    }

II  for (int i=1; i<=6; i++)
    {
        for (int k=1; k<=i-1; k++)
            cout << '-';
        cout << 2*i;
        for (int k=1; k<=6-i; k++)
            cout << '-';
        cout << endl;
    }

III for (int i=1; i<=6; i++)
    {
        for (int k=1; k<=i-1; k++)
            cout << '-';
        cout << 2*i;
        for (int k=i+1; k<=6; k++)
            cout << '-';
        cout << endl;
    }
```

(A) I only
(B) II only
(C) III only
(D) I and II only
(E) I, II, and III

27. Consider this program segment:

```
int newNum = 0, temp;
int num = k;          //k is some predefined integer value
while (num > 10)
{
    temp = num % 10;
    num /= 10;
    newNum = newNum*10 + temp;
}
cout << newNum;
```

Which is a true statement about the segment?

I If $100 \leq num \leq 1000$ initially, the final value of newNum must be in the range $10 \leq newNum \leq 100$.

II There is no initial value of num that will cause an infinite while loop.

III If $num \leq 10$ initially, newNum will have a final value of 0.

(A) I only
(B) II only
(C) III only
(D) II and III only
(E) I, II, and III

28. Consider the function Max, which is defined here:

```
template<class T>
T Max (const T &a, const T &b)
//returns max of a and b
{
    if (a < b)
        return b;
    return a;
}
```

Which of the following correctly uses function Max?

I
```
int main()
{
    T<double>;
    double x = 4.3, y = 2.0, z;
    z = Max(x, y);
        ...
}
```

II
```
int main()
{
    int x = 4, y = -2, z;
    double a = 2.7, b = 3.5;
    z = Max(x, a);
        ...
}
```

III
```
int main()
{
    int x = 4, y = 5, z;
    char c = 'p', d = 'f', k;
    apstring s = "hi", t = "bye", w;
    z = Max(x, y);
    k = Max(c, d);
    w = Max(s, t);
        ...
}
```

(A) I only
(B) II only
(C) III only
(D) II and III only
(E) I, II, and III

29. Consider the function Reverse:

```
int Reverse(int n)
//precondition: n > 0
//postcondition: returns n with its digits reversed
//Example: If n = 234, function Reverse returns 432
{
    int rem, revNum=0;

    <code segment>

    return revNum;
}
```

Which of the following replacements for <code segment> would cause the function to work as intended?

```
I for (int i=0; i<=n; i++)
   {
            rem = n % 10;
            revNum = revNum*10 + rem;
            n /= 10;
   }
II do
   {
            rem = n % 10;
            revNum = revNum*10 + rem;
            n /= 10;
   } while (n != 0);
III do
   {
            rem = n / 10;
            revNum = revNum*10 + rem;
            n %= 10;
   } while (n != 0);
```

(A) I only
(B) II only
(C) I and II only
(D) I and III only
(E) I, II, and III

30. Consider this program:

```
#include <iostream.h>
int count = 0;
void DoSomething();
int main()
{
    int n;
    cout << "How many iterations?";
    cin >> n;
    for (int i=1; i<=n; i++)
    {
        DoSomething();
        cout << count << endl;
    }
    return 0;
}
void DoSomething()
{
    int count = 0;
        ...
    //code to do something - no screen output produced
    count++;
}
```

If the input value for n is 3, what screen output will this program subsequently produce?

(A) 0
    0
    0

(B) 1
    2
    3

(C) 3
    3
    3

(D) ?
    ?
    ?

where ? is some undefined value.

(E) No output will be produced.

Answer Key

1. **C**	11. **A**	21. **D**
2. **D**	12. **B**	22. **D**
3. **E**	13. **D**	23. **B**
4. **E**	14. **A**	24. **C**
5. **C**	15. **B**	25. **B**
6. **C**	16. **E**	26. **E**
7. **D**	17. **C**	27. **D**
8. **D**	18. **A**	28. **C**
9. **A**	19. **A**	29. **B**
10. **A**	20. **C**	30. **A**

Answers Explained

1. **(C)** The enumerators represent integer constants, and their names must follow the rules for identifiers—don't start with a digit and use only letters, digits, and the underscore character. C is the only choice that does all this. Whether you use capital letters or not for the names is a stylistic choice only.

2. **(D)** The enumerators are constants whose values cannot be changed in the course of a program. (In the given declaration, FRI has the default value 0, so SAT = 1, SUN = 2.) Choice A declares the variable day to be of type Weekend and initializes it to SAT. In choice B, the test if (day1 < day2) evaluates to true because FRI < SAT (i.e., 0 < 1). Note that choice C is also correct: integer d will be initialized to 0, the value of FRI. So the loop is equivalent to

   ```
   for (int d=0; d<=2; d++)
   ```

   Choice E will assign numDays a value of SUN - FRI, which is 2 - 0 = 2.

3. **(E)** For this choice, the integer division 13/5 will be evaluated to 2. Then the real value 2.0 will be printed. The compiler needs a way to recognize that real-valued division is required. All the other options provide a way.

4. **(E)** *, /, and % have equal precedence and must be performed first, from left to right.

   ```
         13 - 3 * 6/4 % 3
       = 13 - 18/4 % 3
       = 13 - 4 % 3
       = 13 - 1
       = 12
   ```

5. **(C)** The expression must be evaluated as if parenthesized like this:

   ```
       (2 + 3) * 12/(7 - 4 + 8)
   ```

   This becomes 5 * 12/11 = 60/11 = 5.

6. (**C**) Anytime arithmetic operations are done with floating-point numbers, round-off error occurs. The library functions such as pow and sqrt use various approximations to generate their answers to the required accuracy, but since they do different internal arithmetic, the round-off will usually not result in exactly the same answers. Choice A is wrong because no matter how x was previously calculated, the same x is input to pow and sqrt. Choice B is wrong since round-off error occurs no matter how many bits are used to represent numbers. Choice D is wrong because if x is representable on the machine (i.e., hasn't overflowed), then its square root, $x^{1/2}$, will not overflow.

7. (**D**) Short-circuit evaluation of the boolean expression will occur. (n != 0) will evaluate to false, which makes the entire boolean expression false. (x/n > 100) will not be evaluated, hence no division-by-zero run-time error. When the boolean expression has a value of false, only the else part of the statement, *statement2*, will be executed.

8. (**D**) Each else gets paired with the nearest unpaired if. Thus when (22 % 5 == 0) fails, the else part indicating that 22 is negative will be executed. This is clearly not the intent of the fragment, which can be fixed using delimiters:

```
cin >> num;
if (num > 0)
{
    if (num % 5 == 0)
        cout << num << endl;
}
else
    cout << num << " is negative";
```

9. (**A**) Since (a == 6) is false, the

```
if (c == 6) ...
else
{
    t = 10; ...
```

statement will not be executed. The second else matches up with the first if, which means that p = 9 gets executed. Variables d and t remain undefined.

10. (**A**) Since the first test (x >= 0) is true, the matching else part, y = -x, will not be executed. Since (x <= 100) is true, the matching else part, y = x*2, will not be executed. y will be set to x*3 (i.e., 90) and will now fail the y < 50 test. Thus x will never be altered in this algorithm. Final values are x = 30 and y = 90.

11. (**A**) Beware! Each case segment of a switch statement should be terminated, usually with a break or a return. If a case is not terminated, as in the given code, a fall-through occurs in which every subsequent statement is executed. Only if each cout statement were terminated with a break would the output be as intended, Well done in this case. Choice C is wrong: execution falls though case 3 to case 4, so they both result in Well done being printed. Choice D is wrong: a default case is optional. Choice E is wrong, no statement need be supplied. This is especially true here, where the intention is that case 3 and case 4 give the same output.

12. **(B)** The order of precedence is ! (highest), &&, then || (lowest). Thus, the order of evaluation is (!A), ((!A) && B), and finally ((!A) && B) || C.

13. **(D)** To evaluate to true, the expression must reduce to true && true. We therefore need !(false) && true. Choice D is the only condition that guarantees this: a > b provides !(false) for the left-hand side, and a > b and b > 0 implies both a and b positive, which leads to true for the right-hand side. Choice E, for example, will provide false for the right-hand side only if a > 0. You have no information about a and can't make assumptions about it.

14. **(A)** If (c < a) is false, ((c == a*b) && (c < a)) evaluates to false irrespective of the value of c == a*b. In this case, !(c == a*b && c < a) evaluates to true. Then (a < b) || true evaluates to true irrespective of the value of (a < b). In all the other choices, the given expression may be true. There is not enough information given to guarantee this, however.

15. **(B)** Since k is passed by value, it gets its own memory slot, which initially contains 2, a copy of n, its actual parameter. sum is passed by reference and, therefore, shares memory with total, the actual parameter. When the function is called, k is doubled to equal 4. The first four positive integers are added, and the result 10 is stored in total. Here is a picture of the memory slots just before exiting the function:

```
 n          k         total
┌───┐      ┌───┐      ┌────┐
│ 2 │      │ 4 │      │ 10 │
└───┘      └───┘      └────┘
                        sum
```

After exiting the function, k is erased, along with the local variable i. Therefore, neither k nor i has a value. The values of total and n are 10 and 2, respectively.

16. **(E)** b is passed by reference and will therefore share memory with its actual parameter y. The parameter a is passed by value, and so a copy of x will be placed in a. Just before the function Foo is exited, the memory slots can be pictured like this:

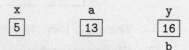

```
 x          a          y
┌───┐      ┌────┐      ┌────┐
│ 5 │      │ 13 │      │ 16 │
└───┘      └────┘      └────┘
                         b
```

When the function is exited, a is erased, and the line cout << x << y << endl; will produce 5 16.

17. **(C)** Choice I is false: void functions and functions without arguments have the same requirements as other functions. Choice II is false: function prototypes must be declared before main(), in order for the compiler to check what types of arguments they need and what their return type is at the point they are invoked in main().

18. **(A)** If n>=1, each of the three segments will print out the integers from 1 through n. If n == 0, segments I and II will fail the test immediately and do nothing. Segment III, however, will execute the loop once and output 1. There's a lesson in this question—always test endpoint situations!

19. **(A)** Since the (value != SENTINEL) test occurs after processing the loop, any value read in will be processed, including the sentinel. Choice B is wrong

because *all* values entered, including the sentinel, are processed. Eliminate choice C: -999 is a fine choice for the sentinel given that only positive integers are valid input data. Choice D is wrong—the computer will patiently keep accepting nonsentinel values. This is not an infinite loop since the problem is not with the code. The user is causing the problem by not terminating the list as instructed. Choice E is wrong—there will be no run-time error. The sentinel value, -999, will be processed, and the loop will then terminate since (value != SENTINEL) will evaluate to false.

20. **(C)** The algorithm generates successive multiples of x, the larger of the two integers x and y, until it finds one that is also a multiple of y. This number will be the smallest common multiple of x and y.

21. **(D)** The problem with the algorithm as given is that it goes too far. When i is equal to n, the loop is executed one more time, causing the (n+1)th integer to be added. This can be fixed by changing the test to while (i < n) *or* by leaving the test alone and interchanging the statements i++ and sum += i. This has the effect of causing the loop to terminate *as soon as* i has the value n+1 (i.e., before n+1 is included in the sum). Notice that making both of the suggested changes leads to the following loop, which won't work properly:

```
do
{
    sum += i;
    i++;
} while (i < n);
```

The loop will terminate before the nth integer is included in the sum.

22. **(D)** Here is a trace of the values of x and y during execution. Note that the condition (y % x == 1) is never true in this example.

x	10				7				4
y		3	6	12		3	6	12	

The while loop terminates when x is 4 since the test while (x > 5) fails.

23. **(B)** The algorithm finds the remainder when the sum of the first three digits of n is divided by 7. If this remainder is equal to the fourth digit, checkDigit, the function returns true, otherwise false. Note that (6+1+4) % 7 equals 4. Thus, only choice B is a valid number.

24. **(C)** As n gets broken down into its digits, nRemaining is the part of n that remains after each digit is stripped off. Thus nRemaining is a self-documenting name that helps describe what is happening. Choice A is false because every digit can be stripped off using some sequence of integer division and mod. Choice B is false because num is passed by value and therefore will not be altered. Eliminate choice D: when the function is exited, all local variables are destroyed. Choice E is nonsense.

25. **(B)** The outer loop produces five rows of output. Each pass through the inner loop goes from i down to 1. Thus five odd numbers starting at 9 are printed in the first row, four odd numbers starting at 7 in the second row, and so on.

26. **(E)** All three algorithms produce the given output. The outer `for (int i ... )` loop produces six rows, and the inner `for (int k ... )` loops produce the symbols in each row.

27. **(D)** Statement I is false, since if `100 <= num <= 109`, the body of the `while` loop will be executed just once. (After this single pass through the loop, the value of `num` will be 10, and the test `if (num > 10)` will fail.) With just one pass, `newNum` will be a one-digit number, equal to `temp` (which was the original `num % 10`). Note that segment II is true: there cannot be an infinite loop because `num /= 10` guarantees termination of the loop. Segment III is true because if `num <= 10`, the loop will be skipped, and `newNum` will keep its original value of 0.

28. **(C)** Code segment I is wrong because `T<double>` is incorrect usage. The variables should be declared in the usual way. Segment II is wrong because the parameter types are mixed. The parameters must be of the same type, both `double` or both `int`.

29. **(B)** The algorithm works by stripping off the rightmost digit of `n` (stored in `rem`), multiplying the current value of `revNum` by 10, and adding that rightmost digit. When `n` has been stripped down to no digits (i.e., `n == 0` is true), `revNum` is complete. Segment III fails because `/` and `%` are confused. Segment I is wrong because the number of passes through the loop depends on the number of digits in `n`, not the value of `n` itself.

30. **(A)** This is a question about the scope of variables. Initially `count` is declared as a global variable that is initialized to 0. The scope of this global variable extends up to the end of the entire file in which it is declared. `count` is also declared as a local variable in `DoSomething()`. After the function call in the `for` loop, the local variable `count` goes out of scope and the value that's being printed is the value of the global `count`, which is unchanged from 0.

CHAPTER TWO
Classes and Structs

Work is the curse of the drinking classes.
—Oscar Wilde

Classes

A *class* is a user-defined type. It combines an abstract data type with its related operations and data members into a single unit. Variables of type class are called *objects*.

Creation of a class requires two parts:

1. A declaration, typically stored in a `.h` file, that names the class and lists the data members and declarations of the member functions.
2. An implementation, typically stored in a `.cpp` file, with code for the member and nonmember functions.

Here is the declaration for a complex number class. Recall that a complex number (a, b) has real part a and imaginary part b.

```
class Complex
{
    public:

// constructors
    Complex();                   //complex number with default value
    Complex(double r, double i); //complex number with specified
                                 //real and imaginary parts
    Complex(const Complex &c);   //copy constructor

// assignment
    const Complex & operator= (const Complex &c); //assign c to
                                            //this complex number
// accessors
    double Real() const; //return real part of this complex
                         //number
    double Imag() const; //return imaginary part of this
                         //complex number
    void Print(ostream & os) const; //print complex number
                                    // in form (a,b)
```

```
    // modifiers
        const Complex & IncrementReal(); //add 1 to real part of
                                            //this complex number
        const Complex & operator+= (const Complex &c);  //add c to
                                                    // this complex number
        const Complex & operator+= (double d); //add d to this
                                                    //complex number
    // similarly -=, *=, /=

        private:
        double myReal,myImag;
    };


    // free (nonmember) functions
    Complex operator+ (const Complex &c1, const Complex &c2); //c1+c2
    Complex operator+ (const Complex &c, double d);           //c+d
    Complex operator+ (double d, const Complex &c);           //d+c
    // similarly -, *, /
    bool operator== (const Complex &c1, const Complex &c2);
        //true if c1==c2, false otherwise
    ostream & operator<< (ostream &os, const Complex &c);   //write c
                                    //to output stream in form (a,b)
    Complex Conj(const Complex &c); //return complex conjugate of c
```

Private and Public Sections

The private section can be accessed only by the class member functions. The public part constitutes the *interface* between the class and a *client program* that uses the class. A client has neither access to the private data members nor knowledge of the class implementation, a principle known as *information hiding* or *encapsulation*.

The Member Functions

In the implementation of the class, all member functions have the class name followed by the *scope resolution operator* :: in their headers.

Constructors

A *constructor* creates an object of the class. Having several constructors provides different ways of initializing class objects. Constructors are recognized by having the same name as the class. They have no return type.

The Complex class shown has three constructors:

1. The *default constructor* has no arguments. It provides reasonable initial values for an object. Here it is implemented using an *initializer list*:

```
//complex number with default value (0,0)
Complex::Complex() : myReal(0), myImag(0) {}
```

In a client program, the declaration

```
Complex c;
```

will create a Complex variable c with real and imaginary parts both equal to 0.

> An **initializer list** in a constructor is a concise and efficient way of assigning values to the private variables of an object. The start of the list is signaled by a colon following the function name; the end of the list is the opening brace for the body of the constructor.
>
> An initializer list can initialize both built-in and user-defined types. `const` data members *must* be initialized in an initializer list. The same is true for private data members that are objects of some other class with no default constructor.

2. The constructor with the real and imaginary parts as parameters sets the private data members of a `Complex` number equal to the values of those parameters. Here again is an implementation using an initializer list:

```
//complex number with specified real and imaginary parts
Complex::Complex(double r, double i) : myReal(r), myImag(i) {}
```

In a client program, a declaration that uses this constructor needs matching parameters:

```
Complex c(-2, 3.5); //sets c to have real part -2, imaginary
                    //part 3.5, ie. initializes c to (-2, 3.5)
```

3. The *copy constructor* initializes a class object by copying another object of the same class. Here is its implementation:

```
//Make a copy of Complex number c
Complex::Complex(const Complex &c)
{
    myReal = c.myReal;
    myImag = c.myImag;
}
```

The copy constructor is called in the following instances:

- A declaration with initialization.

  For example:

  ```
  Complex c2 = c1; //copy constructor initializes c2 to c1
                   //assumes c1 previously initialized
  ```

- An object passed to a function as a value parameter (instead of by reference or `const` reference), necessitating that a copy be made.

- An object returned by value (instead of by reference or `const` reference), likewise requiring a copy.

Here is some code that illustrates the use of the copy constructor:

```
void DoSomething(Complex c)
{
    //body of DoSomething
}
Complex f(double a, double b)
{
```

```
            Complex c1(a,b); //constructor with parameters
            Complex c2=c1;   //copy constructor initializes c2
            Complex c3(c1);  //copy constructor initializes c3
                             //alternative syntax to previous line
            DoSomething(c2); //copy constructor makes copy of c2
              ..
            return c3;       //copy constructor makes copy of c3
        }
```

NOTE
1. If a class has no constructors, the compiler automatically generates a default constructor that initializes variables to default values (such as 0 for numbers).
2. The compiler will also provide a copy constructor that copies each data member. This does not always have the desired effect when the data members are pointers. (See Chapter 8.)
3. If you provide any constructor, it supersedes the system-generated default constructor.

The moral of the story? Whenever you write your own class, be sure to include a default constructor. In that way, *you* will be in control of the default behavior of your class objects!

Accessors

Accessors are *constant member functions* that access a class object without altering the object. An accessor often returns an attribute or feature of the object. The `const` after the argument list in the function declaration indicates that the function does not modify the state of the complex number object.

Here are the implementations of the `Imag` and `Print` functions:

```
//return imaginary part of this complex number
double Complex::Imag() const
{
    return myImag;
}
```

```
//print complex number in form (a,b) to output stream
void Complex::Print(ostream &os) const
{
    os << "(" << myReal << "," << myImag << ")";
}
```

A client program may use these functions as follows:

```
        Complex z;
          ...
        z.Print(cout);
        double x = z.Imag();
```

Modifiers

Modifiers (also called mutators) alter an object in some way. The overloaded `+=` functions, which return a complex number after something has been added to it, are examples of modifiers (see the next section). The return type is typically a reference to the modified class object (`const` reference if the object is to be protected after it has been returned). The implementation in each case uses the keyword this to refer to the current object.

For example, here is the implementation of IncrementReal():

```
// add 1 to real part of complex number
const Complex & Complex::IncrementReal()
{
    myReal++;
    return *this;
}
```

---

this and *this

The keywords this and *this appear only in the implementation code for member functions. Every member function "knows" what object it was invoked on and can refer to it as *this. The keyword this is a pointer to the current object. *this is the object itself, "what this is pointing to."

Here's a good way to think about this. When a member function is invoked on a class object, the object is an implied first parameter of the function. Thus, the example function call z.Print(cout) in the preceding section could be thought of as

```
Print(z,cout);
```

and the declaration of Print could be thought of as

```
void Print(Complex *this, ostream & os) const;
```

If the implementation code for the Print function needs to refer to the object z, it does so as *this.

Overloaded Operator Functions As Member Functions

In general, to overload =, +=, *=, -=, /=, and %=, an existing class object is being modified. In each case, the return type is a const reference to a class object.

Example 1
Overloading +=:
Here is how to use the overloaded operator += in a client program:

```
Complex x, y;
double d;
...
x+=y; //adds a Complex to a Complex
x+=d; //adds a double to a Complex
...
```

These examples are equivalent to

```
x.operator+=(y);
x.operator+=(d);
```

In each case, x is the implied first parameter.

Level AB Only

Here is the implementation for both forms:

```
//add Complex number c to this complex number
const Complex & Complex::operator+= (const Complex &c)
{
    myReal += c.myReal;
    myImag += c.myImag;
    return *this;
}


//add real number d to this complex number
const Complex & Complex::operator+= (double d)
{
    myReal += d;
    return *this;
}
```

Example 2

Overloading the assignment operator:

Usage:

```
int main()
{
    Complex x;   //default constructor
    Complex y=x; //copy constructor (not assignment!)
    ..
    x=y;              //overloaded assignment operator
    ..
}
```

Level AB Only

Implementation:

```
//assign c to this complex no.
const Complex & Complex::operator= (const Complex &c)
{
    if (this != &c) //avoid assigning object to itself
                    //(aliasing).
    {
        myReal = c.myReal;
        myImag = c.myImag;
    }
    return *this;
}
```

Destructor

A *destructor* recycles memory when an object expires, for example at the end of a function call when the object goes out of scope. The destructor is called automatically—you should never call it explicitly. If no destructor is provided, then the compiler provides one that deletes each data member of the object.

Level AB Only

This will work for the Complex class, but it will not work as intended for a class with pointer data members. (See Chapter 8.)

The declaration for a destructor for class `SomeClass` is

```
~SomeClass();
```

Free (Nonmember) Functions

In General

Free (nonmember) functions cannot access the private data members of the class. For example, here is the implementation of the `Conj` function [Note that the conjugate of a complex number (a,b) is (a,-b)]:

```
//return complex conjugate of c
Complex Conj(const Complex &c)
{
    Complex temp(c.Real(),-c.Imag());   //constructor with 2
                                        //parameters used
    return temp;
}
```

Note that the compiler would have given an error message if `myReal` or `myImag` had been used instead of `Real()` and `Imag()`, respectively. This is because `Conj` is a nonmember function and, therefore, cannot access the private data members of the `Complex` class. Also, a statement of the form `temp.Real() = c.Real();` would not be allowed because `Real()` is a `const` member function, an accessor, and cannot change a class object (in this case, `temp`).

Overloaded Binary Operators

Desired Usage

```
int main()
{
    Complex x, y, z;
    ...
    x = y + z;       //Complex plus Complex
    y = z + 8.5;     //Complex plus real
    z = 2 + x;       //real plus Complex
    ...
```

Level AB Only

Why Not Member Functions?

The rule for using an overloaded operator function as a member function of class `SomeClass` is that the left-hand operand must always be of type `SomeClass`. Thus in the three declarations for `operator+`, the first two could have been member functions, but not the third. This is because the statement `c = a + b` is equivalent to `c = a.operator+(b)`, which makes sense only if a is a member of the class. In the statement `z = 2 + x`, `2.operator+(x)` does not make sense because 2 is not a variable of type `SomeClass`.

Typically all related functions are grouped together in a class declaration—thus the three `operator+` functions are usually all declared as nonmember functions.

Return Type

Overloaded binary operator functions always return some value, often of the class type. All the overloaded binary operator functions for the `Complex` class return `Complex` values. Note that the return type cannot be a reference to `Complex`

Level AB
(continued)

(i.e., `Complex &` or `const Complex &`) since the returned value is created locally in the function and destroyed when the function is exited. A reference to a nonexistent object makes no sense and will cause an error.

Implementation

These functions are not member functions and cannot access the private real and imaginary variables of their parameters. They can, however, use the overloaded `+=`, `*=`, ... functions already defined.

A local (temporary) variable is used to store and return the result created by the binary operation.

Here are the implementations of the three different forms of `operator+`:

```
//c1+c2
Complex operator+ (const Complex &c1, const Complex &c2)
{
    Complex temp=c1;
    temp += c2; //calls operator+= (const Complex&)
    return temp;
}


//c+d
Complex operator+ (const Complex &c, double d)
{
    Complex temp=c;
    temp += d;       //calls operator+= (double)
    return temp;
}


//d+c
Complex operator+ (double d, const Complex &c)
{
    Complex temp=c; //can't start with d, not Complex
    temp += d;       //calls operator+= (double)
    return temp;
}
```

Overloaded Boolean Operators

The return type is always `bool`. For example, the `==` operator is overloaded for the `Complex` class.

Usage

```
Complex x, y;
...
if (x==y)
...
```

Level AB Only

Implementation
```
//true if c1==c2, false otherwise
bool operator== (const Complex &c1, const Complex &c2)
{
    return c1.Real()==c2.Real() && c1.Imag()==c2.Imag();
}
```

Overloaded Stream Operators

The overloaded stream operators cannot be member functions because the left-hand operand is not of type `Complex` (e.g., `cout << c`). In fact, the first argument in the function must be a reference to a stream, such as `ostream &` or `istream &`. The return type for these overloaded stream operators is also always a stream reference.

Usage

```
Complex c;
...
cout << c;
```

Level AB Only

Implementation

There are two ways to implement the `operator<<` function. One way uses the accessor functions `Real()` and `Imag()`; the other uses the `Print()` member function.

Here are both implementations:

```
//write c in form (a,b) to output stream
ostream & operator<< (ostream &os, const Complex &c)
{
    os << "(" << c.Real() << "," << c.Imag() << ")";
    return os;
}

//write c in form (a,b) to output stream
ostream & operator<< (ostream &os, const Complex &c)
{
    c.Print(os);
    return os;
}
```

Structs

Definition

A *struct* is a class in which members are by default public. (Members of a class are by default private.) Thus,

```
struct s
{
    ...
```

is equivalent to

```
class s
{
    public:
    ...
```

Typically a struct is used as a collection of related, but potentially different, data types combined into a single type. For example;

```
struct Student
{
    apstring name;
    int studentNum;
    double gpa;
};
```

Each item in the struct is a *member* and is accessed by applying the . *member operator* (dot member operator). For example,

```
Student s;
s.gpa = 3.4;
s.name = "Julian Drix";
s.studentNum = 1408;
```

Initialization

Here is a struct for a point in the coordinate plane:

```
struct Point
{
    double x;   //x-coordinate
    double y;   //y-coordinate
};
```

Points can be initialized in three ways:

1. Using the . member operator:

```
Point P;
P.x = 6.2;
P.y = -3.1;
```

2. Using a list enclosed in braces and separated by commas, where the order of values matches the order in the declaration:

```
Point P = {6.2, -3.1};
```

This method won't work for members of type apvector, apstring, or apmatrix since they have their own class constructors that initialize them.

3. Using constructors:

```
struct Point
{
    double x;   //x-coordinate
    double y;   //y-coordinate
    Point(): x(0.0), y(0.0)  {} //default constructor
    Point(double xValue, double yValue)
          : x(xValue), y(yValue)  {}
};
```

```
Point P;  //initializes P to origin
Point Q (2.3, 9.4);  //initializes Q to (2.3, 9.4)
```

Access

Because the data members of a struct are all public, they can be directly accessed in the implementation code of functions that manipulate struct objects.

Example 1

Here is a function that translates a point horizontally and vertically:

```
void Translate(Point & p, double horiz, double vert)
//translates point p horiz and vert distances
{
    p.x += horiz;
    p.y += vert;
}
```

Level AB Only

Example 2

Here is code to overload the << operator for variables of type `Point`:

```
ostream & operator<< (ostream &os, const Point &p)
// Point p inserted onto os stream
{
    os << "(" << p.x <<"," << p.y << ")";
    return os;
}
```

Usage:

```
Point P(3.4, -0.5);
Translate(P, 2.3, 6.0);
cout << P;
```

This code should cause the ordered pair (5.7, 5.5) to appear on the output screen.

More Complicated Structs

The type of a data member in a struct can be any user-defined type, including an array type or another struct or class.

Example

```
struct Date
{
    int month;
    int day;
    int year;
};
struct Student
{
    apstring name;
    Date birthday;
    int studentNum;
    double gpa;
};
```

Here are some statements that access the members of these structs:

```
Student s;
s.birthday.month = 4;
s.birthday.day = 30;
s.birthday.year = 1980;
```

See Chapter 4 for using apvectors with structs.

Class or Struct Objects as Parameters

When class or struct objects are passed as parameters of functions, they should be passed by reference or const reference to avoid copying the entire structure.

Multiple-Choice Questions on Classes and Structs

1. Refer to the following declarations:

```
struct Address
{
    apstring name;
    apstring street;
    apstring city;
    apstring state;
    int zip;
};
Address adr;
```

Which of the following correctly assigns a zip code of 14580 to adr?
(A) adr = 14580;
(B) zip = 14580;
(C) zip.adr = 14580;
(D) adr.zip = "14580";
(E) adr.zip = 14580;

2. Refer to the following declarations:

```
struct Address
{
    apstring name;
    apstring street;
    apstring city;
    apstring state;
    int zip;
};
struct Student
{
    int idNum;
    Address addr;
    double gpa;
};
Student s;
```

Which of the following correctly assigns the city "Ithaca" to Student s's address?
(A) s.city = "Ithaca";
(B) s.Address.city = "Ithaca";
(C) s.addr.city = "Ithaca";
(D) addr.city = "Ithaca";
(E) Student.addr.city = "Ithaca";

3. Refer to the following declaration:

```
struct Part
{
    int partNumber;
    double price;
    int amount;
};
```

Which of the following is a valid initialization of `Part p`?

  I `Part p = {2597, 32.50, 42};`

 II `Part p;`
   `p.partNumber = 2597;`
   `p.price = 32.50;`
   `p.amount = 42;`

III `Part p(2597, 32.50, 42);`

(A) I only
(B) II only
(C) III only
(D) I and II only
(E) I, II, and III

4. Refer to these declarations:

```
enum City {Berkeley, Boston, Champagne, NewHaven};
```

```
struct BookStore
{
    City branch;
    int numBooks;
};
```

Which of the following code segments will initialize the `Berkeley` branch of a `BookStore` to contain 2500 books?

  I `BookStore b = Berkeley;`
   `b.numBooks = 2500;`

 II `BookStore b;`
   `b.City = Berkeley;`
   `b.numBooks = 2500;`

III `City c = Berkeley;`
   `BookStore b;`
   `b.branch = c;`
   `b.numBooks = 2500;`

(A) I only
(B) II only
(C) III only
(D) I and III only
(E) I, II, and III

For Questions 5 and 6 refer to the following `Ticket` struct:

```cpp
struct Ticket
{
    char row;
    int seat;
    double price;
    Ticket(): row(0), seat(0), price(0.0) {}
    Ticket(char r, int s, double p)
        : row(r),seat(s),price(p) {}
};
```

5. Which of the following would correctly initialize a variable of type `Ticket`?
    I `Ticket t;`
   II `Ticket t();`
  III `Ticket t('a', 10, 14.95);`

   (A) I only
   (B) II only
   (C) III only
   (D) I and III only
   (E) I, II, and III

6. Which would be correct `<code>` for the function

```cpp
void Display(const Ticket & T)
//Display row, seat, and price for Ticket T
{
    <code>
}
```

   (A) `cout << T;`
   (B) `cout << T.row << T.seat << " $" << T.price;`
   (C) `cout << Ticket.row << Ticket.seat << " $" << Ticket.price`
   (D) `cout << T.row() << T.seat() << " $" << T.price();`
   (E) `T.Display();`

Questions 7–9 refer to the `Time` class declared below:

```cpp
class Time
{
    public:
        Time();
        Time (int h, int m, int s);
        void SetTime (int h, int m, int s); //sets time
        void Increment();       //advances time by one second
        bool Equal (const Time &t) const;   //true if this time == t,
                                            //false otherwise
        bool LessThan(const Time &t) const; //true if this time<t,
                                            //false otherwise
        void Write() const;     //display time as hrs:mins:secs
    private:
        int myHrs;
        int myMins;
        int mySecs;
};
```

7. Which of the following is a *false* statement about the member functions?
   (A) Equal, LessThan, and Write are all constant member functions.
   (B) Increment is a mutator member function.
   (C) Time() is the default constructor.
   (D) Time(int h, int m, int s) is the copy constructor.
   (E) There are no free (nonmember) functions in the given declaration for this class.

8. Which of the following represents a correct implementation of the default constructor that sets hours, minutes, and seconds to 0?
   (A) Time:Time()::myHrs(0), myMins(0), mySecs(0) {}
   (B) Time::Time():myHrs(0), myMins(0), mySecs(0) {}
   (C) Time::Time
   ```
   {
       myHrs = 0;
       myMins = 0;
       mySecs = 0;
   }
   ```
   (D) Time::Time():myHrs(0), myMins(0), mySecs(0);
   (E) Time():myHrs(0), myMins(0), mySecs(0) {}

9. A client program has a Display function that writes the time represented by its parameter:

   ```
   void Display (const Time &t)
   //outputs time in the form hrs:mins:secs
   {
       <function body>
   }
   ```

   Which of the following are correct replacements for *<function body>*?

   I Time T(h,m,s);
      T.Write();

   II cout << t.myHrs << ":" << t.myMins << ":" << t.mySecs;

   III t.Write();

   (A) I only
   (B) II only
   (C) III only
   (D) II and III only
   (E) I, II, and III

Questions 10–17 refer to the following `Date` class declaration:

```
class Date
{
    public:
        Date(); //default constructor
        Date(int mo, int day, int yr); //constructor
        Date(const Date &d); //copy constructor
        int Month() const; //returns month of Date
        int Day() const; //returns day of Date
        int Year() const; //returns year of Date
        apstring DateString() const;//string representation
                            // of Date as "m/d/y",
                            // for example, 4/18/1985
    private:
        int myDay;
        int myMonth;
        int myYear;
};
```

10. Which of the following code segments would cause an error message if it were used in a client program of the `Date` class?
    (A) `Date d(2, 13, 1945);`
    (B) `Date d;`
        `int y = d.myYear;`
    (C) `Date d;`
        `int x = d.Year();`
    (D) `Date d;`
        `apstring s = d.DateString();`
    (E) `Date d;`
        `Date e = d;`

Questions 11 and 12 refer to the client program that contains the following lines of code:

```
Date FindBirthdate()
{
    Date bDate;

    <code to get bDate>

    return bDate;
}
int main()
{
    Date d1;
    Date d2(3, 14, 1987);
    Date d3 = d2;
    ...
    d1 = FindBirthdate();
    ...
}
```

11. How many times is the Date class copy constructor invoked when this code is executed?
    (A) 0
    (B) 1
    (C) 2
    (D) 3
    (E) 4

12. Which of the following is a correct replacement for *<code to get bDate>*?

    I   int m, d, y;
        cout << "Enter birthdate: mo, day, yr:" << endl;
        cin >> m >> d >> y;
        bDate = Date (m,d,y);

    II cout << "Enter birthdate: mo, day, yr:" << endl;
        cin >> bDate.Month() >> bDate.Day() >> bDate.Year();

    III cout << "Enter birthdate: mo, day, yr:" << endl;
        cin >> bDate.myMonth >> bDate.myDay >> bDate.myYear;

    (A) I only
    (B) II only
    (C) III only
    (D) I and II only
    (E) I, II, and III

13. Consider the implementation of a Write() member function that is added to the Date class:

    ```
    void Date::Write() const
    //Write the date in the form m/d/y, for example 2/17/1948
    {
        <implementation code>
    }
    ```

    Which of the following could be used as *<implementation code>*?

    I   cout << myMonth << "/" << myDay << "/" << myYear;
    II cout << Month() << "/" << Day() << "/" << Year();
    III cout << DateString();

    (A) II only
    (B) III only
    (C) II and III only
    (D) I and II only
    (E) I, II, and III

14. The following nonmember function is defined for the Date class:

```
bool LeapYear(int year);
//Returns true if year is a leap year, false otherwise.
//A leap year is a year divisible by 4, except for years
//ending in 00, which must also be divisible by 400.
```

LeapYear does not need to be a member function because
(A) Its implementation does not need to access other member functions of the class.
(B) Its implementation does not need to access private data members of the class.
(C) It does not return an object of the Date class.
(D) It has no parameters of type Date.
(E) Boolean functions are generally helper functions, not member functions.

15. Consider modifying the Date class so that it's possible to use assignment statements with Date objects. For example, following the declarations

```
Date d1;
Date d2 (1, 29, 1900);
```

the line

```
d1 = d2;
```

should assign the value of d2 to d1. Which of the following best describes the additional member function that should be provided?
(A) A default constructor
(B) A constructor with three arguments
(C) An overloaded copy constructor
(D) An overloaded assignment operator
(E) A private helper function with two Date arguments

16. The Date class is modified by adding the following member function:

```
void AddYears (int n); // add n years to date
```

Here is a client function that uses the Date class:

```
void f(Date &d, const Date &c)
{
    int i = d.Year();
    d.AddYears(10);
    if (c.Year() == d.Year())
        int j = c.Year();
    c.AddYears(1);
}
```

One of the lines of code has an error. Which one?
(A) int i = d.Year();
(B) d.AddYears(10);
(C) if (c.Year() == d.Year())
(D) int j = c.Year();
(E) c.AddYears(1);

17. The Date class is modified by adding a member function NextYear() that returns the current year plus one. Here is an implementation:

```
int Date::NextYear() const
{
    return ++myYear;
}
```

Why is this incorrect?

(A) The ++ operator is not overloaded for the Date class.

(B) The return type should be Date, not int.

(C) The keyword const indicates that the Date object won't be altered.

(D) NextYear should have an int parameter.

(E) A function that alters a class object should not be a member function.

Questions 18 and 19 refer to the following class declaration:

```
class Student
{
    public:
        Student(); //constructor

        void SetInfo(int idNum, int age, char sex);
        //sets personal data for Student

        void PrintAverage() const;
        // prints Student's current average
        // which is computed by ComputeAverage()

        //other public member functions

    private:
        int myIdNum;
        int myAge;
        char mySex;
        apvector <double> myScores;
        double ComputeAverage();
        //computes Student's current average
};
```

18. A client program has this declaration:

```
Student s;
```

Which of the following statements sets Student s to be a female with idNum 1489 and age 21?

(A) Student s(1489, 21, 'F');

(B) s.Student.SetInfo (1489, 21, 'F');

(C) s.SetInfo(1489, 21, 'F');

(D) s = SetInfo(1489, 21, 'F');

(E) s.SetInfo(1489, 21, F);

19. The function `ComputeAverage()` is a private member function because
    - (A) In order to access `myScores` it should be in the same part of the class declaration as `myScores`.
    - (B) It needs to be accessed by all clients of the class.
    - (C) It needs to be accessed by the `PrintAverage()` function.
    - (D) The class designer did not intend it to be used by clients of the class.
    - (E) Only functions of return type `void` or `Student` can be public member functions.

Questions 20–24 use the following definition of the `BankAccount` class. (Note that a pin is a password that allows you to access your account.)

```
class BankAccount
{
    public:
        BankAccount();
        BankAccount (const apstring & pin, double balance);
        double Balance (const apstring  & pin) const;
            //returns balance in bank account with
            // given pin number
        void Deposit (const apstring & pin, double amount);
        void Withdraw (const apstring & pin, double amount);

        //other public member functions ...

    private:
        apstring myPin;
        double myBalance;
};
```

20. In a client program, which of the following would correctly initialize an account to have pin number 5226 and a balance of $500?
    - (A) `BankAccount b(5226, 500);`
    - (B) `b.BankAccount("5226", 500);`
    - (C) `BankAccount b = ("5226", 500);`
    - (D) `BankAccount b = (5226, 500);`
    - (E) `BankAccount b("5226", 500);`

21. In the client program in Question 20, assume that the `BankAccount` variable `b` has been correctly initialized to have a pin of `"5226"` and a balance of 500. Which of the following would correctly withdraw $250 from this account?
    - (A) `double x = b.Withdraw("5226", 250);`
    - (B) `b.Withdraw("5226", 250);`
    - (C) `Withdraw("5226", 250);`
    - (D) `b.Withdraw(250);`
    - (E) `b.myBalance = b.myBalance - 250;`

22. To enable a client of the `BankAccount` class to make statements of the type

    ```
    BankAccount b1 = b2;
    ```

    what type of member function could be added to the class?
    (A) A copy constructor
    (B) A function `operator=` that overloads the assignment operator
    (C) A default constructor
    (D) A constructor with no parameters
    (E) An accessor that can access the private data members of the class

23. A client program needs to write out the balance in any given bank account. Which of the following correctly does this? You may assume that the variable `acct` has been correctly initialized as type `BankAccount`, and `somePin` of type `apstring` has been verified as the correct pin number for this account. You may also assume correct formatting of the output.
    (A) `cout << "$" << acct.myBalance(somePin);`
    (B) `cout << "$" << myBalance(somePin);`
    (C) `cout << "$" << acct.Balance();`
    (D) `cout << "$" << acct.Balance(somePin);`
    (E) `cout << "$" << acct.Balance(myPin);`

Level AB Only

24. The `BankAccount` class is modified by adding a copy constructor. The following declaration is added to the header file:

    ```
    BankAccount(BankAccount &b); //copy constructor
    ```

    This can be improved. How?
    (A) The copy constructor should be a constant member function.
    (B) The `BankAccount` parameter `b` should be passed by `const` reference.
    (C) The `BankAccount` parameter `b` should be passed by value.
    (D) The return type should be a constant reference to `BankAccount`.
    (E) The return type should be a reference to `BankAccount`.

Questions 25–30 refer to the following definition of the `Rational` class:

```
class Rational
{
public:
    //constructors
    Rational();      //default constructor
    Rational(int n); //an integer that specifies numerator
                     //only. Assumes denominator equals 1
    Rational(int numer, int denom); //constructor
    Rational(const Rational &r);    //copy constructor

    //accessors
    int Numerator() const;   //return numerator
    int Denominator() const; //return denominator
```

```
                        //assignment
                        const Rational & operator=(const Rational &r);
                        const Rational & operator+=(const Rational &r);
                        const Rational & operator+=(int n);
                        //Similarly for -=, *= and /=

                private:
                        int myNum;    //numerator
                        int myDenom; //denominator
                        void FixSigns(); //ensures myDenom > 0
                        void Reduce();   //ensures lowest terms
                };
```

25. The function Reduce() is not a public member function because
    (A) void member functions cannot be public.
    (B) Nonconstant member functions cannot be public.
    (C) Reduce() is not intended for use by clients of the Rational class.
    (D) Reduce() is intended for use only by clients of the Rational class.
    (E) Reduce() uses the private data members of the Rational class.

26. The constructors in the Rational class allow initialization of Rational variables in several different ways. Which of the following is most likely to cause an error?
    (A) Rational r1;
    (B) Rational r2 = r1;
    (C) Rational r(2,-3);
    (D) Rational r(3.5);
    (E) Rational r(10);

Level AB Only

27. The Rational class as shown is incomplete. Arithmetic binary operators need to be overloaded to allow statements of the following type:

```
        Rational r, x, y;
        r = x + y;
        r = 2 + x;
        r = x * 3;
```

and so on.

The following choices are examples of headers for overloaded operator functions declared as nonmember functions for the Rational class. Which of them *cannot* be modified to make the overloaded operator function a member function of the Rational class?
    (A) Rational operator+ (int lhs, const Rational &rhs);
    (B) Rational operator* (const Rational &lhs, const Rational
                                &rhs);
    (C) Rational operator/ (const Rational &lhs, const Rational
                                &rhs);
    (D) Rational operator- (const Rational &lhs, int rhs);
    (E) Rational operator* (const Rational &lhs, int rhs);

28. The insertion operator << is to be overloaded for the Rational class. This will allow the following type of statement in a client program of the Rational class:

```
cout << r; //output Rational number r
```

Here is the declaration for this overloaded function, declared as a nonmember function:

```
ostream & operator<< (ostream &os, const Rational &val);
```

The operator<< function must be declared as a nonmember function because

(A) A call to the function is equivalent to os.operator<<(val), which doesn't make sense for a member function of the Rational class.

(B) A function that has a reference to a stream object in its parameter list cannot be a member function.

(C) It alters the Rational object when the function is called.

(D) Overloaded operator functions must all be nonmember functions.

(E) The operator>> function cannot be a member function, and all related functions must be grouped together.

29. The + operator will be overloaded for the Rational class to enable three different operations:

> Rational number + Rational number
> Rational number + integer
> integer + Rational number

Here is the implementation for the third case, integer + Rational number:

```
Rational operator+ (int a, const Rational &rhs)
{
    <code>
}
```

Which of the following is a correct replacement for *<code>*?

(A) rhs += a;
   return rhs;

(B) Rational r = rhs;
   r += a;
   return r;

(C) int temp = a;
   a += rhs;
   return a;

(D) Rational temp;
   temp = a + rhs;
   return temp;

(E) Rational r =*this;
   r += a;
   return *this;

30. Here is the implementation code to overload the assignment operator for the Rational class:

```
const Rational & Rational::operator= (const Rational &r)
{
    <implementation code>
}
```

Which represents correct *<implementation code>*?

```
I   if (this != &r)
    {
        myNum = r.myNum;
        myDenom = r.myDenom;
    }
    return this;
```

```
II  if (this != &r)
    {
        myNum = r.myNum;
        myDenom = r.myDenom;
    }
    return *this;
```

```
III myNum = r.Numerator();
    myDenom = r.Denominator();
```

(A) I only
(B) II only
(C) III only
(D) II and III only
(E) I, II, and III

31. Which is a *false* statement about the C++ reserved word `this`?
    (A) `this` means the pointer to the current object.
    (B) A programmer should not try to assign a value to `this`.
    (C) `this` is used in the implementation of class member functions only.
    (D) If a class has a data member, `myAttribute`, then the statement
    ```
    myAttribute = someValue;
    ```
    is equivalent to
    ```
    this->myAttribute = someValue;
    ```
    (E) `this` should always be used in the implementation code for overloading a binary arithmetic operator like +.

32. The code for which of the following functions should include the line

    ```
    return *this ?
    ```

    (A) The default constructor
    (B) The copy constructor
    (C) Overloading the + operator
    (D) Overloading the += operator
    (E) Overloading the << operator

33. This question refers to the following class:

```
class IntObject
{
 public:
    IntObject(); //default constructor
    IntObject(int n); //constructor
    IntObject(const IntObject &t); //copy constructor
    void Increment(); //increment by 1

 private:
    int myInt;
};

IntObject::IntObject(): myInt(0) {}
IntObject::IntObject(int n): myInt(n) {}
IntObject::IntObject(const IntObject &t): myInt(t.myInt) {}
void IntObject::Increment()
{
    myInt++;
}
```

Here is a client program that uses this class:

```
IntObject SomeFunction (IntObject obj);

int main()
{
    IntObject x(2), y(7);
    IntObject a = y;
    x = SomeFunction(y);
    a = SomeFunction(x);
    return 0;
}

IntObject SomeFunction (IntObject obj)
{
    IntObject Ans = obj;
    Ans.Increment();
    return Ans;
}
```

How many calls will this program make to the copy constructor of class IntObject?
 (A) 1
 (B) 3
 (C) 5
 (D) 7
 (E) 9

34. A certain class, `SomeClass`, has been defined and contains a void public member function `Print()`. A client program contains the following code:

```
SomeClass x;     //x correctly initialized with default
                 // constructor
x.Print();
```

When the program is run, an error message appears, which starts like this:

```
Link error: Undefined symbol Print ...
```

Which of the following errors in the *implementation* code for the function could be the cause of the error message?

  I Failure to prefix the function definition by the name of its class and the scope operator (two colons).
  II Failure to spell the function name correctly.
  III Complete omission of the function from the class implementation.

  (A) I only
  (B) II only
  (C) III only
  (D) I and III only
  (E) I, II, and III

35. Which of the following is a *correct* statement about classes?
  (A) All class member functions must appear in the public part of a class.
  (B) All classes must have a copy constructor and destructor to avoid compiler errors.
  (C) All overloaded operator functions must be public member functions.
  (D) The private data members of a class can be accessed by public member functions and clients of the class.
  (E) One of the major differences between a class and a struct is that the data members of a struct are by default public, whereas those of a class are by default private.

36. Which of the following is *not* a good reason for overloading an operator in a class?
  (A) Overloading allows the conventional use of the operator to be used for objects of that class.
  (B) Overloading operators in a meaningful way improves code readability.
  (C) Overloading operators allows the programmer to implement sophisticated code.
  (D) Overloading an operator allows the class type to be used as a parameter in a templated function that uses the operator.
  (E) Overloading binary operators for some classes allows concise notation for complicated arithmetic

Answer Key

1. **E**	13. **E**	25. **C**
2. **C**	14. **B**	26. **D**
3. **D**	15. **D**	27. **A**
4. **C**	16. **E**	28. **A**
5. **D**	17. **C**	29. **B**
6. **B**	18. **C**	30. **B**
7. **D**	19. **D**	31. **E**
8. **B**	20. **E**	32. **D**
9. **C**	21. **B**	33. **D**
10. **B**	22. **A**	34. **D**
11. **C**	23. **D**	35. **E**
12. **A**	24. **B**	36. **C**

Answers Explained

1. **(E)** `adr` is an object of type `Address`. Its `zip` field is accessed with `adr.zip`, which eliminates choices A, B, and C. Choice D is wrong because the `zip` data member is of type `int`; therefore, it cannot be assigned in quotes as it would be for a string.

2. **(C)** Since `addr` is of type `Address`, the student's `city` must be accessed with `addr.city`. This eliminates choices A and B. `s` is of type `Student`, which contains the `addr` field. Thus, to assign a `city` value to `s`, you must use `s.addr.city`. This eliminates choices D and E. You should never use the name of the struct in an assignment statement.

3. **(D)** The code in I is an example of an initializer list for a struct. This is valid for the simple types of the data members in the struct, but it is invalid for more complex types that have constructors defined for them, like `apvector`, `apstring`, and `apmatrix`. Segment II uses the .member construct to initialize each field. III *would* be correct if the struct had a constructor with three parameters, but it does not.

4. **(C)** Segment I is wrong because `b`, which is of type `BookStore`, cannot be assigned a value that is of type `City`. Segment II would be correct if `b.City` were changed to `b.branch`. Note that `City` is a type, and just as we don't say `b.int`, we don't say `b.City`.

5. **(D)** Declarations I and III correctly use the default constructor and constructor with parameters, respectively. Declaration II is a common error in declarations that use the default constructor: there should be no parentheses.

6. **(B)** Choice A would be correct if the << operator were overloaded for the `Ticket` struct, but you can't assume that it is. Choice C is wrong because the .member construct must be used with the `Ticket` *object*, not the type. Eliminate D: `row`, `seat`, and `price` are fields of the struct, not functions, so they should not have parentheses. Choice E seems to be treating the `Display` function as a member function of the `Ticket` class, which it is not.

7. **(D)** A copy constructor takes a class object as a parameter. Its declaration would look something like this:

   ```
   Time(const Time & T);
   ```

8. **(B)** Choice A is wrong because the scope resolution operator (2 colons) must precede the function name, not the parameter list. Eliminate choice C because there should be an empty parameter list following the function name (i.e., `Time::Time()`). In choice D function braces, `{}`, should replace the semicolon, whereas choice E is missing the class name and scope resolution operator before the function name, `Time::Time()`.

9. **(C)** I is wrong because it doesn't refer to the parameter, `t`, of the function. II is wrong because a client program may not access private data of the class.

10. **(B)** A client program may not access private data of the class. Note that in choices C, D, and E, `d` is initialized by the default constructor. In choice E, `e` is initialized by the copy constructor.

11. **(C)** The copy constructor would be invoked in these instances:
    - A declaration with initialization. Used in the statement `Date d3=d2;`.
    - A `Date` object passed as a value parameter. Not relevant in this example.
    - A `Date` object returned by value. Used in the statement `d1 = FindBirthdate();`.

12. **(A)** The idea here is to read in three separate variables for month, day, and year and then to construct the required date using the `Date` class constructor with three parameters. Code segment II won't work because `Month()`, `Day()`, and `Year()` are constant member functions and may not be used to read new values into `bDate`. Segment III is wrong because it tries to access private data members in a client program.

13. **(E)** All are correct. Since `Write()` is a member function, it is OK to use the private data members in its implementation code.

14. **(B)** The code for `LeapYear` performs tests on its integer parameter `year` and does not need to access any `Date` private data members.

15. **(D)** The constructors are used to initialize `Date` objects (eliminating choices A and B) and the copy constructor is used as described in the explanation for Question 11, so eliminate choice C. Choice E makes no sense in this context.

16. **(E)** The parameter `c` is passed by `const` reference, which means that the `Date` represented by `c` cannot be modified. The statement `c.AddYears(1)` attempts to modify the `myYear` part of `c`.

17. **(C)** The function `NextYear` should not be a constant member function, since it alters the `myYear` part of the `Date`. Note that the function would be correct if the statement

    ```
    return ++myYear;
    ```

were replaced by

```
return myYear + 1;
```

This is because `return ++myYear` increments `myYear` and returns the result. However, `return myYear+1` leaves `myYear` unchanged while returning the result of adding 1 to it.

18. **(C)** This class has no constructor with parameters, so the only way to assign actual values (nondefault values) to a `Student` object is to use the `SetInfo` member function. Thus, eliminate choice A. Choice D is wrong because it doesn't use the dot member operator with the `SetInfo` member function, whereas choice B uses this operator incorrectly by adding the class name. Choice E is wrong because the third parameter, which is type `char`, should be in single quotes.

19. **(D)** Any member function, irrespective of where it is placed in the class, can access the private data members of that class. A client of the class may not access private member functions.

20. **(E)** Choice A is wrong because the first parameter must be an `apstring`—one of the problems with choice D too. In choice B, `b` has not been declared of type `BankAccount`. Choices C and D both use the constructors incorrectly.

21. **(B)** Choice A is incorrect because the return type of `Withdraw` is `void`. Choice C doesn't have a `BankAccount` object; choice D is missing the `pin` parameter, and choice E is trying to access private data members in a client program.

22. **(A)** The given statement represents initialization of a class object by copying another, existing object. This is one of the uses of the copy constructor.

23. **(D)** Choices A and E try to access private data members in a client program. Eliminate choice C because `Balance` doesn't have a parameter. Choice B commits several sins: it refers to `myBalance` which is (a) private and (b) not a function. It also omits the object, `acct`.

Level AB Only

24. **(B)** In the implementation of this function, the current object will copy the parameter, `b`, without altering `b`. Thus, `b` should be passed by `const` reference. You should reject choices D and E immediately because constructors have no return type.

25. **(C)** `Reduce()` will be used in the implementation of the member functions only.

26. **(D)** None of the constructors in the `Rational` class takes a real-valued parameter. Thus, the real-valued parameter in choice D will be *implicitly converted* to an integer (truncated). This may cause an intent error.

27. **(A)** To be a member function, the left-hand operand of an overloaded binary operator function must be a class object. This is because the statement `a + b`, for example, is equivalent to `a.operator+(b)`, which is meaningless if `a` is not a member of the class. For example, to rewrite choices C and D as headers for member functions, we have

```
Rational operator/ (const Rational &rhs);
//overloads / to perform *this/r, r Rational

Rational operator- (int rhs);
//overloads - to perform *this - n, n an integer
```

This type of modification doesn't work for choice A because `*this` can't be of type `int` for the `Rational` class.

28. **(A)** `os.operator<<(val)` makes no sense as a member function for the `Rational` class since `os` is an `ostream` object. Note that the `ostream` parameter must come first in the function header since in the statement

```
cout << r;
```

the `cout` and `r` operands can't be interchanged. Recall that the left-hand operand is the `*this` of the implementation code, and to be a member function `*this` must refer to a `Rational` class object!

29. **(B)** Eliminate choice A because the `rhs` parameter cannot be altered since it is passed by `const` reference. Eliminate choice C because the left-hand side of `a += rhs` and the return value must both be `Rational` objects. Choice D is wrong because the statement `temp = a + rhs` uses what you're trying to write code for: `operator+` for an integer + `Rational` does not yet exist. Choice E is wrong because `*this` is meaningless here: the function whose implementation is being written is not a member function, so it doesn't make sense to refer to the current object.

30. **(B)** Code segment I uses incorrect syntax for returning a reference to the class object. The correct syntax is `return *this`. Segment III fails to return anything. Nor does it check for aliasing: `if (this != &r)`. This avoids assigning an object to itself. For this simple example, failure to do this test would not cause an error because the values being copied are simple, built-in types. But in general, you should always check for aliasing when defining `operator=`.

31. **(E)** The code for overloading a binary operator typically creates a new value of the class type. No class object is modified, so it makes no sense to use `this`. Note that choice D is correct: `this` is a pointer to the current object, so the pointer notation, while redundant in this example, is nevertheless not wrong. See Chapter 8 for further discussion of pointers.

32. **(D)** The default and copy constructors have no return type, thus it is meaningless to have a `return...` statement. Overloading the + operator returns a value of the class type and should not modify a class object. Overloading the << operator for class X returns a stream type and does not modify an object of type X. Also the keyword `this` is used only in the implementation of member functions, and the `operator<<` function cannot be a member function for class X.

33. **(D)** The line `IntObject a = y;` invokes the copy constructor once. The lines `x=SomeFunction(y);` and `a=SomeFunction(x);` each invoke it three times: once to make a copy of the value parameter of type `IntObject`, once in the line `IntObject Ans =obj;`, and once to return an `IntObject` by value.

34. **(D)** During compilation, if `Print` is misspelled in its implementation code, the compiler will not be able to find a matching header in the `SomeClass` declaration. This will produce a compiler error (something like "undefined identifier"), not a link error. After compilation, a link error occurs if the linker can't find the compiled version of the function implementation. Errors I and III would lead to this error message. Note that the function implementation is not needed for successful compilation of the rest of the program: all that is needed is a correct function declaration, and errors I and III don't preclude this.

35. **(E)** Choice A is incorrect because private member functions are member functions that won't be accessed by clients of the class. Choice B is incorrect because the compiler provides a default copy constructor and default destructor if the class definition omits them. Choice C is incorrect because overloaded operator functions may be nonmember functions. Those whose first (left-hand) parameter is not a class type *must* be nonmember functions. Choice D is incorrect because private data members can *never* be accessed by clients of the class.

36. **(C)** Implementing sophisticated code is often fun and ego-boosting but should never be an end in itself.

CHAPTER THREE

Program Design and Analysis

> *Weeks of coding can save you hours of planning.*
> —*Anonymous*

Students of introductory computer science typically see themselves as programmers. They no sooner have a new programming project in their heads than they're at the computer, typing madly to get some code up and running. (Is this you?)

To succeed as a programmer, however, you have to combine the practical skills of a software engineer with the analytical mindset of a computer scientist. A software engineer oversees the life cycle of software development: initiation of the project, analysis of the specification, and design of the program, as well as implementation, testing, and maintenance of the final product. A computer scientist (among other things!) analyzes the implementation, correctness, and efficiency of algorithms. All these topics are tested on the APCS exam.

The Program Design

Program Specification

The first step in writing a computer program is making sure that you understand the *specification,* a written description of the project.

Abstract Data Type vs. Data Structure

An *abstract data type* (ADT) in a program is an object being created or manipulated by the program, together with the operations needed. There can be more than one ADT in a program. For example, a computer program that maintains a database of all books in a library can be thought of as having two ADTs:

1. The list of books ADT, with operations like Search_List, Sort_By_Author, Remove_Book, and Add_New_Book.
2. A book ADT, with operations like Get_Author, Get_Title, Is_On_Shelf, Get_Location, and How_Many_Copies.

Notice that the ADT is an abstract idea, completely separate from the concrete details of a programming language.

A *data structure,* on the other hand, is a programming construct used to implement an abstract data type. Some examples of data structures are a variable of type `double`, an `apvector` of integers, and an `apmatrix` of type `bool`.

74

Here are some more examples of abstract data types and suitable data structures to implement them.

Example 1

A program must test the validity of a four-digit code number that a person will enter to be able to use a photocopy machine. Rules for validity are provided.

The ADT is a four-digit code number. Some of the operations needed to manipulate the ADT could be Read_Number, Test_Validity, Get_Separate_Digits, and Write_Number.

The data structure used to implement this ADT could be a variable of type `int` or four variables of type `char` to represent the four digits of the code number.

Example 2

A program must produce and print random bridge deals. (A bridge deal consists of four hands each with 13 cards.)

The ADT is a deck of cards, with operations Shuffle, Deal, Sort, Print, and so on. Another ADT here is a card, with operations like Assign_Suit, Assign_Value, and Print_Card.

The data structure for a card could be a variable of type `int` or an enumeration, defined in a `Card` class. For the deck ADT, the data structure could be an `apvector` of 52 elements of type `Card`, defined in a `Deck` class.

Top-down Design

A *top-down design* is a summary of the major tasks to be performed by a program, in order of execution. Each task is further broken down into subtasks, a process known as *stepwise refinement*. A good design provides a fairly detailed overall plan at a glance without including the minutiae of C++ code.

Example

A top-down design for the program that tests the validity of a four-digit code number could be:

Get number
    Prompt user
    Read number   ⎫ Stepwise refinement of "Get number"
    Check number ⎭
      Check for correct symbols (digits) ⎫ Stepwise refinement of "Check number"
      Check range   ⎭
Check validity
  Get separate digits
  <algorithm to check validity>
Write message
  Write number
  State if valid

Algorithm

An *algorithm* is a precise step-by-step procedure that solves a problem or achieves a goal. Don't write any code until your algorithm is completely clear to you.

Program Implementation

Robustness

Always assume that any user of your program is not as smart as you are. You must therefore aim to write a *robust* program, namely one that

- Won't give inaccurate answers for some input data.

- Won't crash if the input data are invalid.

- Won't allow execution to proceed if invalid data are entered.

Examples of bad input data include out-of-range numbers, characters instead of numerical data, and a response of "maybe" when "yes" or "no" was asked for.

Driver Program

Every function must be thoroughly tested before inclusion in a program. A *driver program* is one whose sole purpose is to test a given function.

Stub Function

Sometimes it will make more sense in the development of a program to test a calling function before testing a function it calls. A *stub* is a dummy function that stands in for a function until the actual function has been written and tested. A stub typically has an output statement to show that it was called in the correct place, or it may return some reasonable values if necessary.

Testing and Debugging

Test Data

Not every possible input value can be tested, so a programmer should be diligent in selecting a representative set of *test data*. Typical values in each part of a domain of the program should be selected, as well as endpoint values and out-of-range values.

Example

A program must be written to insert a value into its correct position in this sorted list:

```
2   5   9
```

Test data should include

- A value less than 2

- A value between 2 and 5

- A value between 5 and 9

- A value greater than 9

- 2, 5, and 9

Types of Errors (Bugs)

- A *syntax error* is one that is detected by the compiler. Syntax errors are caused by violating the rules of the programming language, for example, omitting semicolons or braces, using undefined identifiers, using keywords inappropriately, and having parameters that don't match in type and number.

- A *link error* is one detected by the *linker*, a program that links all the pieces of your program into one executable program, even though they might have been compiled in separate files. It also includes the code for the library functions that you use. Link errors occur when you refer to functions that have not been included, or when pieces of code have been incorrectly included more than once.

- A *compile-time error* occurs during compilation of your program. Both syntax and link errors can be thought of as compile-time errors, though, strictly speaking, compilation occurs before linking.

- A *run-time error* occurs during execution of a program. The program usually abruptly halts execution ("crashes"). Typical causes of run-time errors are attempts to divide by zero; using an array index that is out of bounds; attempting to open a file that cannot be found; and so on. An error that causes a program to run forever ("infinite loop") can also be regarded as a run-time error.

- An *intent* or *logic error* is one that fails to carry out the specification of the program. The program compiles and runs but does not do the job. These are sometimes the hardest types of errors to fix.

Program Analysis

Program Correctness

Testing that a program works does not prove that the program is correct. After all, you can hardly expect to test programs for every conceivable set of input data. Computer scientists have developed mathematical techniques to prove correctness in certain cases, but these are beyond the scope of the APCS course. Nevertheless, you are expected to be able to make assertions about the state of a program at various points during its execution.

Assertions

An *assertion* is a precise statement about a program at any given point. The idea is that if an assertion is proved to be true, then the program is working correctly at that point.

An informal step on the way to writing correct algorithms is to be able to make three kinds of assertions about your code.

Precondition

The *precondition* for any piece of code, whether it is a function, loop, or block, is a statement of what is true immediately before execution of that code.

Postcondition

The *postcondition* for a piece of code is a statement of what is true immediately after execution of that code.

Level AB Only

Loop invariant

A *loop invariant* applies only to a loop. It is a precise statement, in terms of the loop variables, of what is true before and after each iteration of the loop. It includes an assertion about the range of the loop variable. Informally, it describes how much of the loop's task has been completed at each stage.

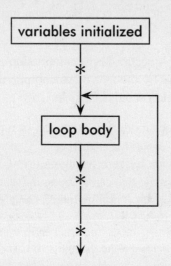

The asterisks show the points at which the loop invariant must be true:

- After initialization

- After each iteration

- After the final exit

Example

```
//function to generate n!
long int Factorial(int n)
//long int not tested on AP exam, but useful here for
//avoiding integer overflow of large factorial numbers
//precondition: n ≥ 0
//postcondition: n! has been returned
{
    long int product = 1;
    int i = 0;
    while (i < n)
    {
        i++;
        product *= i;
    }
    return product;
}
```

Level AB
(continued)

After initialization	`i = 0,`	`product = 1,` i.e., 0!
After first pass	`i = 1,`	`product = 1,` i.e., 1!
After second pass	`i = 2,`	`product = 2,` i.e., 2!
. . .		
After kth pass	`i = k,`	`product = k!`

The loop invariant for the `while` loop is

```
product = i!, 0 ≤ i ≤ n
```

Here is an alternative function body for this function. (Assume the same function header, comment, and pre- and postconditions.)

```
{
    long int product = 1;
    for (int i=1; i<=n; i++)
        product *= i;
    return product;
}
```

The loop invariant for the `for` loop is

```
product = (i-1)!, 1 ≤ i ≤ n+1
```

Here `(i-1)!` (rather than `i!`) is correct because `i` is incremented at the *end* of each iteration of the loop. Also, `n+1` is needed in the second part of the loop invariant because `i` has a value of `n+1` after the final exit from the loop. Remember, the invariant must also be true after the final exit.

Efficiency

An efficient algorithm is one that is economical in the use of

- CPU time. This refers to the number of machine operations required to carry out the algorithm (arithmetic operations, comparisons, data movements, etc.).

- Memory. This refers to the number and complexity of the variables used.

Some factors that affect run-time efficiency include unnecessary tests, excessive movement of data elements, and redundant computations, especially in loops.

Always aim for early detection of output conditions: your sorting algorithm should halt when the list is sorted; your search should stop if the key element has been found.

In discussing efficiency of an algorithm, we refer to the *best case*, *worst case*, and *average case*. The best case is a configuration of the data that causes the algorithm to run in the least possible amount of time. The worst case is a configuration that leads to the greatest possible run time. Typical configurations (i.e., not specially chosen data) give the average case. It is possible that best, worst, and average cases don't differ much in their run times.

For example, suppose that we must search a list of distinct random numbers for a given key value. The algorithm we use is a sequential search starting at the beginning of the list. In the best case, the key will be found in the first position we examine. In the worst case, it will be in the last position or not in the list at all. On average, the key will be somewhere in the middle of the list.

Big-O notation provides a quantitative way of describing the run time or space efficiency of an algorithm. This method is independent of both the programming language and the computer used.

Let n be the number of elements to be processed. For a given algorithm, express the number of comparisons, exchanges, data movements, primitive operations, and the like as a function of n, $T(n)$. (Primitive operations involve simple built-in types and take one unit of time, for example, adding two ints, cin for a double, assigning a char, and performing simple tests.) The type of function that you get for $T(n)$ determines the "order" of the algorithm. For example, if $T(n)$ is a linear function of n, we say the algorithm is $O(n)$ ("order n"). The idea is that for large values of n, the run time will be proportional to n. Here is a list of the most common cases.

Function Type for $T(n)$	Big-O Description
constant	$O(1)$
logarithmic	$O(\log n)$
linear	$O(n)$
quadratic	$O(n^2)$
cubic	$O(n^3)$
exponential	$O(2^n)$

Example 1

An algorithm that searches an unordered list of n elements for the largest value could need n comparisons, and n reassignments to a variable max. Thus, $T(n) \approx 2n$, which is linear, so the search algorithm is $O(n)$.

Example 2

An algorithm that prints out the last five elements of a long list stored as an array (apvector) takes the same amount of time irrespective of the length of the list. Thus, $T(n) = 5$, a constant, and the algorithm is $O(1)$.

Example 3

Algorithm 1 executes with $T(n) = 3n^2 - 5n + 10$ and Algorithm 2 has $T(n) = \frac{1}{2}n^2 - 50n + 100$. Both of these are quadratic, and the algorithms are therefore $O(n^2)$. Constants, low-order terms, and coefficients of the highest order term are ignored in assessing Big-O run times.

NOTE

1. Big-O notation is only meaningful for n large. When n is large, there is some value n above which an $O(n^2)$ algorithm will always take longer than an $O(n)$ algorithm, or an $O(n)$ algorithm will take longer than an $O(\log n)$ algorithm, and so on.
2. The following table shows approximately how many computer operations could be expected given n and the big-O description of the algorithm. For example, an $O(n^2)$ algorithm performed on 100 elements would require on the order of $100^2 = 10^4$ computer operations, whereas an $O(\log_2 n)$ algorithm would require approximately 7 operations.

Level AB
(continued)

n	$O(\log_2 n)$	$O(n)$	$O(n^2)$	$O(2^n)$
16	4	16	256	2^{16}
100	7	100	10^4	2^{100}
1000	10	1000	10^6	2^{1000}

3. Notice that one can solve only very small problems with an algorithm that has exponential behavior. At the other extreme, a logarithmic algorithm is very efficient.

Multiple-Choice Questions on Program Design and Analysis

1. A program is to be written that reads in a five-digit identification number. The specification does not state whether zero can be entered as a first digit. The programmer should
   (A) Write the code to accept zero as a first digit since zero is a valid digit.
   (B) Write the code to reject zero as a first digit since five-digit integers do not start with zero.
   (C) Eliminate zero as a possibility for any of the digits.
   (D) Treat the identification number as a four-digit number if the user enters a number starting with zero.
   (E) Check with the writer of the specification whether zero is acceptable as a first digit.

2. You are required to write a program that balances a checkbook. Which is the best description of the main abstract data type for the program?
   (A) A checkbook
   (B) The bank
   (C) Money
   (D) A check
   (E) An apvector of type double

3. Which of the following would *not* be a suitable operation as part of a checkbook abstract data type?
   (A) Record deposit
   (B) Record withdrawal
   (C) Add amounts
   (D) Subtract amounts
   (E) Initialize amounts of money to 0.0

Refer to the following three program descriptions for this question.

   I Test whether there exists at least one three-digit integer whose value equals the sum of the squares of its digits.
   II Read in a three-digit code number and check if it is valid according to some given formula.
   III License plates consist of three digits and three capital letters. Read in a license plate, and check if there are any repeated characters.

4. Which of the preceding program descriptions have a three-digit number as the abstract data type?
   (A) I only
   (B) II only
   (C) III only
   (D) I and II only
   (E) I, II, and III

5. A program is to be written that manipulates three-digit integers. Some of the operations include reversing digits, finding the sum of digits, and finding the product of digits. Which of the following is the *least* suitable data structure for the implementation of a three-digit number ADT?
    (A) A variable of type `int`
    (B) A variable of type `double`
    (C) An array of three integers
    (D) Three variables of type `char`
    (E) A string of length 3

6. The first step in a top-down design for writing a store inventory program is
    (A) Declare all global variables.
    (B) Make a list of all items in the store.
    (C) List all functions that are necessary for maintaining an inventory.
    (D) Design the input and output of inventory items.
    (E) Write and test the function that will be called most often.

7. Top-down programming is illustrated by which of the following?
    (A) Writing a program from top to bottom in C++
    (B) Writing an essay describing how the program will work, without including any C++ code
    (C) Using driver programs to test all functions in the order that they're called in the program
    (D) Writing and testing the lowest level functions first and then combining them to form appropriate abstract operations
    (E) Writing the program in terms of the operations to be performed and then refining these operations by adding more detail

8. Which of the following should influence your choice of a particular algorithm?
    I The running time of the algorithm.
    II The memory requirements of the algorithm.
    III The ease with which the logic of the algorithm can be understood.

    (A) I only
    (B) III only
    (C) I and III only
    (D) I and II only
    (E) I, II, and III

9. A list of numbers is stored in a sorted array. It is required that the list be maintained in sorted order. This requirement leads to inefficient execution for which of the following processes?

    I Summing the five smallest numbers in the list.
    II Finding the maximum value in the list.
    III Inserting and deleting numbers.

  (A) I only
  (B) III only
  (C) II and III only
  (D) I and III only
  (E) I, II, and III

10. Which of the following is *not* necessarily a feature of a robust program?
  (A) Does not allow execution to proceed with invalid data.
  (B) Uses algorithms that give correct answers for extreme data values.
  (C) Will run on any computer without modification.
  (D) Will not allow division by zero.
  (E) Will anticipate the types of errors that users of the program may make.

11. A large C++ program was thoroughly tested and found to have no bugs. What can be concluded?
  (A) The program has no bugs.
  (B) The program may have bugs.
  (C) All of the preconditions in the program are correct.
  (D) All of the postconditions in the program are correct.
  (E) Every function in the program may safely be used in other programs.

12. A certain freight company charges its customers for shipping overseas according to this scale:

> $80 per ton for a weight of 10 tons or less
> $40 per ton for each additional ton over 10 tons but
>   not exceeding 25 tons
> $30 per ton for each additional ton over 25 tons

For example, to ship a weight of 12 tons will cost 10(80) + 2(40) = $880. To ship 26 tons will cost 10(80) + 15(40) + 1(30) = $1430.
A function takes as parameter an integer that represents a valid shipping weight and outputs the charge for the shipment. Which of the following is the smallest set of input values for shipping weights that will adequately test this function?
  (A) 10, 25
  (B) 5, 15, 30
  (C) 5, 10, 15, 25, 30
  (D) 0, 5, 10, 15, 25, 30
  (E) 5, 10, 15, 20, 25, 30

13. You wish to write a program that will calculate the mean of values stored in integers n1, n2, n3, and n4, and store the result in `average` which is of type `double`. What kind of error will you cause with this statement?

    ```
    double average = n1 + n2 + n3 + n4 /double(4);
    ```

    (A) syntax
    (B) run-time
    (C) overflow
    (D) logic
    (E) type mismatch

14. In a program to find the mean of a list of test scores for a class of students, a programmer forgot to include a test that would check for a given student having a number of scores, `numScores`, equal to zero. If `numScores` equals zero for a student in the class, when will the error be detected?
    (A) At compile time
    (B) While editing the program
    (C) As soon as that student's data are input
    (D) During execution of the program, following input of all students' data
    (E) When an incorrect value for the mean score is output

15. Which best describes a precondition of a function? It is an assertion that
    (A) Describes precisely the conditions that must be true at the time the function is called.
    (B) Initializes the parameters of the function.
    (C) Describes the effect of the function on its postcondition.
    (D) Explains what the function does.
    (E) States what the initial values of the local variables in the function must be.

16. Consider the following code fragment:

    ```
    //precondition: a1, a2, a3 contain 3 distinct integers
    //postcondition: max contains the largest of a1,a2,a3

    //first set max equal to larger of a1 and a2
    if (a1 > a2)
        max = a1;
    else
        max=a2;
    //set max equal to larger of max and a3
    if (max < a3)
        max = a3;
    ```

    Which of the following initial setups for a1, a2, a3 will cause (1) the least number of computer operations (best case) and (2) the greatest number of computer operations (worst case) for this algorithm?
    (A) (1) largest value in a1 or a2   (2) largest value in a3
    (B) (1) largest value in a2 or a3   (2) largest value in a1
    (C) (1) smallest value in a1   (2) largest value in a2
    (D) (1) largest value in a2   (2) smallest value in a3
    (E) (1) smallest value in a1 or a2   (2) largest value in a3

Refer to the following code segment for Questions 17 and 18.

```
//compute the mean of integers 1 .. N
//N is an integer ≥ 1 and has been initialized
int k = 1;
double mean, sum=1.0;
while (k < N)
{
    <loop body>
}
mean = sum/N;
```

17. What is the precondition for the `while` loop?
    (A) $N \geq 1$, k = 1, sum = 1.0
    (B) sum = 1 + 2 + 3 + ... + k
    (C) k < N, sum = 1.0
    (D) k ≥ N, sum = 1.0
    (E) mean = sum/N

Level AB Only

18. What should replace `<loop body>` so that the following is the loop invariant for the `while` loop:

$$sum = 1 + 2 + ... + k, \; 1 \leq k \leq N$$

    (A) sum += k;
        k++;

    (B) k++;
        sum += k;

    (C) sum++;
        k += sum;

    (D) k += sum;
        sum++;

    (E) sum += k;

Questions 19 and 20 refer to the Fibonacci sequence described here. The sequence of Fibonacci numbers is $1, 1, 2, 3, 5, 8, 13, 21, \ldots$. The first two Fibonacci numbers are each 1. Each subsequent number is obtained by adding the previous two. Consider this function:

```
int Fib(int n)
//precondition: n ≥ 1
//postcondition: the nth Fibonacci number has been returned
{
    int prev=1, next=1, sum=1;
    for (int i=3; i<=n; i++)
    {
        sum = next + prev;
        prev = next;
        next = sum;
    }
    return sum;
}
```

19. Which of the following is a correct assertion about the loop variable i?
    (A) `1 ≤ i ≤ n`
    (B) `0 ≤ i ≤ n`
    (C) `3 ≤ i ≤ n`
    (D) `3 ≤ i ≤ n+1`
    (E) `3 < i < n+1`

20. Which of the following is a correct loop invariant for the `for` loop, assuming the correct bounds for the loop variable i?
    (A) `sum =` ith Fibonacci number
    (B) `sum = (i+1)`th Fibonacci number
    (C) `sum = (i-1)`th Fibonacci number
    (D) `sum = (prev-1)`th Fibonacci number
    (E) `sum = (next+1)`th Fibonacci number

21. An efficient algorithm that must delete the last two elements in a long list of n elements stored as an array is
    (A) $O(n)$
    (B) $O(n^2)$
    (C) $O(1)$
    (D) $O(2)$
    (E) $O(\log n)$

22. An algorithm to remove all negative values from a list of n integers sequentially examines each element in the array. When a negative value is found, each element is moved down one position in the list. The algorithm is
    (A) $O(1)$
    (B) $O(\log n)$
    (C) $O(n)$
    (D) $O(n^2)$
    (E) $O(n^3)$

Level AB
(continued)

23. A certain algorithm is $O(\log_2 n)$. Which of the following will be closest to the number of computer operations required if the algorithm manipulates 1000 elements?
    (A) 10
    (B) 100
    (C) 1000
    (D) 10^6
    (E) 10^9

24. A certain algorithm examines a list of n random integers and outputs the number of times the value 5 appears in the list. Using big-O notation, this algorithm is
    (A) $O(1)$
    (B) $O(5)$
    (C) $O(n)$
    (D) $O(n^2)$
    (E) $O(\log n)$

Refer to the following function for Questions 25 and 26.

```
int Mystery(int a, int b)
//precondition: a and b are initialized integers
{
    int total=0, count=1;
    while (count <= b)
    {
        total += a;
        count++;
    }
    return total;
}
```

25. What is the postcondition for function `Mystery`?
    (A) $\text{total} = a + b$
    (B) $\text{total} = a^b$
    (C) $\text{total} = b^a$
    (D) $\text{total} = a * b$
    (E) $\text{total} = a/b$

Level AB Only

26. Which is a loop invariant for the `while` loop?
    (A) `total = (count-1)*a`, $0 \le \text{count} \le b$
    (B) `total = count*a`, $1 \le \text{count} \le b$
    (C) `total = (count-1)*a`, $1 \le \text{count} \le b$
    (D) `total = count*a`, $1 \le \text{count} \le b+1$
    (E) `total = (count-1)*a`, $1 \le \text{count} \le b+1$

Answer Key

1. **E**	10. **C**	19. **D**
2. **A**	11. **B**	20. **C**
3. **E**	12. **C**	21. **C**
4. **D**	13. **D**	22. **D**
5. **B**	14. **D**	23. **A**
6. **C**	15. **A**	24. **C**
7. **E**	16. **A**	25. **D**
8. **E**	17. **A**	26. **E**
9. **B**	18. **B**	

Answers Explained

1. (**E**) A programmer should never make unilateral decisions about a program specification. When in doubt, check with the person who wrote the specification.

2. (**A**) The abstract data type is the major object that is being created or manipulated by the program, in this case a checkbook. Choice E is wrong because it is a *data structure* (which may be used for implementing a checkbook), not an ADT.

3. (**E**) Initializing variables may be done as part of the implementation of operations, but it is not an abstract operation associated with the checkbook ADT (as are the operations in choices A–D).

4. (**D**) In I and II a three-digit number is the object being manipulated and is therefore the ADT. For III, however, the ADT is a license plate consisting of three digits and three letters.

5. (**B**) It is unwise to store the original number in a variable of type `double` because, in order to access each digit, you will need to use the integer operators / and % (integer division and mod).

6. (**C**) A top-down design is an overall plan of the program. It is therefore essential to start with a list of the functions that will be used for the inventory. Eliminate choices A and E: no code should be written until the design is in place. Eliminate B and D: input and output are secondary considerations that need to be addressed as part of the plan, but not until the main functions have been decided upon.

7. (**E**) Top-down programming consists of listing the functions for the abstract data type and then using stepwise refinement to break each function into a list of subtasks. Eliminate choices A, C, and D: top-down programming refers to the design and planning stage and does not involve any actual writing of code. Choice B is closer to the mark, but "top-down" implies a list of functions, not an essay describing the functions.

8. (**E**) All three considerations are valid when choosing an algorithm. III is especially important if your code will be part of a larger project created by several programmers. Yet even if you are the sole writer of a piece of software, be aware that your code may one day need to be modified by others.

9. (**B**) A process that causes excessive data movement is inefficient. Inserting an element into its correct (sorted) position involves moving elements to create a slot for this element. In the worst case, the new element must be inserted into the first slot, which involves moving every element up one slot. Similarly, deleting an element involves moving elements down a slot to close the "gap." In the worst case, where the first element is deleted, all elements in the array will need to be moved. Summing the five smallest elements in the list means summing the first five elements. This requires no testing of elements and no excessive data movement, so it is efficient. Finding the maximum value in a sorted list is very fast—just select the element at the appropriate end of the list.

10. (**C**) "Robustness" implies the ability to handle all data input by the user and to give correct answers even for extreme values of data. A program that is not robust may well run on another computer without modification, and a robust program may need modification before it can run on another computer.

11. (**B**) Testing a program thoroughly does not prove that a program is correct. Usually it is impossible to test every possible set of input data. (Think of the Y2K bug!)

12. (**C**) Eliminate choice D because 0 is an invalid weight, and you may infer from the function description that invalid data have already been screened out. Eliminate choice E because it tests two values in the range 10–25. (This is not wrong, but choice C is better.) Eliminate choice A since it tests only the endpoint values. Eliminate B because it tests *no* endpoint values.

13. (**D**) The statement is syntactically correct, but as written it will not find the mean of the integers. The bug is therefore an intent or logic error. To execute as intended, the statement needs parentheses:

```
double average = (n1 + n2 + n3 + n4)/double(4);
```

14. (**D**) This is a run-time error caused by an attempt to divide by zero.

15. (**A**) A precondition does not concern itself with the action of the function, the local variables, the algorithm, or the postcondition. Nor does it initialize the parameters. It simply asserts what must be true directly before execution of the function.

16. (**A**) The best case causes the fewest computer operations, and the worst case leads to the maximum number of operations. In the given algorithm, the initial test if (a1 > a2) and the assignment to max will occur irrespective of which the largest value is. The second test, if (max < a3), will also always occur. The final statement, max = a3, will occur only if the largest value is in a3; thus, this represents the worst case. So the best case must have the biggest value in a1 or a2.

17. (**A**) The precondition is an assertion about the variables in the loop just before the loop is executed. Variables N, k, and sum have all been initialized to the values shown in choice A. Choice C is wrong because k may equal N. Choice

D is wrong because k may be less than N. Choice E is wrong because mean is not defined until the loop has been exited. Choice B is wrong because no adding has been done at the start of the loop.

Level AB Only

18. **(B)** Note that A and B are the only reasonable choices. Choice E results in an infinite loop, and choices C and D increment sum by 1 instead of by k. For choice A, 1 is added to sum in the first pass through the loop, which is wrong; 2 should be added. Thus, k should be incremented before updating sum. Note that for choice B after the first pass k = 2 and sum = 1 + 2. After the second pass, k = 3 and sum = 1 + 2 + 3. Also note that k's initial value is 1 and final value on exiting the loop for the last time is N, as in the given loop invariant.

19. **(D)** Eliminate choices A, B, and E since i is initialized to 3 in the for loop. Choice C is wrong because the value of i after final exit from the loop is n+1.

20. **(C)** Eliminate choices D and E, since the loop invariant should include the loop variable in its statement. Notice that the first exit from the for loop has i = 4 and sum = 2, which is the third Fibonacci number. In general, at each exit from the loop, sum is equal to the (i-1)th Fibonacci number.

21. **(C)** Deleting a constant number of elements at the end of an array is independent of n, and therefore $O(1)$. Don't let yourself be caught by choice D: there is no such thing as $O(2)$!

22. **(D)** In the worst case, every element in the array is negative. Thus the number of data moves will be $(n-1) + (n-2) + \ldots + 2 + 1 = n(n-1)/2$. This is a quadratic function, so the algorithm is $O(n^2)$. Alternatively, you can see that each of the n elements must be examined, and in the average case it is moved about $n/2$ places. So again you get $O(n^2)$. Note that unless you are specifically asked, you should not quote the order of the best case—always assume worst case or average case behavior. Here in the best case there are no negative values in the list and so no data movements. The algorithm is $O(n)$.

23. **(A)** If $n = 1000$, $\log_2 n \approx 10$ since $2^{10} \approx 1000$.

24. **(C)** The entire list of n integers must be examined once; thus, the algorithm is $O(n)$.

25. **(D)** a is being added to total b times, which means that at the end of execution total = a*b.

Level AB Only

26. **(E)** Since count is incremented at the end of the loop, total = (count-1)*a, not count*a. Thus, eliminate choices B and D. Choice A is wrong because count is initialized to 1, not 0. Note that after the final exit from the loop, count has value b+1, which eliminates choice C.

CHAPTER FOUR

One- and Two-Dimensional Arrays

ARRAYED: Drawn up and given an orderly disposition,
as a rioter hanged to a lamppost.
—Ambrose Bierce, The Devil's Dictionary *(1911)*

One-Dimensional Arrays

An array is a data structure that can be used to implement any list abstract data type, where the elements in the list are of the same type; for example, a class list of 25 test scores, a membership list of 100 names, or a store inventory of 500 items.

For an array of N elements in C++, index values ("subscripts") go from 0 to $N - 1$. A major disadvantage of built-in arrays (also called C-style arrays) is that they have no checking for indexes that are out of range. Out-of-range errors can cause disastrous system crashes. For this reason, the use of built-in arrays is discouraged, and they are not included on the AP exam.

The apvector Class

Arrays will be implemented with the apvector class. This is a class of "safe" (range-checked) arrays created by the APCS Development Committee. You will be provided with a copy of the header file apvector.h during the AP exam. (An updated version of the AP classes can be found on the College Board web site, *http://www.collegeboard.org/ap/computer-science/*.

Templated Classes

The apvector class is an example of a *templated class*, a "container" that allows the class to be declared with a parameter of any type. So we can declare an array of itemType, where itemType is any specified type.

Note that for a templated class,

1. template <class itemType> must precede the class declaration:

   ```
   template <class itemType>
   class SomeClass
   ```

   Here template and class are keywords; itemType and SomeClass are identifiers that you choose.

2. The itemType parameter becomes concrete when variables of the class are declared, as in the following example. The actual data type is placed in <>

brackets after the class name, and the compiler then generates an instance of `SomeClass` with `itemType` replaced by the actual type. For example,

```
//MyProgram.cp
#include "apvector.h"

struct SomeStruct
{
    ...
};

int main()
{
    apvector <double> realList;
    apvector <int> intList;
    apvector <apstring> wordList;
    apvector <SomeStruct> StructList;
    ...
```

NOTE   A user-defined type used as a template argument (such as `apstring` and `SomeStruct` in this example) should have a default constructor.

Implementation of apvector Class

The complete implementation (`apvector.cpp`) can be found at the College Board web site, *http://www.collegeboard.org/ap/computer-science/*. This will *not* be provided to you on the AP exam.

Both Level A and AB students should be able to

- Read and understand the implementation code

- Use the apvector functions in client programs

An `apvector` object is implemented with a C-style array called `myList` and an `int` variable `mySize` that keeps track of the number of elements in the array.

Each member function of a templated class is a templated function. Thus, the phrase `template <class itemType>` must precede the definition of every function in the implementation. In general, the header for each function has this format:

```
template <class itemType>
return_type apvector <itemType>  ::  function_name (parameter list)
```
                  class name   scope resolution operator

The Functions in apvector

Here is a summary of all the functions in the apvector class.

1. Constructors
   Recall that a constructor has no return type. Thus, the first four member functions in apvector are constructors.

```
apvector()
```

This is the default constructor. It allows you to declare a zero-element array that will need to be resized as soon as you use it. For example,

```
apvector <int> a;    //array a has no elements
```

```
apvector (int size)
```

This allows you to declare an array that can hold `size` elements. Each element is initialized to some default value. For example,

```
apvector <double> d(100);    //array d has 100 slots
```

```
apvector (int size, const itemType & fillValue)
```

This allows you to declare an array with `size` items, each initialized to `fillValue`. For example,

```
apvector <int> a(500,0);      //array a has 500 slots
                              //each initialized to 0
```

```
apvector (const apvector <itemType> & vec)
```

This is the copy constructor, which allows an `apvector` object to be declared by copying an existing `apvector`. For example,

```
apvector <int> v(200,5);
apvector <int> b = v;    //copy constructor used
                         //here. b now contains 200
                         //elements each equal to 5
```

2. Destructor

```
~apvector()
```

The destructor recycles memory every time an `apvector` object goes out of scope. It is called automatically—you should never call it explicitly.

3. Assignment

```
const apvector & operator= (const apvector & vec)
```

This function overloads the assignment operator so that you can use assignment for `apvector` objects as you do for built-in types. For example,

```
apvector <int> a,b;
//code to initialize a and b
   ...
b = a; //assignment overload used here
```

4. Accessors

```
int length() const
```

This is a constant member function that returns the length of the array. (More precisely, it is the number of memory slots currently allocated to the array, which is not necessarily the number of slots you have filled with meaningful data.) For example,

```
apvector <double> d(100);
int x = d.length(); //x gets assigned the value 100
```

5. Indexing

```
itemType & operator [] (int k)
const itemType & operator [] (int k) const
```

These functions both overload the subscripting brackets, which allows `apvector` objects to mimic built-in arrays. Thus, after declaring

```
apvector <int> a(10);
```

we can refer to a[0], a[1], ... , a[9] in a meaningful way. The first form of the function is invoked for a non-`const` vector and allows assignment to individual elements, for example a[2]=5. The second is invoked for a `const` vector. Both functions will abort if you use an out-of-range index.

6. Modifiers

```
void resize(int newSize)
```

This function resizes the vector to `newSize` elements. If `newSize` is less than the current length, then elements may be lost. For example,

```
apvector <int> b(100);
cout << b.length();      //outputs 100
b.resize(50);
cout << b.length();      //outputs 50
```

Notice two features about the implementation of the `resize` function.

- The statement

  ```
  int numToCopy = newSize < mySize ? newSize : mySize;
  ```

  is equivalent to

  ```
  int numToCopy;
  if (newSize < mySize)
      numToCopy = newSize;
  else
      numToCopy = mySize;
  ```

  The ? : construct is not part of the APCS C++ subset and won't be tested on the exam.

- The algorithm to resize an `apvector` copies each element into a new block of memory slots. This is quite inefficient, especially if you add elements to your array one at a time and resize after each addition! Here are two possible approaches to improving efficiency by minimizing calls to `resize()`:

(i) Declare an apvector that is considerably larger than the length you'll need and have a variable n that keeps track of the actual number of elements. Whenever you add an element, n++ will reflect this. In this case a.length() no longer refers to the number of meaningful elements in the vector a.

(ii) If you can't be sure of declaring an array that is large enough, start with some reasonable initial length and keep track of the number of elements with n again. Test n against a.length() each time n is incremented. If n ever becomes bigger than the length, use resize() to double the size of a. If you like, you can do a final resize so that a.length equals n.

Level AB Only

Modifying apvector

AB students should be able to modify the apvector class by adding new member functions.

Example

Add a member function MaxValue() to the apvector class that returns the largest value in the array. You may assume as a precondition that the apvector has at least one element.

(a) How would you modify the apvector.h file?

(b) Give the complete implementation in apvector.cpp.

(c) Write a driver program to test function MaxValue() for an array of integers. You may assume the existence of functions GetList(a) and WriteList(a) that perform the following tasks: GetList(a) initializes array a to integer values, and then resizes a appropriately; WriteList(a) writes a[0], a[1],... a[a.length()-1] to the screen.

Solution.

(a) MaxValue() is an accessor and so should be declared as a constant member function. The following header should be added under //accessors:

```
itemType MaxValue() const;
```

The following comment should be added to the documentation section:

```
//itemType MaxValue() const
//precondition: vector contains at least one element
//postcondition: Returns the largest value in the vector
```

Note: These comments are added so that the new member function is written in a style that conforms with the style of the apvector class. On the AP exam, you are not generally required to comment your code, but you may be asked to write pre- and postconditions.

Level AB
(*continued*)

```
(b) template <class itemType>
    itemType apvector <itemType> :: MaxValue ()const
    // Returns the largest value in the vector
    {
        itemType max = myList[0];
        for (int i=1; i<mySize; i++)
            if (myList[i] > max)
                max = myList[i];
        return max;
    }

(c) //Driver program to test MaxValue
    int main()
    {
        apvector <int> a;

        GetList(a);
        WriteList(a);

        cout << "Largest value is " << a.MaxValue() << endl;

        return 0;
    }
```

Using Arrays

Arrays may be passed as parameters in functions. Like any nonsimple object, an apvector should be passed by reference if it may be modified and by const reference if it should not be changed. The type of the element is explicitly provided in the header.

Example 1

```
int CountNegs(const apvector <int> & a)
//precondition: a[0],...,a[a.length()-1] contain integers
//postcondition: number of negative values in a has been
//               returned
{
    int count = 0;
    for (int i=0; i<a.length(); i++)
        if (a[i] < 0)
            count++;
    return count;
}
```

Level AB Only

NOTE

1. This algorithm sequentially examines each element in the array, and so it is $O(n)$.
2. The loop invariant for the `for` loop is

count = number of negative values in a[0], ..., a[i-1], and
$$0 \le i \le a.length()$$

Loop invariants for array algorithms can be nicely illustrated with a diagram showing a snapshot of what is happening. Each rectangle represents a portion of array a. The labels on top of the rectangle are array indexes for elements at the beginning and end of each portion.

```
0                                       i-1  i            a.length()-1
                                                              ↘
┌──────────────────────────────────────────┬──────────────────────┐
│  count = number of negatives in here      │  still to be examined │
└──────────────────────────────────────────┴──────────────────────┘
```

Example 2

```
void InsertNum(apvector <int> & a, int & n, int num)
//precondition: a[0], ..., a[n-1] contain integers sorted in
//increasing order. n < a.length()-1
//postcondition: num has been inserted in its correct position
{
    //find insertion point
    int i = 0;
    while (i < n && num > a[i])
        i++;
    //if necessary, move elements a[i]...a[n-1] up 1 slot
    for (int j=n; j>=i+1; j--)
        a[j] = a[j-1];
    //insert num in i-th slot and update n
    a[i] = num;
    n++;
}
```

NOTE

1. This algorithm illustrates a disadvantage of the array data structure: insertion and deletion of an element in an ordered list is inefficient, since, in the worst case, it may involve moving all the elements in the list.

Level AB Only

2. Insertion or deletion of a single element in an ordered list is $O(n)$. If n elements must be inserted (or deleted) with this algorithm, the algorithm becomes $O(n^2)$.
3. The loop invariant for the `while` loop is

num > a[0], num > a[1], ... num > a[i-1], where $0 \le i \le n$

Here is the diagram that illustrates this loop invariant:

```
0                              i-1  i                    n-1
┌──────────────────────────────────┬──────────────────────┐
│  num > all elements in here       │  still to be examined │
└──────────────────────────────────┴──────────────────────┘
```

apvectors and Structs

An apvector As a Data Member

Example

```
struct Student
{
    apstring name;
    apvector <int> testScores;  //scores for one Student
};

Student s;
...
//print out all test scores for Student s
for (int i = 0; i<s.testScores.length(); i++)
    cout << s.testScores[i];
```

You may be wondering how the testScores apvector got (a) sized and (b) initialized. A good way is with a constructor in the Student struct to declare the apvector. Then in your program you use the . member construct to read in or assign actual testScores values. For example,

```
const int NUMSCORES = 10;
struct Student
{
    apstring name;
    apvector <int> testScores;
    Student() : //default constructor
        name(), //empty string
        testScores(NUMSCORES)   //NUMSCORES slots
        {}
};

int main()
{
    Student s;
    s.name = "Mathilda Concia";
    s.testScores[0] = 56;
    s.testScores[1] = 92;
        ...
```

Note: If the NUMSCORES parameter is omitted from the constructor, you need the statement

```
    s.testScores.resize(NUMSCORES);
```

in main before assigning values to the apvector.

An apvector of Structs

Let's expand the preceding example to include an array of structs.

```
apvector <Student> AllStudents;
...
//print a list of all the students' names
for (int i = 0; i<AllStudents.length(); i++)
    cout << AllStudents[i].name << endl;

//print the third score of the 100th student
//assumes that the first index of each array is 0
cout << AllStudents[99].testScores[2];
```

Vector Objects in a Class

The following simple example of a deck class (for a deck of cards) shows how an apvector can be used as a private data member for a class object. This example provides the framework to which other member functions like Shuffle and Deal can later be added.

Here is the header file, deck.h.

```
//deck class. array of 52 cards
#include "apvector.h"

typedef int CARD;

class deck
{
    public:
        deck();                  //constructor
        void NewDeck();          //initialize deck
        void WriteDeck() const; //write deck elements
    private:
        apvector <CARD> myDeck;
};
```

The typedef statement (useful, but not tested) is included to enhance the readability of the code. We think of a deck of cards, not a deck of ints.

Here is the implementation file, deck.cpp.

```
#include <iostream.h>
#include "deck.h"

const int NUMCARDS = 52;

deck::deck(): myDeck(NUMCARDS)
{}

void deck::NewDeck()
{
    for (int i=0; i<NUMCARDS; i++)
        myDeck[i] = i;
}

void deck::WriteDeck() const
{
    for (int i=0; i<NUMCARDS; i++)
        cout << myDeck[i] << " ";
    cout << endl;
}
```

Note that the default constructor creates (with an initializer list) a deck object using one of the apvector constructors. If it had been desirable to initialize each deck element to 0, say, the apvector constructor with the fillValue parameter could have been used:

```
deck :: deck() : myDeck(NUMCARDS,0) {}
```

Here is a driver program that tests the simple member functions shown earlier:

```
#include <iostream.h>
#include "deck.h"

int main()
{
    deck d;
    d.NewDeck();
    d.WriteDeck();
    return 0;
}
```

Note that the actual apvector is a private variable and is nowhere in sight in the client program shown.

apvector of Class Objects

Suppose a large card tournament needs to keep track of many decks. The abstract data type is a list of decks, and this could be implemented with an apvector of deck objects:

```
const int MAXDECKS = 500;
apvector <deck> allDecks(MAXDECKS); //creates 500 decks

//initialize the decks
for (int i=0; i<MAXDECKS; i++)
    allDecks[i].NewDeck();
```

Two-Dimensional Arrays

A two-dimensional array (matrix) is often the data structure of choice for abstract data types like board games, tables of values, theatre seats, and mazes.

As with one-dimensional arrays, two-dimensional arrays are implemented for the AP exam with a user-defined class of "safe" (range-checked) arrays, the apmatrix class. The complete header file apmatrix.h will be provided during the AP exam. It is available at *http://www.collegeboard.org/ap/computer-science/*.

The apmatrix Class

A Templated Class

A program using the apmatrix class needs to include the apmatrix.h header file:

```
#include "apmatrix.h"
```

As for `apvector`, `apmatrix` is a templated class. This allows you to declare a matrix of `itemType`, where `itemType` is any type you choose.

In the `apmatrix` class, the matrix object is implemented as an `apvector` of `apvectors`:

```
private:
    ...
    apvector<apvector<itemType> > myMatrix;
```

This means that each row of the matrix is an `apvector` of `itemType`. The space before the final angle bracket > prevents confusion with >>, the extraction operator.

Functions in `apmatrix`

The complete implementation (`apmatrix.cpp`) can be found at the College Board web site, *http://www.collegeboard.org/ap/computer-science/*. This will not be provided to you on the AP exam. You are, however, expected to be familiar with the member functions.

1. Constructors

   > `apmatrix()`

   This is the default constructor. It allows you to declare a 0-element matrix, which will need to be resized when you use it. For example,

   ```
   apmatrix <double> m;      //0 x 0 matrix (no elements)
   ```

   > `apmatrix(int rows, int cols)`

   This creates a `rows` × `cols` matrix, uninitialized. For example,

   ```
   apmatrix <int> m(50,40);     //50 x 40 matrix of ints
   ```

   > `apmatrix(int rows, int cols, const itemType & fillValue)`

   This constructor allows you to declare a `rows` × `cols` matrix with each element initialized to `fillValue`. For example,

   ```
   apmatrix <char> m(100,200,'f'); //100 x 200 matrix of
                                   //elements 'f'
   ```

   > `apmatrix(const apmatrix & mat)`

   This is the copy constructor. For example,

   ```
   apmatrix <int> m(10,15);
   //code to initialize m
   apmatrix <int> k = m;        //copy constructor invoked
   ```

2. Destructor

```
~apmatrix()
```

The destructor recycles memory. A reminder—you never invoke this explicitly.

3. Assignment

```
const apmatrix & operator = (const apmatrix & rhs)
```

This is the overloaded assignment operator. For example,

```
apmatrix <int> m1,m2;
//code to initialize m1 and m2
   ...
m2 = m1;    //overloaded assignment used here
```

4. Accessors

```
int numrows() const
int numcols() const
```

These constant member functions return the number of rows and columns of an apmatrix. For example,

```
apmatrix <int> m(25,30);
int x = m.numrows();        //x assigned value 25
int y = m.numcols();        //y assigned value 30
```

5. Indexing

```
const apvector <itemType> & operator [] (int k) const
apvector <itemType> & operator [] (int k)
```

As for apvector, these functions overload the indexing operator. This allows you to use the brackets to refer to matrix elements as for built-in arrays. For example, m[3][2]. The first index, 3, refers to a row; the second refers to a column. Note that m[i] refers to the entire ith row of the matrix.

6. Modifier

```
void resize(int newRows, int newCols)
```

This resizes the matrix to newRows × newCols. If newRows is less than the current number of rows, then elements may be lost; the same is true for newCols. For example,

```
apmatrix <int> m(20,60);
cout << m.numrows() << " " << m.numcols();     //outputs 20 60
m.resize(10,100);
cout << m.numrows() << " " << m.numcols();     //outputs 10 100
```

Matrix Algorithms

Look at the following 3 × 4 matrix:

$$
\begin{array}{cccc}
2 & 6 & 8 & 7 \\
1 & 5 & 4 & 0 \\
9 & 3 & 2 & 8
\end{array}
$$

If m is the apmatrix variable, the row subscripts go from 0 to 2 and the column subscripts go from 0 to 3. The element m[1][2] is 4, whereas m[0][2] and m[2][3] are both 8. In general, rows go from 0 to numrows()-1 and columns go from 0 to numcols()-1.

Example 1

You can access every element in a matrix as follows:

```
void AccessByRow(apmatrix <int> & m)
//row-by-row traversal of m
{
    for (int row=0; row<m.numrows(); row++)
        for (int col=0; col<m.numcols(); col++)
            Process m[row][col];
}
```

Note that interchanging the two for loops gives a column-by-column traversal of m.

Example 2

The major and minor diagonals of a square matrix are defined as follows:

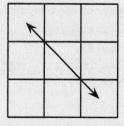 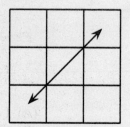

Major diagonal   **Minor diagonal**

You can process the diagonals as follows:

```
apmatrix <int> m(SIZE,SIZE);    //SIZE is a const int value

void ProcessDiagonals(apmatrix <int> & m)
{
    for (int i=0; i< SIZE; i++)
        Process m[i][i];            //major diagonal
            OR
        Process m[i][SIZE-i-1];     //minor diagonal
}
```

Multiple-Choice Questions on One- and Two-Dimensional Arrays

1. Given the following global declarations:

    ```
    enum SomeType {word0, word1, word2};

    class c
    {
        //class declaration, including default constructor
    };
    ```

    Which of the following is an illegal declaration?
    (A) ```
        struct s
        {
                SomeType t;
                c element1, element2;
        };
        ```
    (B) `apvector <c> someArray;`
    (C) `apvector <SomeType> v(100);`
    (D) `apmatrix <c> m(20, 10);`
    (E) `apvector <int> a(SomeType);`

2. Which of the following correctly initializes a vector v of integers to contain four elements each with value 25?

    I  `apvector <int> v(4,25);`

    II  ```
    apvector <int> a(4,25);
    apvector <int> v = a;
    ```

    III ```
    apvector <int> v(10);
    v.resize(4);
    for (int i=0; i<v.length(); i++)
        v[i] = 25;
    ```

    (A) I only
    (B) II only
    (C) III only
    (D) I and III only
    (E) I, II, and III
    ```

3. Given that MAX is some positive integer constant, which of the following code segments correctly initializes apvector a to contain integers from 0 to MAX-1?

   I
   ```
   apvector <int> a;
   for (int i=0; i<MAX; i++)
           a[i] = i;
   a.resize(MAX);
   ```

   II
   ```
   apvector <int> a;
   a.resize(MAX);
   for (int i=0; i<MAX; i++)
           a[i] = i;
   ```

   III
   ```
   apvector <int> a(MAX);
   for (int i=0; i<MAX; i++)
           a[i] = i;
   ```

   (A) I only
   (B) II only
   (C) III only
   (D) II and III only
   (E) I and II only

4. Consider the following code fragment that initializes vector v with numbers read in from the keyboard:

   ```
   int num;
   apvector <int> v;
   while (cin >> num)
   {
       <code to read current value of num into v>
   }
   ```

   Which of the following is a correct replacement for *<code to read current value of num into v>*?

   I
   ```
   v.resize(v.length()+1);
   v[v.length()-1] = num;
   ```

   II
   ```
   v.resize(v.length()+1);
   v[v.length()] = num;
   ```

   III
   ```
   v[v.length()-1] = num;
   v.resize(v.length()+1);
   ```

   (A) I only
   (B) II only
   (C) III only
   (D) I and II only
   (E) I and III only

5. The following program segment is intended to find the index of the first negative integer in `v[0] ... v[N-1]`, where `v` is an apvector of `N` integers.

```
int i = -1;
do
{
    i++;
} while (v[i] >= 0);
location = i;
```

This segment will work as intended
(A) Always.
(B) Never.
(C) Whenever v contains at least one negative integer.
(D) Whenever v contains at least one non-negative integer.
(E) Whenever v contains no negative integers.

6. Refer to the following code segment. You may assume `a` is an apvector of `n` integers, `n = a.length()`.

```
int sum = a[0], i = 0;
while (i < n)
{
    i++;
    sum += a[i];
}
```

Which of the following will be the result of executing the segment?
(A) Sum of `a[0], a[1], ... , a[n-1]` will be stored in `sum`.
(B) Sum of `a[1], a[2], ... , a[n-1]` will be stored in `sum`.
(C) Sum of `a[0], a[1], ... , a[n]` will be stored in `sum`.
(D) An infinite loop will occur.
(E) A run-time error will occur.

7. The following code fragment is intended to find the smallest value in a[0] ... a[n-1].

```
//precondition: a[0]...a[n-1] initialized with integers
//  a is an apvector, a.length() = n
//postcondition: min = smallest value in a[0]...a[n-1]
    int min = a[0];
    int i = 1;
    while (i < n)
    {
        i++;
        if (a[i] < min)
            min = a[i];
    }
```

This code is incorrect. For the segment to work as intended, which of the following modifications could be made?

I Change the line
```
    int i = 1;
```
to
```
    int i = 0;
```
Make no other changes.

II Change the body of the while loop to
```
    {
        if (a[i] < min)
            min = a[i];
        i++;
    }
```
Make no other changes.

III Change the test for the while loop as follows:
```
    while (i <= n)
```
Make no other changes.

(A) I only
(B) II only
(C) III only
(D) I and II only
(E) I, II, and III

Questions 8 and 9 refer to the following function:

```
void DoSomething(apvector <int> & a)
{
    int count = 0;
    for (int i=0; i<a.length(); i++)
        if (a[i] != 0)
        {
            a[count] = a[i];
            count++;
        }
    a.resize(count);
}
```

8. If apvector a initially contains the elements 0, 6, 0, 4, 0, 0, 2 in this order, what will a contain after the function call DoSomething(a)?
    (A) 6, 4, 2
    (B) 0, 0, 0, 0, 6, 4, 2
    (C) 6, 4, 2, 4, 0, 0, 2
    (D) 0, 6, 0, 4, 0, 0, 2
    (E) 6, 4, 2, 0, 0, 0, 0

Level AB Only

9. If a contains N elements, then the algorithm in DoSomething has run time
    (A) $O(N^2)$
    (B) $O(N)$
    (C) $O(1)$
    (D) $O(\log N)$
    (E) $O(N \log N)$

10. Consider this program segment:

```
for (int i=2; i<=k; i++)
    if (a[i] < someValue)
        cout << "SMALL";
```

    What is the maximum number of times that SMALL can be printed?
    (A) 0
    (B) 1
    (C) k-1
    (D) k-2
    (E) k

11. Let v be an `apvector` that contains n integers sorted in increasing order. What does the following program fragment do?

```
int m = 0;
for (int j=1; j<n; j++)
    if (v[j] != v[m])
    {
        m++;
        v[m] = v[j];
    }
m++;
v.resize(m);
```

(A) It computes m, the number of duplicate elements in v, and reverses the order of v while removing all duplicates. Note, for example, if v contains 2, 3, 3, 5, 5, 5, 5, there are four duplicate elements in v, one 3, and three 5s.

(B) It leaves v unchanged, and sets m = n.

(C) It computes m, the number of duplicate elements in v, and places these duplicate elements in v[0] ... v[m-1].

(D) It computes m, the number of distinct elements in v[0] ... v[n-1], and places these elements in v[0] ... v[m-1].

(E) It computes m, the number of elements that are larger than v[0], and places these elements in v[0] ... v[m-1].

Level AB Only

12. A new member function, `min()`, is to be added to the `apvector` class. Function `min()` will return the smallest value in the current `apvector` object. Which of the following is the correct way to start the implementation of function `min()`?

(A) `int apvector<itemType>::min()`

(B) `itemType apvector<itemType>::min()`

(C) `template <class itemType>`
`itemType apvector<itemType> min()`

(D) `template <class itemType>`
`itemType apvector<itemType>::min()`

(E) `template <class itemType>`
`apvector<itemType>::min()`

13. A member function `CountNegs` is to be added to the `apvector` class. It will return the number of negative values in the `apvector` object. Which of the following is the best declaration for this new function?

(A) `int CountNegs();`

(B) `int CountNegs() const;`

(C) `int CountNegs(apvector <itemType> & vec);`

(D) `int CountNegs(const apvector <itemType> & vec);`

(E) `int CountNegs(const apvector <itemType> & vec) const;`

14. A function `DeleteKey` must delete all occurrences of `key` from its `apvector` parameter. `key` is any integer value, variable, or expression. The most suitable header for this function would be

(A) `void DeleteKey(apvector <int> & v, int key);`
(B) `void DeleteKey(apvector <int> & v, int & key);`
(C) `void DeleteKey(apvector <int> v, int key);`
(D) `void DeleteKey(const apvector <int> & v, int key);`
(E) `void DeleteKey(const apvector <int> & v, int & key);`

Questions 15–17 refer to program segments I and II. Each segment reads integers from `infile` and stores them in an `apvector` called `list`. (See Chapter 6 for reading numbers from `infile`.)

```
I apvector <int> list(1);
  int value, count=0;
  while (infile >> value)
  {
      list.resize(count+1);
      list[count]=value;
      count++;
  }
```

```
II apvector <int> list(1);
   int value, count=0;
   while (infile >> value)
   {
       if (count == list.length())
           list.resize(2*count);
       list[count]=value;
       count++;
   }
   list.resize(count);
```

Recall that whenever an `apvector` is resized, its elements are copied into a new block of memory. For example, `a.resize(50)` for an `apvector` `a` that has 35 elements will cause 35 elements to be copied into an `apvector` with 50 slots.

15. Suppose that ten elements are read into `list` using program segment I. How many copies of `apvector` elements will be made because of resizing?

(A) 9
(B) 10
(C) 45
(D) 55
(E) 100

16. Suppose that ten elements are read into `list` using program segment II. How many copies of `apvector` elements will be made because of resizing?

(A) 5
(B) 10
(C) 15
(D) 20
(E) 25

Level AB Only

17. If the `apvector` originally contains N elements, what are the run-time efficiencies for (1) segment I, and (2) segment II?
    (A) (1) $O(N^2)$ (2) $O(N^2)$
    (B) (1) $O(N^2)$ (2) $O(N)$
    (C) (1) $O(N)$ (2) $O(N^2)$
    (D) (1) $O(N)$ (2) $O(N)$
    (E) (1) $O(N)$ (2) $O(1)$

18. Refer to the following declaration:

```
struct Address
{
    apstring name;
    apstring street;
    apstring city;
    apstring state;
    int zip;
};
apvector <Address> a(100);
```

Which of the following code segments prints out a list of addresses?

```
 I for (int i = 0; i<100; i++)
        cout << a[i].Address << endl;

 II for (int i = 0; i<100; i++)
        cout << a[i] << endl;

III for (int i = 0; i<100; i++)
    {
        cout << a[i].name << endl;
        cout << a[i].street << endl;
        cout << a[i].city << ", ";
        cout << a[i].state << " ";
        cout << a[i].zip << endl;
    }
```

   (A) I only
   (B) II only
   (C) III only
   (D) I and III only
   (E) II and III only

Refer to the following declarations for Questions 19 and 20:

```
struct Address
{
    apstring name;
    apstring street;
    apstring city;
    apstring state;
    int zip;
};
struct Student
{
    int idNum;
    Address addr;
    double gpa;
};


apvector<Student> s(100);
```

19. Here is a code segment to generate a list of Student names only:

```
for (int i = 0; i < 100; i++)
    <line of code>;
```

Which of the following is a correct *<line of code>*?

   I `cout << s[i].addr.name << endl;`

   II `cout << s[i].Address.name << endl;`

   III `cout << s.addr.name[i] << endl;`

  (A) I only

  (B) II only

  (C) III only

  (D) I and II only

  (E) I and III only

20. Here is a function that locates the Student with the highest idNum:

```
Student Locate(const apvector <Student> &s)
//precondition: apvector s of Student is initialized and
//              contains 100 elements
//postcondition: Student with highest idNum has been returned
{
    <function body>
}
```

Which of the following could replace <*function body*> so that the function works as intended?

```
I   int max = s[0].idNum;
    for(int i=1; i<100; i++)
        if(s[i].idNum > max)
        {
        max = s[i].idNum;
        return s[i];
        }
    return s[0];

II  int index = 0;
    int max = s[0].idNum;
    for(int i=1; i<100; i++)
        if(s[i].idNum > max)
        {
            max= s[i].idNum;
            index = i;
        }
    return s[index];

III int max = 0;
    for(int i=1; i<100; i++)
        if(s[i].idNum > s[max].idNum)
        max = i;
    return s[max];
```

(A) I only
(B) II only
(C) III only
(D) I and III only
(E) II and III only

Questions 21–23 refer to the following declarations:

```
struct Ticket
{
    char row;
    int seat;
    double price;
};

struct Transaction
{
    int numTickets;
    apvector <Ticket> tickList;
};
```

21. Which of the following modifications to the `Transaction` struct will create 20 slots for the `tickList` array?

```
    I  struct Transaction
       {
               int numTickets(20);
               apvector <Ticket> tickList;
       };
   II  struct Transaction
       {
               int numTickets;
               apvector <Ticket> tickList(20);
       };
  III  struct Transaction
       {
               int numTickets;
               apvector <Ticket> tickList;
               Transaction() : numTickets(0), tickList(20) {}
       };
```

(A) None
(B) I only
(C) II only
(D) III only
(E) II and III only

22. A function `TotalPaid` returns the total amount paid for a given ticket transaction.

```
double TotalPaid (const Transaction &trans)
// precondition: a transaction trans has occurred
// postcondition: returns total amount paid
{
    int total = 0;
        <code>
    return total;
}
```

Which of the following represents correct *<code>* for this function?

(A) `for (int i = 0; i < numTickets; i++)`
`        total += trans.tickList[i].price;`

(B) `for (int i = 0; i < trans.numTickets; i++)`
`        total += tickList[i].price;`

(C) `for (int i = 0; i < trans.numTickets; i++)`
`        total += trans.tickList[i].price;`

(D) `Ticket t;`
`    total += t.price;`

(E) `Transaction T;`
`    for (int i = 0; i < T.numTickets; i++)`
`            total += T.tickList[i].price;`

23. Suppose it is necessary to keep a list of all ticket transactions. A suitable declaration would be:

(A) `apvector <Ticket> Transaction;`
(B) `apvector <Transaction> Ticket;`
(C) `apvector <Transaction> ListOfSales;`
(D) `apvector <Ticket> ListOfSales;`
(E) `apvector <ListOfSales> Transaction;`

24. Consider this class:

```
class BingoCard
{
    public:
        BingoCard();        //default constructor
        void CreateCard();  //create bingo card with
                            //20 integers
        void DisplayCard(); //display bingo card
    private:
        apvector <int> myCard;
};
```

The default constructor creates a bingo card array with 20 slots. Which of the following represents a correct implementation?

(A) `BingoCard::myCard(20) {}`

(B) `BingoCard::BingoCard() : myCard(20) {}`

(C) `BingoCard::BingoCard() : apvector <int> myCard(20) {}`

(D) `BingoCard::BingoCard() : apvector <int> (20) {}`

(E)
```
BingoCard::BingoCard()
{
    apvector <int> myCard(20);
}
```

25. Consider the following class:

```
class Book
{
    public:
        Book();
        Book(apstring title, apstring author);
        void Display() const;   //displays title, author
    private:
        apstring myTitle;
        apstring myAuthor;
};
```

A program has this declaration:

```
apvector <Book> bookList;
```

Suppose `bookList` is initialized so that each `Book` in the list has a title and author. Which of the following will display the title and author of each book in `bookList`?

(A)
```
for (int i=0; i<bookList[i].length(); i++)
    bookList[i].Display();
```

(B)
```
for (int i=0; i<bookList.length(); i++)
    bookList[i].Display();
```

(C)
```
for (int i=0; i<bookList.length(); i++)
    bookList.Display();
```

(D)
```
for (int i=0; i<bookList.length(); i++)
    Book.Display();
```

(E)
```
for (int i=0; i<bookList.length(); i++)
    Book[i].Display();
```

Level AB Only

26. The following code segment reverses the elements of a[first] ... a[last].

```
int k=first, j=last;
while (k < j)
{
    Swap(a[k],a[j]);    //interchanges a[k] and a[j]
    k++;
    j--;
}
```

Which of the following diagrams represents the loop invariant for the while loop? (Each rectangle represents a segment of array a. The labels above the rectangles represent the indexes of array elements at the beginning and end of each segment.)

(A)

first		k k+1		j-1 j		last
swapped		original elements		swapped		

(B)

first		k k+1		j-1 j		last
original elements		swapped		original elements		

(C)

first		k-1 k		j j+1		last
swapped		original elements		swapped		

(D)

first		k-1 k		j j+1		last
original elements		swapped		original elements		

(E)

first		k-1 k		j-1 j		last
swapped		original elements		swapped		

27. The following algorithm sets min equal to the smallest value in a[0] ... a[n-1]:

```
min = a[0];
i = 1;
while (i < n)
{
    if (a[i] < min)
        min = a[i];
    i++;
}
```

The loop invariant for the while loop is
(A) min is smallest value in a[0] ... a[i], $1 \le i \le n$
(B) min is smallest value in a[0] ... a[i-1], $1 \le i \le n-1$
(C) min is smallest value in a[0] ... a[i], $1 \le i \le n-1$
(D) min is smallest value in a[0] ... a[i-1], $1 < i \le n$
(E) min is smallest value in a[0] ... a[i-1], $1 \le i \le n$

28. Which of the following initializes an 8×10 matrix with integer values that are perfect squares? (0 is a perfect square.)

    I `apmatrix <int> m(8,10,25);`

    II `apmatrix <int> m(10,20);`
    ```
        for (int i=0; i< m.numrows(); i++)
            for (int j=0; j<m.numcols(); j++)
                m[i][j] = i*i;
        m.resize(8,10);
    ```

    III `apmatrix <int> m(4,6);`
    ```
        for (int i=0; i< m.numrows(); i++)
            for (int j=0; j<m.numcols(); j++)
                m[i][j] = j*j;
        m.resize(8,10);
    ```

    (A) I only
    (B) II only
    (C) III only
    (D) II and III only
    (E) I and II only

29. Consider the following function that will alter its `apmatrix` parameter:

    ```
    void MatStuff(apmatrix <int> & m, int row)
    //precondition: m is initialized
    {
        for (int col=0; col<m.numcols(); col++)
            m[row][col] = row;
    }
    ```

    Suppose m is originally

    ```
    1   4   9   0
    2   7   8   6
    5   1   4   3
    ```

    After the function call `MatStuff(m,2)`, m will be

    (A)
    ```
    1   4   9   0
    2   7   8   6
    2   2   2   2
    ```

    (B)
    ```
    1   4   9   0
    2   2   2   2
    5   1   4   3
    ```

    (C)
    ```
    2   2   2   2
    2   2   2   2
    2   2   2   2
    ```

    (D)
    ```
    1   4   2   0
    2   7   2   6
    5   1   2   3
    ```

    (E)
    ```
    1   2   9   0
    2   2   8   6
    5   2   4   3
    ```

30. Assume that a square matrix m is defined by

```
apmatrix <int> m(SIZE,SIZE);    //SIZE is an integer const ≥ 2
```

What does the following code segment do? (You may assume the existence of a Swap function that interchanges its parameters.)

```
for (int i=0; i<SIZE-1; i++)
    for (int j=0; j<SIZE-i-1; j++)
        Swap(m[i][j],m[SIZE-j-1][SIZE-i-1];
```

(A) Reflects m through its major diagonal. For example,

$$\begin{matrix} 2 & 6 \\ 4 & 3 \end{matrix} \longrightarrow \begin{matrix} 2 & 4 \\ 6 & 3 \end{matrix}$$

(B) Reflects m through its minor diagonal. For example,

$$\begin{matrix} 2 & 6 \\ 4 & 3 \end{matrix} \longrightarrow \begin{matrix} 3 & 6 \\ 4 & 2 \end{matrix}$$

(C) Reflects m through a horizontal line of symmetry. For example,

$$\begin{matrix} 2 & 6 \\ 4 & 3 \end{matrix} \longrightarrow \begin{matrix} 4 & 3 \\ 2 & 6 \end{matrix}$$

(D) Reflects m through a vertical line of symmetry. For example,

$$\begin{matrix} 2 & 6 \\ 4 & 3 \end{matrix} \longrightarrow \begin{matrix} 6 & 2 \\ 3 & 4 \end{matrix}$$

(E) Leaves m unchanged.

31. A square matrix is declared as

```
apmatrix <int> m(SIZE,SIZE);
```

where SIZE is an appropriate integer constant. Consider the following function:

```
void Mystery(apmatrix <int> & m, int value, int top,
    int left, int bottom, int right)
{
    for (int i=left; i<=right; i++)
    {
        m[top][i] = value;
        m[bottom][i] = value;
    }
    for (int i=top+1; i<=bottom-1; i++)
    {
        m[i][left] = value;
        m[i][right] = value;
    }
}
```

Assuming that there are no out-of-range errors, which best describes what function Mystery does?

(A) Places value in corners of the rectangle with corners (top, left) and (bottom, right)

(B) Places value in the diagonals of the square with corners (top, left) and (bottom, right)

(C) Places value in each element of the rectangle with corners (top, left) and (bottom, right)

(D) Places value in each element of the border of the rectangle with corners (top, left) and (bottom, right)

(E) Places value in the topmost and bottommost rows of the rectangle with corners (top, left) and (bottom, right)

32. This question refers to the following program segment:

```
const int SIZE = 8;
apmatrix <char> m(SIZE,SIZE);

bool IsThere(const apmatrix <char> & m, int row,
        int col, char symbol)
{
    bool yes;
    int i, count=0;
    for (i=0; i<SIZE; i++)
        if (m[i][col] == symbol)
            count++;
    yes = (count == SIZE);
    count = 0;
    for (i=0; i<SIZE; i++)
        if (m[row][i] == symbol)
            count++;
    return (yes || count == SIZE);
}
```

Which of the following conditions on a matrix m of the type declared in the program segment will by itself guarantee that

```
IsThere(m, 2, 2, '$')
```

will have the value true when evaluated?

I The element in row 2 and column 2 is '$'
II All elements in both diagonals are '$'
III All elements in column 2 are '$'

(A) I only
(B) III only
(C) I and II only
(D) I and III only
(E) II and III only

Level AB Only

33. Which of the following is *not* a templated class? (apstring is discussed in Chapter 5; apstack and apqueue are discussed in Chapter 9.)
(A) apvector
(B) apmatrix
(C) apstring
(D) apstack
(E) apqueue

Answer Key

1. **E**	12. **D**	23. **C**
2. **E**	13. **B**	24. **B**
3. **D**	14. **A**	25. **B**
4. **A**	15. **C**	26. **C**
5. **C**	16. **E**	27. **E**
6. **E**	17. **B**	28. **E**
7. **B**	18. **C**	29. **A**
8. **A**	19. **A**	30. **B**
9. **B**	20. **E**	31. **D**
10. **C**	21. **D**	32. **B**
11. **D**	22. **C**	33. **C**

Answers Explained

1. **(E)** Since the data members of a struct can be of any type, including user-defined types, choice A is correct. Choices B, C, and D all correctly initialize variables that match the constructors of apvector or apmatrix. Choice E is wrong because the parameter SomeType should be some positive integer that allocates the number of slots for array a.

2. **(E)** Choice I uses the fillValue constructor. Choice II uses the copy constructor to initialize v by copying a. Choice III correctly resizes v and then assigns the value 25 to each of its slots.

3. **(D)** Segments I and II both use the default constructor to create array a with 0 elements. The array a must be resized to MAX slots before it can be filled, so segment II is correct. Segment I, however, will cause an out-of-range error: the for loop tries to refer to a[i] when a has no elements. Segment III is correct because the constructor in the declaration creates array a with MAX slots.

4. **(A)** After the declaration

```
apvector <int> v;
```

v contains zero elements. It must be resized before any elements can be added. Without resizing, segment III will cause an out-of-range error. The second line of segment II will also cause an out-of-range error: after the resize, v.length() is the current length, and so the last element is v[v.length()-1]. For example, if the current length of v is 4, the last available slot is v[3].

5. **(C)** If v contains no negative integers, the value of i will eventually exceed N-1, causing an out-of-range error in v[i].

6. **(E)** The intent is to sum array elements a[0], a[1], ... , a[n-1]. Notice, however, that when i has the value n-1 it is incremented to n in the loop. Now the statement sum += a[i]; refers to a[n] (out of range).

7. **(B)** There are two problems with the segment as given:

 1. `a[1]` is not tested.
 2. When `i` has a value of `n-1`, incrementing `i` will lead to an out-of-range error for the `if(a[i] < min)` test.

 Change II corrects both these errors. The change suggested in III corrects neither of these errors. The change in I corrects (1) but not (2).

8. **(A)** `DoSomething` removes all occurrences of 0 from array `a` and then resizes `a`.

Level AB Only

9. **(B)** The algorithm is linear. It passes once through the array, making a single assignment if a nonzero element is found. Resizing of `a` is done just once at the end, and it too is $O(N)$.

10. **(C)** If `a[i] < SomeValue` for all `i` from 2 to `k`, `SMALL` will be printed on each iteration of the `for` loop. Since there are `k-1` iterations, the maximum number of times that `SMALL` can be printed is `k-1`.

11. **(D)** When the `for` loop finds an element that is different from the previous elements, it increments `m` and places the new element in `v[m]`. This results in `v[0] ... v[m-1]` containing distinct elements. The quantity `m` is the number of distinct elements. For example, if the original array is 1 1 4 6 6, then

 First pass compares `v[0]` and `v[1]`. No change: 1 1 4 6 6
 Second pass compares `v[0]` and `v[2]`. v changes to: 1 4 4 6 6
 Third pass compares `v[1]` and `v[3]`. v changes to: 1 4 6 6 6
 Fourth pass compares `v[2]` and `v[4]`. No change: 1 4 6 6 6
 Exit loop and increment `m` to 3 (three distinct elements)
 Resize array, which becomes 1 4 6

Level AB Only

12. **(D)** `apvector` is a templated class, so any new member function is a templated function that should be preceded with `template<class itemType>`. This eliminates choices A and B. Choice C is missing the scope resolution operator (`::`) in front of `min()`, and choice E is missing the return type `itemType`.

13. **(B)** `CountNegs` is a member function that will directly access its `apvector` object through its private variables. There should therefore be no `apvector` parameter. This eliminates choices C, D, and E. Since `CountNegs` is an accessor that will not modify its `apvector` object, it should be declared as a constant member function, which eliminates choice A. (Note: Choice A is not *wrong*. Choice B is better!)

14. **(A)** The `apvector` `v` may be modified and must therefore be passed by reference, not by `const` reference or by value. Eliminate choices C, D, and E. Since `key` can be a value or an expression, it must be passed by value, not reference, which eliminates choice B. If `key` were restricted to being a variable, passing by reference would be legal. Since `key` should not be modified, passing by value would still be better (a copy is made, the original value is protected).

15. **(C)** During the first pass though the loop, no elements will be copied.
During the second pass though the loop, one element will be copied.

. . .

During the tenth pass though the loop, nine elements will be copied.
Total number of copies $= 0 + 1 + \cdots + 9 = 45$

16. **(E)** When `list.length()` and `count` both $= 1$, one element is copied.
When `list.length()` and `count` both $= 2$, two elements are copied.
When `list.length()` and `count` both $= 4$, four elements are copied.
When `list.length()` and `count` both $= 8$, eight elements are copied.
Total so far $= 1 + 2 + 4 + 8 = 15$.
Final resizing copies ten more elements, so the total is 25.

Level AB Only

17. **(B)** For the algorithm in segment I:
During the first pass though the loop, no elements will be copied.
During the second pass though the loop, one element will be copied.

. . .

During the Nth pass though the loop, $N - 1$ elements will be copied.
Total number of copies $= 0 + 1 + \ldots + N - 1 = N(N - 1)/2$, which is $O(N^2)$.
For the algorithm in segment II:
Resizing will be done whenever `count` and `list.length()` both equal the same power of 2, 2^p say. In that case, 2^p elements will be copied.

$$
\begin{aligned}
\text{Total number of copies} \quad &= \quad 1 + 2 + 4 + \ldots + 2^k, \\
&\qquad\qquad \text{where } 2^k < N \le 2^{k+1}, \\
&= \quad 2^{k+1} - 1
\end{aligned}
$$

Notice that
$$
\begin{aligned}
2^k \quad &< \quad N \\
\implies \quad (2)2^k \quad &< \quad 2N \\
\implies \quad 2^{k+1} \quad &< \quad 2N \\
\implies \quad 2^{k+1} - 1 \quad &< \quad 2N - 1
\end{aligned}
$$

This means that the total number of copies is no more than $2N - 1$, and so the algorithm is $O(N)$. For example, if $N = 10$,

$$
\begin{aligned}
\text{Total number of copies} \quad &= \quad 1 + 2 + 4 + 8 = 1 + 2 + 4 + 2^3, \\
&\qquad\qquad \text{where } 2^3 < N \le 2^4 \\
&= \quad 2^4 - 1 \ (\text{i.e., } 15)
\end{aligned}
$$

Informally, for segment I, in a typical pass through the loop the length of the list is about $N/2$, and all of these elements get copied. Since there are N passes through the loop, the number of copies is $O(N^2)$. For segment II, copying is done only when necessary. And each time it is done, the sum of all copies is roughly double the length of the copy to be made at that stage. Since the last list to be copied is at most of length N, the maximum number of copies is at most $2N$, which is $O(N)$.

18. **(C)** To print out an `Address` each field must explicitly be printed, which eliminates code segments I and II. Segment II would be correct if the `<<` operator were overloaded for the `Address` struct, but you can't assume this.

19. **(A)** `s[i]` is an element of type `Student`. `s[i].addr` is the `Address` field of student `s[i]`. The name part of student `s[i]`'s address is `s[i].addr.name`. Line I of code is the only line that uses this construct correctly.

20. **(E)** Code segment I is incorrect because it returns the first student whose `idNum` is greater than `max`, not necessarily the student with the highest `idNum` in the list.

21. **(D)** To create the `tickList` apvector slots, the `Transaction` struct needs a constructor. Declaration III is the only choice that provides one.

22. **(C)** Eliminate choices D and E since they don't mention the parameter, `trans`. `trans.numTickets` represents the number of tickets in this transaction. Eliminate choice A because it incorrectly refers to this quantity as `numTickets`. The price for each `Ticket` in the `tickList` for this transaction is represented by `trans.tickList[i].price`. This eliminates choice B.

23. **(C)** An array of type `Transaction` is required. This eliminates choices A, D, and E. Choice B is not suitable because it names the array `Ticket`, which is the identifier used in the `Ticket` struct.

24. **(B)** Choices C, D, and E are wrong because they do not have the correct syntax to create `myCard`, which has already been declared of type `apvector<int>`. Choice A is wrong because the class name must follow the scope resolution operator (`::`). That is, you need `BingoCard::BingoCard(): ...`

25. **(B)** It is required to display `bookList[0]`, `bookList[1]`, ... `bookList[bookList.length()-1]`. Thus, the correct loop body is

    ```
    bookList[i].Display();
    ```

    This eliminates choices C, D, and E. Choice A is wrong because `bookList[i].length()` has no meaning. `length()` applies to the apvector `bookList`, not to the single element `bookList[i]`.

Level AB Only

26. **(C)** Since `k` and `j` are changed at the *end* of the loop, the invariant is: `a[first]...a[k-1]` have been swapped with `a[last]` down to `a[j+1]`. The middle part of the array has not been processed, and these elements are still in their original positions.

27. **(E)** `i` is incremented at the end of the loop, which means that on exiting the loop `a[i]` has not yet been examined. This eliminates choices A and C. The loop invariant must be true on the final exit from the loop, at which time `i=n`. This eliminates choice B. Choice D is wrong because `i` is initialized to 1. Thus, $1 \le i ...$

28. **(E)** Declaration I uses the `fillValue` constructor that initializes each slot in an 8 × 10 matrix with the value 25. Code segment II places a perfect square in each slot of a 10 × 20 matrix and then resizes to 8 × 10. Values are lost in the resizing, but the smaller matrix still fulfills the condition of the problem. Code segment III, which first initializes a 4 × 6 matrix and then resizes to 8 × 10, will contain slots in the larger matrix that are not defined. They may be perfect squares (zero), but you can't count on it. So III is incorrect.

29. **(A)** `MatStuff` processes the row selected by the row parameter, 2 in the function call. The row value, 2, overwrites each element in row 2. Don't make the mistake of selecting choice B—the row labels are 0, 1, 2.

30. **(B)** Hand execute this for a 2 × 2 matrix. i goes from 0 to 0, j goes from 0 to 0, so the only interchange is Swap(m[0][0],m[1][1]), which suggests choice B. Check with a 3 × 3 matrix:

```
i = 0    j = 0    Swap(m[0][0],m[2][2]);
         j = 1    Swap(m[0][1],m[1][2]);
i = 1    j = 0    Swap(m[1][0],m[2][1]);
```

The elements to be interchanged are shown paired in the following figure. The result will be a reflection through the minor diagonal.

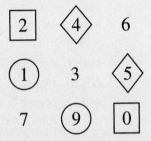

31. **(D)** The first for loop places value in the top and bottom rows of the defined rectangle. The second for loop fills in the remaining border elements on the sides. Note that the top+1 and bottom-1 initializer and terminating conditions avoid filling in the corner elements twice.

32. **(B)** For the function call IsThere (m, 2, 2, '$') the code counts how many times '$' appears in row 2 and how many times in column 2. The function returns true only if count == SIZE for either the row or column pass (i.e., the whole of row 2 or the whole of column 2 contains the symbol '$'). This eliminates choices I and II.

Level AB Only

33. **(C)** Choices A, B, D, and E all have a generic itemType parameter in their class definition that can be replaced with any appropriate type. This is not true of the apstring class.

CHAPTER FIVE

Strings

I usually start with a repulsive character and go on from there.
—Chester Gould, on his Dick Tracy cartoons (1955)

Type char

Characters are the building blocks of strings and text files. Variables of type char hold single characters only. A character value, such as one used in an assignment, is denoted by single quotes. For example,

```
char vowel = 'e';
const char blank = ' ';
```

The ASCII Character Set

The legal characters that comprise type char are ordered according to the ASCII table (see Appendix B). C++ treats characters as integers: the integer value of a character is its position in the ASCII table. Thus, 'A' has a value of 65, and '!' has a value of 33. Because the characters are ordered, variables of type char can be compared, incremented, used in for loops, and so on.

Example 1

The boolean expression ('!' < '%') is true because 33, the value of '!', is less than 37, the value of '%'.

Example 2

This program segment prints all the "printable" characters:

```
for (char k='!'; k<='~'; k++)
    cout << k;
```

The following segment does the same:

```
for (char k=33; k<=126; k++)
    cout << k;
```

And if you want a list of the printable characters and their integer equivalents in the ASCII table, just cast each char to int:

```
for (char k='!'; k<='~'; k++)
    cout << k << "  " << int(k) << endl;
    //outputs !    33
    //        "    34
    //       ...
    //        ~   126
```

You are not expected to know the ASCII value of any given character. Here are some general features of the ASCII table that you should know, however:

1. The digits '0' through '9' follow each other consecutively, as do the capital (uppercase) letters 'A' through 'Z' and the lowercase letters 'a' through 'z'. This means that the "gap" between any uppercase letter and its lowercase equivalent is constant (i.e., 'a' - 'A' = 'b' - 'B' = ... equals 32 for ASCII). Also, if char variable d is a digit, its integer value can be obtained with the statement

   ```
   int value = d - '0';
   ```

2. All capital letters (values 65–90) are less than all lowercase letters (values 97–122).

3. Addition or subtraction of characters means addition or subtraction of their integer ASCII values. For example,

   ```
   'Z' - 'A' = 90 - 65 = 25
   '9' - '0' = 57 - 48 = 9
   ```

   If an integer value is added to (or subtracted from) a character, the result is a character. For example,

'A' + 2 → 'C':	(the character 2 "slots" higher than 'A')
'8' - 3 → '5':	(the character 3 "slots" lower than '8')

Strings

The apstring **Class**

For the APCS course, strings are implemented with the apstring class. You will be provided with a copy of the header file apstring.h during the AP exam. (An up-to-date copy can be found at *http://www.collegeboard.org/ap/computer-science/*.)

An apstring s is a safe (range-checked) array of characters indexed from 0 to s.length()-1. For example, if s = "car", then s[0] = 'c', s[1] = 'a', and s[2] = 'r'. A reference to s[3] will cause an out-of-range error.

The attributes (private data members) of an apstring are

- myLength, the number of characters in the string.

- myCapacity, the number of memory slots for storing characters of the string. The implementation uses myCapacity = myLength + 1, which allows termination of the string with the null character '\0'. These implementation details are hidden from a client program that uses an apstring.

- myCstring, which stores the characters of the string in a C-style string. You don't need to be familiar with C-style strings to use the apstring class.

Additionally, the apstring class defines the following global constant:

```
const int npos = -1;
```

It is returned by the find member functions to indicate "not a position in the string."

The Functions in
`apstring`

The complete implementation (`apstring.cpp`) is available on the College Board web site, *http://www.collegeboard.org/ap/computer-science/*. It will not be provided on the AP exam. You should, however, be familiar with all the functions in the apstring class. Here is a summary.

Constructors

The first three functions have no return type and are therefore constructors.

```
apstring()
```

This is the default constructor that creates an empty string. For example,

```
apstring s; //s equals the empty string ""
```

```
apstring(const char * s)
```

This constructor allows you to construct a nonempty string from a string literal. For example,

```
apstring s = "pqrs";
```

```
apstring(const apstring & str)
```

This is the copy constructor, which allows you to declare an apstring by copying an existing apstring. For example,

```
apstring s1 = "cat";
apstring s2 = s1;   //copy constructor used in this line
                    //s2 contains "cat"
```

Destructor

```
~apstring()
```

The destructor automatically recycles memory when an apstring object goes out of scope. You never call it explicitly.

Assignment

There are three different functions that overload the assignment operator.

```
const apstring & operator = (const apstring & str)
```

This allows an apstring variable to be assigned to another apstring variable. For example,

```
apstring s, t;
//code to initialize t
    ...
s = t;  //assignment overload used here
```

```
const apstring & operator = (const char * s)
```

This allows a string literal to be assigned to an apstring. For example,

```
apstring s;
s = "newThing";
```

```
const apstring & operator = (char ch)
```

This allows a character to be assigned to an apstring. For example,

```
apstring s;
s = 'p';
```

Accessors

The following five accessor functions are all constant member functions.

```
int length() const
```

This returns the length of the string.

```
int find(const apstring & str) const
```

This returns the index of the first character of the first occurrence of str in the current string. If str does not occur in the current string, −1 is returned (the value of the constant npos).

```
int find(char ch) const
```

This returns the index of the first occurrence of ch in the current string, or npos if ch does not occur.

```
apstring substr(int pos, int len) const
```

This returns the substring of length len that starts at the index pos of the current string. If pos < 0, the substring starts at the beginning of the current string. If the values of pos and len would take you off the end of the string, the returned substring is truncated at the end of the current string. If pos $\geq$ s.length(), the substr function returns an empty string.
Examples:

```
apstring s = "tapestry";
int x = s.length();        //x has the value 8
x = s.find("pest");        //x has the value 2
x = s.find("tryst");       //x has the value npos (-1)
x = s.find('t');           //x has the value 0
x = s.find('A');           //x has the value npos (-1)
apstring st;
st = s.substr(5,3);        //st contains "try"
st = s.substr(5,4);        //st contains "try"
st = s.substr(-1,3);       //st contains "tap"
st = s.substr(8,2);        //st contains ""
```

```
const char* c_str() const
```

This converts the current `apstring` object to a C-style string. It lets you use C library functions that take a C-style string parameter. For example,

```
ifstream infile;
apstring myFile;
cout << "Enter file name" << endl;
cin >> myFile;
infile.open(myFile.c_str());
```

The `ifstream` member function `open` takes a C-style string parameter, so you have to convert `myFile` to a C-style string.

Indexing

```
char operator[] (int k) const
char & operator[] (int k)
```

These functions both overload the subscripting operator, which allows individual characters in an `apstring` s to be accessed: `s[0]`, `s[1]`, ... `s[s.length()-1]`. The first form of the function is invoked for a `const apstring`; the second, for a non-`const apstring`. Both functions abort if you use an out-of-range index.

Modifiers (Overloaded +=)

```
const apstring & operator += (const apstring & str)
const apstring & operator += (char ch)
```

These functions allow you to append either a string or a character to the current `apstring`. For example,

```
apstring s1 = "candy";
apstring s2 = "apple";
char c = 't';
s1 += s2;        //s1 contains "candyapple"
s2 += c;         //s2 contains "applet"
```

All the following functions operate on `apstrings`, but are nonmember (free) functions.

Input/Output

```
ostream & operator << (ostream & os, const apstring & str)
istream & operator >> (istream & is, apstring & str)
```

The insertion << and extraction >> operators are overloaded so that an `apstring` can be written to an output stream or read from an input stream.

```
istream & getline(istream & is, apstring & str)
```

This function allows a line from the input stream to be read into an apstring.

Examples

```
apstring s;
getline(input, s);   //reads line s from input
cout << s;           //prints s to screen
cin >> s;            //reads s from keyboard, up to
                     //whitespace (see Chapter 6)
```

Comparison

```
bool operator == (const apstring & lhs, const apstring & rhs)
```

This compares strings for equality. For example,

```
if (str1 == str2)
    ...
```

The other boolean operators, !=, <, <=, >, and >= are similarly overloaded. Note that two strings s1 and s2 are compared as follows: starting at s1[0] and s2[0], a character-by-character comparison is done until you reach the first character in which the strings differ, s1[k] and s2[k] say. If s1[k] > s2[k], then s1 > s2 and vice versa. If s1 and s2 have identical characters, then s1 == s2. If they have identical characters except that s1 terminates before s2, then s1 < s2. For example,

```
apstring s1 = "HOT", s2 = "HOTEL", s3 = "dog";
if (s1 < s2)         //true, s1 terminates first
    ...
if (s1 < s3)         //true, 'H' < 'd'
```

Concatenation

The following three functions overload the + operator, which is called the *concatenation* operator when used with strings.

```
apstring operator + (const apstring & lhs, const apstring & rhs)
apstring operator + (char ch, const apstring & str)
apstring operator + (const apstring & str, char ch)
```

These functions allow the following concatenations, respectively:

> string + string
> character + string
> string + character

In each case, an apstring value is returned. The apstring parameters, which are passed by const reference, remain unchanged. For example,

```
apstring s1 = "roly", s2 = "poly", s3 = "Malcolm", s4;
s4 = s1 + s2;        //s4 contains "rolypoly"
s4 = 'X' + s2;       //s4 now contains "Xpoly"
s4 = s3 + 'X';       //s4 now contains "MalcolmX"
```

Multiple-Choice Questions on Strings

1. Consider this function:

```
int ToLower(int c)
//Returns the lowercase equivalent of character c.
//If c is not uppercase, returns c unchanged.
{
    if (c >= 'A' && c <= 'Z')
        return c + ('a' - 'A');
    else
        return c;
}
```

Which properties of the ASCII table are assumed in order for this function to work as intended?

   I 'A' through 'Z' are consecutive with no intervening characters
   II 'a' through 'z' are consecutive with no intervening characters
   III Each character in the table corresponds to a unique integer value

(A) I only
(B) II only
(C) III only
(D) I and II only
(E) I, II, and III

2. What will occur as a result of executing the following code? You may assume that the capital letters 'A' through 'Z' correspond to positions 65–90 in the ASCII able.

```
char k;
for (k=65; k<=90; k++)
    cout << k << " ";
```

(A) The integers 65 through 90 will be output to the screen.
(B) The characters 'A' through 'Z' will be output to the screen.
(C) The characters 'a' through 'z' will be output to the screen.
(D) There will be a syntax error because of type mismatch.
(E) There will be a run-time error.

3. Consider this function:

```
int GetDigitValue(char d)
//precondition: d is a digit, i.e., in the range '0' to '9'
//postcondition: integer equivalent of the digit d has
//been returned
{
    return <code>
}
```

Which is a correct replacement for <code>?

(A) '0' - d
(B) d - '0'
(C) d - 0
(D) 0 - d
(E) 'd' - '0'

4. Consider these declarations:

```
 I apstring s1 = "crab";
 II apstring s2 = "A";
III apstring s3 = s2;
```

Which declaration uses the default constructor of the apstring class?

(A) I only
(B) II only
(C) III only
(D) I and II only
(E) None

5. Suppose that strA = "TOMATO", strB = "tomato", and strC = "tom". Given that the integer value of 'A' in the ASCII table is 65 and that of 'a' is 97, which is true?

(A) (strA < strB) && (strB < strC)
(B) (strB < strA) || (strC < strA)
(C) (strC < strA) && (strA < strB)
(D) !(strA == strB) && (strC < strB)
(E) !(strA == strB) && (strC < strA)

6. This question refers to the following code segment:

```
apstring line;
line = "Some more silly stuff on strings!";
//the words are separated by a single space
```

What string will be stored in str after execution of the following?

```
int x = line.find('m');
apstring str = line.substr(10,5) + line.substr(25,x);
```

(A) " sill s"
(B) "sillystrin"
(C) "sillyst"
(D) " sillstrin"
(E) "silly st"

7. Refer to the following function:

```
void ChangeString(apstring & s, int N, char ch)
{
    int k = s.find(ch);
    s = s.substr(k,N) + s.substr(N,k);
    for (int i=0; i < s.length(); i++)
        if (s[i] < ch)
            s[i] = ch;
}
```

What will str contain after the following code is executed?

```
apstring str("conglomeration");
ChangeString(str, 6, 'g');
```

(A) "glomgromgr"
(B) "glomeromer"
(C) "glomgrmgr"
(D) "lomromr"
(E) "mgrglomgr"

8. One of the rules for converting English to Pig Latin states: If a word begins
   with a consonant, move the consonant to the end of the word and add "ay".
   Thus "dog" becomes "ogday," and "crisp" becomes "rispcay". Suppose s is
   an apstring containing an English word that begins with a consonant. Which
   of the following creates the correct corresponding word in Pig Latin? Assume
   the declarations

   ```
   apstring ayString = "ay", pigString;
   ```

   (A) `pigString = s.substr(s.length()-1) + s[0] + ayString;`
   (B) `pigString = s.substr(1,ayString.length()) + s[0] +`
       `ayString;`
   (C) `pigString = s.substr(1,s.length()-1) + s[0] + ayString;`
   (D) `pigString = s.find(1,s) + s[0] + ayString;`
   (E) `pigString = s.find(s.substr(1,s.length()-1)) + s[0]+`
       `ayString;`

9. This question refers to function GetString:

   ```
   apstring GetString(const apstring & s1, const apstring & s2)
   {
       int index = s1.find(s2);
       return s1.substr(index, s2.length());
   }
   ```

   Which is true about GetString? It may return a string that

     I Is equal to s2.
    II Has no characters in common with s2.
   III Is equal to s1.

   (A) I only
   (B) II only
   (C) III only
   (D) I and III only
   (E) I, II, and III

10. This question refers to the following function:

```
apstring StringStuff(const apstring & strA,
    const apstring & strB, const apstring & strC)
{
    apstring temp = strA;
    temp += strB;
    temp += strC;
    return temp;
}
```

What will be contained in newString after execution of the following code?

```
apstring newString;
apstring s1 = "xy", s2 = "pqr", s3 = "abc";
newString = StringStuff(s2, s1, s3);
```

   (A) "pqrxyabc"
   (B) "abcxypqr"
   (C) "xypqrabc"
   (D) "abcpqr"
   (E) "pqrabc"

11. Consider this function:

```
apstring DoSomething(const apstring & s)
{
    const char blank = ' ';
    apstring temp;
    for (int i=0; i<s.length(); i++)
        if (s[i] != blank)
            temp += s[i];
    return temp;
}
```

Which of the following is the most precise description of what DoSomething does?

   (A) It returns s with all its blanks removed.
   (B) It returns s unchanged.
   (C) It returns an apstring that is an exact copy of s.
   (D) It returns an apstring that is equivalent to s with all its blanks removed.
   (E) It returns an apstring that contains s.length() blanks.

12. Function `Replace` is designed to replace a target substring in its first parameter s with a replacement string.

```
void Replace(apstring & s, const apstring & target,
    const apstring & replStr)
//precondition: s contains exactly one occurrence of target
//postcondition: target in s has been replaced with replStr
{
    <function body>
}
```

Which of the following can replace *<function body>* so that the postcondition is always satisfied?

```
 I  int k = s.find(target);
    apstring firstPart = s.substr(0,k);
    apstring lastPart = s.substr(k+target.length(),s.length()
            - (k+target.length()));
    s = firstPart + replStr + lastPart;
```

```
II  int k = s.find(target);
    apstring temp;
    for (int i=0; i<k; i++)
        temp += s[i];
    temp += replStr;
    for (int i=k+target.length(); i<s.length(); i++)
        temp += s[i];
    s = temp;
```

```
III int k = s.find(target);
    apstring temp;
    for (int i=0; i<k; i++)
        temp += s[i];
    temp += replStr;
    for (int i=k+replStr.length(); i<s.length(); i++)
        temp += s[i];
    s = temp;
```

(A) I only
(B) II only
(C) III only
(D) I and II only
(E) I and III only

13. Here is a function that returns the sum of all elements in a vector:

```
template <class someType>
someType Sum (const apvector<someType> &v)
{
    someType total(0);
    int n = v.length();
    for (int i = 0; i < n; i++)
        total += v[i];
    return total;
}
```

This function works correctly for `apvector<int>` and `apvector<double>`. Why does it fail for `apvector<apstring>`?

(A) The `apstring` class does not have a constructor with a single integer argument.

(B) The `apstring` class does not have an overloaded += operator.

(C) Adding elements of type `apstring` is meaningless.

(D) It is illegal to use a class type as the parameter of a templated function.

(E) `apvector <apstring>` is an illegal C++ construct.

Answer Key

1. **E**	6. **C**	11. **D**
2. **B**	7. **C**	12. **D**
3. **B**	8. **C**	13. **A**
4. **E**	9. **E**	
5. **D**	10. **A**	

Answers Explained

1. **(E)** The test `if(c >= 'A' && c <= 'Z')` assumes property I is true: `c` must remain unchanged if it's not an uppercase letter. The expression `c + ('a' - 'A')` assumes that the gap between a lowercase character and its uppercase equivalent is constant, which means that given property I is true, property II must be true. This expression also assumes that a unique integer will be returned for any particular character, which assumes III to be true.

2. **(B)** If `k` were declared to be of type `int`, the integers 65–90 would be printed. Since `k` is of type `char`, the character equivalents of 65–90, namely the letters `'A'` through `'Z'`, are printed.

3. **(B)** Subtraction of two characters returns the difference of their integer equivalents in the ASCII table. Since the digits are consecutive, `'9' - '0' = 9`, `'8' - '0' = 8`, etc. Choice E is wrong because if `d` is a *variable* of type `char`, it is wrong to use quotes.

4. **(E)** I and II use the constructor that allows initialization from a string literal. III uses the copy constructor. The default constructor constructs an empty string:

   ```
   apstring s; //s is the empty string ""
   ```

5. **(D)** Note that `strA < strB` and also `strA < strC` since `'T' < 't'`. `strC < strB` since the length of `strC` is less than the length of `strB`. Thus, all the choices are eliminated except choice D.

6. **(C)** `x` contains the index of the first occurrence of `'m'` in `line`, namely 2. (Remember that `'s'` is at index 0.) `line.substr(10,5)` contains `"silly"` (the substring starts at index 10 and contains five characters), and `line.substr(25,2)` contains `"st"`. The concatenation operator + joins these.

7. **(C)** The first occurrence of `'g'` in `str` is at index 3, thus `k = 3`. The substring `s.substr(3,6) = "glomer"` (6 characters starting at index 3). The substring `s.substr(6,3) = "mer"` (3 characters starting at index 6). Thus the concatenated string is `"glomermer"`. Now each character of the string that is less than `'g'` is replaced by `'g'`. Since `'e'` is the only character that gets replaced in this case, the final string is `"glomgrmgr"`.

8. **(C)** Suppose `s` contains `"cat"`. You want `pigString = "at" + "c" + "ay"`. `"at"` is the substring of `s` starting at position 1 and 2 letters long (i.e.,

s.length() - 1 characters). We thus want s.substr(1,s.length()-1). (Here the first parameter is the starting position and the second is the number of characters.) Note that you can eliminate choices D and E immediately since find returns an integer, not a string.

9. **(E)** I is true whenever s2 occurs in s1. For example, if s1 = "catastrophe" and s2 = "cat", then GetString returns "cat". II may be true if s2 is not contained in s1. For example, if s1 = "empire" and s2 = "cat", the string "emp" will be returned. III will be true whenever s1 = s2.

10. **(A)** Matching the parameters correctly will cause this pairing: strA ↔ s2, strB ↔ s1, strC ↔ s3. Thus, temp will be assigned s2, or "pqr". Then, temp += strB → "pqrxy" and temp += strC → "pqrxyabc".

11. **(D)** The function examines each character in s and, if it is a nonblank, appends it to apstring temp (temp starts out empty). Thus, temp ends up as a copy of s but without the blanks. A copy of temp is returned. Choice A is not precise since s is passed by const reference and cannot be modified. Choice B, in a sense, is correct in that s is left unchanged, but it is not the *best* characterization of what the function does. Choices C and E are simply wrong because the function removes blanks.

12. **(D)** Take a concrete example to test the algorithms. For example, let s = "caroline", target = "rolin", and replStr = "pet". For segment I,

    ```
    k = 2
    firstPart = s.substr(0,2) → "ca"
    lastPart = s.substr(7,1) → "e"
    s = "ca" + "pet" + "e", which satisfies the postcondition.
    ```

    For segment II,

    ```
    k = 2, temp = ""
    ```
    In the first loop, i goes from 0 to 1.
    temp so far is "ca".
    Then temp += "pet" → "capet".
    In the second loop, i goes from 7 to 7.
    temp += s[7] → "capete", which satisfies the postcondition.

    Segment III is the same as II except that in the second loop i is initialized to the wrong value, k + replStr.length(). You want to pick up the letters in s following the *target* string, so the correct initialization for i is k + target.length().

13. **(A)** The problem is with the line someType total(0). It is meaningful to initialize total to 0 if someType is int or double, but it is undefined with the current apstring class. The problem could be solved by adding a constructor that initializes an apstring with a single integer parameter, its length. For example,

    ```
    apstring(int n);    // creates a string of length n, filled
                        // with n dummy characters, spaces, say.
    ```

    Then the statement someType total (0); would declare total to be an empty string, and function Sum would work correctly by concatenating all the apstrings in its apvector parameter.

CHAPTER SIX
Files and Streams

Don't change streams in mid-horse.
—Anonymous

Computers have become indispensable for many reasons, not the least of which is their ability to handle huge amounts of data. You, the programmer (and AP exam taker), need to know how a program accomplishes each of the following:

- Creates and stores new data

- Retrieves existing data from a file

- Accepts data entered at the keyboard and writes data to the screen

Streams

Input/Output Streams

In C++ all data are transmitted on input or output streams. These streams and the operations performed on them are made available to the program by including the `iostream.h` library file.

The variable `cin` and the extraction operator `>>` get data from the *standard input stream*. The variable `cout` and the insertion operator `<<` send data to the *standard output stream*. (These streams were introduced in Chapter 1.)

$$\text{keyboard} \xrightarrow{\text{standard input stream cin}} \text{program}$$

$$\text{program} \xrightarrow{\text{standard output stream cout}} \text{screen}$$

To read from and write to files, you use `>>` and `<<` with *file streams* that connect data to a disk device. To do this, you must include two new classes from the C++ library, `ofstream` (output file stream) and `ifstream` (input file stream). The header file is `fstream.h`.

$$\text{disk} \xrightarrow{\text{input file stream ifstream}} \text{program}$$

$$\text{program} \xrightarrow{\text{output file stream ofstream}} \text{disk}$$

Creating an Output File

You need the following three lines of code:

```
#include <fstream.h>
...
ofstream outfile;
outfile.open("myfile");
```

NOTE

1. outfile is declared to be an ofstream object (output file stream variable) and can be any valid identifier of your choice.
2. The last line connects outfile to an external file called myfile in this example.
3. open is a member function of the ofstream class that takes a string parameter (hence the . member syntax). The open function will not be tested on the AP exam.
4. When the open function is called, one of two things happens.

   (i) If a file named myfile exists on disk, it will be opened for output and connected to the output stream outfile. *Any data in the file are erased.*

   (ii) If myfile does not exist on disk, a new file with that name is opened for output and connected to outfile.

Once a file is open for output, you can use the same operations that you use for screen output. Just replace cout with your file variable name.

Example
Here is a program that creates a file of 24 random integers, one per line.

```
#include <iostream.h>
#include <stdlib.h>      //needed for rand()
#include <fstream.h>

int main()
{
    int num;
    ofstream outfile;

    outfile.open("ints.dat");
    for (int i=1; i<25; i++)
    {
        num = rand()%100 +1;    //random int from 1 to 100
        outfile << num << endl;
    }
    outfile.close();         //close is not tested on AP exam
    return 0;
}
```

Reading from an Input File
You need the same code as for writing to an output file, except ofstream is replaced by ifstream:

```
#include <fstream.h>
    ...
ifstream infile;
infile.open("somefile");
```

When the last line is executed, the file somefile is opened for reading and connected to the input stream infile.

How you extract data from infile depends on the application and the type of data. Numbers only? Words only? You need to know the various types of text processing: line by line, word by word, or character by character.

Reading Numbers

A program receives data from the keyboard when a user types in one or more characters separated by whitespace, typically blanks, tabs, or carriage returns. Similarly, numerical data in an input file is separated by whitespace. Each line is terminated with the newline character '\n', which you can think of as having been inserted into the file by typing a carriage return.

The >> operator extracts characters from the input stream until it encounters whitespace, including a carriage return. The computer converts the characters to the data value represented depending on the type of variable for input. For example, consecutive characters '5' and '6' followed by a space will be converted to the integer value 56 if the variable is type int.

Example 1

If infile contains

```
25 13\n
 6\n
```

the statements

```
int n1, n2, n3;
infile >> n1 >> n2 >> n3;
```

will assign n1 = 25, n2 = 13, and n3 = 6.

If the number of integers entered at the keyboard is initially unknown, you can terminate the list with a sentinel like −999. (See Chapter 1.) Alternatively, the following construct can be used:

```
while (infile >> num)    //for input file stream
```

or

```
while (cin >> num)       //for standard input stream
```

Example 2

```
//count the number of integers in infile
//assumes infile contains only integers
//and is open for reading at the top of the file
int num, fileCount = 0;
while (infile >> num)        //while there is still a number
{                            //on the infile stream
    fileCount++;
}
```

Example 3

```
//count number of integers entered at the keyboard
int num, kbdCount = 0;
cout << "Enter integers separated by spaces." << endl;
cout << "Terminate with any non-digit character." << endl;
while (cin >> num)  //while there are still numbers
{                   //on the cin stream, get a number
    kbdCount++;
}
```

1. For Example 2, the `while` loop terminates when end-of-file is reached. Attempting to read a `num` from the `infile` stream fails, and the expression `infile >> num` evaluates to `false`.

2. For Example 3, the `while` loop terminates similarly when a non-numeric character is entered. The expression `cin >> num` evaluates to `false`, and the `cin` stream is left in a failed state. This should be cleared with the statement

```
cin.clear();
```

`clear()` will not be tested on the AP exam.

Reading Numbers and Words

In C++ a *word* is a sequence of characters separated from other words by whitespace. The `>>` operator is ideal for extracting words, since it reads all the characters up to and not including whitespace.

Example

Suppose `infile` contains `NUMLINES` lines with mixed data types in a consistent order: `item idNumber price`. For example,

```
hat          296 10.59
scarf        304  6.95
    ...
```

Then the following code segment will read each line for processing:

```
apstring item;
int idNum;
double price;
for (int i=0; i<NUMLINES; i++)
{
    infile >> item >> idNum >> price;
    <process item>
}
```

Alternatively, replace the `for` loop with

```
while (infile >> item >> idNum >> price)
    <process item>
```

This too will read all lines in the file, but it doesn't depend on knowing how many lines there are.

Files, Streams, and Strings

Word-by-Word
Processing

Example

Suppose wordFile contains the following (remember: '\n' = newline):

```
If ifs and       ands,\n
   were\n
   pots and pans\n
```

Then the following code fragment will list the first six words of wordFile:

```
//assume wordFile open for reading
apstring word;
for (int i=0; i<6; i++)
{
    wordFile >> word;
    cout << word << endl;
}
```

The output that appears on the screen is

```
If
ifs
and
ands,
were
pots
```

NOTE

1. Punctuation is included as part of a word.
2. Suppose that the text in the file were instead typed from the keyboard, with carriage returns replacing newline characters. Then, replacing wordFile with cin in the code segment would produce the same output.

If the number of words in a text file is unknown, the while(wordFile >> word) construct can be used:

```
//wordFile open for reading
apstring word;
while (wordFile >> word)
{
    <process word>
}
```

Again, this works because the test wordFile >> word becomes false when the end of file is reached.

Reading an unknown number of words from the *keyboard* requires a string sentinel for termination. Be sure that the sentinel is not a word that could appear in the list! (There are system-dependent ways of terminating keyboard input without a sentinel, but these are neither standard nor part of the APCS curriculum.)

Example

```
const apstring SENTINEL = "zzz";
apstring word;
cin >> word;
while (word != SENTINEL)
{
    <process word>
    cin >> word;
}
```

Line-by-Line Processing

The `getline( )` Function

The >> operator cannot be used to read in a string that contains spaces. The `apstring` class provides the `getline()` function to read a string of characters into a string variable:

```
getline(input, str);
```

The first parameter is an `istream`; the second is an `apstring`. Function `getline` reads all characters, including spaces and tabs up to a newline character, '\n'. The newline character is removed from the stream but not stored in `str`.

Example 1

```
apstring name;
cout << "Enter your full name on 1 line" << endl;
getline(cin, name);
```

Example 2

```
//infile opened
apstring line;
getline(infile, line);  //reads first line of infile
getline(infile, line);  //reads second line of infile
    ...
```

Example 3

```
//infile opened
apstring line;
while (getline(infile, line))
{
    <process line>
}
```

Example 3 works because `getline` returns the state of the stream as a side effect. When there are no more lines in `infile`, the attempted read leaves the stream in a failed state and terminates the `while` loop. The state of the stream is restored with `infile.clear()`. (It is not tested on the AP exam.)

The >> Operator and `getline`

Beware of `getline` and `>>` in the same stream! Here is an example reading numbers and strings:

```
int age;
apstring name;
cout << "Enter your age" << endl;
cin >> age;
cout << "Enter your full name" << endl;
getline(cin, name);
cout << name << " you are " << age;
```

Suppose you enter 16 followed by a carriage return, then "Louise Wachs" followed by a carriage return. You might expect this output:

```
Louise Wachs you are 16
```

What you actually get is

```
you are 16
```

What happened is that the carriage return you entered after the 16 is still in the `cin` stream. The `getline` call read all characters up to the next `'\n'`, so it read nothing! You can fix this in two ways. Immediately following the `cin >> age;` statement, add either

```
getline(cin, dummy);   OR   cin.ignore(100,'\n');
```

The `getline` works by reading an empty string into `dummy` and throwing away the `'\n'` character. The stream is now ready for the "real" `getline` statement.

The function `ignore(100,'\n')` will read (and ignore) up to 100 characters, until it finds and gobbles up the first newline character. The `ignore` function is very useful, but will not be tested on the AP exam.

Note that the problem described here occurs only when `getline` follows `>>` for the same stream. There is no problem if `>>` follows `getline`, or `getline` follows `getline`.

Character-by-Character Processing

Any line of text in a file can be accessed with `getline(infile, line)`. The individual characters in the `line` string can then be processed using the `apstring` functions. Note that the newline characters in the file will not be processed with this method.

Example 1

To process all characters in a file, except the `'\n'` characters.

```
//infile open for reading
apstring line;
while (getline(infile, line))
    for (int i=0; i<line.length(); i++)
    {
        <process line[i]>        //process each character
    }                            //in line
```

Any nonwhitespace character in a text file can be accessed with `infile >> ch`.

Example 2

```
//infile open for reading
char ch;
while (infile >> ch)
{
    <process ch>      //process each character that
}                     //is not whitespace
```

An alternative method for character-by-character processing is to use the stream member functions get and put. (These will not be tested on the AP exam.)

Example 3

Process *every* character in `infile` and write to `outfile`:

```
while (infile.get(ch))  //gets every character in file,
{                       //including '\n'
    <process ch>
    outfile.put(ch);    //writes ch to outfile
}
```

Example 4

Count the number of lines and characters in `infile`.

Method I

```
//infile is open at top of file
int numLines = 0, numChars = 0;
while (getline(infile, line))
{
    numLines++;
    numChars += line.length();
}
numChars += numLines;       //include the '\n' characters
```

Method II

```
//infile is open at top of file
int numLines = 0, numChars = 0;
while (infile.get(ch))
{
    numChars++;
    if (ch == '\n')
        numLines++;
}
```

Input/Output of User-Defined Objects

You can input or output user-defined objects by writing nonmember functions that overload the operators << and >> (see Chapter 2).

Streams as Parameters

Remember that whenever a stream is passed as an argument, it should be passed by reference.

Multiple-Choice Questions on Files and Streams

1. An external file contains real numbers randomly spaced in the file.
   For example,

   ```
   2.6     7.84     10
        13
   8.9      2.753
        . . .
   ```

   Which of the following program segments will print a list of all numbers in
   the file to the screen?

   (A) ```
       ofstream numFile;
       <code to open numFile>
       double d;
       while (numFile >> d)
           cout << d << endl;
       ```

   (B) ```
       ifstream numFile;
       <code to open numFile>
       double d;
       while (numFile >> d)
           cout << d << endl;
       ```

   (C) ```
       ifstream numFile;
       <code to open numFile>
       double d;
       while (cin >> d)
           cout << d << endl;
       ```

   (D) ```
       ofstream numFile;
       <code to open numFile>
       double d;
       while (cin >> d)
           numFile << d << endl;
       ```

   (E) ```
       ifstream numFile;
       <code to open numFile>
       double d;
       while (numFile >> d)
           numFile << d << endl;
       ```
       ```

2. Suppose that the stream `itemFile` is open for input and the following line in `itemFile` is to be read:

```
dog 30 42.35
```

Which of the following correctly reads the data into an `apstring`, `int`, and `double` variable, respectively? You may assume the declarations

```
apstring s, line;
int n;
double d;
```

    (A) `getline(itemFile, s, n, d);`
    (B) `getline(itemFile, line);`
    (C) `getline(itemFile, line, s, n, d);`
    (D) `cin >> s >> n >> d;`
    (E) `itemFile >> s >> n >> d;`

3. Consider the code segment

```
char ch1, ch2;
int num;
cin >> ch1 >> ch2 >> num;
```

Suppose the user inputs "A<space>2<carriage return>3":

```
A 2\n
3
```

Which represents the variable contents after execution of the code segment?
    (A) ch1 = 'A', ch2 = ' ', num = 2
    (B) ch1 = 'A', ch2 = '2', num = 3
    (C) ch1 = 'A', ch2 = '2', num = '3'
    (D) ch1 = 'A', ch2 = ' ', num = some undefined value
    (E) No values assigned. Type mismatch error at run time.

4. Suppose that a program has `int` variables `i`, `j`, and `k`, whose contents are currently 15, 30, and 45, respectively. The program now executes the following two statements:

```
cin >> i >> j >> k;
cout << "i = " << i << " j = " << j << " k = " << k;
```

A user types the following input data:

```
10.26 4 11
```

What output is produced by the program? (Ignore spacing.)
(A) i = 10.26 j = 4 k = 11
(B) i = 10   j = 4 k = 11
(C) i = 10   j = 30 k = 45
(D) i = 10   j = 26 k = 4
(E) No output produced. Type mismatch error at run time.

Questions 5–7 refer to the following text file, `owl.txt`:

```
The Owl
and the Pussy-Cat
went to sea
```

You may assume that

- `infile`, the stream variable for `owl.txt`, is open for input at the top of this file.

- Each line is terminated with a carriage return.

- There are no blanks following the last letter in each line.

- There is exactly one blank between words on the same line.

5. Which of the following program segments correctly counts the number of words in `infile`?

```
I  int wordCount = 0;
   apstring line;
   while (getline(infile, line))
       for (int i=0; i<line.length(); i++)
           if (line[i] == ' ')
               wordCount++;
```

```
II int wordCount = 0;
   apstring word;
   while (infile >> word)
       wordCount++;
```

```
III int wordCount = 0;
    apstring line;
    int blanks_in_line;
    while (getline(infile, line))
    {
        blanks_in_line = 0;
        for (int i=0; i<line.length(); i++)
            if (line[i] == ' ')
                    blanks_in_line++;
        wordCount += blanks_in_line + 1;
    }
```

(A) I only
(B) II only
(C) I and II only
(D) II and III only
(E) I, II, and III

6. Suppose `outfile` has just been opened for writing. What will `outfile` contain after execution of this code?

```
//infile is open for input at the top of owl.txt
apstring str;
while (getline(infile, str))
    outfile << str;
```

(A) The Owl
    and the Pussy-Cat
    went to sea
(B) The Owl and the Pussy-Cat went to sea
(C) The Owland the Pussy-Catwent to sea
(D) TheOwlandthePussy-Catwenttosea
(E) The
    Owl
    and
    the
    Pussy-Cat
    went
    to
    sea

7. Suppose `outfile` has just been opened for writing. What will `outfile` contain after execution of this code?

```
//infile is open for input at the top of owl.txt
apstring str;
while (infile >> str)
    outfile << str;
```

(A) The Owl
     and the Pussy-Cat
     went to sea

(B) The Owl and the Pussy-Cat went to sea

(C) The Owland the Pussy-Catwent to sea

(D) TheOwlandthePussy-Catwenttosea

(E) The
     Owl
     and
     the
     Pussy-Cat
     went
     to
     sea

8. Consider the function

```
void CopyFile (ifstream & inf, ofstream & outf)
//copies contents of inf to outf
//precondition: inf is open for input at the beginning
//              of the file.
//              outf is empty and open for output
//postcondition: outf is an exact copy of inf
{
    apstring str;
    <code to copy inf to outf>
}
```

Which of the following is correct *<code to copy inf to outf>*?

```
I   while (getline(inf, str))
        outf << str << endl;

II  while (getline(inf, str))
        outf << str;

III while (inf >> str)
        outf << str << endl;
```

(A) I only
(B) II only
(C) III only
(D) I and III only
(E) II and III only

9. In the following code segment, you may assume that `Area(length, width)` and `Perim(length, width)` correctly find the area and perimeter of the rectangle defined by the parameters `length` and `width`.

```
int length, width;
apstring operation;
cout << "Enter length and width of rectangle" << endl;
cin >> length >> width;
cout << "Enter operation: perimeter or area" << endl;
getline(cin, operation);
if (operation == "area")
    cout << operation << " is " << Area(length, width);
else if (operation == "perimeter")
    cout << operation << " is " << Perim(length, width);
else
    cout << "Oops! An error occurred!";
```

What output will be produced after the user enters the following input?

```
6   8
area
```

(A) "Oops! An error occurred!"
(B) area is 48
(C) is 48
(D) perimeter is 28
(E) No output because of run-time error

10. Suppose that `infile` has just been opened for input and contains the following:

```
Canned Snow Crab
25
3.95
C456
```

What will be output after execution of the following lines of code?

```
apstring item, idNum;
int quantity;
double price;

getline(infile, item);
cout << item << endl;
infile >> quantity;
cout << quantity << endl;
infile >> price;
cout << price << endl;
getline(infile, idNum);
cout << idNum << endl;
```

(A) Canned Snow Crab
    25
    3.95
    C456

(B) Canned Snow Crab
    25
    3.95

(C) 25
    3.95
    C456

(D) Canned Snow Crab
    25

(E) Canned Snow Crab

11. This question refers to the function Compress:

```
void Compress(ifstream & inf)
//outputs the contents of inf without whitespace
//   (e.g. blanks and carriage returns)
//precondition:  inf is open for input at the top of the file
//               inf contains no whitespace other than blanks
//               or newline characters
//postcondition: inf output to screen with no whitespace
{
    apstring s;
    <code>
}
```

Which of the following replacements for <*code*> will satisfy the postcondition of function Compress?

```
 I while (getline(inf, s))
       cout << s;

 II while (inf >> s)
       cout << s;

III apstring temp;
    while (getline(inf, s))
    {
        for (int i=0; i<s.length(); i++)
            if (s[i] != ' ')
                temp += s[i];
        cout << temp;
    }
```

(A) I only
(B) II only
(C) III only
(D) I and II only
(E) II and III only

12. This question refers to the function KeyCount:

```
int KeyCount(ifstream & inf, const apstring & keyWord)
//precondition:  inf open for input at top of file
//               inf contains no hyphenated words
//               keyWord contains no spaces or punctuation
//postcondition: number of occurrences of keyWord in inf
//               has been returned
{
    int count = 0;
    apstring word;
    while (inf >> word)
        if (word == keyWord)
            count++;
    return count;
}
```

This function does not work as intended. For example, if inf contains

```
The fortune teller said I would drown in a pit of slime.
Slime is not an attractive thought. I would not use "slime"
to refer to my worst enemies.
```

then the code segment

```
apstring key = "slime";
int x = KeyCount(inf, key);
```

results in x having the value 0. The programmer's intent is that x should have the value 3 in this case. The programmer proposes to fix KeyCount so that it works as intended. Which of the following changes are necessary?

  I word should be stripped of punctuation.
  II word should be stripped of blanks.
  III A lowercase copy of word should be compared with a lowercase copy of keyWord.

(A) I only
(B) II only
(C) III only
(D) I and III only
(E) I, II, and III

13. The following program segment counts the number of lines in `infile`:

```
//infile is open for reading at the top of the file,
// and contains at least two lines of text
int count = 0;
apstring line;
while (getline(infile, line))
    count++;
```

The segment does not provide the correct answer. It returns a count that is one fewer than the actual number of lines in `infile`. Which of the following is the most likely cause of the error?

(A) None of the lines in `infile` were terminated by carriage returns.

(B) The function to open `infile` caused the first line to be skipped.

(C) The final line in `infile` was not terminated with a carriage return.

(D) An incorrect pathname was given for `infile` and the file could not be opened.

(E) `getline` was used incorrectly. Replacing

```
while (getline(infile, line))
```

with

```
while (infile >> line)
```

would have produced the correct number of lines.

Answer Key

1. **B**	6. **C**	11. **E**
2. **E**	7. **D**	12. **D**
3. **B**	8. **A**	13. **C**
4. **C**	9. **A**	
5. **D**	10. **B**	

Answers Explained

1. **(B)** The file variable `numFile` must be an *input* file stream object, namely of type `ifstream`. This eliminates choices A and D. Also, numbers must be read in from `numFile`, which requires `while (numFile >> d)`. This eliminates choice C. Choice E is wrong because writing d to screen requires `cout << d`.

2. **(E)** Choices A, B, and C are wrong mainly because `getline` inserts an entire line into a string. The `>>` operator must be used to extract the different parts of the line. Choice D is wrong because the data are coming from `itemFile`, not the keyboard.

3. **(B)** Since `>>` skips over whitespace, including `'\n'`, `ch1` will be assigned `'A'`, `ch2` will be assigned `'2'`, and `num` will be assigned the integer value 3.

4. **(C)** When reading an `int`, the `>>` operator stops reading at the first character that is inappropriate for type `int`, in this case the decimal point. Thus, the value 10 is stored in `i`. The input operation then fails for `j`, since `j` can't start with a decimal point. The `cin` stream goes into a failed state. Both `j` and `k` retain their current values. All future statements in the program that refer to `cin` will be ignored until `cin` is cleared.

5. **(D)** Segment III is clunky but it works. Notice that the number of words in a line is one more than the number of blanks. Thus, segment I gives an incorrect word count.

6. **(C)** `getline` does not read the newline character into `str`. This means that there will be no newlines in `outfile`. This eliminates choices A and E. Choice D is wrong since nothing in the given code removes spaces from each string. B is wrong because nothing in the code inserts a space in `outfile` between each `str`.

7. **(D)** The `>>` operator skips any initial whitespace and then reads into `str` all characters up to whitespace. Thus, `while (infile >> str)` does a word-by-word reading. `outfile << str` outputs these words without spaces. Note that the newline character is counted as whitespace, thus there are no newlines in the output.

8. **(A)** Since `getline` returns `str` with no carriage return, newlines need to be inserted at the end of each `str` in `outf`. Hence, `outf << str;` in segment II is wrong. `outf << str << endl;` is correct. Segment III will produce a list of

words, one per line, in `outf` since `while (inf >> str)` reads one word at a time into `str`.

9. **(A)** After 6 and 8 are entered, the carriage return character is still in the `cin` stream. `getline(cin, operation)` then reads the empty string into `operation`. Thus, `operation` has neither the value "area" nor "perimeter," which leads to `Oops! An error has occurred!`

10. **(B)** `getline(infile, item)` will read `Canned Snow Crab` into `item` and will throw away the newline character. Then `infile >> quantity` will read 25 into `quantity`. The newline character is still in the `infile` stream. The statement `infile >> price` will skip over the newline character and read 3.95 into `price`. The newline character following 3.95 is still in the stream. Now `getline(infile, idNum)` will read up to that newline character, so `idNum` will be assigned the empty string. Therefore, the final line of the file won't be printed.

11. **(E)** `getline(inf, s)` preserves the spaces in `s`, which eliminates segment I. Note that segment III doesn't need to test `s` for newline characters (`'\n'`) since `getline` does not store `'\n'` into `s`.

12. **(D)** Since `inf >> word` reads in a word attached to surrounding punctuation (as in `"slime"` and `slime.`), correction I is necessary. Correction III is necessary since `Slime` is not equal to `slime`, but the programmer wants to count them both. Note that comparing uppercase copies of `word` and `keyWord` would work equally well. Correction II is redundant since `keyWord` contains no spaces and `inf >> word` will read nonspace characters only.

13. **(C)** `getline(infile, line)` should read a line from `infile` up to the newline character *or* the end-of-file character. In many systems this is exactly what happens, and the given code returns the correct number of lines. In some systems, however, if the last line of `infile` is not terminated with a carriage return, reading the last line is not completed and the line count has an off-by-one error. The point of this question is to realize that the other choices are highly unlikely causes of the error, so C must be the answer. For choice A, if none of the lines were terminated by carriage returns the count will be no greater than 1! Choice B is a highly improbable cause of the error, especially if a (previously tested) library file function is used to open the file. For choice D, an incorrect pathname for `infile` will lead to an inability to locate the file, *not* an off-by-one error in the line count. For choice E, `while(infile >> line)` will produce a count of the number of *words* in the file.

CHAPTER SEVEN

Recursion

Men have become the tools of their tools.
—Henry David Thoreau (1817–1862)

Recursive Functions

A *recursive function* is a function that calls itself. For example, here is a program that calls a recursive function StackChars().

```
#include <iostream.h>
void StackChars();          //Recursive function
int main()
{
    cout << "Enter a sentence terminated with a period" << endl;
    StackChars();
    cout << endl;
    return 0;
}

void StackChars()
{
    char ch;
    cin.get(ch);    //reads a single char from keyboard
    if (ch = '.')
        cout << endl;
    else
        StackChars();
    cout << ch;
}
```

Here is what appears on the screen if you enter "Oh hi."

```
Enter a sentence terminated with a period
Oh hi.
.ih hO
```

The program reads in a string terminated with a period and echoes its reverse to the screen. How does this happen?

Each time the recursive call to StackChars() is made, execution goes back to the start of a new call of the function. The computer must remember to complete all the pending calls to the function. It does this by stacking the statements that must still be executed as follows: The first time StackChars() is called, the 'O'

164

is read and tested for being a period. No it's not, so StackChars() is called again. The statement cout << 'O' (which has not yet been executed) goes on a stack and execution goes to the start of the function. The 'h' is read. No, it's not a period, so cout << 'h' goes on the stack. And so on. The stack looks something like this before the call in which the period is read:

cout << 'i';
cout << 'h';
cout << ' ';
cout << 'h';
cout << 'O';

Imagine that these statements are stacked like plates. In the final StackChars() call, ch has the value '.'. Yes, it *is* a period, so the StackChars() line is skipped, the period is printed on the screen, and the function call terminates. The computer now completes each of the previous function calls in turn by "popping" the statements off the top of the stack. It prints the 'i', the 'h', the space, the 'h', and the 'O', and execution of StackChars() is complete.[1]

NOTE

1. With each new call of StackChars() a new local variable ch is created.
2. The first time the function actually terminates, the program returns to complete the most recently invoked previous call. That's why the characters get reversed in this example.

General Form of Simple Recursive Functions

Here is the framework for a simple recursive function that has no specific return type.

```
void RecursiveFunc( ... )
{
    if (termination condition)
        Output some values
    else
    {
        Perform some action
        RecursiveFunc( ... ); //recursive function call
    }
}
```

NOTE

1. The termination condition is called the *base case*. It typically occurs for the simplest case of the problem, such as when an integer has a value of 0 or 1. Other examples of base cases are when some terminating character is encountered, or an end-of-file is reached.

---

[1]Actually, the computer stacks the pending statements in a recursive function call more efficiently than the way described. But *conceptually* this is how it is done.

2. In the else part of this framework, *Perform some action* and RecursiveFunc can sometimes be interchanged without altering the net effect of the algorithm. What changes is the order of executing statements. This can sometimes be significant, or even disastrous. See the KillBlob example at the end of this chapter, or the tree traversals and recursive tree algorithms in Chapter 10.

Example 1

```
void Drawline(int n)
{
    if (n == 0)
        cout << "That's all, folks!" << endl;
    else
    {
        for (int i=1; i<=n; i++)
            cout << '*';
        cout << endl;
        DrawLine(n-1);
    }
}
```

The function call DrawLine(3) produces this output:

```
***
**
*
That's all, folks!
```

NOTE

1. A function that has no pending statements following the recursive call is an example of *tail recursion*. Function DrawLine is such a case, but StackChars is not.
2. The base case in the DrawLine example is n equal to 0. Notice that each subsequent call, DrawLine(n-1), makes progress toward termination of the function. If your function has no base case, or if you never reach the base case, you will create *infinite recursion*. This is a catastrophic error that will cause your computer eventually to run out of memory and give you heart-stopping messages like STACK OVERFLOW or SEGMENTATION FAULT (CORE DUMPED).

Example 2

```
//illustrates infinite recursion
void Catastrophe(int n)
{
    cout << n << endl;
    Catastrophe(n+1);
}
```

Try running the case Catastrophe(1) if you have lots of time to waste!

Writing Recursive Functions

To come up with a recursive algorithm, you have to be able to frame a process *recursively* (i.e., in terms of a simpler case of itself). This is different from framing it *iteratively*, which repeats a process until a final condition is met. So a good strategy for writing recursive functions is first to state the algorithm recursively in words or pictures.

Example 1

Write a function that returns $n!$ (n factorial).

$n!$ defined iteratively	$n!$ defined recursively
$0! = 1$	$0! = 1$
$1! = 1$	$1! = (1)(0!)$
$2! = (2)(1)$	$2! = (2)(1!)$
$3! = (3)(2)(1)$	$3! = (3)(2!)$
$\cdots$	$\cdots$

The general recursive definition for $n!$ is

$$n! = \begin{cases} 1, & n = 0 \\ n(n-1)!, & n > 0 \end{cases}$$

The definition seems to be circular until you realize that if 0! is defined, all higher factorials are defined. Code for the recursive function follows directly from the recursive definition:

```
long int Fac(int n)
//returns n!  long int used to avoid integer overflow.
//  long int not tested on AP exam
//precondition: n ≥ 0
{
    if (n == 0)      //base case
        return 1;
    else
        return n*Fac(n-1);
}
```

Example 2

Write a recursive function `RevDigs` that outputs its integer parameter with the digits reversed. For example,

$$\begin{array}{lll} \text{RevDigs(147)} & \text{outputs} & 741 \\ \text{RevDigs(4)} & \text{outputs} & 4 \end{array}$$

First describe the process recursively. Output the rightmost digit. Then if there are still digits left in the remaining number, reverse its digits. You get the remaining number at each stage by using n/10. Here is the function:

```
void RevDigs(int n)
//Outputs n with digits reversed
//precondition: n ≥ 0
{
    cout << n % 10;        //rightmost digit
    if (n/10 != 0)         //base case
        RevDigs(n/10);
}
```

Example 3

Suppose `infile` is open for input. Write a recursive function `FindString` that prints out all lines in `infile` that contain a given substring.

In words, recursively:

> If there is another line in `infile`,
> > if the substring is in that line, output the line;
> > in either case, recursively `FindString` in rest of `infile`.

```
void FindString(ifstream & infile, const apstring & substr)
//prints all lines in infile that contain substr
//precondition: infile open for reading
{
    apstring line;
    if (getline(infile, line))
    {
        if (line.find(substr) != npos)  //if substr in line
            cout << line << endl;
        FindString(infile, substr);
    }
}
```

Example 4

Let `a[0]` ... `a[n-1]` be initialized with integers. Write a recursive algorithm to do a linear search for the integer `key`. Return the index of `key` or −1 if `key` is not in the list.

Recursive description of linear search, in words:

> To `LinearSearch` list of n elements:
> > If the list is empty, return -1;
> > Otherwise, if the nth element is the key, return n-1;
> > Otherwise, recursively `LinearSearch` the first n-1 elements.

```
int LinearSearch(const apvector <int> & a, int n, int key)
//Do a linear search for key in a[0] ... a[n-1]
//precondition: a[0] ... a[n-1] initialized with integers
//postcondition: index returned such that a[index] == key
//               -1 returned if key not in a
{
    if (n == 0)                //empty list
        return -1;
```

```
        else if (a[n-1] == key) //check last element in a
            return n-1;
        else
            return LinearSearch(a,n-1,key);
    }
```

Analysis of Recursive Functions

Recall the Fibonacci sequence 1, 1, 2, 3, 5, 8, 13, ... The nth Fibonacci number equals the sum of the previous two numbers if $n \geq 3$. Recursively,

$$\text{Fib}(n) = \begin{cases} 1, & n = 1 \text{ or } 2 \\ \text{Fib}(n-1) + \text{Fib}(n-2), & n \geq 3 \end{cases}$$

Here is the function:

```
int Fib(int n)
//Returns the nth Fibonacci number, n ≥ 1
{
    if (n == 1 || n == 2)
        return 1;
    else
        return Fib(n-1) + Fib(n-2);
}
```

Notice that there are two recursive calls in the last line of the function. So to find Fib(5), for example, takes eight recursive calls to Fib!

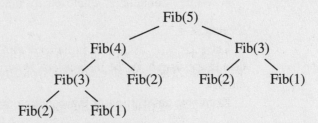

Level AB Only

In general, each call to Fib(n) makes two more calls. This is the tipoff for an exponential algorithm (i.e., the run time is $O(2^n)$). This is much slower than the $O(n)$ run time of the corresponding iterative algorithm (see Chapter 3, Question 20).

This leads to the question: Since every recursive algorithm can be written iteratively, when should one use recursion? Bear in mind that recursive algorithms have two disadvantages: extra run time and memory. Their major plus is elegance and simplicity of code. Here are some general rules:

1. Avoid recursion for algorithms that involve large local arrays—just a few recursive calls can cause memory overflow.
2. Avoid recursion if run time is important.

3. Use recursion when it significantly simplifies code without costing too much in extra time and memory.
4. Recursion is especially useful for branching processes like traversing trees or directories.
5. Avoid recursion for simple iterative functions like factorial, Fibonacci, and the linear search in Example 4.
6. Tail recursive algorithms (recursive call is the last statement of the function) are often better as iterative algorithms. In tail recursion, when a return is all that needs to be done to terminate a function, it seems wasteful to stack up all those local variables!

Sorting Algorithms That Use Recursion

Mergesort and Quicksort are discussed in Chapter 11.

Recursion in 2-D Grids

A certain type of problem crops up occasionally on the AP exam: using recursion to traverse a two-dimensional array. The problem comes in several different guises. For example,

1. A game board from which you must remove pieces.
2. A maze with walls and paths from which you must try to escape.
3. White "containers" enclosed by black "walls" into which you must "pour paint."

In each case you will be given a starting position (row, col) and instructions on what to do. The recursive solution typically involves these steps:

Check that the starting position is not out of range:
If (starting position satisfies some requirement)
Perform some action to solve problem
RecursiveCall(row+1, col)
RecursiveCall(row−1, col)
RecursiveCall(row, col+1)
RecursiveCall(row, col−1)

Example

On the right is an image represented as a grid of black and white cells. Two cells in an image are part of the same Blob if each is black and there is a sequence of moves from one cell to the other, where each move is either horizontal or vertical to an adjacent black cell. For example, the diagram represents an image that contains two Blobs, one of them consisting of a single cell.

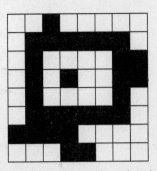

Assuming the following declarations, you are to write a recursive algorithm for function KillBlob whose header is given.

```
const int SIZE = 200;
enum CellType {black, white};
apmatrix <CellType> image(SIZE, SIZE);

void KillBlob(apmatrix<CellType> & image, int row, int col);
```

If $0 \leq$ row $\leq$ SIZE-1 and $0 \leq$ col $\leq$ SIZE-1 and image[row][col] is black, then KillBlob should set all cells in the same Blob to white. Otherwise, image is unchanged.

Solution.

```
{
    if (row >= 0 && row < SIZE && col >= 0 && col < SIZE)
        if (image[row][col] == black)
        {
            image[row][col] = white;
            KillBlob(image, row-1, col);
            KillBlob(image, row+1, col);
            KillBlob(image, row, col-1);
            KillBlob(image, row, col+1);
        }
}
```

Note: If you put the statement

```
image[row][col] = white;
```

after the four recursive calls, you get an infinite loop if your Blob has more than one cell. This is because, when you visit an adjacent cell, one of its recursive calls visits the original cell. If this cell is still black, yet more recursive calls are generated, *ad infinitum*.

A final thought: recursive algorithms can be tricky. Try to state the solution recursively *in words* before you launch into code. Oh, and don't forget the base case!

Multiple-Choice Questions on Recursion

1. Which of the following statements about recursion are true?
   - I Every recursive algorithm can in principle be written iteratively.
   - II Tail recursion is always used in "divide-and-conquer" algorithms.
   - III In a recursive definition, an object is defined in terms of a simpler case of itself.

   (A) I only
   (B) III only
   (C) I and II only
   (D) I and III only
   (E) II and III only

2. Which of the following is a valid reason for using a recursive algorithm rather than the corresponding iterative algorithm?
   - I The iterative algorithm requires very complicated code.
   - II The recursive algorithm, being shorter, is likely to save on run time.
   - III The recursive algorithm, being shorter, is likely to save on memory.

   (A) I only
   (B) II only
   (C) III only
   (D) II and III only
   (E) I, II, and III

3. Which of the following, when used as the <*body*> of function Sum, will enable that function to compute $1 + 2 + \ldots + n$ correctly for any $n > 0$?

```
int Sum(int n)
//precondition: n > 0
//postcondition: 1+2+...+n has been returned
{
    <body>
}
```

```
 I return n + Sum(n-1);
 II if (n == 1)
        return 1;
    else
        return n + Sum(n-1);
III if (n == 1)
        return 1;
    else
        return Sum(n) + Sum(n-1);
```

   (A) I only
   (B) II only
   (C) III only
   (D) I and II only
   (E) I, II, and III

4. Refer to the function `StringRecur`:

```
void StringRecur(apstring s)
{
    if (s.length() < 15)
        cout << s;
    StringRecur(s + '*');
}
```

When will function `StringRecur` terminate without error?
(A) Only when the length of the input string is less than 15
(B) Only when the length of the input string is greater than or equal to 15
(C) Only when an empty string is input
(D) For all string inputs
(E) For no string inputs

5. Refer to function `StrRecur`:

```
void StrRecur(apstring s)
{
    if (s.length() < 15)
    {
        cout << s;
        StrRecur(s + '*');
    }
}
```

When will function `StrRecur` terminate without error?
(A) Only when the length of the input string is less than 15
(B) Only when the length of the input string is greater than or equal to 15
(C) Only when an empty string is input
(D) For all string inputs
(E) For no string inputs

Questions 6 and 7 refer to function `Result`:

```
int Result(int n)
{
    if (n == 1)
        return 2;
    else
        return 2*Result(n-1);
}
```

6. What value does `Result(5)` return?
(A) 64
(B) 32
(C) 16
(D) 8
(E) 2

7. If $n > 0$, how many times will Result be called to evaluate Result(n) (including the initial call)?

(A) 2

(B) $2n$

(C) 2^n

(D) n^2

(E) n

8. Refer to function Mystery:

```
int Mystery(int n, int a, int d)
{
    if (n == 1)
        return a;
    else
        return d + Mystery(n-1, a, d);
}
```

What value is returned by the call Mystery(3, 2, 6)?

(A) 20

(B) 14

(C) 10

(D) 8

(E) 2

9. Refer to function F:

```
int F(int k, int n)
{
    if (n == k)
        return k;
    else
        if (n > k)
            return F(k, n-k);
        else
            return F(k-n, n);
}
```

What value is returned by the call F(6, 8)?

(A) 8

(B) 4

(C) 3

(D) 2

(E) 1

10. What does function Recur do?

```
int Recur(apvector <int> & x, int n)
//x is an array of n integers
{
    int t;
    if (n == 1)
        return x[0];
    else
    {
        t = Recur(x, n-1);
        if (x[n-1] > t)
            return x[n-1];
        else
            return t;
    }
}
```

(A) It finds the largest value in x and leaves x unchanged.
(B) It finds the smallest value in x and leaves x unchanged.
(C) It sorts x in ascending order and returns the largest value in x.
(D) It sorts x in descending order and returns the largest value in x.
(E) It returns x[0] or x[n-1], whichever is larger.

11. Refer to the function Power:

```
double Power(double base, int expo)
//precondition: expo is any integer, base is not zero
//postcondition: base raised to expo power returned
{
    if (expo == 0)
        return 1;
    else if (expo > 0)
        return base*Power(base, expo-1);
    else
        return <code>;
}
```

Which <code> correctly completes function Power?
(Recall that $a^{-n} = (1/a)^n$, $a \neq 0$; for example, $2^{-3} = 1/2^3 = 1/8$.)
(A) (1/base) * Power(base, expo+1)
(B) (1/base) * Power(base, expo-1)
(C) base * Power(base, expo+1)
(D) base * Power(base, expo-1)
(E) (1/base) * Power(base, expo)

12. Consider the following function:

```
void DoSomething(int n)
{
    if (n > 0)
    {
        DoSomething(n-1);
        cout << n;
        DoSomething(n-1);
    }
}
```

What would be output following the call `DoSomething(3)`?
  (A) 3211211
  (B) 1121213
  (C) 1213121
  (D) 1211213
  (E) 1123211

13. Refer to function `WriteEven`:

```
void WriteEven(ifstream & s)
//precondition: s is open for input at the top of the file.
//             s contains a list of integers, both even and odd
//postcondition: all even integers in s have been listed on
//               the screen in the reverse order that they
//               are read, i.e., last even integer in s
//               printed first, ..., first even integer in s
//               printed last
{
    int num;
    <code>
}
```

Which `<code>` satisfies the postcondition of function `WriteEven`?

```
 I if (s >> num)
   {
       if (num % 2 == 0)
           cout << num << endl;
       WriteEven(s);
   }

II if (s >> num)
   {
       WriteEven(s);
       if (num % 2 == 0)
           cout << num << endl;
   }

III if (s >> num)
    {
        if (num % 2 == 0)
            WriteEven(s);
        cout << num << endl;
    }
```

(A) I only
(B) II only
(C) III only
(D) I and II only
(E) I, II, and III

Questions 14–16 refer to function T:

```
int T(int n)
//precondition: n ≥ 1
{
    if (n == 1 || n == 2)
        return 2*n;
    else
        return T(n-1) - T(n-2);
}
```

14. What will be returned by T(5)?
   (A) 4
   (B) 2
   (C) 0
   (D) −2
   (E) −4

15. For the function call T(6), how many calls to T will be made, including the original function call?
   (A) 6
   (B) 7
   (C) 11
   (D) 15
   (E) 25

Level AB Only

16. The run time of function T is
   (A) $O(n)$
   (B) $O(n^2)$
   (C) $O(2^n)$
   (D) $O(n^3)$
   (E) $O(\log n)$

17. This question refers to functions F1 and F2:

```
int F1(int a, int b);
int F2(int p, int q);

int F1(int a, int b)
{
    if (a == b)
        return b;
    else
        return a + F2(a-1,b);
}

int F2(int p, int q)
{
    if (p < q)
        return p + q;
    else
        return p + F1(p-2,q);
}
```

What value will be returned by a call to F1(5, 3)?
 (A) 5
 (B) 6
 (C) 7
 (D) 12
 (E) 15

18. Consider function Foo:

```
int Foo(int x)
{
    if (x == 1 || x == 3)
        return x;
    else
        return x*Foo(x-1);
}
```

Assuming no possibility of integer overflow, what will be the value of z after execution of the following statement?

```
        int z = Foo(Foo(3) + Foo(4));
```

 (A) (15!)/(2!)
 (B) 3! + 4!
 (C) (7!)!
 (D) (3! + 4!)!
 (E) 15

Questions 19 and 20 refer to the following functions:

```
void WriteThreeDigits(int n)
{
    cout << n/100;
    cout << ((n/10) % 10);
    cout << n % 10;
}

void WriteWithCommas(int n)
//precondition: n ≥ 0
{
    if (n<1000)
        cout << n;
    else
    {
        WriteThreeDigits(n % 1000);
        cout << ",";
        WriteWithCommas(n/1000);
    }
}
```

19. The function WriteWithCommas is supposed to print its non-negative int argument with commas properly inserted (every three digits, starting at the right). For example, the integer 27048621 should be printed as 27,048,621. WriteWithCommas does not always work as intended, however. Assuming no integer overflow, which of the following integer arguments will *not* be printed correctly?

    (A) 896
    (B) 251462251
    (C) 365051
    (D) 278278
    (E) 4

20. Which change in the code of the given functions will cause function WriteWithCommas to work as intended?

    (A) Interchange the lines cout << n/100 and cout << n % 10 in function WriteThreeDigits.
    (B) Interchange the lines WriteThreeDigits(n % 1000) and WriteWithCommas(n/1000) in function WriteWithCommas.
    (C) Change the test in WriteWithCommas to if (n > 1000).
    (D) In the function WriteWithCommas, change the line WriteThreeDigits(n % 1000) to WriteThreeDigits(n/1000).
    (E) In the function WriteWithCommas, change the recursive call WriteWithCommas(n/1000) to WriteWithCommas(n % 1000).

Answer Key

1.	**D**	8.	**B**	15.	**D**
2.	**A**	9.	**D**	16.	**C**
3.	**B**	10.	**A**	17.	**E**
4.	**E**	11.	**A**	18.	**A**
5.	**D**	12.	**C**	19.	**C**
6.	**B**	13.	**B**	20.	**B**
7.	**E**	14.	**E**		

Answers Explained

1. (**D**) Tail recursion is when the recursive call of a function is made in the last line of the function definition. Divide-and-conquer algorithms like those used in binary search, mergesort, or quicksort have recursive calls *before* the last line. Thus, statement II is false.

2. (**A**) Because of the stacking of pending statements in recursive algorithms, they take longer to execute. Recursive algorithms also tend to use more memory since new local variables are created for each call. Thus, statements II and III are wrong.

3. (**B**) Code segment I is wrong because there is no base case. Code segment III is wrong because, besides anything else, Sum(n) prevents the function from terminating—the base case n = 1 will not be reached.

4. (**E**) When StringRecur is invoked, it calls itself irrespective of the length of s. Since there is no action that leads to termination, the function will not terminate until the computer runs out of memory (run-time error).

5. (**D**) The base case is s.length() $\geq$ 15. Since s gets longer on each function call, the function will eventually terminate. If the original length of s is $\geq$ 15, the function will terminate without output on the first call.

6. (**B**) Letting R denote the function Result, we have

$$
\begin{aligned}
R(5) &= 2 * R(4) \\
&= 2 * (2 * (R(3))) \\
&= \cdots \\
&= 2^5 \\
&= 32
\end{aligned}
$$

7. (**E**) For Result(n) there will be $(n-1)$ recursive calls before Result(1), the base case, is reached. Adding the initial call gives a total of n function calls.

8. **(B)** Letting M denote function Mystery, we have

$$
\begin{aligned}
M(3, 2, 6) &= 6 + M(2, 2, 6) \\
&= 6 + (6 + M(1, 2, 6)) \quad \text{(base case)} \\
&= 6 + 6 + 2 \\
&= 14
\end{aligned}
$$

9. **(D)** Here are the recursive calls that are made, in order: $F(6, 8) \rightarrow F(6, 2) \rightarrow F(4, 2) \rightarrow F(2, 2)$, base case. Thus, 2 is returned.

10. **(A)** If there is only one element in x, then Recur returns that element. Having the recursive call at the beginning of the else part of the algorithm causes the if part for each function call to be stacked until t eventually gets assigned to x[0]. The pending if statements are then executed, and t is compared to each element in x. The largest value in x is returned.

11. **(A)** The required code is for expo negative. For example, Power(2, -3) should return $2^{-3} = 1/8$. So expo+1 for the second parameter must be correct, otherwise you will never reach expo = 0, the base case. This eliminates choices B, D, and E. The recursive definition for b^n where $n < 0$ is

$$
b^n = \begin{cases} 1, & n = 0 \\ (1/b) \cdot b^{n+1}, & n < 0 \end{cases}
$$

which eliminates choice C. For example, $2^{-3} = (1/2) \cdot 2^{-2}$.

12. **(C)** The boxes and arrows show the order of execution of the statements.

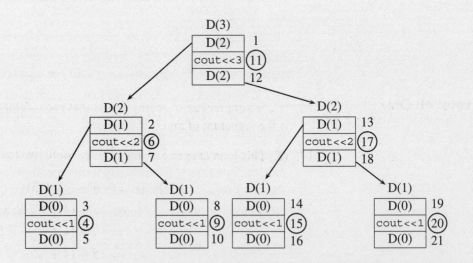

Each box represents a function call to DoSomething. The numbers in the box refer to that function call only. D(0) is the base case, so the statement immediately following it is executed next. When all statements in a given box (function call) have been executed, backtrack along the arrow to find the statement that gets executed next. The circled numbers represent the output statements. Following them in order, statements 4, 6, 9, 11, 15, 17, and 20 produce the output in choice C.

13. **(B)** Since even numbers are printed *before* the recursive call in segment I, they will be printed in the order in which they are read from the file. Contrast

this with the correct choice, segment II, in which the recursive call is made before the test for evenness. These tests will be stacked until the last number is read from the file. Recall that the pending statements are removed from the stack in reverse order (most recent recursive call first), which leads to even numbers being printed in reverse order. Segment III is wrong because all numbers from s will be printed, irrespective of whether they are even or not. Note that segment III would work if the file contained only even numbers.

14. **(E)** The first two terms, $T(1)$ and $T(2)$, are 2 and 4. Subsequent terms are generated by subtracting the previous two terms. Thus, the sequence goes 2, 4, 2, -2, -4, -2, 2, 4, ... Thus, $T(5) = -4$. Alternatively,

$$\begin{aligned} T(5) &= T(4) - T(3) \\ &= [T(3) - T(2)] - T(3) \\ &= -T(2) \\ &= -4 \end{aligned}$$

15. **(D)** 15. Count them! (Note that you stop at $T(2)$ since it's a base case.)

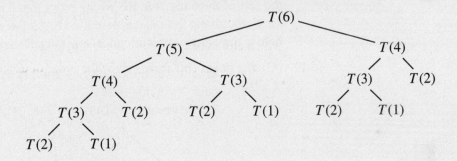

Level AB Only

16. **(C)** A simple way of seeing this is that each call makes two more calls. This is the signature of an $O(2^n)$ process.

17. **(E)** This is an example of *mutual recursion*, two functions that call each other.

$$\begin{aligned} F1(5, 3) &= 5 + F2(4, 3) \\ &= 5 + (4 + F1(2, 3)) \\ &= 5 + (4 + (2 + F2(1, 3))) \\ &= 5 + (4 + (2 + 4)) \\ &= 15 \end{aligned}$$

Note that $F2(1, 3)$ is a base case.

18. **(A)** Foo(3) = 3 (base case). Foo(4) = 4 * Foo(3) = 12. So you need to find
    Foo(Foo(3) + Foo(4)) = Foo(15).

$$
\begin{aligned}
\text{Foo}(15) &= 15 * \text{Foo}(14) \\
&= 15 * (14 * \text{Foo}(13)) \\
&= \cdots \\
&= 15 * 14 * \cdots * 4 * \text{Foo}(3) \\
&= 15 * 14 * \cdots * 4 * 3 \\
&= (15)!/(2!)
\end{aligned}
$$

19. **(C)** Suppose that $n = 365051$. `WriteWithCommas(365051)` will write 051 and
    then execute the function call `WriteWithCommas(365)`. This is a base case, so
    365 will be written out, resulting in 051,365. A number like 278278 (two sets
    of three identical digits) will be written out correctly, as will a "symmetrical"
    number like 251462251. Also, any $n < 1000$ is a base case and the number
    will be written out correctly as is.

20. **(B)** The cause of the problem is that the numbers are being written out with
    the sets of three digits in the wrong order. Interchanging `WriteThreeDigits`
    `(n % 1000)` and `WriteWithCommas(n/1000)` fixes the problem. For example,
    here is the order of execution for `WriteWithCommas(365051)`.

    ```
    WriteWithCommas(365) → Base case. Writes 365
    cout << ","; → 365,
    WriteThreeDigits(051) → 365,051 which is correct
    ```

CHAPTER EIGHT
Pointers and Linked Lists

As some day it may happen that a victim must be found,
I've got a little list—I've got a little list.
—*Gilbert and Sullivan*, The Mikado *(1885)*

Pointers

Why use pointers? Their great advantage is that they allow the *dynamic allocation* of memory. This means that you can assign memory during execution of a program as opposed to setting aside large chunks at compile time (*static allocation*). The built-in functions `new` and `delete` take new memory slots from the memory heap as needed and return them when done.

A *pointer* is a simple built-in type that contains the address of another variable. The actual value of a pointer is usually irrelevant. Of greater interest is the object being pointed to. Accessing the variable that a pointer points to is called *dereferencing* the pointer.

The *null pointer* has the value `NULL` (or 0) and points to nothing. If you try to dereference the null pointer you get a run-time error.

Linear Linked Lists

Features of a Linked List

People often just say "linked list" for a linear linked list. Picture a linked list as follows:

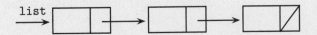

It has these features:

1. A collection of memory slots, called *nodes*, each of which has a data field and a pointer field.
2. Each pointer field contains the address of the next node in the list.

3. An *external pointer*, in this case called `list`, provides access to the linked list.
4. The pointer field of the last node in the list has the value `NULL`.

Struct Implementation of a Linked List

Struct Declaration, Node Creation and Deletion

A linked list can be implemented in C++ using a struct for each node. For example, here is a declaration for a linked list of integers:

```
struct node
{
    int info;        //integer data
    node *next;      //link to the next node
};
node *list;          //external pointer list is of type
                     //"points to node"
```

NOTE

1. `next` and `list` are both pointers.
2. If a pointer `p` will point to an element of this linked list, it must be declared of type `node *`, as follows:

```
node *p;
```

The following declarations create a single node in a linked list:

```
node *p;
p = new node;
```

These two statements are equivalent to the single statement

```
node *p = new node;
```

which results in `p` pointing to an empty node:

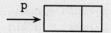

This node can be filled as follows:

```
p->info = 8;
p->next = NULL;
```

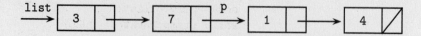

The notation `p->info` denotes "the info in the node that `p` points to," and `p->next` denotes "the pointer value in the node that `p` points to."

Suppose a linear linked list is as follows:

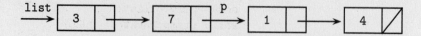

1. You cannot use p to access any values in nodes preceding the node p points to.
2. p->next->info denotes "the info in the node after the node p points to." In this case, it has the value 4. Similarly, p->next->next has the value NULL.
3. list->next->next has the same value as p since they both point to the node containing 1.

---

new and delete

When a node is created with new, that node will exist independently inside and outside the scope in which it was created. The only way to return the memory to the memory heap is with the built-in function delete:

```
delete p;   //recycle the memory slot that p points to
            //p becomes undefined
```

Here are some good rules to remember. Only use delete for a pointer slot that was obtained with new. Always recycle dynamic variables with delete when they are no longer needed. If you don't, you'll cause a *memory leak* in your program (and perhaps lose points on the AP exam!).

Initialization of a Linear Linked List

A linked list can be created with the following function GetNode, which initializes a single node, and the function Append, which attaches a node to the end of the list.

```
node *GetNode(int num)
//Creates a new node containing num and a NULL pointer
//Returns a pointer to this node
{
    node *p = new node; //get empty node pointed to by p
    p->info = num;
    p->next = NULL;
    return p;
}


void Append(node * & list, int num)
//precondition: list points to a linked list
//postcondition: new node with num appended to end of list
{
    if (list == NULL)          //empty list?
        list = GetNode(num);   //create first node
    else
    {
        //advance temp until it points to the last node
        node *temp = list;
        while (temp->next != NULL)
            temp = temp->next;
        temp->next = GetNode(num);  //append new node
    }
}
```

NOTE
1. The external pointer parameter, `list`, must be passed by reference since its value will be changed if the linked list was initially empty.
2. The precondition of `Append` says nothing about the linked list being nonempty, so you must do the `if (list == NULL)` test.
3. When traversing a linked list, beware of going too far. There is no turning back!

Insertion and Deletion

Example 1

Suppose that you are asked in a Part II question to write the body of function `Delete` whose header is

```
void Delete(node * & list, node * & p)
//precondition: list contains at least 1 node
//              p points to a node in the list
//postcondition: node that p points to deleted from list
```

First draw a picture with all the possibilities. Watch out for first node/last node situations. Don't assume that the node to be deleted is in the "middle" of the list. Check if "middle of the list" code works for the last node—it often does. It seldom works for the first node, however. Here are the four cases you need to worry about in the given problem:

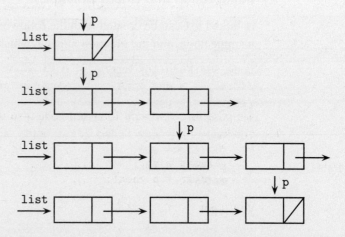

Notice that if p points to the first node (first two illustrated cases), you can simply reassign `list`. If p is further along, however, you need a temporary pointer to access the node preceding p whose pointer field will need to be adjusted. Also, notice that the same piece of code will take care of the last two cases.

```
void Delete(node * & list, node * & p)
{
    if (list == p)      //first node to be deleted.
        list = p->next; //handles 1 node case too
    else
    {
        node *q = list;
```

```
        while (q->next != p)
            q = q->next;
        q->next = p->next;
    }
    delete p;   //pointers OK, so recycle node p
}
```

Here's a diagram showing how the pointers are reassigned, and how the node magically vanishes when `delete p` is executed:

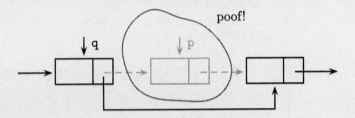

Now a look at insertion. Here's a hint. Adjust the pointer connections of the *new* node *first*. Then change the pointer connections in the linked list nodes. This avoids having part of your list float off into space. Consider the following setup:

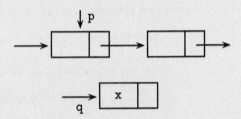

Suppose that you want to attach node q so that it immediately follows node p. If you say

```
    p->next = q;
    q->next = p->next;
```

you'll get

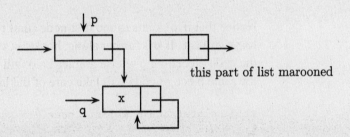

Suppose that you say instead

```
q->next = p->next;   //attach new node first
p->next = q;         //now attach list to new node
```

Then you get the correct setup

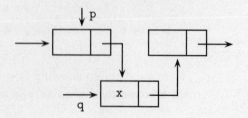

Example 2

Write the body of function `Insert`:

```
void Insert(node * & list, node * p, int x)
//precondition:  list points to a nonempty linked list
//               p points to a node in list
//postcondition: x inserted into list directly following
//               the node that p points to
```

If p points to the first node in the list, the code will be the same as for a node in the middle of the list, since the new node is being inserted *after* node p. The code may be different if p points to the *last* node, but checking the code for the general case shows that it works here too. So we have

```
void Insert(node * & list, node * p, int x)
{
    node *q = new node; //initialize new node with x
    q->info = x;
    q->next = p->next;  //attach new node to linked list
    p->next = q;        //attach linked list to new node
}
```

Struct with Constructor

Adding a constructor to the node struct makes creation of nodes very convenient:

```
struct node
{
    int info;
    node *next;
    node();                      //default constructor
    node(int val, node * link);  //constructor
};
node :: node() : info(0), next(NULL) {}
node :: node(int val, node *link) : info(val), next(link) {}
```

Since the implementation of the two constructors is simple (just initializer lists), they are often included in the struct declaration:

```
struct node
{
    int info;
    node *next;
    node() : info(0), next(NULL) {}
    node(int val, node *link) : info(val), next(link) {}
};
```

Using this declaration, we can initialize a node pointed to by `list` in two ways:

```
node *list = new node;
```

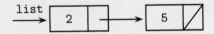

```
node *list = new node(6,NULL);
```

Suppose that a linked list exists. For example,

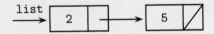

The statement

```
list = new node(7,list);
```

adds a node containing 7 to the front of the list. This is because the right-hand side of the statement is evaluated first. A new node gets value 7, and its pointer field has the same address as `list`:

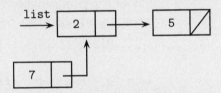

Then the left-hand side is executed. `list` is assigned to point to this new node:

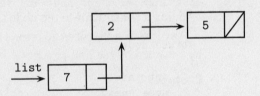

Having a node constructor in the struct means that you don't need the function `GetNode` anymore. Here is a modified `Append` function:

```
void Append(node * & list, int num)
//precondition: list points to a linked list
//postcondition: new node with num appended to end of list
{
    if (list == NULL)                //empty list?
        list = new node(num,NULL);  //create first node
    else
    {
        node *temp = list;
        while (temp->next != NULL)  //advance to end
            temp = temp->next;
```

```
                    temp->next = new node(num,NULL);
            }
    }
```

The dashed pointer connection shows the last step of Append:

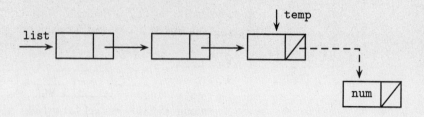

Templated Struct

Up until now the info fields of the linked lists have been integers. A templated struct allows flexibility in the type of data:

```
template <class type>
struct node
{
    type info;
    node <type> *next;
    node() : next(NULL) {}  //default constructor
    node(const type & val, node <type> *link = NULL)
        : info(val), next(link) {}
};
```

Notice that the second constructor is defined with *link = NULL. This is an optional default parameter. The next field is set to NULL if you specify only the val parameter; for example,

```
node<int> *p = new node<int>(5);
```

Any function that uses this struct as a parameter is a templated function and must be preceded by the line template <class type>.

Example

Print all the elements of a linked list. Assume the previous declaration.

```
template <class type>
void Print(node <type> *list)
//precondition: list points to a linked list
//postcondition: all values of the list printed, 1 per line
{
    if (list == NULL)
        cout << "Empty list" << endl;
    else
        while (list != NULL)
        {
            cout << list->info;
            list = list->next;
        }
}
```

NOTE

1. The `list` parameter is passed by value, so we can use it as the traveling pointer in the function. On exit, the copy of `list` will be discarded, and `list` will have its original value.
2. The function assumes that `<<` is defined for `type`. If `type` is a class in which `<<` has not been overloaded, you may cause an error.
3. As with templated classes, the type for an instance of a templated struct is decided when the variable is declared. Assuming the previous struct declaration, you could write

```
int main()
{
    node <int> *intList = NULL;
    node <char> *charList = new node <char>('$',NULL);
    node <char> *charList = new node <char>('z',charList);
```

The last two lines of code produce

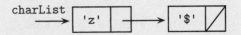

Header and Trailer Nodes

Header and *trailer nodes* are nodes at the front and end of a linked list that do not contain values of the list. Often these are dummy nodes with fake values or no value. Sometimes the header node contains useful information about the list, its length for example.

The effect of having headers and trailers is that insertion and deletion is always done in the "middle" of the list, which means no special tests for first node/last node conditions.

Circular Linked Lists

A linear linked list allows easy access to the first node but requires traversal of the whole list to reach the final node. A small change converts a linear linked list into a *circular linked list,* which allows easy access to both the first and last nodes. Let the pointer field of the last node point to the first node, instead of being NULL.

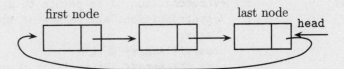

NOTE

1. In a circular linked list, the external pointer customarily points to the last node. In the preceding picture, `head->next->info` accesses the data in the first node.
2. Since there is no longer a NULL pointer value in the last node, the external pointer is the stoplight for list traversal. This means no traveling with the external pointer!

Example

Write out the contents of a circular linked list.

```
template <class type>
void Print(node <type> *head)
//precondition: head points to a circular linked list
//              << overloaded for printing type object
//postcondition: contents of list printed, 1 per line
{
    if (head == NULL)
        cout << "Empty list" << endl;
    else
    {
        node <type> *p = head;
        do
        {
            cout << p->next->info << endl;
            p = p->next;
        } while (p != head);
    }
}
```

Doubly Linked Lists

Why Doubly Linked Lists?

Singly linked linear and circular lists have several disadvantages:

1. Traversal is in just one direction.
2. To access previous nodes, you must go to the external pointer and start again.
3. Given a pointer to a node, you cannot easily delete that node. There is no direct access to the previous pointer field.

A data structure that overcomes these disadvantages is a *doubly linked* list, where each node has three fields: a data field, a pointer to the next node, and a pointer to the previous node. The price we pay is storage for the extra pointer.

Struct for a Doubly Linked List

```
template <class T>
struct node
{
    T data;
    node <T> *next;
    node <T> *prev;
    node() : next(NULL), prev(NULL) {}
    node(const T & val, node <T> *N, node <T> *P)
        : data(val), next(N), prev(P) {}
};
```

Note that next and prev can be declared in one line instead of two in the struct, but beware, don't omit a '*':

```
node<T> *next, *prev;
```

The pointers for this scheme look like this:

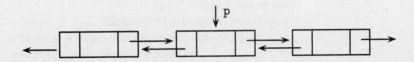

Note that p->next->prev and p->prev->next are both equivalent to p.

Insertion and Deletion

Example 1

Insert an element in a doubly linked list.

```
template <class T>
void InsertAfter(node <T> *current, const T & item)
//precondition: current points to a node in a doubly linked list.
//              Assume header and trailer, i.e., node in middle of
//              list
//postcondition: item inserted after node pointed to by current
{
    //get new node and attach it to the list
    node <T> *q = new node<T>(item,current->next,current);
    //adjust the list pointer connections
    q->next->prev = q;
    current->next = q;
}
```

In this algorithm, the line

```
node <T> *q = new node <T>(item,current->next,current);
```

does the following:

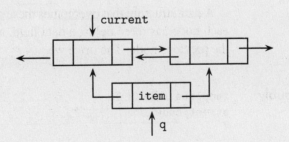

The statement is equivalent to the statements

```
node <T> *q = new node <T>;
q->data = item;
q->next = current->next;
q->prev = current;
```

Example 2

Delete an element from a doubly linked list.

```
template <class T>
void Delete(node <T> *current, T & item)
//precondition: current points to a node in a doubly linked list.
//              Assume header and trailer, i.e., node in middle of
//              list
//postcondition: node pointed to by current deleted and contents
//               stored in item
{
    item = current->data;
    //adjust pointers to skip node that current points to
    current->prev->next = current->next;
    current->next->prev = current->prev;
    delete current;
}
```

The two statements after the `//adjust pointers ...` comment perform the dashed pointer connections shown in the figure:

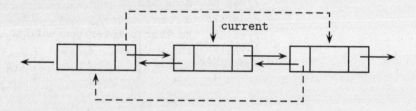

Designs for Doubly Linked Lists

Here are some of the designs possible for doubly linked lists.

Linear doubly linked list:

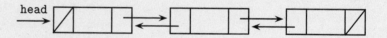

Linear doubly linked list with header and trailer:

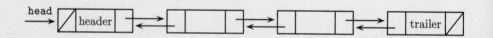

Circular doubly linked list:

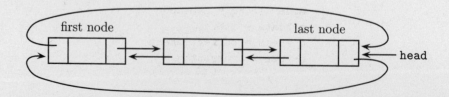

Run Time of Linked List vs. Array Algorithms

In each case, assume n elements in a singly linked linear linked list (LLL) and also in an `apvector` that does not require resizing.

Algorithm	LLL	Array	Comment
Add or remove element at end	$O(n)$	$O(1)$	For LLL, must traverse whole list. For array, simple assignment: `a[n+1]` = element. (Assumes no resizing.)
Add or remove element at front	$O(1)$	$O(n)$	For array, must move each element up one slot to create empty slot in `a[0]`. For LLL, simple pointer adjustment.
Linear search for key	$O(n)$	$O(n)$	In worst case, need to search entire LLL or array.
Insert element in correct position in sorted list (a) Find insertion point (b) Insert element	$O(n)$ $O(1)$	$O(n)$ $O(n)$	Insertion in LLL requires just pointer adjustments. For array, may have to move n elements to create a slot.
Delete all occurrences of value from list	$O(n)$	$O(n)$	For LLL, find value, adjust pointers, find value, adjust pointers, etc. For array, $O(n^2)$ if all elements moved each time you find value. $O(n)$ algorithm in Chapter 4, Question 8.

Multiple-Choice Questions on Pointers and Linked Lists

For Questions 1–13 assume that linked lists are implemented using the following declaration:

```
struct ListNode
{
    int info;
    ListNode *next;
};
```

1. The following segment is supposed to search and delete from a linear linked list all nodes whose data fields are less than val, a previously defined integer. Assume that head points to the first node in the list, and that the list is nonempty.

```
ListNode *q, *p = head;
do
{
    if (p->info < val)
    {
        q = p->next;
        p->next = p->next->next;
        delete q;
    }
    else
        p = p->next;
} while (p->next != NULL);
```

Which is true about this code segment?

(A) It works for all the nodes of the linked list.
(B) It fails for only the first node of the list.
(C) It fails for only the last node of the list.
(D) It fails for the first and last nodes of the list but works for all others.
(E) It fails for all nodes of the list.

2. Consider function WriteList:

```
void WriteList(ListNode *L)
//precondition: L is not NULL
//              L points to the last node in a circular
//              linked list
//postcondition: all elements of list L printed to
//               screen, 1 per line, first through last
{
    <code>
}
```

Which of the following could replace <code> so that WriteList works as intended?

```
 I ListNode *p = L->next;
   do
   {
       cout << p->info << endl;
       p = p->next;
   } while (p != L);

II ListNode *p = L;
   do
   {
       cout << p->next->info << endl;
       p = p->next;
   } while (p != L);

III ListNode *p = L;
    while (p != L)
    {
        cout << p->next->info << endl;
        p = p->next;
    }
```

(A) I only
(B) II only
(C) III only
(D) I and II only
(E) I, II, and III

3. Refer to function FindKey:

```
bool FindKey(ListNode *list, int key)
//precondition: list points to a linear linked list
//postcondition: returns true if key in list, else false
{
    while (list != NULL && list->info != key)
        list = list->next;
    return (list != NULL);
}
```

Which is true about function FindKey?

(A) FindKey works as intended only if key is in the list.
(B) FindKey works as intended only if the list is nonempty.
(C) FindKey works as intended only if key is not in the last node of the list.
(D) FindKey does not work under any circumstances.
(E) FindKey always works as intended.

4. Consider function Insert:

```
void Insert (ListNode *current, int num)
//precondition:  current points to a node in a nonempty
//               linked list sorted in increasing order
//               current represents the insertion point for num
//postcondition: num inserted in a node directly after the
//               node to which current points
{
    <code>
}
```

What is the run time of <code>, assuming the most efficient algorithm?

(A) $O(1)$
(B) $O(n)$
(C) $O(n^2)$
(D) $O(\log n)$
(E) $O(n \log n)$

5. A circular linked list has external pointer `head`. The following segment is intended to count the number of nodes in the list:

```
int count = 0;
ListNode *p = head->next;
while (p != head)
{
    count++;
    p = p->next;
}
```

Which statement is true?

(A) The segment works as intended whenever the list is nonempty.
(B) The segment works as intended when the list has just one element.
(C) The segment works as intended only when the list is empty.
(D) The segment fails in all cases.
(E) The segment works as intended in all cases.

6. Consider the following function for removing a value from a linear linked list:

```
void Del(ListNode *p)
//precondition:  p points to a node in a nonempty
//               linear linked list
//postcondition: the value that p points to has been removed
//               from the list
{
    ListNode *q = p->next;
    p->info = q->info;
    p->next = q->next;
    delete q;
}
```

In which of the following cases will function `Del` fail to work as intended?

  I   p points to any node in the list other than the first or last node.
  II p points to the last node in the list.
  III p points to the first node, and there is more than one node in the list.

(A) I only
(B) II only
(C) I and II only
(D) I and III only
(E) I, II, and III

7. Suppose that the precondition of function `Del` in Question 6 is changed so that the function always works as intended. What is the run time of the algorithm?

(A) $O(n)$
(B) $O(4)$
(C) $O(1)$
(D) $O(n^2)$
(E) $O(\log n)$

8. Consider two circular linked lists, list1 and list2, in which the external pointers point to the last node in each list. Function Concat appends list2 to list1 and results in an augmented list1. For example, for the lists

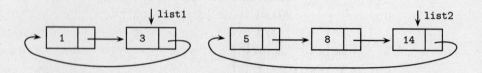

Concat(list1,list2) will produce

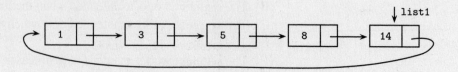

```
void Concat(ListNode * & list1, ListNode * list2)
//precondition: list1 and list2 are circular linked lists
//postcondition: list2 has been appended to list1
{
    if (list1 == NULL)
        list1 = list2;
    else
        if (list2 != NULL)
        {
            <more code>
        }
}
```

Which could replace <*more code*> so that the postcondition of Concat is satisfied? You may assume the existence of the Swap function

```
void Swap(ListNode * & p, ListNode * & q)
//interchanges p and q
```

```
  I list1->next = list2->next;
    list2->next = list1->next;
    list1 = list2;
```

```
 II ListNode *p = list1->next;
    list1->next = list2->next;
    list2->next = p;
    list1 = list2;
```

```
III Swap(list1->next, list2->next);
    list1 = list2;
```

(A) I only
(B) II only
(C) III only
(D) II and III only
(E) I and II only

9. Suppose that list1 and list2 point to the first nodes of two linear linked lists, and that q points to some node in the first list. The first piece of the first list, namely all the nodes up to and including the one pointed to by q, is to be removed and attached to the front of list2, maintaining the order of the nodes. After removal, list1 should point to the remaining nodes of its original list. list2 should point to the augmented list. If neither q nor list1 is originally NULL, then this task is correctly performed by which of the following program segments? Assume that p is a correctly declared pointer.

```
  I q->next = list2;
    list2 = list1;
    list1 = q->next;

 II while (list1 != q->next)
    {
        p = list1;
        list1 = list1->next;
        p->next = list2;
        list2 = p;
    }
    list1 = p;

III p = q->next;
    q->next = list2;
    list2 = list1;
    list1 = p;
```

(A) None
(B) III only
(C) I and III only
(D) II and III only
(E) I, II, and III

10. Refer to function Remove:

```
void Remove(ListNode * & L, int val)
{
    if (L != NULL)
    {
        Remove(L->next, val);
        if (L->info == val)
        {
            ListNode *temp = L->next;
            delete L;
            L = temp;
        }
    }
}
```

What does function Remove do?

(A) It deletes all values in list L that are not equal to val.
(B) It deletes all occurrences of val in list L.
(C) If the first value in the list is val, it deletes just this node.
(D) If the last value in the list is val, it deletes just this node.
(E) It deletes all occurrences of val in list L that start at the second node of the list.

11. Refer to function Search:

```
ListNode *Search(ListNode *list, int key)
//Returns pointer to first occurrence of key in list
//Returns NULL if key not in list
{
    <code>
}
```

Which of the following replacements for <code> will result in function Search working as intended?

I
```
if (list->info == key)
    return list;
else
    return Search(list->next,key);
```

II
```
ListNode *p = list;
do
{
    p = p->next;
} while (p->info != key);
return p;
```

III
```
ListNode *p = list;
while (p != NULL && p->info != key)
    p = p->next;
return p;
```

(A) I only
(B) II only
(C) III only
(D) II and III only
(E) I, II, and III

12. This question refers to function `Mystery`:

```
void Mystery(ListNode * & list)
{
    ListNode *grab, *hold;
    hold = list;
    list = NULL;
    while (hold != NULL)
    {
        grab = hold;
        hold = hold->next;
        grab->next = list;
        list = grab;
    }
}
```

Assume an initial list

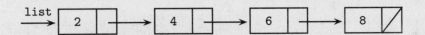

After the function call `Mystery(list)`, what will the list look like?

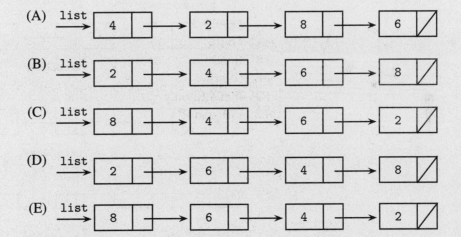

13. Function `Minimum` returns a pointer to the smallest value in a linear linked list.

```
ListNode *Minimum(ListNode *Head)
//precondition: Head points to a nonempty linear linked list
//postcondition: Pointer returned to node with smallest value
{
    ListNode *minSoFar = Head, *p = Head->next;
    while (p != NULL)
    {
        if (p->info < minSoFar->info)
            minSoFar = p;
        p = p->next;
    }
    return minSoFar;
}
```

Suppose `Minimum(Head)` is called for the following list:

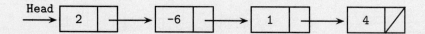

Which of the following does *not* satisfy the loop invariant for the `while` loop?

(A)
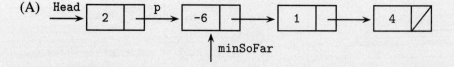

(B)
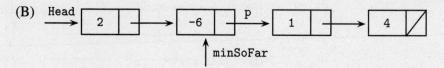

(C)
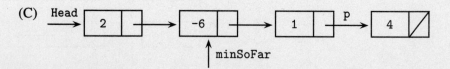

(D)
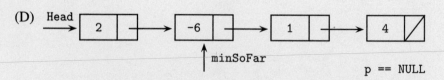

(E)
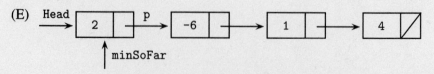

Questions 14–17 refer to the following definition:

```
struct node
{
    int info;
    node *next;
    node(int val, node *link);
};
node :: node(int val, node *link)          //constructor
    : info(val), next(link) {}
```

14. Consider a linear linked list of integers with external pointer head. Which of the following statements will have the effect of inserting the value 3 at the front of the list? For example, before execution of the statement:

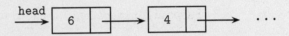

After execution of the statement:

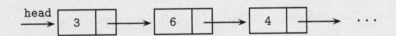

(A) head = new node(3, head);
(B) head = new node(3, head->next);
(C) head->next = new node(3, head);
(D) head->next = new node(3, head->next);
(E) head = new node(3, NULL);

15. Consider function `InsertSecond`:

```
void InsertSecond(node *L)
//precondition: L is not NULL
//postcondition: new node inserted in second position of the
//       list, with value 1 more than that of the first node
{
    <code>
}
```

For example, before calling `InsertSecond(L)`:

After calling `InsertSecond(L)`:

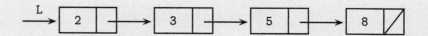

Which of the following could replace *<code>* so that `InsertSecond` works as intended?

(A) `L = new node(L->info + 1, L->next);`

(B) `L = new node(L->info + 1, L);`

(C) `L->next = new node(L->info + 1, L);`

(D) `L = new node(L->next->info + 1, L->next);`

(E) `L->next = new node(L->info + 1, L->next);`

16. Consider function Append:

```
void Append(node *list, int num)
//precondition: list is not NULL
//postcondition: num has been added to end of list
{
    node *p = list;
    <more code>
}
```

Which correctly replaces <*more code*> so that the postcondition of Append is satisfied?

(A) ```
while (p != NULL)
      p = p->next;
p->next = new node(num, NULL);
```

(B) ```
while (p->next != NULL)
      p = p->next;
p = new node(num, p);
```

(C) ```
while (p->next != NULL)
      p = p->next;
p = new node(num, p->next);
```

(D) ```
while (p->next != NULL)
      p = p->next;
p->next = new node(num, NULL);
```

(E) ```
while (p != NULL)
      p = p->next;
p->next = new node(num, p->next);
```

17. Refer to the function Print:

```
void Print()
{
    node *List = NULL;
    for (int i=1; i<=5; i++)
        List = new node(i, List);
    node *temp = List;
    while (temp != NULL)
    {
        cout << temp->info;
        temp = temp->next;
    }
}
```

What will be printed as a result of calling function Print?

(A) 12345
(B) 54321
(C) 2345
(D) 5
(E) 1
```

The following declarations apply to Questions 18–22:

```
struct ListNode
{
    int data;
    ListNode *next;
    ListNode *back;
    ListNode(int D, ListNode *N, ListNode *B)
        : data(D), next(N), back(B) {}
};
```

18. Suppose p and q point to two adjacent nodes in the middle of a doubly linked list as shown:

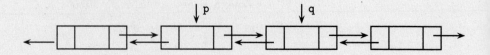

A code segment that deletes both of these nodes from the list is

```
 I p->back->next = q->next;
   q->next->back = p->back;
   delete p;
   delete q;

II p->next = q->next;
   q->back = p->back;
   delete p;
   delete q;

III p->next->back = q->back;
    q->back->next = p->next;
    delete p;
    delete q;
```

(A) I only
(B) II only
(C) I and II only
(D) I and III only
(E) II and III only

19. Suppose a doubly linked list does not have header or trailer nodes. Consider function DeleteNode:

```
void DeleteNode(ListNode *p)
//precondition:  p points to a node in a nonempty
//               doubly linked list
//postcondition: node pointed to by p has been deleted
{
    p->back->next = p->next;
    p->next->back = p->back;
    delete p;
}
```

In which of the following cases will DeleteNode fail to work as intended?

   I p points to the first node in the list.

   II p points to the last node in the list.

   III p points to a node other than the first or last node in the list.

(A) I and II only

(B) III only

(C) I and III only

(D) I, II, and III

(E) None. DeleteNode will always work as intended.

20. Consider a doubly linked list with three nodes as shown:

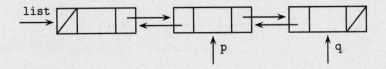

Which of the following program segments converts this list into a doubly linked circular list with three nodes? (Assume that after execution the external pointer list may point to any node.)

   I
```
q->next = list;
q = q->next;
list->back = q;
```

   II
```
list->back = p->next;
p->next->next = list;
```

   III
```
p->back->back = q;
q->next = p->back;
```

(A) I only

(B) II only

(C) III only

(D) II and III only

(E) I, II, and III

21. Refer to function `DLLStuff`:

```
int DLLStuff(ListNode *head)
//precondition:  head points to a doubly linked list with
//               at least 4 nodes
//postcondition: an integer value has been returned
{
    ListNode *p = head, *r = head->next;
    if (p->data % 2 == 1)
    {
        p->data -= 1;
        p = p->next->next;
        r = p->back->back;
    }
    if (r->next->data % 2 == 1)
    {
        p = r->next;
        r->data += 6;
        r = p->next->next;
    }
    else
        r = p->next;
    return p->data + r->data;
}
```

What will be returned if `DLLStuff(head)` is called for the following doubly linked list?

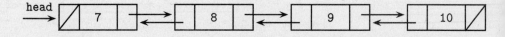

(A) 17
(B) 18
(C) 19
(D) 21
(E) An error will occur.

22. Suppose pointer p points to a node in the middle of a doubly linked list of integers as shown:

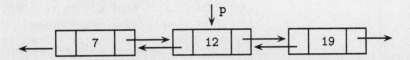

The value 9 is to be inserted between 7 and 12. Which code segment correctly achieves this?

```
 I ListNode *q = new ListNode(9, p, p->back);
   p->back->next = q;
   p->back = q;

II ListNode *q = new ListNode(9, p, p->back);
   p->back = q;
   q->back->next = q;

III ListNode *q = new ListNode(9, p, p->back);
    p->back = q;
    p->back->next = q;
```

(A) I only
(B) II only
(C) III only
(D) I and II only
(E) I, II, and III

23. NameSlots is an array of structs used to implement several linear linked lists. Each struct contains a name and the array index of the next element in the list, with 0 denoting the end of the list. NameSlots[0] is not used for storage. Consider the following example of 18 array elements in NameSlots:

Smith	3	Berg	7	Jones	18	Frank	0	Herm	17	Vann	9
1		2		3		4		5		6	

Finn	13	Plett	11	Clem	15	Em	0	Hoyt	14		
7		8		9		10		11		12	

Gross	5	Brown	16	Jed	0	Sid	0	Schot	0	Kay	4
13		14		15		16		17		18	

This example contains five linked lists, beginning at array slots 1, 2, 6, 8, and 10 respectively. What is the length of the longest linked list in NameSlots?

(A) 3
(B) 4
(C) 5
(D) 17
(E) 18

24. A list of items is to be maintained in random order. Operations performed on the list include

    - insertion of new items at the front of the list
    - deletion of old items from the rear of the list.

    A programmer considers using a linear singly linked list (LLL), a circular singly linked list (CLL), or an array to store the items. Which of the following correctly represents the run-time efficiency of (1) insertion and (2) deletion for this list? (You may assume that no resizing of the array is necessary, and that the most efficient algorithm possible is used in each case.)

    (A) array: (1) $O(n)$ (2) $O(1)$
         LLL: (1) $O(1)$ (2) $O(n)$
         CLL: (1) $O(1)$ (2) $O(n)$

    (B) array: (1) $O(n)$ (2) $O(1)$
         LLL: (1) $O(1)$ (2) $O(n)$
         CLL: (1) $O(1)$ (2) $O(1)$

    (C) array: (1) $O(1)$ (2) $O(1)$
         LLL: (1) $O(1)$ (2) $O(1)$
         CLL: (1) $O(1)$ (2) $O(1)$

    (D) array: (1) $O(n)$ (2) $O(n)$
         LLL: (1) $O(1)$ (2) $O(n)$
         CLL: (1) $O(1)$ (2) $O(n)$

    (E) array: (1) $O(1)$ (2) $O(n)$
         LLL: (1) $O(n)$ (2) $O(1)$
         CLL: (1) $O(n)$ (2) $O(1)$

25. Assume that linked lists are implemented with the following templated struct:

```
template <class T>
struct Node
{
    T data;
    Node <T> *link;
    Node(const T & D, Node <T> *L = NULL)
        : data(D), link(L) {}
};
```

Suppose that you want to write a program that uses a linked list of apstrings. What must be done to declare an external pointer head for such a list?

(A) Have the following statements in main():
```
T <apstring>;
Node *head;
```

(B) Have just one statement in main():
```
Node <apstring> *head;
```

(C) Alter the struct declaration by changing template <class T> to template <class apstring>. Then in main() have the declaration
```
Node <apstring> *head;
```

(D) Alter the constructor in the struct declaration to be
```
Node(const apstring & D, Node <apstring> *L = NULL)
    : data(D), link(L) {}
```
Then in main() have the declaration
```
Node *head;
```

(E) Alter the entire struct declaration by replacing every occurrence of T with apstring. Then in main() have the declaration
```
Node *head;
```

Answer Key

1. **E**	10. **B**	19. **A**
2. **B**	11. **C**	20. **D**
3. **E**	12. **E**	21. **C**
4. **A**	13. **A**	22. **D**
5. **D**	14. **A**	23. **C**
6. **B**	15. **E**	24. **A**
7. **C**	16. **D**	25. **B**
8. **D**	17. **B**	
9. **B**	18. **A**	

Answers Explained

1. **(E)** Here is what happens if p is pointing to a node that must be deleted:

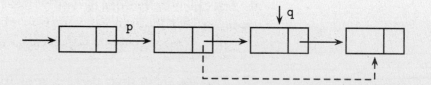

The algorithm deletes the node *following* the node that should be deleted.

2. **(B)** Segment I does not output the last element in the list. Segment III does not print anything—the test fails immediately!

3. **(E)** If list is NULL, the test will be short-circuited, and there will be no dereferencing of a null pointer in the second half of the test. Also, if list is NULL, key was not found and the function will return false, which is correct. Notice that traversing the list with the list pointer is OK because list is passed by value. This means that a copy of the list pointer is made, and list will have its original value when the function is exited.

4. **(A)** The function does not find the insertion point; it merely attaches a new node. This is a constant $O(1)$ operation.

5. **(D)** When there are no elements in the circular linked list (i.e., head is NULL), a run-time error will occur: head->next tries to dereference a null pointer. If there's just one element in the list:

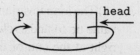

The test will fail immediately, leaving a count of 0. In all other cases, count will have a value one less than the actual number of nodes.

6. **(B)** If p points to the last node, q = p->next will give q a value of NULL. Referring to q->info will then cause a run-time error (dereferencing a null pointer).

7. **(C)** Provided p doesn't point to the last node in the list, this is a nifty algorithm that requires no list traversal. It is independent of the number of nodes in the list and is therefore $O(1)$. Note: There is no such thing as $O(4)$. Don't be caught just because the function has four steps!

8. **(D)** Segment I fails because the first line breaks the connection to the first node of list1. Now list2->next gets connected to the first node of list2. Segment II avoids this problem in its first line by using a temporary pointer to hold the address of the first node in list1. Notice that the first three lines of segment II are exactly the code to interchange list1->next and list2->next correctly, so segment III is also correct.

9. **(B)** In segment I the statement q->next = list2 maroons the second piece of the first list: list1 can no longer be reassigned. The first statement of segment III, p = q->next, is crucial to avoid losing that piece of the first list. The pointer movements in segment II make no sense.

10. **(B)** Remove is a recursive function that reaches the base case at the last node. It backtracks along the list, deleting all nodes that contain val. Notice that in the first call of the function the test if (L->info == val) guarantees that if the first node of the list is val, it too will be deleted.

11. **(C)** Segment I has no base case. It would be correct if preceded by

```
if (list == NULL)
    return NULL;
else
{
```

Besides the fact that segment II misses the first node, it has other problems, too. If p becomes NULL, the test (p->info != key) will cause a run-time error (dereferencing a null pointer).

12. **(E)** This breathless-sounding algorithm reverses pointers in the list. Here is a picture of the loop invariant for the while loop:

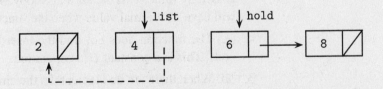

In words, list points to the part of the list that's already been reversed, and hold points to the part of the original list that still needs to be taken care of.

13. **(A)** The loop invariant for the while loop is that minSoFar points to the smallest value up to and excluding the node that p points to. Notice that p is advanced right at the end of the loop (last statement), so the node that p points to on exiting the loop has not yet been examined.

14. **(A)** The right-hand side of the statement is evaluated first. The new node's pointer field gets the same address as `head`:

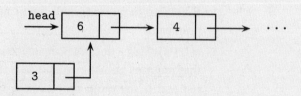

The last thing done is that `head` is assigned to point to the new node.

15. **(E)** Remember, the right-hand side is evaluated first:
`new node(L->info + 1, L->next)`.

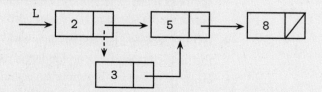

Finally `L->next` points to the new node (shown dashed in the figure).

16. **(D)** The test must be `while (p->next != NULL)` so that `p` eventually points to the last node. This eliminates choices A and E. Choices B and C are wrong because assigning the new node to `p` means that the node won't get attached to the list.

17. **(B)** Each pass through the `for` loop creates a new node at the front of the linked list, resulting in

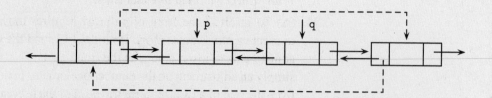

Thus, `54321` will be printed.

18. **(A)** The dashed arrows show the pointer connections that must be made before nodes `p` and `q` are recycled:

The only way to access the `next` field of the node to the left of `p` is with `p->back->next`. Similarly, the `back` field for the node to the right of `q` is `q->next->back`. Thus, segment II is wrong. Segment III is pure garbage!

19. **(A)** Cases I and II both fail because a null pointer is being dereferenced. For the first node, p->back is NULL. For the last node, p->next is NULL.

20. **(D)** Choice I changes the pointer connections incorrectly, as shown:

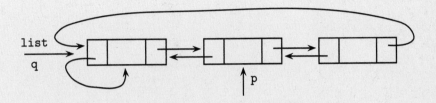

21. **(C)** After initialization p points to 7 and r points to 8. Then 7 % 2 is 1, so 7 gets changed to 6, p gets to point to 9, and r points to 6. Then 8 % 2 != 1, so the else part is executed: r points to 10. Finally, p->data + r->data = 9 + 10 = 19.

22. **(D)** In segment III, here's the situation after p->back = q:

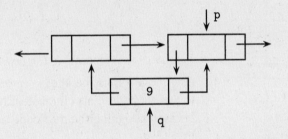

p->back->next is now equivalent to p, which does not give node q the correct pointer connection to the node on the left.

23. **(C)** The linked list starting in slot 2 can be represented schematically like this:

The 0 in Schot's slot indicates the end of the list. Tracing through each of the other lists that start in slots 1, 6, 8, and 10 yields lists with lengths 4, 3, 4, and 1, all with fewer than five elements.

24. **(A)** To insert at the front of an array requires movement of all n elements to create a slot—thus, $O(n)$. Both the LLL and the CLL require just pointer adjustments to insert a node at the front: $O(1)$. To remove at the rear requires simply an adjustment on the number of elements in the array, $O(1)$. To remove from the rear of a LLL requires traversal of the list to reach the last node, $O(n)$. It would seem that a CLL would be $O(1)$ for removing an element from the rear, since the external pointer points to the last element. The problem is, to remove the last element requires accessing the pointer field of the previous node, which requires traversal along the entire list, $O(n)$.

25. **(B)** The point about a template is that it remains unchanged, with type T as a parameter. Thus, all choices that change the template declaration are wrong (choices C, D, and E). The actual data type is declared in `main()`, as shown in choice B. There is no such statement as the one in choice A.

CHAPTER NINE

Stacks and Queues

The other line moves faster.
—Ettore

Stacks

The Stack ADT

Think of a stack of plates or cafeteria trays. The last one added to the stack is the first one removed: last in first out (LIFO). And you can't remove the second tray without taking off the top one!

A *stack* is an ordered collection of items of the same type, in which items can be added and removed only at one end. In theory, there is no limit to the number of items on the stack.

Changes to the stack are controlled by two operations, *push* and *pop*. To push an item onto the stack is to add that item to the top of the stack. To pop the stack is to remove an item from the top of the stack. Imagine that the top of the stack floats up and down as items are pushed onto or popped off the stack. Push and pop are ideally $O(1)$ operations.

Another useful operation for a stack is an *isEmpty* test that returns true or false. If you try to pop an empty stack, you get an *underflow* error.

Array Implementation of a Stack

For the AP exam, stacks are implemented with the apstack class. You will be provided with a copy of the header file apstack.h during the exam. An updated version of this file can be found at *http://www.collegeboard.org/ap/computer-science/*.

apstack is a templated class that allows a stack of any data type, itemType. Using an array to hold the items of the stack is reasonable, since all elements are of the same type. Hence apstack has the private variable myElements, which is an apvector of itemType. The other private variable, myTop, is the index of the top element at any given time. If the stack is empty, myTop is -1.

**Functions in
apstack**

The complete implementation (apstack.cpp) is on the College Board web site. You will not receive a copy of this on the AP exam, but you *should* be familiar with all the functions.

1. Constructors

   ```
   apstack()
   ```

   This is the default constructor; it creates an empty stack.

   ```
   apstack(const apstack & s)
   ```

   The copy constructor creates a copy of s. For example,

   ```
   apstack <char> s1;  //default constructor creates empty
                       //stack s
   apstack <char> s2 = s1; //copy constructor initializes
                           //s2 to s1
   ```

2. Destructor

   ```
   ~apstack()
   ```

   The destructor deletes the stack. No implementation code is required since the apvector destructor takes care of the memory allocated to myElements. As usual, you should never call the destructor explicitly—it is invoked automatically whenever an apstack object goes out of scope.

3. Assignment overload

   ```
   const apstack & operator= (const apstack & rhs)
   ```

   This allows variables of type apstack to be assigned to each other. For example,

   ```
   apstack <int> s1,s2;
       ...
   s1 = s2;
   ```

4. Accessors
   The three accessors are all constant member functions.

   ```
   const itemType & top() const
   ```

   This returns the top element of the stack but leaves the stack unchanged. Think of it as a function that takes a peek at the top element and returns to tell what it saw. If, however, it peeks and the stack is empty, an underflow error occurs. The precondition for top() is that the stack is not empty.

   ```
   bool isEmpty() const
   ```

   This returns true if the stack is empty, false otherwise.

   ```
   int length() const
   ```

   This returns the number of elements on the stack.

5. Modifiers

```
void push(const itemType & item)
```

This pushes item onto the top of the stack.

```
void pop()
```

This pops the top element off the stack without storing it.

```
void pop(itemType & item)
```

This pops the top element and stores it in item. Think of it as a combination of pop() and top().

```
void makeEmpty()
```

This clears the stack. After makeEmpty(), the stack contains no elements.

Example (Statements are numbered for reference.)

```
1    apstack <int> s;
2    for (int i=1; i<=4; i++)
         s.push(2*i);     //pushes 2,4,6,8 onto stack
3    s.pop();             //throws away the 8
     int x = s.length(); //stores 3 in x
4    s.pop(x);            //pops the 6 and stores it in x
5    x = s.top();         //stores the 4 in x. stack unchanged
     if (s.isEmpty())
         cout << "Bye!";
     else
         cout << "Still cool!";  //this is output; s has 2 items
6    s.makeEmpty();          //empties s
     if (s.isEmpty())
         cout << "Bye!";        //"Bye!" output this time
     else
         cout << "Still cool!";
```

Here are snapshots of the stack s.

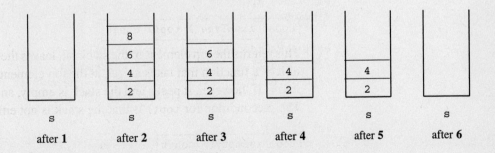

When to Use a Stack

Consider using a stack for any problem that involves backtracking (last in first out). Some examples include retracing steps in a maze and keeping track of nested structures, such as

- Expressions within other expressions.

- Functions that call other functions.

- Traversing directories and subdirectories.

In each case the stack mechanism untangles the nested structure.

Example

Write a program to test if a C++ expression has valid parentheses. An expression is valid if the number of openers (left parentheses '(') equals the number of enders (right parentheses ')'). For example, 3/(a+(b*2)) is valid, but (x-(y*(z+4) is invalid. (Note that simply checking if the number of openers equals the number of enders is insufficient: the expression)3+4(is not valid. To be valid, each ender must be preceded by a matching opener.)

Assume that the expression will be entered as an apstring. The program will include a function isValid() to test if the string is valid. Here's where the stack comes in. Do a character-by-character processing. If expr[i] is an opener, push it onto the stack s. If it's an ender and the stack is empty, the expression is invalid since there is no matching opener. If the stack is not empty, however, pop the stack. When the end of the expression is reached, the stack should be empty if the expression is valid.

Suppose that the expression to be examined is (3+4*(5%2)). Here is the state of the stack at various stages of the processing:

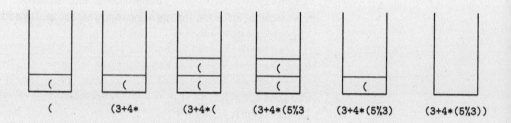

Here's the complete program.

```
//Check parentheses in expression
#include <iostream.h>
#include "apstring.h"
#include "apstack.h"

bool isValid(const apstring & expr);
//precondition: expr is a C++ expression
//postcondition: returns true if parentheses in expression
//               are valid, false otherwise

int main()
{
    apstring expr;
    cout << "Enter expression" << endl;
    getline(cin, expr);
    if (isValid(expr))
        cout << "Valid parentheses";
```

```
        else
            cout << "Invalid parentheses";
        return 0;
}

bool isValid(const apstring & expr)
{
    const char OPENER = '(', ENDER = ')';
    apstack <char> s;
    for (int i=0; i<expr.length(); i++)
        if (expr[i] == OPENER)
            s.push(expr[i]);
        else if (expr[i] == ENDER)
            if (s.isEmpty())     //no matching opener
                return false;
            else
                s.pop();         //pop matching opener
    if (s.isEmpty())
        return true;
    else
        return false;            //too many openers
}
```

Pointer Implementation of a Stack

Notice the similarity between stacks and linear linked lists.

- Both are accessible only at one end.

- A stack is accessed through the top element; a linked list through an external pointer to the first node.

- s.push(x) is equivalent to adding an element to the front of a linked list.

- s.pop() is equivalent to removing an element from the front of a linked list.

All this suggests implementing a stack with a linked list. Think of the first node in the linked list as being the top of the stack.

What changes should be made to the apstack class to implement a stack as a linked list? Ideally, the *specifications* for the functions in apstack.h should remain unchanged. The main change in the header file is in the declaration of the private variables, namely the data structure that represents the stack. Recall that in the array implementation we have

```
private:
    int myTop;
    apvector <itemType> myElement;
```

Now we have

```
private:
    struct stackNode
    {
        itemType info;
        stackNode *next;
        stackNode() : next(NULL) {}    //default constructor
                                       //for stackNode
```

```
          stackNode(const itemType & item, stackNode *n = NULL)
              : info(item), next(n) {}     //constructor
    };
    stackNode *stackPtr;          //external pointer to stack
    int size;                     //number of elements in stack
```

Here is an additional change; it is useful to have a private helper function to copy linear linked lists:

```
void copy(stackNode * & newList, stackNode * oldList);
//makes copy of oldList in newList
//precondition: oldList points to a linear linked list
//postcondition: newList points to a linear linked list
//that is an exact copy of the list pointed to by oldList
```

This change will simplify the implementation of the copy constructor and overloaded assignment operator, where you will need to copy not only the external pointer but also the nodes in the linked list.

All other changes to the apstack class are made only in apstack.cpp, the implementation code. An advantage of the linked list implementation over the array implementation is that you do not have to specify a maximum size for the stack in the header file.

Here are some of the key stack functions implemented with pointers. The new class will be called apLLstack (for Linked List) to distinguish it from apstack. Note that apLLstack is *not* part of the AP Committee materials.

1. Default Constructor

```
template <class itemType>
apLLstack <itemType> :: apLLstack()
    : size(0), stackPtr(NULL) {}
//postcondition: stack is empty
```

2. isEmpty()

```
template <class itemType>
bool apLLstack <itemType> :: isEmpty() const
//postcondition: returns true if stack empty, false otherwise
{
    return stackPtr == NULL;
}
```

3. push(x)

```
template <class itemType>
void apLLstack <itemType> :: push(const itemType & item)
//precondition: stack is [e1, e2...en] with n ≥ 0
//postcondition: stack is [e1, e2, ... en, item]
{
    stackPtr = new stackNode(item, stackPtr);
    size++;
}
```

4. pop(x)

```cpp
template <class itemType>
void apLLstack <itemType> :: pop(itemType & item)
//precondition: stack is [e1,e2,...en] with n ≥ 1
//postcondition: stack is [e1,e2,...e(n-1)] and item == en
{
    if (isEmpty())
    {
        cerr << "error, popping an empty stack" << endl;
        abort();
    }
    item = stackPtr->info;
    stackNode * p = stackPtr;
    stackPtr = stackPtr->next;
    delete p;
    size--;
}
```

5. top()

```cpp
template <class itemType>
const itemType & apLLstack <itemType> :: top() const
//precondition: stack is [e1, e2, ... en] with n ≥ 1
//postcondition: returns en
{
    if (isEmpty())
    {
        cerr << "error, accessing top of empty stack" << endl;
        abort();
    }
    return stackPtr->info;
}
```

You will find the complete files apLLstack.h and apLLstack.cpp in Appendix C. Note that these will *not* be provided to you on the AP exam. You are, however, expected to be able to implement the stack functions with pointers.

Many of the functions in apLLstack have fairly straightforward implementations. The three that do not are the copy constructor, the destructor, and the assignment overload.

Notice how simple the copy constructor is to implement in the original apstack: the variables myTop and myElements are simply copied from those of the stack s.

```cpp
template <class itemType>
apstack<itemType> :: apstack(const apstack <itemType> &s)
    : myTop(s.myTop), myElements(s.myElements) {}
```

The linked list version is not so simple. The initializer myElements(s.myElements) will not copy the whole stack s, it'll just make stackPtr for the current object point to the parameter stack s. The elements of two stacks will share memory rather than be separate lists, which is required. The reason myElements(s.myElements) works for apstack, by contrast, is that the copy constructor of apvector makes an element-by-element copy of myElements.

We use the private helper function copy to solve this problem in apLLstack.

```
template <class itemType>
apLLstack <itemType> ::
    apLLstack(const apLLstack <itemType> & s)
//postcondition: stack is a copy of s
{
    size = s.size;
    copy(stackPtr, s.stackPtr);
}
```

Similarly, the implementation of `operator=` uses the `copy` function.

The implementation of the destructor in the original `apstack` class is again simple because it implicitly invokes the `apvector` destructor.

```
template <class itemType>
apstack <itemType> :: ~apstack()
//postcondition: stack is destroyed
{
//apvector destructor frees memory
}
```

There is no such luck in the pointer implementation. `delete stackPtr;` won't do it—just the front node will be recycled, and the rest of the list will be left dangling. You need a node-by-node destructor, which is provided by the function `makeEmpty()`.

Once the pointer implementation of the `apstack` class is tested and running, use in a client program couldn't be easier. The earlier "check parentheses in expression" program could be run by replacing `apstack` with `apLLstack`. Notice that there are no pointers in sight. The implementation is hidden from the client.

Queues

The Queue ADT

Think of a line of well-behaved people waiting to board a bus. New arrivals go to the back of the line. The first one in line arrived first and is the first to board the bus: first in first out (FIFO).

A *queue* is an ordered collection of items of the same type in which new items are added at one end, the back, and removed at the other end, the front. In theory, there is no limit to the number of items in a queue.

Changes to the queue are controlled by operations *enqueue* and *dequeue*. To enqueue an item is to add that item to the *back* of the queue. To dequeue is to remove an item from the *front* of the queue. As for a stack, an *isEmpty* operation tests for an empty queue. If you try to dequeue from an empty queue you get an underflow error.

Array Implementation of a Queue

For the AP exam, queues are implemented with the `apqueue` class. You will be provided with a copy of the header file `apqueue.h` during the exam. An updated version can be found at *http://www.collegeboard.org/ap/computer-science/*.

apqueue is a templated class allowing a queue of any data type, itemType. A queue is implemented with an apvector and three int variables. mySize keeps track of the number of elements currently in the queue. myFront and myBack are the indexes of the current front and back elements. This allows the front and back to "float" as items are removed or added, both $O(1)$ operations. For example, consider the queue

q
		J	A	B	C		
	2	3	4	5	6	7	
		f			b		

After q.dequeue():

q
			A	B	C		
	2	3	4	5	6	7	
			f		b		

After q.enqueue('K'):

q
			A	B	C	K
	2	3	4	5	6	7
			f			b

Notice that dequeue results in myFront being incremented by one, whereas enqueue increments myBack by one. If either is in the last array slot, *wraparound* occurs, and the new index value becomes 0. For example, the initial queue size in apqueue is 10, set by the integer constant QDEFAULT_SIZE. Suppose that the current state of the queue is

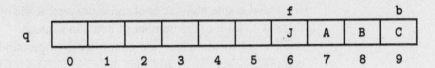

q
						J	A	B	C
0	1	2	3	4	5	6	7	8	9

`q.enqueue('K')` will result in

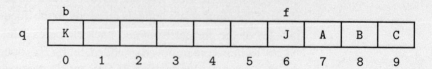

If the current state of the queue is

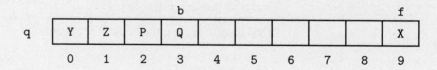

`q.dequeue()` will result in

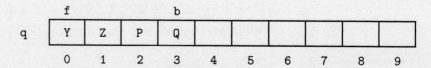

Functions in apqueue

The complete implementation (`apqueue.cpp`) can be found on the College Board web site. Again, you will not get a copy of this on the AP exam, but you are expected to be familiar with the functions.

1. Constructors and Destructor

```
apqueue() //default constructor, creates empty queue
```

Notice that for an empty queue `myFront` is 0 and `myBack` is -1.

```
apqueue(const apqueue <itemType> & q) //copy constructor
```

This creates a copy of q. Again, as for `apstack`, the `apvector` copy constructor is invoked.

```
~apqueue() //destructor
```

As with `apstack`, the `apvector` destructor is implicitly invoked to destroy an `apqueue` that goes out of scope.

2. Assignment Overload

```
const apqueue & operator= (const apqueue & rhs)
```

This allows variables of type `apqueue` to be assigned to each other.

3. Accessors

```
const itemType & front() const
```

This returns the front element of the queue, leaving the queue unchanged. (It is analogous to `top()` in `apstack`.)

```
bool isEmpty() const
```

This returns `true` if the queue is empty, `false` otherwise.

```
int length() const
```

This returns the number of elements in the queue.

4. Modifiers

```
void enqueue(const itemType & item)
```

This inserts `item` at the back of the queue.

```
void dequeue()
```

This removes an element from the front of the queue.

```
void dequeue(itemType & item)
```

This removes an element from the front of the queue and stores it in `item`.

```
void makeEmpty()
```

This empties the queue.

5. Private Helper Functions

```
void DoubleQueue()
```

This doubles the storage available for a queue. The algorithm copies the elements of the current `apvector` to a temporary `apvector` that is double the current size. Then it reassigns `myElements = temp`.

```
void Increment(int & val) const
```

This is used to add 1 to `myFront` or `myBack` when a `dequeue` or `enqueue` occurs. If `val` is at the last slot of the array before incrementing, `val` is reset to `0`. See the description of wraparound in the previous section.

Example

How to use the apqueue class. Some lines are numbered for reference.

```
1    apqueue <char> q;              //default constructor
     char ch;
     for (char c='a'; c<='f'; c++)
2        q.enqueue(c);
3    apqueue <char> k = q;          //copy constructor
     for (int i=1, i<3; i++)
4        k.dequeue();
5    k.dequeue(ch);                 //assigns ch the value 'c'
6    k.enqueue('r');
     int x = k.length();           //assigns x the value 4
     ch = k.front();               //assigns ch the value 'd'
```

The state of the queues is shown in the following figure. Here f and b denote the front and back of each queue.

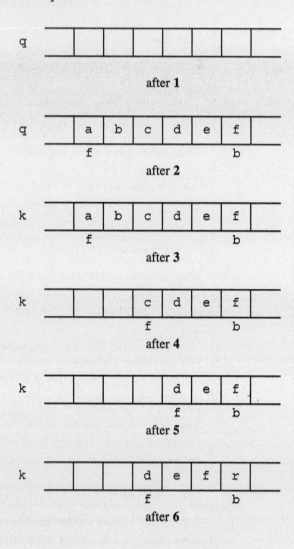

q

after **1**

q | a | b | c | d | e | f
  f   b

after **2**

k | a | b | c | d | e | f
  f   b

after **3**

k | | | c | d | e | f
        f   b

after **4**

k | | | | d | e | f
            f   b

after **5**

k | | | | d | e | f | r
            f   b

after **6**

When to Use a Queue

Think of a queue for any problem that involves processing data in the order in which it was entered. Some examples include

- Going back to the beginning and retracing steps.

- Simulations of lines—cars waiting at a car wash, people standing in line at a bank, and so on.

Example

Write a program that simulates the redial feature of a telephone. Each digit that is entered is treated as a separate element and placed in a queue. When it's time to redial, the queue is emptied, and the digits are printed in the order that they were entered.

```
//Simulate redial feature of a phone
#include <iostream.h>
```

```
#include "apqueue.h"
int main()
{
    apqueue <char> q;
    char ch;
    cout << "Enter phone no. Terminate with a period ";
    cout << "and a carriage return." << endl;
    cin >> ch;
    while (ch != '.')
    {
        q.enqueue(ch);
        cin >> ch;
    }
    cout << "The number dialed was ";
    while (!q.isEmpty())
    {
        q.dequeue(ch);
        cout << ch;
    }
    cout << endl;
    return 0;
}
```

Pointer Implementation of a Queue

There are two designs that make sense in implementing a queue with pointers:

1. A circular singly linked list. Since the external pointer points to the last node, easy access is provided to both the front and the back of the queue.
2. A linear singly linked list with external pointers to both the first and last nodes.

We will use the second method since it more closely mirrors the original apqueue implementation. The implementations of apqueue.h and apqueue.cpp with pointers are called apLLqueue.h and apLLqueue.cpp. They are given in their entirety in Appendix C. They are *not* part of the AP Committee materials and will *not* be provided to you on the AP exam. Nevertheless, you are expected to be able to implement the queue functions with pointers.

Since a queue, in theory, is never full, and memory is allocated dynamically when pointers are used, you can dispense with the private helper functions DoubleQueue and Increment. You do, however, still need a private copy function as for apLLstack.

Here is the private section of apLLqueue.h:

```
private:
    int mySize;              // # of elements currently in queue
    struct queueNode         // Nodes for storage of queue elements
    {
        itemType info;
        queueNode * next;
        queueNode():next(NULL) {}       //default constructor
        queueNode(const itemType & item, queueNode * n = NULL)
              : info(item), next(n) {}    //constructor
    };
    queueNode * myFront;     // External pointer to front of queue
    queueNode * myBack;      // External pointer to back of queue
```

```
void copy(queueNode * &newFront,
    queueNode * &newBack, queueNode * oldFront);
//copies list oldFront into new list newFront
//newBack points to last node of newFront list
```

Here is the pointer implementation of some of the key queue functions.

1. Default Constructor

```
template <class itemType>
apLLqueue <itemType> :: apLLqueue()
    : mySize(0), myFront(NULL), myBack(NULL)
//postcondition: the queue is empty
{}
```

2. isEmpty()

```
template <class itemType>
bool apLLqueue<itemType>::isEmpty() const
//postcondition: returns true if queue empty, false otherwise
{
    return myFront == NULL;
}
```

3. enqueue(x)

```
template <class itemType>
void apLLqueue <itemType> :: enqueue(const itemType & item)
//precondition: queue is [e1, e2, ..., en] with n ≥ 0
//postcondition: queue is [e1, e2, ..., en, item]
{
    if (isEmpty())
        myBack = myFront = new queueNode(item, NULL);
    else                //add element at back of queue
        myBack = myBack->next = new queueNode(item, NULL);
    mySize++;
}
```

4. dequeue(x)

```
template <class itemType>
void apLLqueue <itemType> :: dequeue(itemType & item)
//precondition: queue is [e1, e2, ..., en] with n ≥ 1
//postcondition:  queue is [e2, ..., en] and item == e1
{
    if (isEmpty())
    {
        cerr << "dequeue from empty queue" << endl;
        abort();
    }
    item = myFront->info;
    queueNode * p = myFront;
    myFront = myFront->next;
    delete p;
    if (myFront == NULL) //there was just 1 element in the queue
        myBack = NULL;
    mySize--;                //one fewer element
}
```

5. front()

```
template <class itemType>
const itemType & apLLqueue <itemType> :: front() const
//precondition: queue is [e1, e2, ..., en] with n ≥ 1
//postcondition: returns e1
{
    return myFront->info;
}
```

Note that we have the same situation for the copy constructor, the destructor, and the assignment overload as we had for apLLstack. A node-by-node copy must be made in the code for the copy constructor and assignment overload. For this we use the private helper function copy. For the destructor, we again need a node-by-node deletion, which is provided by makeEmpty().

As for apLLstack, the pointers in apLLqueue are hidden from a client program. If the word apqueue is replaced by apLLqueue in the preceding redial program, the program should run without change.

Pointer vs. Array Implementation of Stacks and Queues

For *small objects* the array implementation is preferable since the algorithms are faster and don't have the overhead of new and delete that linked lists have. Doubling the array length for insertion of *n* items is in the worst case $O(\log_2 n)$, and the time cost for recopying elements is small.

For large objects a linear linked list is preferable, since

- The time for recopying array items becomes significant.

- When the array size is doubled, memory needed to store the old and new (double-sized) arrays is expensive.

- A significant amount of memory is wasted since the array capacity is larger than the actual number of elements.

Priority Queue

What Is It?

A *priority queue* is a collection of items of the same type, each of which contains a data field and an integer priority. Items with the highest priority are removed first.

Operations for the Priority Queue ADT

The operations associated with a priority queue are

```
1. Insert(x, pri)    //Insert element x with priority pri
2. FindHighest(x)    //Find element with highest priority
3. DeleteHighest()   //Delete element with highest priority
```

```
4. DeleteHighest(x)    //Delete element with highest priority
                       //Store this element in x
5. isEmpty()           //True if queue empty, false otherwise
```

Data Structures for a Priority Queue

The data structure selected for a priority queue should allow for

- Rapid insertion of elements that arrive in arbitrary order.

- Rapid retrieval of the item with the highest priority.

Some possible data structures for a priority queue follow:

1. A linear linked list with elements in random order. Insertion is done at the front of the list, $O(1)$. Deletion requires a linear search for the element with highest priority, $O(n)$.
2. A linear linked list with elements sorted by priority number, highest priority in front. Deletion means removal of the first node, $O(1)$. Insertion requires a linear scan to find the insertion point, $O(n)$.
3. An array with elements in random order. Insertion is done at the end of the list, $O(1)$, if resizing is not necessary. Deletion requires a linear search, $O(n)$.
4. An array with elements sorted by priority, highest priority at the end. Deletion means removing the last element in the array, $O(1)$. Insertion requires finding the insertion point and then creating a slot by moving array elements—$O(n)$ irrespective of the type of search.
5. The classic data structure for a priority queue: a *binary heap*. (See Chapter 11 for a description of a heap and an array representation of a heap.) For a priority queue, a *minimum heap* is used. The value in every node is less than or equal to the value in each of its children. For example,

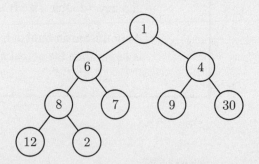

The numbers in the heap represent the *priorities* of the elements. (The lower the number, the higher the priority.) The idea is that the element with the highest priority is kept in the root of the tree, so deleting an element means removing the root element. Then restoring the heap ("reheaping") is an $O(\log n)$ operation. Insertion of an element also requires reheaping, $O(\log n)$. (It is possible to have an $O(1)$ insertion by simply adding an element to the end of the array, but then reheaping will be required before an item can be deleted.)

When to Use a Priority Queue

Think of using a priority queue in any problem where elements enter in a random order but are removed according to priority number. For example,

- A data base of patients awaiting liver transplants, where the sickest patients have the highest priority.

- Scheduling events. Events are generated in random order and each event has a time stamp denoting when the event will occur. The scheduler retrieves the events in the order they will occur.

Here is a final thought (from Mark Allen Weiss): A priority queue is not a queue, it just sounds like one.

Multiple-Choice Questions on Stacks and Queues

1. A stack s of integers contains 1, 4, 5, 8, 9 in the order given, with 1 on top. What will be output by the following code segment?

```
while (s.top() % 2 == 1)
{
    s.pop();
    cout << s.top();
}
```

   (A) 1
   (B) 4
   (C) 14
   (D) 159
   (E) 48

2. Functions `Add(s)` and `Multiply(s)` do the following to a stack s when invoked:

   > The stack is popped twice.
   > The two popped items are added or multiplied accordingly.
   > The result is pushed onto the stack.

   What will stack s contain following execution of the following code segment?

   ```
   int x = 3, y = 5, z = 7, w = 9;
   s.push(x);
   s.push(y);
   Add(s);
   s.push(w);
   s.push(z);
   Multiply(s);
   Add(s);
   ```

   (A) Nothing
   (B) 31
   (C) 71
   (D) 78
   (E) 128

3. Assume these declarations:

```
apqueue <int> q;
int x, sum = 0;
```

If q is initialized, which of the following code segments will correctly sum the elements of q and leave q unchanged?

```
 I  for (int i=1; i<=q.length(); i++)
    {
        q.dequeue(x);
        sum += x;
        q.enqueue(x);
    }
 II while (!q.isEmpty())
    {
        q.dequeue(x);
        sum += x;
        q.enqueue(x);
    }
III apqueue <int> temp(q);
    while (!temp.isEmpty())
    {
        temp.dequeue(x);
        sum += x;
    }
```

(A) I only
(B) II only
(C) III only
(D) I and III only
(E) II and III only

4. Consider the following sequence of statements:

```
int a = 2, b = 5, c = 4;
apqueue <int> q;
q.enqueue(a);
q.enqueue(b);
q.enqueue(c);
a++;
q.dequeue(a);
q.enqueue(c);
q.enqueue(a);
b = a;
q.enqueue(b);
while (!q.isEmpty())
{
    q.dequeue(a);
    cout << a;
}
```

What output will be produced?

(A) 254422
(B) 54433
(C) 25433
(D) 54422
(E) 25444

5. Suppose that a queue q contains the numbers 1, 2, 3, 4, 5, 6 in that order, with 1 at the front of q. Suppose that there are just three operations that can be performed using only one stack, s.

(i) `q.dequeue(x)` then print x
(ii) `q.dequeue(x)` then `s.push(x)`
(iii) `s.pop(x)` then print x

Which of the following is not a possible output list using just these operations?

(A) 123456
(B) 654321
(C) 234561
(D) 125643
(E) 345612

6. Let `intStack` be a stack of integers and `opStack` be a character stack of arithmetic operators. A function `DoOperation()` exists that

   (i) Pops two values from `intStack`.

   (ii) Pops an operator from `opStack`.

   (iii) Performs the operation.

   (iv) Pushes the result onto `intStack`.

   Assume that the integers 5, 8, 3, and 2 are pushed onto `intStack` in that order (2 pushed last), and *, -, and + are pushed onto `opStack` in that order (+ pushed last). The `DoOperation()` function is invoked three times. The top of `intStack` contains the result of evaluating the expression

   (A) $((2 * 3) - 8) + 5$

   (B) $((2 + 3) - 5) * 8$

   (C) $((2 + 3) - 8) * 5$

   (D) $((5 * 8) - 3) + 2$

   (E) $((5 + 8) - 3) * 2$

7. Suppose that `s` and `t` are both stacks of `itemType` and that `x` is a variable of type `itemType`. Assume that `s` initially contains n elements, where n is large, and that `t` is initially empty. Which is true after execution of the following code segment?

```
int len = s.length()-2;
for (int i=1; i<=len; i++)
{
    s.pop(x);
    t.push(x);
}
len = s.length()-2;
for (int i=1; i<=len; i++)
{
    t.pop(x);
    s.push(x);
}
```

   (A) `s` is unchanged. `x` equals the third item from the bottom of `s`.

   (B) `s` is unchanged. `x` equals `s.top()`.

   (C) `s` contains two elements. `x` equals `s.top()`.

   (D) `s` contains two elements. `x` equals the bottom element of `s`.

   (E) `s` contains two elements. `x` equals `t.top()`.

8. Refer to the following program segment:

```
apqueue <int> Q;
int x;
for (int i=1; i<6; i++)
    Q.enqueue(i*i);
do
{
    if (Q.front() % 2 == 0)
    {
        cout << Q.front() << ' ';
        Q.dequeue();
    }
    else
    {
        Q.dequeue(x);
        Q.enqueue(x);
    }
} while (!Q.isEmpty());
```

Which will be true after this segment is executed?

(A) 4 16 has been printed, and the queue contains 1 9 25, with 1 at the front and 25 at the back.

(B) 16 4 has been printed, and the queue contains 1 9 25, with 1 at the front and 25 at the back.

(C) 1 4 9 16 25 has been printed, and the queue is empty.

(D) 4 16 has been printed, and the segment continues to run without termination.

(E) 4 16 4 16 4 16 ... has been printed, and the segment was forcibly terminated.

9. Consider a stack s and queue q of integers. What must be true following execution of this code segment?

```
int x;
q.makeEmpty();
s.makeEmpty();
for (int i=1; i<=4; i++)
    s.push(i);
for (int i=1; i<=4; i++)
{
    s.pop(x);
    if (x % 2 == 0)
        q.enqueue(x);
    else
    {
        q.dequeue(x);
        s.push(x);
    }
}
```

(A) 2 is at the back of q.

(B) s.top() is 2.

(C) s is empty.

(D) q is empty.

(E) An error has occurred.

10. Consider this code segment:

```
apstring str = "racketeer";
char x;
apstack <char> s;
for (int i=0; i<str.length(); i++)
    s.push(str[i]);
for (int i=0; i<str.length(); i++)
    if (isVowel(str[i]))   //test if character is a
        //lowercase vowel, 'a', 'e', 'i', 'o', or 'u'
    {
        s.pop(x);
        cout << x;
    }
    else
        s.push(str[i]);
```

What output will be produced?

(A) rckt

(B) rcktr

(C) t

(D) rktc

(E) rkct

11. Assume that linked lists are implemented with this declaration:

```
struct node
{
    int data;
    node *link;
};
```

Refer to the following function, Reverse:

```
void Reverse(node *First)
//precondition: First points to a linear linked list
//postcondition: list elements printed in reverse order
{
    <code>
}
```

Which < code > will successfully achieve the postcondition of function Reverse?

```
 I  if (First != NULL)
    {
        cout << First->data;
        Reverse(First->link);
    }
```

```
 II  int x;
     apstack <int> s;
     while (First != NULL)
     {
         s.push(First->data);
         First = First->link;
     }
     while (!s.isEmpty())
     {
         s.pop(x);
         cout << x;
     }
```

```
III  int x;
     apqueue <int> q;
     while (First != NULL)
     {
         q.enqueue(First->data);
         First = First->link;
     }
     while (!q.isEmpty())
     {
         q.dequeue(x);
         cout << x;
     }
```

(A) I only
(B) II only
(C) III only
(D) I and II only
(E) I and III only

12. The `apstack` class defines two forms of `pop`: one that saves the top item and one that does not. This is an example of

    (A) Operator overloading
    (B) Function overloading
    (C) A helper member function
    (D) Stack overflow
    (E) Using a `stackTop` function

13. In the apqueue class queues are implemented with an `apvector` of `itemType` and integer variables `myFront` and `myBack` that keep track of the front and back indexes of the queue. An alternative design is to let the front index always equal 0, and just keep track of the back index of the queue. This design would cause which member function to be less efficient than in the actual design?

    (A) `dequeue`
    (B) `enqueue`
    (C) `front`
    (D) `length`
    (E) `makeEmpty`

14. The apqueue class has a private helper function `DoubleQueue()`, which doubles the storage for `myElements`. If `DoubleQueue()` is not working correctly, which member function in apqueue is likely to fail as well?

    (A) The copy constructor
    (B) `dequeue(x)`
    (C) `enqueue(x)`
    (D) `Increment(x)`
    (E) `makeEmpty()`

15. The apqueue class has a private helper function `Increment(val)`, which adds 1 to `val` with wraparound. If `Increment(val)` does not work as intended, which member functions in apqueue are likely to fail as well?

    I `enqueue(x)`
    II `dequeue(x)`
    III `DoubleQueue()`

    (A) I only
    (B) II only
    (C) III only
    (D) I and II only
    (E) I, II, and III

For questions 16–18, suppose that the `apstack` class is to be implemented with pointers. Here is the declaration of the private variables to be used:

```
struct stackNode          //nodes for storage of stack elements
{
    itemType info;
    stackNode *next;
    stackNode() : next(NULL) {}
    stackNode(const itemType & item, stackNode *n = NULL)
        : info(item), next(n) {}
};
stackNode *stackPtr;       //external pointer to stack
int size;                  //number of elements in stack
```

16. The following code to implement the copy constructor for the pointer implementation of the `apstack` class is incorrect.

```
template <class itemType>
apstack <itemType> :: apstack(const apstack <itemType> & s)
//postcondition: stack is a copy of s
{
    size = s.size;
    stackPtr = s.stackPtr;
}
```

What is wrong with this code?

(A) Stack s has not been correctly copied.
(B) A test for aliasing is missing.
(C) The `return` statement of the function is missing.
(D) A copy of s is being constructed, so s should not be passed by `const` reference.
(E) The return type of the function has been omitted.

17. Here is the implementation of pop() for the pointer implementation of the apstack class.

```
template <class itemType>
void apstack <itemType> :: pop()
//precondition: stack is [e1,e2,...en] with n ≥ 1
//postcondition: stack is [e1,e2,...e(n-1)]
{
    if (isEmpty())
    {
        cerr << "error, popping an empty stack" << endl;
        abort();
    }

    <popping code>

    size--;
}
```

Which of the following is correct *<popping code>*?

```
 I stackNode *p = stackPtr;
   stackPtr = stackPtr->next;
   delete p;

 II stackNode *p = stackPtr;
    delete p;
    stackPtr = stackPtr->next;

III delete stackPtr;
    stackPtr = stackPtr->next;
```

(A) I only
(B) II only
(C) III only
(D) I and III only
(E) II and III only

18. Suppose apstack has been rewritten so that stacks are implemented as linear linked lists with pointers. A driver program is written to test the new implementation. Which of the following declarations of stacks s1 and s2 in main() are correct?

```
  I stackPtr s1, s2;
 II stackNode *s1, *s2;
III apstack s1, s2;
```

(A) None
(B) I only
(C) II only
(D) III only
(E) I and III only

19. Suppose the `apqueue` class is to be implemented with pointers. Here is a possible declaration of the private variables to be used:

```
private:
    int mySize;          // # of elements currently in queue
    struct queueNode     // Nodes for storage of queue elements
    {
        itemType info;
        queueNode * next;
        queueNode():next(NULL) {}
        queueNode(const itemType & item, queueNode * n = NULL)
            : info(item), next(n) {}
    };
    queueNode * myFront;   // External pointer to front of queue
    queueNode * myBack;    // External pointer to rear of queue
```

A new member function `back` is to be added with the following specifications:

precondition: Queue contains n elements, $n \geq 1$.
postcondition: The element at the back of the queue has been returned. The queue remains unchanged.

Assuming that the line `template <class itemType>` precedes the implementation code, which of the following is the *best* implementation for function `back`?

(A)
```
const itemType & apqueue <itemType> :: back()
{
        return myBack->info;
}
```

(B)
```
const itemType & apqueue <itemType> :: back() const
{
        return myBack;
}
```

(C)
```
const itemType & apqueue <itemType> :: back() const
{
        return myBack->info;
        mySize--;
}
```

(D)
```
const itemType & apqueue <itemType> :: back() const
{
        return myBack->info;
}
```

(E)
```
const itemType & apqueue :: back() const
{
        return myBack->info;
        mySize--;
}
```

20. Consider the following two implementations of a queue class:

    (1) An `apvector` of `itemType` to hold the elements of the queue. Integer variables `mySize`, `myFront`, and `myBack` contain the size, front index, and back index, respectively. (Queue functions are implemented as in the `apqueue` class.)

    (2) A linear linked list to hold the elements of the queue. Pointers `myFront` and `myBack` point to the front and back elements.

    Which of the following is a legitimate reason to use implementation (2) rather than implementation (1), given that `itemType` is a large user-defined class object?

      I The pointer implementation is more memory efficient.

     II The queue operation `enqueue()` is faster for large objects when implemented with pointers.

    III The implementation code for the constructors and destructor for the linked list implementation is simpler than that for the `apvector` implementation.

    (A) I only

    (B) II only

    (C) III only

    (D) I and II only

    (E) I, II, and III

21. Which of the following is true of a priority queue?

    (A) If elements are inserted in increasing order of priority (i.e., lowest priority element inserted first), and all elements are inserted before any are removed, it works like a queue.

    (B) If elements are inserted in increasing order of priority (i.e., lowest priority element inserted first), and all elements are inserted before any are removed, it works like a stack.

    (C) If all elements are inserted before any are removed, it works like a queue.

    (D) If elements are inserted in decreasing order of priority (i.e., highest priority element inserted first), and all elements are inserted before any are removed, it works like a stack.

    (E) If elements are inserted in increasing order of priority, then it works like a queue whether or not all insertions precede any removals.

22. Refer to the following priority queue class and the given driver program that tests the member functions:

```
template <class T>
class PriorityQueue
{
    public:
        PriorityQueue();          //default constructor
        ~PriorityQueue();         //destructor
        void Insert(const T & x);       //insert x
        void DeleteHighest(T & x);      //remove item of
                    //highest priority and store in x
        bool IsEmpty(); //true if empty, otherwise false
        //other member functions ...
    private:
        //variables that implement priority queue
            ...
};

#include <iostream.h>
#include "PriorityQueue.h"
int main()
{
    int x;
    PriorityQueue <int> PQ;
    //integer elements represent priorities,
    //smallest = highest priority
    PQ.Insert(4);
    PQ.Insert(1);
    PQ.Insert(3);
    PQ.Insert(2);
    PQ.Insert(5);
    do
    {
        DeleteHighest(x);
        cout << x << ' ';
    } while (!PQ.IsEmpty());
    return 0;
}
```

Assuming that the code works as intended, what is the output?

(A) 5 4 3 2 1
(B) 4 1 3 2 5
(C) 1 2 3 4 5
(D) 5 2 3 1 4
(E) 3 1 2 4 5

Questions 23–25 refer to the following class declaration and the program segment:

```
template <class T>
class C
{
    public:
        C();                //constructor
        void Insert(const T & x);      //insert x into C
        void Delete(T & x); //delete item from C.
                            //store in x
            ...
    private:
        //appropriate data structure to implement C
};
```

Program segment that uses C above:

```
C <apstring> words;
apstring w1 = "Tom";
apstring w2 = "Dick";
apstring w3 = "Harry";
apstring w4 = "Moe";
apstring s;
words.Insert(w1);
words.Insert(w2);
words.Insert(w3);
words.Insert(w4);
words.Delete(s);
words.Delete(s);
cout << s;
```

23. What will the output be if C is a stack?

   (A) Tom
   (B) Dick
   (C) Harry
   (D) Moe
   (E) There is insufficient information to determine the output.

24. What will the output be if C is a queue?

   (A) Tom
   (B) Dick
   (C) Harry
   (D) Moe
   (E) There is insufficient information to determine the output.

25. What will the output be if C is a priority queue?

   (A) Tom
   (B) Dick
   (C) Harry
   (D) Moe
   (E) There is insufficient information to determine the output.

Answer Key

1. **B**	10. **D**	19. **D**
2. **C**	11. **B**	20. **D**
3. **D**	12. **B**	21. **B**
4. **D**	13. **A**	22. **C**
5. **E**	14. **C**	23. **C**
6. **C**	15. **E**	24. **B**
7. **E**	16. **A**	25. **E**
8. **D**	17. **A**	
9. **A**	18. **A**	

Answers Explained

1. **(B)** When 1 is `s.top()`, it passes the `while` test and gets popped. The current `s.top()` is then 4, which gets printed. Now the test fails on 4, and the `while` loop is not executed again.

2. **(C)** After the first call to `Add(s)`, the stack will contain 8. After the call to `Multiply(s)`, it will contain 63 (on top), then 8. Therefore, after the second `Add(s)`, it will contain 71.

3. **(D)** It seems like a fine idea to take an element out of q, sum it, and then insert it at the back. This works well in segment I. The trouble is that the `while` loop in segment II will be an infinite loop since q will never be empty. Segment III uses the copy constructor of the `apqueue` class to make a temporary copy of q. Though `temp` is changed, q correctly remains unchanged.

4. **(D)** Here is the state of the queue just before it is emptied:

Note that the variable a starts out with value 2. Then a++ results in a=3. The operation `q.dequeue(a)` stores the front element of the queue in a (i.e., a=2). The queue is a first-in-first-out structure, which means that elements are removed in the order they were inserted, from front to back as shown.

5. **(E)** For 3456 to have been printed means that 1 and 2 where dequeued and pushed onto s in that order. The order of printing would then have to be 21, not 12. Note that this means that 345621 would have been OK.

6. **(C)** The first call to `DoOperation()` pops 2 and 3, pops +, and pushes 5, the result. The second call pops 5 and 8, pops -, and pushes -3. The third call pops -3 and 5, pops *, and pushes -15. The expression in C is the only choice that evaluates to -15.

7. **(E)** The first `for` loop removes the top `s.length()-2` elements from s, leaving two elements. `x` currently equals the top element of t, `t.top()`, and `s.length()` equals 2. The second `for` loop is for `i` equals 1 to 0, so nothing is done in this loop! This leaves s with two elements and `x` equal to `t.top()`.

8. **(D)** Here is Q initially:

1 fails the test and is removed (from the front) and inserted at the back of the queue.
4 passes the test and is printed and removed.
9 fails and is removed and inserted at the back.
16 passes and is printed and removed.
25 fails and is removed and inserted at the back.
Q now looks like this:

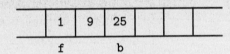

None of the elements in the queue will now pass the `if` test, which means that there will be an infinite sequence of removals and insertions in Q. The `while` loop never terminates.

9. **(A)** Initially s contains 1, 2, 3, 4 with 4 on top. Here is the state of s and q after each pass through the second `for` loop:

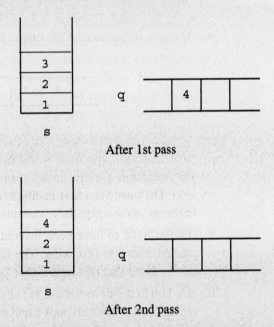

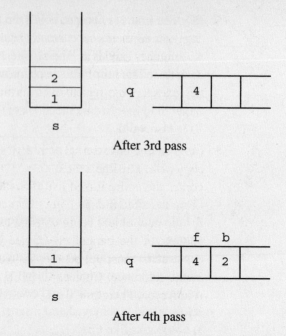

After 3rd pass

After 4th pass

10. **(D)** Here's what happens for each letter of the word:
    r: r pushed onto stack
    a: stack popped and r printed
    c: c pushed onto stack
    k: k pushed onto stack
    e: stack popped and k printed
    t: t pushed onto stack
    e: stack popped and t printed
    e: stack popped and c printed
    r: r pushed onto stack

11. **(B)** Remember that a stack is a last-in-first-out structure, which means that elements placed in it are retrieved in reverse order. So segment II is correct. A queue is a first-in-first-out structure, so the elements will be printed in the order they were received. Thus, segment III is wrong. Segment I would be correct if the cout and Reverse statements were interchanged. As it is, an element is printed *before* the recursive call, which means that elements will be printed out in the given order rather than being reversed.

12. **(B)** Two (or more) forms of the same function in a given class or program is an example of function overloading. The compiler distinguishes the functions by matching parameter types.

13. **(A)** The current implementation of dequeue requires a simple adjustment of myFront, $O(1)$. By contrast, maintaining the front at 0 would require all elements of the queue to be moved down one slot every time the front element is removed, an $O(n)$ operation. None of the other functions would be affected as far as efficiency is concerned.

14. **(C)** DoubleQueue() is needed when storage for the queue is to be enlarged. enqueue(x) is the only function given in which this happens.

15. (**E**) Increment(x) is used every time the front or back index has to be adjusted (i.e., whenever elements are added or removed from the queue). This explains why choices I and II are valid choices. DoubleQueue() works by using a loop to copy the elements of the queue into a temporary array. In this loop, every time the index k of the current queue is incremented, you have to use Increment(k) rather than k++, in case the index of the current queue wraps around. So choice III is also valid.

16. (**A**) Copying the external pointer of stack s is not equivalent to a node-by-node copy of s. The line stackPtr = s.stackPtr should be replaced by code that copies the entire linked list of s, including the external pointer s.stackPtr. (This is called a *deep copy*.) Choice B is wrong because memory allocated for the new object being constructed (i.e., this) will not be the same as the address of the parameter. Choice D is wrong; the parameter for the copy constructor must not be altered, just copied. It is therefore *always* passed by const reference. Choices C and E are wrong because constructors have no return type. Therefore, there should be neither a return statement nor a return type.

17. (**A**) The delete p statement in segment II will delete the first node, which is also pointed to by stackPtr. This means that pointers p and stackPtr will both become undefined. Thus, the pointer to the rest of the linked list representing the stack will be lost. Segment III uses delete incorrectly; it cannot delete just a data field (see Chapter 8).

18. (**A**) The pointer implementation is hidden in the apstack.cpp file and should be invisible to a client program. Thus, declarations I and II are wrong. Declaration III is almost correct, but apstack is a templated class and, therefore, needs an actual type in the declaration. Something like this would have been correct:

```
apstack <char> s1, s2;
```

19. (**D**) Choice A can be improved: because function back() is an accessor, it should be written as a constant member function. Choice B is wrong—it returns a pointer instead of an item. Choices C and E alter the queue with the (wrong) statement mySize--.

20. (**D**) Reason I is correct. For a large itemType, when the array size is doubled, memory needed to store the old and new (double-sized) apvectors is expensive. Also, a significant amount of memory is wasted since the array capacity is larger than the actual number of elements. Reason II is correct for large objects, when time for recopying an apvector becomes expensive. Reason III is false: writing code for the copy constructor, destructor, and assignment overload is *more* complicated for linked lists—a node-by-node deletion or copying must be done. In the apvector implementation, by contrast, the apvector destructor takes care of memory, and the apvector copy constructor can be invoked to copy all the elements of the queue.

21. (**B**) If elements are inserted in increasing order of priority, the last one in will have top priority and will be the first one out, and so on. Thus, the priority queue will work just like a stack. Choice C would be correct only if the elements were inserted in decreasing order of priority, since the first one in would then be the first one out. Choice D is wrong because the first element entered (top

priority) would have to be the first one out—not a stack! Choices A and E are both wrong because higher priority elements would land at the back of the queue. Removing these would violate the first-in-first-out property of a queue.

22. **(C)** The smaller the integer, the higher the priority. Elements are deleted from a priority queue according to their priority number, highest priority (lowest number) first. This is independent of the order of the insertion.

23. **(C)** Here is the stack:

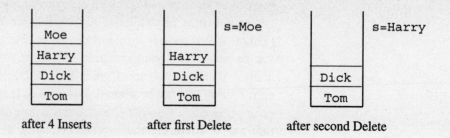

after 4 Inserts   after first Delete   after second Delete

24. **(B)** Here is the queue:

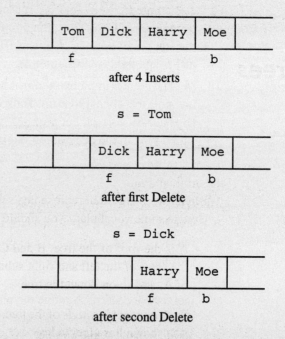

after 4 Inserts

s = Tom

after first Delete

s = Dick

after second Delete

25. **(E)** Since the program segment offers no information about the relative priorities of Tom, Dick, Harry, and Moe, there is not enough information to determine the order of removal of items.

CHAPTER TEN

Trees

TREE: A tall vegetable ...
—*Ambrose Bierce,* The Devil's Dictionary *(1911)*

In arrays and matrices there is a certain equality to the elements, with easy and speedy access to any given element. A tree, on the other hand, is a hierarchy in the way it represents data, with some elements "higher" and easier to access than others. A tree is also a structure that allows branching.

Binary Trees

A *binary tree* is a finite set of elements that is either empty or contains a single element called the *root*, and whose remaining elements are partitioned into two disjoint subsets. Each subset is itself a binary tree, called the left or right *subtree* of the original tree.

Binary trees are often represented schematically as shown.

Here is some vocabulary you should know:

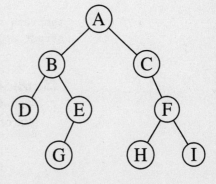

- A is the *root* of the tree. B and C are the roots of the left and right subtrees of A, and so on down the tree.

- Each element is a *node* of the tree. The tree shown has nine nodes.

- Any node whose left and right subtrees are empty is called a *leaf*. Thus, D, G, H, and I are leaves.

- The *depth* of a node is the length of the path from the root to that node. Thus, the depth of A is 0, of B is 1, and of H and I is 3.

- The *level of a node* is equal to its depth. Thus, nodes D, E, and F are all at level 2. The *level of a tree* is equal to the depth of its deepest leaf. Thus, the level of the tree shown is 3.

- The *height* of a tree is the number of nodes on the longest path from the root to a leaf. Thus, the height is one more than the level of the tree. The height is defined to be 0 for an empty tree. The height is 1 for a single node tree. The height of the tree shown on page 257 is 4.

- A *balanced tree* has approximately the same number of nodes in the left and right subtrees rooted at each level. The tree shown on page 257 is balanced.

- A *full binary tree* has every leaf on the same level; and every nonleaf node has two children.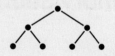

- A *complete binary tree* is either full or full through the next-to-last level, with the leaves as far left as possible.

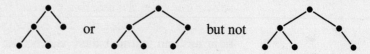

- Note the following family relationships among nodes. A is the *parent* of B and C. B and C are the *children* of A, called the left and right child, respectively. C has no left child, just a right child, F. D and E, the children of B, are called *siblings*. Note that F is not a sibling of either D or E since it has a different parent. A node with no children is a leaf.

- Any node that occurs in a subtree of node k is a *descendant* of k. Thus every node except A is a descendant of A. Node I is a descendant of C but not of B.

- If node k is a descendant of node j, then j is an *ancestor* of node k. Thus, B is an ancestor of D, E, and G, but not of F, H, and I.

Implementation of Binary Trees

Trees are typically implemented with an external pointer to the root node through which the tree is accessed. Each node in the tree has a data field as well as left and right pointers to its children. We use a templated struct to provide flexibility for the type of data, and constructors in the struct that allow for quick and convenient construction of tree nodes:

```
template <class T>
struct node
{
    T data;
    node <T> *left;
    node <T> *right;
    node() : left(NULL), right(NULL) {}
    node(const T & d, node <T> *L, node <T> *R)
        : data(d), left(L), right(R) {}
};
```

Here's how we use this struct to create a root node with an integer element in it:

```
int main()
{
    node <int> *root;
    root = new node <int> (7, NULL, NULL);
        ...
```

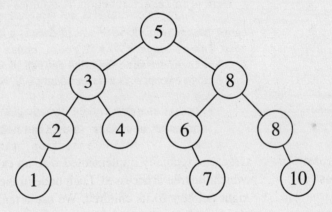

Binary Search Trees

A *binary search tree* is a binary tree that stores elements in an ordered way that makes it efficient to find a given element and easy to access the elements in sorted order. The ordering property is conventional. The following definition of a binary search tree gives the ordering property used most often.

A binary search tree is either empty or has just one node, the root, with left and right subtrees that are binary search trees. Each node has the property that all nodes in its left subtree are less than it, and all nodes in its right subtree are greater than or equal to it.

Here is an example:

Inserting an Element into a Binary Search Tree

Insertion Algorithm

Suppose that we wish to insert the element 9 into the preceding tree. Start by comparing with the root:

> 9 > 5, go right
> 9 > 8, go right
> 9 > 8, go right
> 9 < 10, insert to left of 10

The resulting binary search tree is shown on page 260.

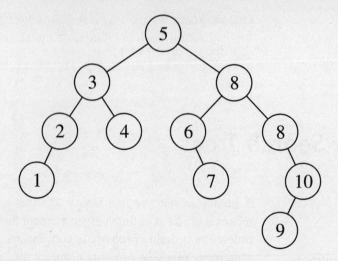

An algorithm for inserting an element uses two pointers, p and q, say, following each other to find the insertion point. The "front" pointer q is like a kamikaze pilot plunging downward until it is NULL, at which point p points to the node at which the new data will be attached. A simple comparison tells whether the new node goes left or right.

Here is an Insert function. It assumes the struct declared previously for trees.

```
template <class T>
void Insert(node <T> * & root, const T & item)
//inserts item into binary search tree pointed to by root
{
    node <T> *p, *q;
    if (root == NULL)        //create root node
        root = new node <T> (item, NULL, NULL);
    else          //find insertion point and insert item
    {
        q = root;
        while (q != NULL)
        {
            p = q;
            if (item < p->data)
                q = p->left;
            else
                q = p->right;
        }
        if (item < p->data)
            p->left = new node <T> (item, NULL, NULL);
        else
            p->right = new node <T> (item, NULL, NULL);
    }
}
```

Run-time Analysis

To insert a single element in an existing binary search tree of n elements:

1. Balanced tree: Insertion will require at most one comparison per level (i.e., no more than $\log_2 n$ comparisons). Thus, the algorithm is $O(\log n)$.

2. Unbalanced tree: As many as n comparisons may be required if the tree consists of a long chain of children. Thus, the algorithm is $O(n)$ in the worst case. For example,

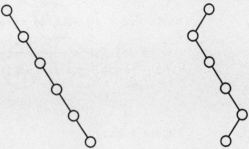

Creating the Tree

The preceding `Insert` function makes creation of a binary search tree quite easy. Assuming that you have a file of numbers or characters or any type that can be compared, here is a function that will slot them into a binary search tree.

```
template <class T>
void CreateBST (node <T> * & root, ifstream & inf)
// Create BST from elements in inf
// Assume inf open for reading at top of file
{
    T element;
    root = NULL;
    while (inf >> element)
        Insert(root, element);
}
```

Run-time Analysis

1. The best case occurs if the elements are in random order, leading to a tree that is reasonably balanced, with the level of the tree approximately equal to $\log_2 n$. To create the tree each of the n elements will require no more than $\log_2 n$ comparisons, so the run time is $O(n \log n)$.

2. Worst case occurs if the elements are initially sorted or sorted in reverse order. To create the tree, insertion of nodes requires $0+1+2+\cdots+n-1 = n(n-1)/2$ comparisons, which is $O(n^2)$. The tree thus formed is a sequence of left or right links as shown.

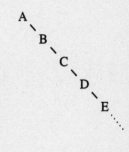

The special ordering property of a binary search tree allows for quick and easy searching for any given element. If the target is less than the current node value, go left; otherwise go right.

The following function returns a pointer to the first node that it encounters with the target value. It returns `NULL` if the target is not in the tree.

```
template <class T>
node <T> * Find(node <T> *root, const T & target)
//Returns a pointer to target, NULL if target not in tree
{
    while (root != NULL && target != root->data)
    {
        if (target < root->data)
            root = root->left;
        else
            root = root->right;
    }
    return root;
}
```

NOTE
1. The algorithm is $O(\log n)$ if the tree is balanced and $O(n)$ for an unbalanced tree.
2. Since the root pointer parameter is passed by value, it is OK to use it as a traveling pointer inside the function. When the function is exited, the original value of root will be retained.

Tree Traversal

There is no natural order for accessing all the elements of a binary tree. Three different methods of traversal are used, each with its own applications.

Inorder:	left - root - right	A
Recursively:	If root is not NULL:	/ \
	Traverse the left subtree inorder	B C
	Visit the root	
	Traverse the right subtree inorder	BAC
Preorder:	root - left - right	
Recursively:	If root is not NULL:	
	Visit the root	
	Traverse the left subtree preorder	
	Traverse the right subtree preorder	ABC
Postorder:	left - right - root	
Recursively:	If root is not NULL:	
	Traverse the left subtree postorder	
	Traverse the right subtree postorder	
	Visit the root	BCA

Example 1

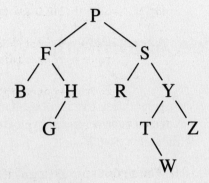

Inorder: BFGHPRSTWYZ
Preorder: PFBHGSRYTWZ
Postorder: BGHFRWTZYSP

Example 2

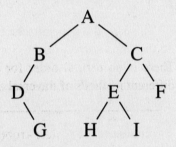

Inorder: DGBAHEICF
Preorder: ABDGCEHIF
Postorder: GDBHIEFCA

The C++ recursive algorithms follow the definitions for each traversal. We use a tree pointer. The base case is when it's NULL. In the following sample function, the "Visit the root" step of the definition simply writes out the data in the node with cout.

```cpp
template <class T>
void Postorder(node <T> *tree)
//does a postorder traversal of tree
{
    if (tree != NULL)
    {
        Postorder(tree->left);
        Postorder(tree->right);
        cout << tree->data;
    }
}
```

1. Similar functions can be written for inorder and preorder traversals.
2. If the tree is a binary search tree (as in Example 1), an inorder traversal will print out the elements in increasing sorted order.

Recursive Tree Algorithms

Most algorithms that involve binary trees are recursive because the trees themselves are recursive structures. A typical recursive function DoTreeStuff has the following structure in pseudocode:

```
DoTreeStuff
{
    if (root != NULL)          //handles base case
    {
        Visit the root         //Important! Don't forget this.
        DoTreeStuff to left subtree      //recursive call
        DoTreeStuff to right subtree     //recursive call
    }
}
```

This is just a general scheme. Often visiting the root postorder or inorder leads to the same correct result. Sometimes order *is* important; it depends on the actual application.

For the following examples, assume that trees of integers are implemented using the following simple node struct:

```
struct TreeNode
{
    int info;
    TreeNode *left;
    TreeNode *right;
};
```

Example 1

```
void Destroy(TreeNode *tree)
//destroys tree
{
    if (tree != NULL)
    {
        Destroy(tree->left);
        Destroy(tree->right);
        delete tree;
    }
}
```

In Example 1 order is important. If the delete statement comes before the recursive calls (preorder), the root node will be destroyed, and the tree pointer will become undefined. The parameters tree->left and tree->right in the two recursive calls to Destroy will now attempt to dereference the undefined pointer. This is a run-time error with unpredictable consequences, including the possibility of a system crash!

Example 2

```
int TreeSum(TreeNode *tree)
//returns sum of values in tree, 0 if tree empty
{
    if (tree == NULL)   //base case
        return 0;
    else
        return tree->info + TreeSum(tree->left)
                + TreeSum(tree->right);
}
```

Example 3

Two trees are *similar* if they have the same pointer structure. Thus, the following two trees are similar:

whereas these two trees are not similar:

```
bool Similar(TreeNode *tree1, TreeNode *tree2)
//returns true if tree1 is similar to tree2, false otherwise
{
    if (tree1 == NULL && tree2 == NULL) //both NULL
        return true;
    else
        if (tree1 == NULL || tree 2 == NULL)    //one NULL
            return false;
        else
            return Similar(tree1->left, tree2->left) &&
                Similar(tree1->right, tree2->right);
}
```

Example 4

```
TreeNode *NewTree(TreeNode *tree)
//creates identical tree and returns pointer to it
{
    if (tree == NULL)    //base case
        return NULL;
    else
    {
        TreeNode *temp = new TreeNode;
        temp->info = tree->info;
        temp->left = NewTree(tree->left);
        temp->right = NewTree(tree->right);
        return temp;
    }
}
```

This example can be done with fewer statements if we have a constructor for creating new nodes. To the preceding TreeNode struct, add the constructor

```
TreeNode :: TreeNode(int I, TreeNode *L, TreeNode *R)
    : info(I), left(L), right(R) {};
```

Then Example 4 can be written

```
TreeNode *NewTree(TreeNode *tree)
{
    if (tree == NULL)    //base case
        return NULL;
    else
    {
        TreeNode *temp = new TreeNode(tree->info,
            NewTree(tree->left), NewTree(tree->right));
        return temp;
    }
}
```

Binary Expression Trees

Infix, Postfix, and Prefix Expressions

A common application of trees is the storage and evaluation of mathematical expressions. A mathematical expression is made up of *operators* like +, −, *, /, and % and *operands*, which are numbers and variables.

There are three different representations of expressions: *infix:* A+B; *prefix:* +AB; and *postfix:* AB+. The "in," "pre," and "post" describe the position of the operator with respect to the operands. To convert the familiar infix form to postfix, for example, convert the pieces of the expression with highest precedence to postfix first. Then continue that way in stages.

Example 1
Convert (A+B)∗(C−D) to postfix.

(A+B)∗(C−D) = (AB+)∗(CD−)   //parentheses have highest precedence
            = AB+CD−∗   //treat AB+ and CD− as single operands

Example 2
Convert (A−B)/C∗D to prefix.

(A−B)/C∗D = ((−AB)/C)∗D   // ∗ and / have equal precedence. Work
                          // from left to right
         = (/−ABC)∗D
         = ∗/−ABCD

Example 3
Convert A−B/(C+D∗E) to postfix.

A−B/(C+D∗E) = A−B/(C+(DE∗))
            = A−(B/CDE∗+)
            = A−BCDE∗ + /
            = ABCDE∗ + /−

Example 4
Same as Example 3 for prefix.

A−B/(C+D∗E) = A−B/(C+(∗DE))
            = A−(B/(+C∗DE))
            = A−/B+C∗DE
            = −A/B+C∗DE

Binary Expression Tree

A *binary expression tree* either consists of a single root node containing an operand or it stores an expression as follows. The root contains an operator that will be applied to the results of evaluating the expressions in the left and right subtrees, each of which is a binary expression tree.

A node containing an operator must have two nonempty subtrees. A node containing an operand must be a leaf. For example,

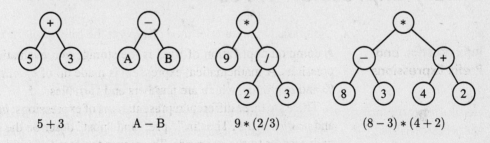

$$5 + 3 \qquad A - B \qquad 9 * (2/3) \qquad (8-3)*(4+2)$$

NOTE

1. The level of the nodes indicates the precedence: operations in the highest level nodes are performed first. The operation at the root will always be the last operation performed.
2. An expression can be generated in its infix form by an inorder traversal of the tree. (But *you* must provide the brackets!) A preorder traversal yields the prefix form, whereas a postorder traversal yields the postfix form.

Example 1

Write the infix, prefix, and postfix form of the expression represented by each binary expression tree.

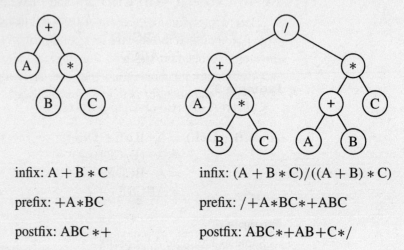

infix: $A + B * C$ infix: $(A + B * C)/((A + B) * C)$

prefix: $+A*BC$ prefix: $/+A*BC*+ABC$

postfix: $ABC*+$ postfix: $ABC*+AB+C*/$

Example 2

Evaluate the expression in the following tree.

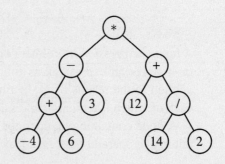

Solution: Do an inorder traversal to get the following infix form:

$$[(-4 + 6) - 3] * [12 + 14/2] = (2 - 3) * (12 + 7) = -19$$

Evaluating a Binary Expression Tree

Consider a program that evaluates a binary expression tree for some given expression. (We assume the tree has already been created.) Note that

(Value of tree) = (Value of left subtree) ∘ (Value of right subtree)

where ∘ is some operation. But

(Value of left subtree) = (Value of *its* left subtree) • (Value of *its* right subtree) where ● is some other operation. Clearly the process is recursive. The base case is reached at a leaf, when the node contains an operand as opposed to an operator.

Suppose that operators and operands are represented by character strings in tree nodes:

```
struct exprNode
{
    apstring info;  //either an operator or operand
    exprNode *left;
    exprNode *right;
};
```

Before applying an `Eval` function to evaluate the tree, you need an `IsOperand` function that tells if you have an operator or an operand; a `GetValue` function that converts an operand string to a numerical value, and a `DoOperation` function to apply the particular operation required. Here are the headers for `IsOperand` and `GetValue`, and code for `DoOperation` and `Eval`:

```
bool IsOperand(exprNode *treePtr);
//returns true if treePtr points to an operand,
//false if it points to an operator

double GetValue(const apstring &s);
//converts s to a real number value

double DoOperation(char op, double lhs, double rhs)
//applies binary operation op to left-hand side and
// right-hand side. Returns result
{
    switch(op)
    {
        case '+': return lhs + rhs;
        case '-': return lhs - rhs;
        case '*': return lhs * rhs;
        case '/':
            if (rhs != 0)
                return lhs / rhs;
            else
                <error message>
    }
}
```

```
double Eval(exprNode *root)
//Returns value of binary expression tree
{
    if (IsOperand(root))
        return GetValue(root->info);
    else            //root->info is an operator
        return DoOperation(root->info[0],
            Eval(root->left), Eval(root->right));
}
```

Note that `root->info[0]` is the first character of the `apstring` `root->info`. For an operator, this is the only character in the string.

Multiple-Choice Questions on Trees

1. A full binary tree with k leaves contains how many nodes?
   (A) k
   (B) k^2
   (C) 2^k
   (D) $\log_2 k$
   (E) $2k - 1$

2. A binary tree has level k. Which represents
   1. The maximum possible number of nodes, and
   2. The minimum possible number of nodes in the tree?
   (A) (1) 2^{k+1} (2) $2^k + 1$
   (B) (1) 2^{k+1} (2) k
   (C) (1) $2^{k+1} - 1$ (2) k
   (D) (1) $2^{k+1} - 1$ (2) $k + 1$
   (E) (1) $2^k + 1$ (2) 2^k

3. Which of the following represents (1) inorder, (2) preorder, and (3) postorder traversals of the tree shown?
   (A) (1) GRAPES   (2) RAGPES   (3) GAESPR
   (B) (1) GRAEPS   (2) RGAPES   (3) GESPAR
   (C) (1) EPSARG   (2) PESRGA   (3) ESPGAR
   (D) (1) GRAEPS   (2) GESPAR   (3) RGAPES
   (E) (1) GRAPES   (2) GAESPR   (3) RAGPES

4. The tree shown is traversed postorder and each element is pushed onto a stack s as it is encountered. The following program fragment is then executed:

```
for (int i=1; i<=5; i++)
    s.pop(x);
```

   What is the value of x after the segment is executed?
   (A) D
   (B) G
   (C) A
   (D) F
   (E) B

5. Each of the following lists of numbers is inserted, in the order given, into a binary search tree. Which list produces the most balanced tree?
   (A) 2 4 7 5 8 10
   (B) 9 7 2 1 4 0
   (C) 5 1 2 6 3 4
   (D) 2 5 1 4 0 3
   (E) 6 4 1 8 10 5

6. The element 10 is to be inserted into the binary search tree shown.

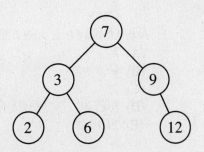

After insertion, the tree is as follows:

(A)

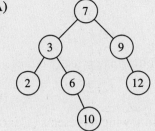

(D)

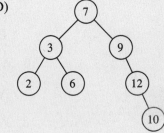

(B)

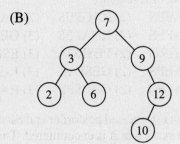

(E)

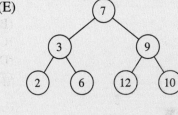

(C)

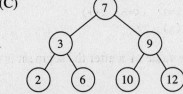

7. Array elements a[0], a[1], ... , a[n-1] are inserted into a binary search tree. The elements will then be used for searching the array for a given element. In the *worst* case, the insertion and search, respectively, will be
   (A) $O(n^2)$, $O(n)$
   (B) $O(n \log n)$, $O(n \log n)$
   (C) $O(n^2)$, $O(n \log n)$
   (D) $O(n^2)$, $O(n^2)$
   (E) $O(n \log n)$, $O(n)$

8. Worst-case performance of the search of a *balanced* binary search tree is
    (A) $O(n^2)$
    (B) $O(n)$
    (C) $O(\log n)$
    (D) $O(2^n)$
    (E) $O(n \log n)$

9. The value of the binary expression tree shown is
    (A) 1
    (B) 4
    (C) 10
    (D) 11
    (E) 25

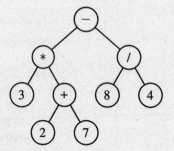

10. Which of the following correctly represents the expression A / B * C % D?

(A)

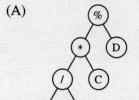

(B)

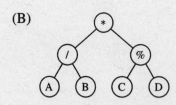

(C)

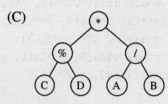

(D)

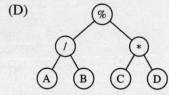

(E)

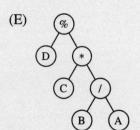

11. The (1) prefix, and (2) postfix forms of the expression P + (Q − R) * A / B are:

    (A) (1) +P*−QR/AB   (2) PQR−AB/ * +

    (B) (1) PQR−AB/ * +   (2) +P*−QR/AB

    (C) (1) PQR−A*B/+   (2) +P/ * −QRAB

    (D) (1) +P/ * −QRAB   (2) PQR−A*B/+

    (E) (1) +*P−QR/AB   (2) PQRA−*B/+

For Questions 12 and 13 assume that binary trees are implemented using this declaration:

```
struct node
{
    int info;
    node *left;
    node *right;
    node(int D, node *L, node *R);
};
node :: node(int D, node *L, node *R)        //constructor
        : info(D), left(L), right(R) {}
```

12. Suppose that pointer p points to a node as shown. Which of the following correctly inserts the number 5 as the right child of the node that p points to?

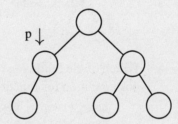

    (A) `p->right = new node(5, NULL, NULL);`

    (B) `p = new node(5, p->left, p->right);`

    (C) `p->right = new(5, NULL, NULL);`

    (D) `p->right = new node(5, p->left, p->right);`

    (E) `p = new node(5, NULL, NULL);`

13. Two trees are *mirror images* of each other if their roots and left and right subtrees are reflected across a vertical line as shown:

Example 1   Example 2

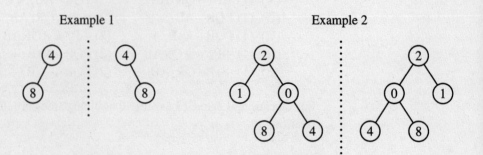

Refer to the following function `MirrorTree`:

```
node *MirrorTree(node *tree)
//precondition: tree points to a binary tree
//postcondition: a mirror image of tree is created and
//a pointer to it is returned
{
    if (tree == NULL)
        return NULL;
    else
    {
        <more code>
    }
}
```

Which of the following replacements for <*more code*> correctly achieves the postcondition for function `MirrorTree`?

```
 I node *temp = new node;
   temp->info = tree->info;
   temp->left = MirrorTree(tree->right);
   temp->right = MirrorTree(tree->left);
   return temp;

II return new node(tree->info, MirrorTree(tree->right),
                   MirrorTree(tree->left));

III return new node(tree->info, MirrorTree(tree->left),
                    MirrorTree(tree->right));
```

(A) I only
(B) II only
(C) III only
(D) I and II only
(E) I and III only

For Questions 14–22 assume that binary trees are implemented using the following declaration:

```
struct TreeNode
{
    int info;
    TreeNode *left;
    TreeNode *right;
};
```

14. Refer to function NumNodes:

    ```
    int NumNodes(TreeNode *tree)
    //returns the number of nodes in tree
    {
        if (tree == NULL)
            return 0;
        else
        {
            <code>
        }
    }
    ```

    Which replacement for <code> will cause the function to work as intended?

    I return 1 + NumNodes(tree->left) + NumNodes(tree->right);

    II return NumNodes(tree) + NumNodes(tree->left) +
              NumNodes(tree->right);

    III return NumNodes(tree->left) + NumNodes(tree->right);

    (A) None
    (B) I only
    (C) II only
    (D) III only
    (E) II and III only

15. Refer to function LeafSum:

```
int LeafSum(TreeNode *tree)
//returns sum of leaves in tree, 0 for empty tree
{
    if (tree == NULL)
        return 0;
    else
    {
        <code>
    }
}
```

Which replacement for <code> is correct?

(A) ```
if (tree->left == NULL && tree->right == NULL)
    return tree->info;
else
    return 1 + LeafSum(tree->left) + LeafSum(tree->right);
```

(B) ```
if (tree->left == NULL || tree->right == NULL)
    return tree->info;
else
    return 1 + LeafSum(tree->left) + LeafSum(tree->right);
```

(C) ```
if (tree->left == NULL && tree->right == NULL)
    return tree->info;
else
    return tree->info + LeafSum(tree->left) +
           LeafSum(tree->right);
```

(D) ```
if (tree->left == NULL || tree->right == NULL)
    return tree->info;
else
    return LeafSum(tree->left) + LeafSum(tree->right);
```

(E) ```
if (tree->left == NULL && tree->right == NULL)
    return tree->info;
else
    return LeafSum(tree->left) + LeafSum(tree->right);
```
```

16. Which is true about function `Find`?

```
TreeNode *Find(TreeNode *root, int target)
//return pointer to node with target value,
// or NULL if target not found
{
    if (root == NULL)
        return NULL;
    else if (target == root->info)
        return root;
    else if (target < root->info)
        return Find(root->left, target);
    else
        return Find(root->right, target);
}
```

(A) Function `Find` will never work as intended.
(B) Function `Find` will always work as intended.
(C) Function `Find` will only work as intended if `target` is not in the tree.
(D) Function `Find` will always work as intended if the tree is a binary search tree.
(E) Function `Find` will only work as intended if the tree is a binary search tree and `target` occurs no more than once in the tree.

17. Refer to function `DoSomething`:

```
int DoSomething(TreeNode *root)
{
    if (root != NULL)
        if (root->right == NULL)
            return root->info;
        else
            return DoSomething(root->right);
}
```

Which best describes what `DoSomething` does?

(A) It returns the largest element in a nonempty binary search tree.
(B) It returns the largest element in a nonempty tree.
(C) It returns an element at the highest level of a nonempty tree.
(D) It returns the smallest element in a nonempty binary search tree.
(E) It returns the smallest element in a nonempty tree.

18. Refer to function `Traverse`, and to the binary tree shown:

```
void Traverse(TreeNode *T)
{
    if (T != NULL)
    {
        <code>
    }
}
```

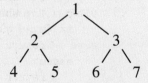

By replacing `<code>` with the three statements `Traverse(T->left)`, `Traverse(T->right)`, and `cout << T->info` in some order, we can cause function `Traverse` to execute one of six traversals. For example, by replacing `<code>` with

```
Traverse(T->left);
Traverse(T->right);
cout << T->info;
```

we would cause `Traverse` to execute a postorder traversal. Which of the following replacements for `<code>` will cause the numbers 1 through 7 to be printed in ascending order when `Traverse(T)` is called?

(A) ```
Traverse(T->left);
cout << T->info;
Traverse(T->right);
```

(B) ```
cout << T->info;
Traverse(T->left);
Traverse(T->right);
```

(C) ```
Traverse(T->right);
Traverse(T->left);
cout << T->info;
```

(D) ```
Traverse(T->right);
cout << T->info;
Traverse(T->left);
```

(E) It is impossible to print the numbers 1 through 7 in ascending order using this method.

19. Refer to function `WhatsIt`:

```
int WhatsIt(TreeNode *tree)
{
    int x, y;
    if (tree == NULL)
        return -1;
    else
    {
        x = 1 + WhatsIt(tree->left);
        y = 1 + WhatsIt(tree->right);
        if (x >= y)
            return x;
        else
            return y;
    }
}
```

Function `WhatsIt` returns -1 for an empty tree. What does function `WhatsIt` do when invoked for a nonempty tree?

(A) It returns the largest value in the tree.

(B) It returns the number of nodes in the subtree that has the greatest number of nodes.

(C) It returns the level of the tree.

(D) It returns 1 plus the level of the tree.

(E) It returns either the leftmost value or the rightmost value of a tree, whichever is larger.

20. Refer to function `ChangeTree`. You may assume function `HasOneChild`, whose header is given, works as specified.

```cpp
bool HasOneChild(TreeNode *t);
//postcondition: returns true if t has exactly one child;
//               otherwise returns false

void ChangeTree(TreeNode * & T)
{
    if (T != NULL)
    {
        ChangeTree(T->left);
        ChangeTree(T->right);
        if (HasOneChild(T))
        {
            TreeNode *p = T;
            if (T->left != NULL)
                T = T->left;
            else
                T = T->right;
            delete p;
        }
    }
}
```

Suppose function `ChangeTree` is applied to the binary tree shown:

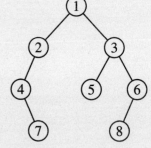

Which of the following represents the resulting tree?

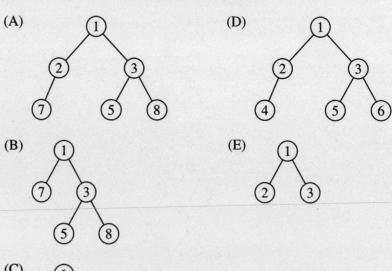

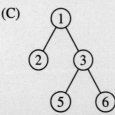

21. Refer to function `Number`:

```
void Number(TreeNode *tree, int & nextNum)
{
    if (tree != NULL)
        if (tree->left == NULL && tree->right == NULL)
        {
            tree->info = nextNum;
            nextNum++;
        }
        else
        {
            Number(tree->right, nextNum);
            Number(tree->left, nextNum);
        }
}
```

Which of the following trees is a possible result of executing the next two statements? (You may assume that `nextNum` and `tree` are correctly declared.)

```
nextNum = 3;
Number(tree, nextNum);
```

(A)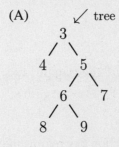

(D)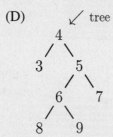

(B)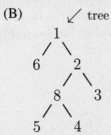

(E)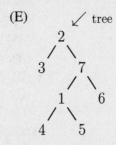

(C)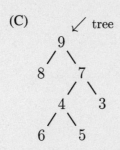

22. Recall that the height of a binary tree is defined as follows: the height of an empty tree is 0; the height of a nonempty tree is the number of nodes on the longest path from the root to a leaf of the tree. Thus, the height of the tree shown is 5.

Refer to function F:

```
int F(TreeNode *t)
{
    if (t == NULL)
        return 0;
    else
        return Max(Height(t->left) + Height(t->right),
            F(t->left), F(t->right));
}
```

You may assume that function Max returns the largest of its integer arguments and that function Height returns the height of its tree argument. What value is returned when F(t) is called for this tree?

(A) 4

(B) 5

(C) 6

(D) 7

(E) 8

23. Assume that the binary tree shown has been implemented with this declaration:

```
struct node
{
    char info;
    node *left;
    node *right;
};
```

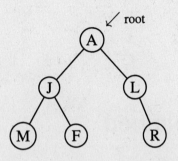

What will be output by the following code segment?

```
node *current;
apqueue <node *> q;
if (root == NULL)
    cout << "Empty tree" << endl;
else
{
    q.enqueue(root);
    do {
        q.dequeue(current);
        cout << current->info;
        if (current->left != NULL)
            q.enqueue(current->left);
        if (current->right != NULL)
            q.enqueue(current->right);
    } while (!q.isEmpty());
}
```

(A) MJFALR
(B) MFRJLA
(C) AJLMFR
(D) MFJRLA
(E) AJMFLR

Answer Key

1. **E**	9. **E**	17. **A**
2. **D**	10. **A**	18. **E**
3. **B**	11. **D**	19. **C**
4. **A**	12. **A**	20. **B**
5. **E**	13. **D**	21. **B**
6. **B**	14. **B**	22. **C**
7. **A**	15. **E**	23. **C**
8. **C**	16. **D**	

Answers Explained

1. **(E)** Draw some pictures and count!

# of leaves	# of nodes
1	1
2	3
4	7
8	15
16	31
32	63
. . .	. . .
k	$2k - 1$

2. **(D)** For the maximum possible number of nodes, each node must have two children. Notice the pattern:

Level	Max possible # of nodes
0	1
1	3
2	7
3	15
. . .	. . .
k	$2^{k+1} - 1$

For the minimum possible number of nodes, each node must have no more than one child. Thus, for example, a level 3 tree with the minimum number of nodes will look like this:

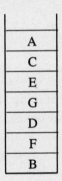

or   or   and so on.

In each case there will be $k + 1$ nodes.

3. **(B)**
   (1) For inorder think left-root-right (i.e., G-R-right). When we now traverse the right subtree inorder, there is no left, so A comes next. Then traverse the P-E-S subtree inorder, which gives E-P-S.
   (2) For preorder think root-left-right (i.e., R-G-right). When we now traverse the right subtree, A is now the root and comes next. There is no left, so traverse the P-E-S subtree preorder, which gives P-E-S.
   (3) Similarly for postorder, thinking left-right-root produces GESPAR.

4. **(A)** A postorder traversal yields BFDGECA, so here's the stack:

A
C
E
G
D
F
B

The fifth pop will remove element D.

5. **(E)** In each case the first number in the list will go into the root node. Subsequent numbers that are less than the first number will go into the left subtree; those greater than or equal to the first will go into the right subtree. Eliminate choices A and B, which are almost in sorted order. Each of these will form trees that are virtually long chains:

Choice A   Choice B

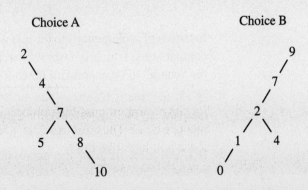

Choice C won't form a balanced tree either: all elements but one will go into the left subtree.

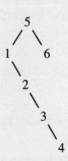

You should be able to eliminate choices A, B, and C by inspection. Comparing the trees in choices D and E shows that E yields the more balanced tree:

6. **(B)** Starting at the root, compare the new element with the current node. Go left if the element is less than the current node; otherwise go right. Insert at the first available empty slot. For the tree shown, start by comparing 10 with 7. $10 > 7$, so go right. Then $10 > 9$, so go right. Then $10 < 12$. 12 is a leaf, so insert left.

7. **(A)** Worst case for insertion into a binary search tree occurs when the numbers are already sorted. The resulting tree will be unbalanced, a long chain of numbers:

Insertion of n elements into the tree will require $0+1+\cdots+n-1 = n(n-1)/2$ comparisons, which is $O(n^2)$. Searching this tree will require each "link" in the "chain" to be examined, much like a sequential search. This is $O(n)$.

8. **(C)** If the tree is balanced, the worst case occurs when the key is found in a leaf (i.e., at the highest level of the tree). The maximum level of a balanced tree is $\log_2 n$. Therefore, the search is $O(\log n)$.

9. **(E)** The infix form of the expression is $3 * (2 + 7) - 8/4$, which equals $(3 * 9) - 2 = 25$.

10. **(A)** The operators /, *, and % all have equal precedence and must therefore be performed from left to right. Thus, the order of performing the operations is /, followed by *, then %. Now recall the general rule: the earlier an operation is performed, the higher its node level in the tree. In particular, the last operation performed is always the root node. So % must be in the root node, which eliminates choices B, C, and E. Since / is performed before *, the node containing / must have a higher level than the node containing *, which eliminates choice D. Choice D fails for another reason: C * D is not part of the given expression. Note that if the given expression had been (A/ B) * (C % D), choice B would have been correct, since / and % would have equal first precedence and * would be the last operation performed.

11. **(D)** For both pre- and postfix, perform the operations in order of precedence, changing each subexpression to prefix or postfix as you go.

    (1) prefix:
    $$\begin{aligned} P + (Q - R) * A/B &= P + [(- QR) * A]/B \\ &= P + (*- QRA)/B \\ &= P + (/ * - QRAB) \\ &= + P / * - QRAB \end{aligned}$$

    To go from the first to the second line, note that * and / have equal precedence, so we use the leftmost one first.

    (2) postfix:
    $$\begin{aligned} P + (Q - R) * A/B &= P + [(QR -) * A]/B \\ &= P + (QR - A *)/B \\ &= P + (QR - A * B/) \\ &= PQR - A * B/+ \end{aligned}$$

12. **(A)** The right-hand side of the assignment statement is evaluated first. `new node(5, NULL, NULL)` uses the constructor to create a new node with `info` equal to 5 and left and right pointer fields each set to `NULL`. Choice C almost gets it right, but omits `node`, the name of the new object. `p->right` is then assigned to point to this node, attaching the node to the tree. Choices B and E, which begin `p=`, must be wrong because they fail to attach the new node to the tree. The left and right pointer fields for the new node must be `NULL`, which eliminates choices B and D.

13. **(D)** Segments I and II are equivalent, but segment II takes advantage of the constructor for the struct. The order of the pointer parameters in the constructor is left, right, so in segment II the recursive call `MirrorTree(tree->right)` will attach as the left subtree of the new tree a copy of the right subtree of `tree`. Similarly, `MirrorTree(tree->left)` will cause a copy of the left subtree of `tree` to be attached as the right subtree of the new tree. Segment III is wrong because it creates an *exact* copy of the tree rather than a mirror image.

14. **(B)** Eliminate segment III; it forgot to count the root node! Segment II calls `NumNodes(tree)`, which leads to infinite recursion. Segment I correctly adds 1 for the root node, and adds the number of nodes in the left and right subtrees.

15. **(E)** This is an example where you *don't* automatically add the `info` in the root node. Thus, eliminate choices A, B, and C, which all add something to `LeafSum(tree->left) + LeafSum(tree->right)`. The correct test for a leaf is that both the left and right pointers must be `NULL`. Thus, eliminate choice D, which has an "or" in the test instead of an "and."

16. **(D)** The algorithm uses the binary search tree property and searches only the left subtree if `target` is less than the current root value, or only the right subtree if `target` is greater than or equal to the current root value. In a general (i.e., not a binary search) tree, the given algorithm may miss the target. Note that choice E is false; the postcondition specifies that a pointer is returned to `target`, which the algorithm will do irrespective of the number of times `target` occurs in the tree.

17. **(A)** The algorithm is actually returning the rightmost element of the tree, which is not one of the choices. Note that the rightmost element of a binary search tree is the largest (check it out!), which makes A the best choice. None of the other choices *must* be true. For example, if the tree in choice C looks like the following tree, C will be false.

18. **(E)** Choice A is an inorder traversal yielding 4251637. Choice B is a preorder traversal: 1245367. Choice C is a right-to-left postorder traversal: 7635421. Choice D is a right-to-left inorder traversal: 7361524. Trying the regular postorder and the right-to-left preorder traversals (the two remaining possibilities) does not yield the required output either.

19. **(C)** For the line `x = 1 + WhatsIt(tree->left)`, 1 is added for each recursive call until `tree->left` is NULL. The same is true for the line `y = 1 + WhatsIt(tree->right)`. Look at an example like the following tree:

    Here x will end up with value 1 (2 recursive calls plus −1 for the base case), whereas y will end up with the value 2 (3 recursive calls plus −1 for the base case). The function in this case will return 2, the maximum of x and y, which is the level of the tree.

20. **(B)** The `ChangeTree` function removes from `T` all nodes that have exactly one child, replacing the removed node with that child. Thus, nodes 2, 4, and 6 will be removed. First 7 will replace 4, then 7 will replace 2, and finally 8 will replace 6.

21. **(B)** This function numbers all the leaves of the tree beginning with the right subtree. The starting number given in this case is 3. The rightmost leaf becomes 3, and leaves are numbered in ascending order from right to left.

22. **(C)** The function call F(t) returns the maximum of the following three quantities:
    (1) Sum of heights of left and right subtrees of root node t. Here $4 + 1 = 5$.
    (2) Maximum of sum of heights of left and right subtrees for *any* node in the right subtree of node t. Here this is 1.
    (3) Maximum of sum of heights of left and right subtrees for *any* node in the left subtree of node t.

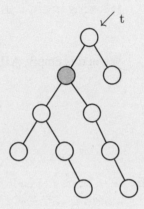

Note that the shaded node in the left subtree of node t has height of left subtree = 3, and height of right subtree = 3. No other node in the subtree returns a higher total, so the function call F(t->left) returns 6. Since Max(5, 1, 6) = 6, F(t) returns 6.

23. **(C)** The algorithm yields a horizontal traversal of the tree, starting at the root. Suppose that the pointers to the nodes are labeled with small letters as shown:

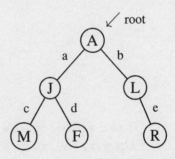

After the first pass through the do-while loop, A has been printed and q is

	a	b		
	f	b		

q

After the second pass, J has been printed and q is

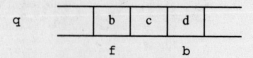

After the third pass, L has been printed and q is

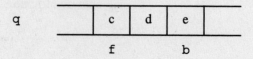

When q is empty, AJLMFR has been printed.

CHAPTER ELEVEN
Sorting and Searching

Critics search for ages for the wrong word, which,
to give them credit, they eventually find.
—Peter Ustinov (1952)

In each of the following sorting algorithms, assume that an array of n elements, a[0], a[1], ... , a[n-1] is to be sorted in ascending order.

O(n²) Sorts: Selection and Insertion Sorts

Selection Sort

This is a "search-and-swap" algorithm. Here's how it works.

Find the smallest element in the array and exchange it with a[0], the first element. Now find the smallest element in the subarray a[1] ... a[n-1], and swap it with a[1], the second element in the array. Continue this process until just the last two elements remain to be sorted, a[n-2] and a[n-1]. The smaller of these two elements is placed in a[n-2], the larger in a[n-1], and the sort is complete.

Trace these steps with a small array of four elements. The unshaded part is the subarray still to be searched.

8	1	4	6	
1	8	4	6	after first pass
1	4	8	6	after second pass
1	4	6	8	after third pass

NOTE

Level AB Only

1. For an array of n elements, the array is sorted after $n - 1$ passes.
2. After the kth pass, the first k elements are in their final sorted position.
3. Number of comparisons in first pass: $n - 1$
   Number of comparisons in second pass: $n - 2$
   ... and so on.
   Total number of comparisons $= (n-1) + (n-2) + \cdots + 2 + 1 = n(n-1)/2$, which is $O(n^2)$.
4. Irrespective of the initial order of elements, selection sort makes the same number of comparisons. Thus, best, worst, and average cases are all $O(n^2)$.

291

Insertion Sort

Think of the first element in the array, a[0], as being sorted with respect to itself. The array can now be thought of as consisting of two parts, a sorted list followed by an unsorted list. The idea of insertion sort is to move elements from the unsorted list to the sorted list one at a time; as each item is moved, it is inserted into its correct position in the sorted list. In order to place the new item, some elements may need to be moved down to create a slot.

Here is the array of four elements. In each case, the boxed element is "it," the next element to be inserted into the sorted part of the list. The shaded area is the part of the list sorted so far.

8	1	4	6	
1	8	4	6	after first pass
1	4	8	6	after second pass
1	4	6	8	after third pass

NOTE

1. For an array of n elements, the array is sorted after $n - 1$ passes.
2. After the kth pass, a[0], a[1], ... , a[k] are sorted with respect to each other but not necessarily in their final sorted positions.

Level AB Only

3. The worst case for insertion sort occurs if the array is initially sorted in reverse order, since this will lead to the maximum possible number of comparisons and moves:

   Number of comparisons in first pass: 1
   Number of comparisons in second pass: 2

   $$\vdots$$

   Number of comparisons in $(n - 1)$th pass: $n - 1$

   Total number of comparisons $= (n-1) + (n-2) + \cdots + 2 + 1 = n(n-1)/2$, which is $O(n^2)$.

4. The best case for insertion sort occurs if the array is already sorted in increasing order. In this case, each pass through the array will involve just one comparison, which will indicate that "it" is in its correct position with respect to the sorted list. Therefore, no elements will need to be moved.
   Total number of comparisons $= n - 1$, which is $O(n)$.

5. For the average case, insertion sort must still make $n - 1$ passes (i.e., $O(n)$ passes). Each pass makes $O(n)$ comparisons, so the total number of comparisons is $O(n^2)$.

Recursive Sorts: Mergesort and Quicksort

Selection and insertion sorts are inefficient for large n, requiring approximately n passes through a list of n elements. More efficient algorithms can be devised using a "divide-and-conquer" approach, which is used in all the sorting algorithms that follow.

Mergesort

Here is a recursive description of how mergesort works:

If there is more than one element in the array
> Break the array into two halves.
> Mergesort the left half.
> Mergesort the right half.
> Merge the two subarrays into a sorted array.

Mergesort uses a `Merge` function to merge two sorted pieces of an array into a single sorted array. For example, suppose array `a[0] ... a[n-1]` is such that `a[0] ... a[k]` is sorted and `a[k+1] ... a[n-1]` is sorted, both parts in increasing order. Example:

a[0]	a[1]	a[2]	a[3]	a[4]	a[5]
2	5	8	9	1	6

In this case, `a[0] ... a[3]` and `a[4] ... a[5]` are the two sorted pieces. The function call `Merge(a,0,3,5)` should produce the "merged" array:

a[0]	a[1]	a[2]	a[3]	a[4]	a[5]
1	2	5	6	8	9

The middle numerical parameter in `Merge` (the 3 in this case) represents the index of the last element in the first "piece" of the array. The first and third numerical parameters are the lowest and highest index, respectively, of array `a`.

Here's what happens in mergesort:

1. You start with an unsorted list of n elements.
2. The recursive calls break the list into n sublists, each of length 1. Note that these n arrays, each containing just one element, are sorted!
3. Recursively merge adjacent pairs of lists. You will then have approximately $n/2$ lists of length 2; then, you will have approximately $n/4$ lists of approximate length 4, and so on, until you have just one list of length n.

An example of mergesort follows:

5	−3	2	4	0	6

Break list into
n sublists of
length 1

5	−3	2		4	0	6

5	−3		2		4	0		6

5		−3		2		4		0		6

Merge adjacent
pairs of lists

−3	5		2		0	4		6

−3	2	5		0	4	6

−3	0	2	4	5	6

Level AB Only

Analysis of Mergesort:

1. The Merge function compares each element in the subarrays, an $O(n)$ process. It also copies the elements from a temporary array back into the original list, another $O(n)$ process. This total of $2n$ operations makes the merge part of the algorithm $O(n)$.

2. To break the array of n elements into n arrays of one element each requires $\log_2 n$ divisions, an $O(\log n)$ process. For each of the $\log_2 n$ divisions of the array, the $O(n)$ Merge function is called to put it together again. Thus, mergesort is $O(n \log n)$.

3. The major disadvantage of mergesort is that it needs a temporary array that is as large as the original array to be sorted. This could be a problem if space is a factor.

4. Mergesort is not affected by the initial ordering of the elements. Thus, best, worst, and average cases are $O(n \log n)$.

Quicksort

For large n, quicksort is, on average, the fastest known sorting algorithm. Here is a recursive description of how quicksort works:

If there are at least two elements in the array
    Partition the array.
    Quicksort the left subarray.
    Quicksort the right subarray.

The Partition function splits the array into two subarrays as follows: a *pivot* element is chosen at random from the array (often just the first element) and placed so that all items to the left of the pivot are less than or equal to the pivot, whereas those to the right are greater than or equal to it.

For example, if the array is 4 1 2 7 5 −1 8 0 6, and a[0] = 4 is the pivot, the Partition function produces

$$-1 \quad 1 \quad 2 \quad 0 \quad \boxed{4} \quad 5 \quad 8 \quad 7 \quad 6$$

Here's how the partitioning works: Let a[0], 4 in this case, be the pivot. Markers up and down are initialized to index values 1 and $n - 1$, as shown. Move the up marker until a value less than the pivot is found, or down equals up. Move the down marker until a value greater than the pivot is found, or down equals up. Swap a[up] and a[down]. Continue the process until down equals up. This is the pivot position. Swap a[0] and a[pivotPosition].

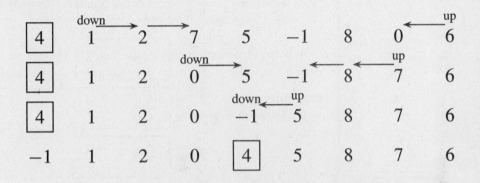

Notice that the pivot element, 4, is in its final sorted position.

Level AB Only

Analysis of Quicksort
1. For the fastest run time, the array should be partitioned into two parts of roughly the same size. In this case, and on average, there are $\log_2 n$ splits. The Partition algorithm is $O(n)$. Therefore the best- and average-case run times are $O(n \log n)$.
2. If the pivot happens to be the smallest or largest element in the array, the split is not much of a split—one of the subarrays is empty! If this happens repeatedly, quicksort degenerates into a slow, recursive version of selection sort and is $O(n^2)$ (worst case).
3. The worst case for quicksort occurs when the partitioning algorithm repeatedly divides the array into pieces of size 1 and $n - 1$. An example is when the array is initially sorted in either order and the first or last element is chosen as the pivot. Some algorithms avoid this situation by initially shuffling up the given array (!) or selecting the pivot by examining several elements of the array (such as first, middle, and last) and then taking the median.

Note that for both quicksort and mergesort, when a subarray gets down to some small size m, it becomes faster to sort by straight insertion. The optimal value of m is machine-dependent, but it's approximately equal to 7.

A Binary Tree Sort: Heapsort

Level AB Only

Heapsort is an elegant algorithm that uses the *concept* of a binary tree without the pointer implementation!

Recall the following definitions from Chapter 10:

A *full binary tree* has every leaf on the same level; and every nonleaf node has two children.

A *complete binary tree* is either full or full through the next-to-last level, with the leaves as far left as possible.

A *heap* (sometimes called a *max heap*) is a complete binary tree in which every node has a value greater than or equal to each of its children.

Example

Is each of the following a heap?

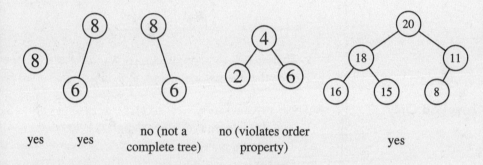

| yes | yes | no (not a complete tree) | no (violates order property) | yes |

NOTE

1. The largest value in a heap is in the root node.
2. A heap has $n/2$ subtrees that have at least one child. This counts the tree itself.

To sort array a[1], a[2], a[3], ..., a[n], heapsort has three main steps:

I. Slot the elements into a "mental" binary tree, level by level, from left to right as shown here. This creates a *complete* binary tree in your head, with the property that if node a[k] has children, its left child is a[2*k] and its right child is a[2*k + 1]. To maintain this "children" property is the reason we do not use the C++ convention of starting the array with a[0]. In fact, a[0] remains unused.

a[1]	a[2]	a[3]	a[4]	a[5]	a[6]
2	1	4	9	3	7

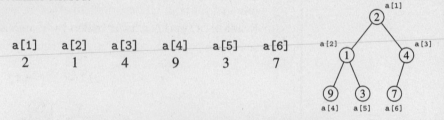

II. Transform the tree into a heap. Notice that a[n/2] down to a[1] are roots of nonempty subtrees. We work from the "bottom" subtree up:

Level AB
(continued)

```
for (int rootIndex = n/2; rootIndex >= 1; rootIndex--)
    FixHeap(a, rootIndex, n);
```

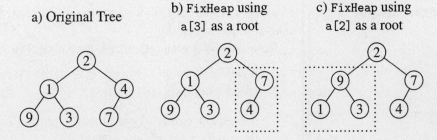

a) Original Tree   b) FixHeap using a[3] as a root   c) FixHeap using a[2] as a root

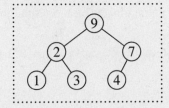

d) FixHeap using a[1] as a root   e) Tree is now a heap

This mental picture gives meaning to what is happening to the array—a sequence of swaps.

	a[1]	a[2]	a[3]	a[4]	a[5]	a[6]
Original array	2	1	4	9	3	7
FixHeap(a,3,6)	2	1	7	9	3	4
FixHeap(a,2,6)	2	9	7	1	3	4
FixHeap(a,1,6)	9	2	7	1	3	4
	9	3	7	1	2	4

III. Sort the array using the heap property that the biggest element is at the top of the tree: Swap a[1] and a[n]. Now a[n] is in its final sorted position in the array. Reduce *n* by one (think of it as an apple that has dropped off the tree), and restore the heap using one fewer elements. Eventually there will be just one element in the tree, at which stage the array will be sorted.

```
while(n > 1)
{
    Swap(a[1], a[n]);
    n--;
    FixHeap(a,1,n); //rootIndex is 1 in each case
}
```

a) Tree is a heap

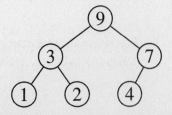

Level AB
(*continued*)

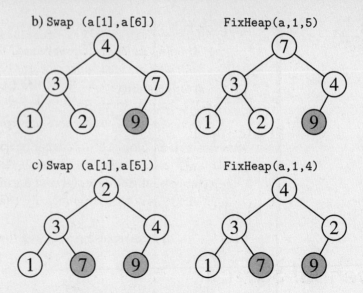

b) Swap (a[1],a[6])   FixHeap(a,1,5)

c) Swap (a[1],a[5])   FixHeap(a,1,4)

... and so on until Swap(a[1],a[2]) yields

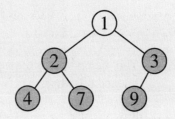

Here is the sequence of swaps in the array, starting after the tree has been formed into a heap.

	a[1]	a[2]	a[3]	a[4]	a[5]	a[6]
heap	9	3	7	1	2	4
swap	4	3	7	1	2	9
fix	7	3	4	1	2	9
swap	2	3	4	1	7	9
fix	4	3	2	1	7	9
swap	1	3	2	4	7	9
fix	3	1	2	4	7	9
swap	2	1	3	4	7	9
sorted!	1	2	3	4	7	9

Note that the FixHeap function in parts I and II of this algorithm assumes that the heap property is violated only by the root node (i.e., if you cover the root, the rest of the tree looks like a heap).

Analysis of Heapsort

1. For small n, this is not very efficient because of the initial overhead: Array elements must be rearranged to satisfy the heap property—the largest element must be moved to the "top" of the heap, and then moved again to the end of the array.

Level AB
(continued)

2. Heapsort is very efficient for large n.

    a) Building the original heap has $n/2$ iterations, each containing a FixHeap call, which, in the worst case, travels to the bottom (highest level) of the tree, $\log_2 n$ iterations. Thus, building the original heap is $O(n \log n)$.

    b) The sorting loop: $(n-2)$ iterations of an $O(1)$ swap and $O(\log n)$ Fixheap-ing. Thus the sorting piece of the algorithm is also $O(n \log n)$.

3. Heapsort is an "in-place" sort requiring no temporary storage. Its best, average, and worst case running times are all $O(n \log n)$. The worst case is only 20 percent worse than its average running time! This means that the order of the input elements does not significantly affect the running time.

Sequential Search

Assume that you are searching for a key in a list of n elements. A sequential search starts at the first element and compares the key to each element in turn until the key is found or there are no more elements to examine in the list. If the list is sorted, in ascending order, say, stop searching as soon as the key is less than the current list element.

Level AB Only

Analysis:
1. The best case has key in the first slot, and the search is $O(1)$.
2. Worst case occurs if the key is in the last slot or not in the list. All n elements must be examined, and the algorithm is $O(n)$.
3. On average, there will be $n/2$ comparisons, which is also $O(n)$.

Binary Search

If the elements are in a *sorted* array, a divide-and-conquer approach provides a much more efficient searching algorithm. The following recursive pseudo-code algorithm shows how the *binary search* works.

    Assume that a[low] ... a[high] is sorted in ascending order and that a function BinSearch returns the index of key. If key is not in the array, it returns -1.

```
if (low > high) //Base case. No elements left in array
    return -1;
else
    mid = (low + high)/2;
    if (key == a[mid]) //found the key
        return mid;
    else if (key < a[mid]) //key in left half of array
        <BinSearch for key in a[low] to a[mid - 1]>
    else // key in right half of array
        <BinSearch for key in a[mid + 1] to a[high]>
```

NOTE   When `low` and `high` cross, there are no more elements to examine and `key` is not in the array.

For example, suppose 5 is the key to be found in the following array:

a[0]	a[1]	a[2]	a[3]	a[4]	a[5]	a[6]	a[7]	a[8]
1	4	5	7	9	12	15	20	21

First pass: `mid = (8+0)/2 = 4`.   Check `a[4]`.
Second pass: `mid = (0+3)/2 = 1`.   Check `a[1]`.
Third pass: `mid = (2+3)/2 = 2`.   Check `a[2]`. Yes! Key is found.

Level AB Only

Analysis of Binary Search:

1. In the best case, we find the key on the first try (i.e., `(low + high)/2` is the index of `key`.) This is $O(1)$.
2. In the worst case, the key is not in the list or is at either end of a sublist. Here the n elements must be divided by 2 until there is just one element and then that last element must be tested. This equals $1 + \log_2 n$ comparisons. Thus, in the worst case, the algorithm is $O(\log n)$. An easy way to find the number of comparisons in the worst case is to round n up to the next power of 2 and take the exponent. For example, in the array above $n = 9$. Suppose 21 were the key. Round 9 up to 16, which equals 2^4. Thus, you would need four comparisons to find it. Try it!
3. In the average case, you need about half the comparisons of the worst case, so the algorithm is still $O(\log n)$.

Hash Coding

Level AB Only

Description

A *hash table* stores data of some type (`tableElementType`) with an associated *key field* of type `keyType`. Ideally, a hash table should provide for efficient insertion and retrieval of items.

Here is a simple example of hash coding. A catalog company stores customer orders in an array as follows. The last two digits of the customer's phone number provide the index in the array for that particular customer's order. Thus, two customers with phone numbers 257-3178 and 253-5169 will have their orders stored in `list[78]` and `list[69]`, respectively. In this example, the *hash table* is an array, the *key field* is a phone number, the *hash function* is (phone number mod 100), and the *hash address* is the array index.

The simplest implementation of the hash table ADT is an array of data items. To insert or retrieve any given item, a *hash function* is performed on the key field of the item, which returns the array index or *hash address* of that item. This method cannot guarantee a unique address for each data item.

For example, suppose a small business maintains employee data in an employeeList. If socialSecurityNo is the key field, and (socialSecurityNo % 100) is the hash function, 567350347 and 203479247 both hash to the same address: employeeList[47].

A good hash function minimizes such *collisions* by spreading them uniformly through the key field values.

Resolving
Collisions

Hash and Search (or Open Addressing with Linear Probing)

Store the colliding element in the next available slot. An example for storing data with keyValue 556677003 is shown in the following table.

employeeList

[00]	empty
[01]	453614001
[02]	empty
[03]	123467003
[04]	689286004
[05]	empty
⋮	
[99]	618272899

The hash function yields hash address 03. employeeList[03] already contains data, so we try slot [04] and so on. In this example, the new data gets stored in employeeList[05]. If the key hashes to the last slot in the array and is filled, treat it as a circular structure and go back to the beginning of the array to search for an empty slot.

In this scheme, searching for a given data item involves
1. Hash and compare.
2. If keys don't match, do a sequential search starting at that slot in the array.

Rehashing

If the first computation causes a collision, compute a new hash address using the old hash address as input. Repeat if necessary. Typically, a rehash function has form (hash address + <const>) % <number of slots> where "const" and "number of slots" are relatively prime (i.e., no common factors greater than 1). This ensures that every index will be covered.

Level AB
(continued)

For example, the hash function for this table is key % 10. The rehash function is (hash address + 3) % 10. (Note that 3 and 10 are relatively prime.) Here are the steps to insert 26402 into the table:

26402 % 10 = 02	(taken)	
(2 + 3) % 10 = 05	(taken)	
(5 + 3) % 10 = 08,	which becomes the hash address of the new item.	

[00]	
[01]	27401
[02]	68902
[03]	
[04]	
[05]	67905
[06]	
[07]	
[08]	
[09]	27309

These methods are simple to implement but are less than ideal in resolving collisions. What follows is more elegant.

Chaining

In this method, the hash address is the index for an array of pointers called *buckets*. Each bucket points to a linear linked list of data items that share the same hash address.

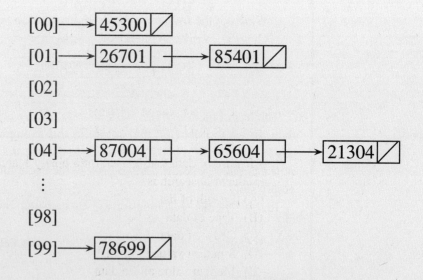

To insert an item, hash to the appropriate bucket and insert at the front of the list. Thus, insertion is $O(1)$. To search for an item, apply the hash function and do a sequential search of the appropriate list. Assuming that items are uniformly distributed in the hash table, a search should occur in constant time, which is $O(1)$.

In summary, a good hash function should

1. Distribute data items uniformly throughout the hash table.
2. Provide for $O(1)$ insertion and searching.

Multiple-Choice Questions on Sorting and Searching

1. The decision to choose a particular sorting algorithm should be made based on

     I Run-time efficiency of the sort
    II Size of the array
   III Space efficiency of the algorithm

   (A) I only
   (B) II only
   (C) III only
   (D) I and II only
   (E) I, II, and III

2. The following code fragment does a sequential search to determine whether a given integer, `value`, is stored in an array `a[0] ... a[n-1]`.

```
int i = -1;
do
{
    i++;
} while ( < boolean expression > );
return i;
```

   Which of the following should replace < *boolean expression* > so that the algorithm works as intended?
   (A) `value == a[i]`
   (B) `value != a[i]`
   (C) `value != a[i] && i < n`
   (D) `i < n && value != a[i]`
   (E) `i < n || value != a[i]`

3. A feature of data that is used for a binary search but not necessarily used for a sequential search is
   (A) Length of list
   (B) Type of data
   (C) Order of data
   (D) Smallest value in the list
   (E) Median value of the data

4. An unsorted list of integers is stored in an array. Having the list unsorted leads to inefficient execution for which of the following operations?
   I Inserting a new element
   II Searching for a given element
   III Computing the mean of the elements

   (A) I only
   (B) II only
   (C) III only
   (D) I and II only
   (E) I, II, and III

5. An algorithm for searching a large sorted array for a specific value x compares every third item in the array to x until it finds one that is greater than or equal to x. Whenever a larger value is found, the algorithm compares x to the previous two items. If the array is sorted in increasing order, which of the following describes all cases when this algorithm uses fewer comparisons to find x than would a binary search?
   (A) It will never use fewer comparisons.
   (B) When x is in the middle position of the array
   (C) When x is very close to the beginning of the array
   (D) When x is very close to the end of the array
   (E) When x is not in the array

6. Assume that A[0] ... A[N-1] is an array of N positive integers and that the following assertion is true:

   $$\text{A[0]} > \text{A[k]} \text{ for all } k \text{ such that } 0 < k < N$$

   Which of the following *must* be true?
   (A) The array is sorted in ascending order.
   (B) The array is sorted in descending order.
   (C) All values in the array are identical.
   (D) A[0] holds the smallest value in the array.
   (E) A[0] holds the largest value in the array.

7. The following code is designed to set index to the location of the first occurrence of key in array a and to set index to -1 if key is not in a.

```
index=0;
while (a[index] != key)
    index++;
if (a[index] != key)
    index = -1;
```

   In which case will this program *definitely* fail to perform the task described?
   (A) When key is the first element of the array
   (B) When key is the last element of the array
   (C) When key is not in the array
   (D) When key is 0
   (E) When key equals a[key]

8. Refer to function Search.

```
int Search(const apvector <int> & v, int key)
//precondition: v[0]...v[v.length()-1] are initialized
//postcondition: Returns k such that -1 ≤ k ≤ v.length()-1
//   If k ≥ 0 then v[k] = key
//   If k = -1 then key != any of the elements in v
{
    int index = 0;
    while (index < v.length()-1 && v[index] < key)
        index++;
    if (v[index] == key)
        return index;
    else
        return -1;
}
```

Which of the following should be added to the precondition of Search?
(A) v is sorted smallest to largest.
(B) v is sorted largest to smallest.
(C) v is unsorted.
(D) There is at least one occurrence of key in v.
(E) key occurs no more than once in v.

Questions 9–14 are based on the following code and the given list a[0] ... a[7].

```
int BinSearch(const apvector <int> &a, int n, int key)
// Does binary search for key in array a[0]...a[n-1], sorted
// in ascending order.
// Returns index such that a[index]=key. If key not in a,
// returns -1

int low,high,mid;
{
    low = 0;
    high = n-1;
    while (low <= high)
    {
        mid = (low + high)/2;
        if (a[mid] == key)
            return mid;
        else if (a[mid] < key)
            low = mid + 1;
        else
            high = mid - 1;
    }
    return -1;
}
```

A binary search will be performed on the following list.

a[0]	a[1]	a[2]	a[3]	a[4]	a[5]	a[6]	a[7]
4	7	9	11	20	24	30	41

9. To find the key value 27, the search interval *after* the first pass through the while loop will be
   (A) a[0] ... a[7]
   (B) a[5] ... a[6]
   (C) a[4] ... a[7]
   (D) a[2] ... a[6]
   (E) a[6] ... a[7]

10. Approximately how many iterations will be required to determine that 27 is not in the list?
    (A) 1
    (B) 4
    (C) 8
    (D) 27
    (E) an infinite loop since 27 is not found

11. What will be stored in y after executing the following?
    ```
    int y = BinSearch(a, 8, 4);
    ```
    (A) 20
    (B) 7
    (C) 4
    (D) 0
    (E) -1

12. If the test for the while loop is changed to
    ```
    while (low < high)
    ```
    the BinSearch function does not work as intended. Which value in the given list will not be found?
    (A) 4
    (B) 7
    (C) 11
    (D) 24
    (E) 30

13. For BinSearch which of the following assertions will be true following every iteration of the while loop?
    (A) key = a[mid] or key is not in a.
    (B) a[low] ≤ key ≤ a[high]
    (C) low ≤ mid ≤ high
    (D) key = a[mid], or a[low] ≤ key ≤ a[high]
    (E) key = a[mid], or a[low] ≤ key ≤ a[high], or key is not in array a.

Level AB Only

14. A loop invariant for the while loop is: key is not in array a or
    (A) a[low] < key < a[high],   0 ≤ low ≤ high+1 ≤ n
    (B) a[low] ≤ key ≤ a[high],   0 ≤ low ≤ high+1 ≤ n
    (C) a[low] ≤ key ≤ a[high],   0 ≤ low ≤ high ≤ n
    (D) a[low] < key < a[high],   0 ≤ low ≤ high ≤ n
    (E) a[low] ≤ key ≤ a[high],   0 ≤ low ≤ high ≤ n-1

Consider the following code for Questions 15–19.

```
void InsertionSort(apvector <int> &a, int n)
//precondition: a[0],a[1]...a[n-1] is an unsorted list of
//                integers
//postcondition: list a is sorted in descending order

{
    int i,j, temp;

    for (i=1; i<=n-1; i++)
    {
        temp = a[i];
        j = i - 1;
        while (j>=0 && temp>a[j])
        {
            a[j+1] = a[j];
            j--;
        }
        a[j+1] = temp;
    }
}
```

15. An array is to be sorted biggest to smallest using the InsertionSort function. If the array originally contains

    1   7   9   5   4   12

    what will it look like after the third pass of the for loop?
    (A) 9 7 1 5 4 12
    (B) 9 7 5 1 4 12
    (C) 12 9 7 1 5 4
    (D) 12 9 7 5 4 1
    (E) 9 7 12 5 4 1

16. When sorted biggest to smallest with InsertionSort, which list will need the fewest changes of position for individual elements?
    (A) 5, 1, 2, 3, 4, 9
    (B) 9, 5, 1, 4, 3, 2
    (C) 9, 4, 2, 5, 1, 3
    (D) 9, 3, 5, 1, 4, 2
    (E) 3, 2, 1, 9, 5, 4

17. When sorted biggest to smallest with InsertionSort, which list will need the greatest number of changes in position?
    (A) 5, 1, 2, 3, 4, 9
    (B) 9, 5, 1, 4, 3, 2
    (C) 9, 4, 2, 5, 1, 3
    (D) 9, 3, 5, 1, 4, 2
    (E) 3, 2, 1, 9, 5, 4

18. While typing the `InsertionSort` function, a programmer by mistake enters

    `while (temp > a[j])`

    instead of

    `while (j >= 0 && temp > a[j])`

    Despite this mistake, the function works as intended the first time the programmer enters an array to be sorted in descending order. Which of the following could explain this?
       I The first element in the array was the largest element in the array.
      II The array was already sorted in descending order.
     III The first element was less than or equal to all the other elements in the array.

    (A) I only
    (B) II only
    (C) III only
    (D) I and II only
    (E) None

Level AB Only

19. A loop invariant for the outer loop (the `for` loop) is
    (A) `a[0]` $\geq$ `a[1]` $\geq$ ... $\geq$ `a[i-1]`, $0 \leq i \leq n$
    (B) `a[0]` $>$ `a[1]` $>$ ... $>$ `a[i-1]`, $1 \leq i \leq n$
    (C) `a[0]` $\geq$ `a[1]` $\geq$ ... $\geq$ `a[i]`, $0 \leq i \leq n - 1$
    (D) `a[0]` $>$ `a[1]` $>$ ... $>$ `a[i]`, $1 \leq i \leq n$
    (E) `a[0]` $\geq$ `a[1]` $\geq$ ... $\geq$ `a[i-1]`, $1 \leq i \leq n$

Consider the following code for Questions 20 and 21.

```
void SelectionSort(apvector <int> &a, int n)
//precondition: a[0],a[1]...a[n-1] is an unsorted list of
//              integers
//postcondition: list a is sorted in descending order
{
    int i,j, maxPos, max;

    for (i=0; i<=n-2; i++)
    {
        //find max element in a[i+1] to a[n-1]
        max = a[i];
        maxPos = i;
        for (j=i+1; j<n; j++)
            if (a[j] > max)
            {
                max = a[j];
                maxPos = j;
            }
        Swap(a[i], a[maxPos]);
    }
}
```

20. If an array contains the following elements, what would the array look like after the third pass of SelectionSort, sorting from high to low?

$$89 \quad 42 \quad -3 \quad 13 \quad 109 \quad 70 \quad 2$$

    (A) 109   89   70   13   42   -3   2

    (B) 109   89   70   42   13   2   -3

    (C) 109   89   70   -3   2   13   42

    (D) 89   42   13   -3   109   70   2

    (E) 109   89   42   -3   13   70   2

Level AB Only

21. A loop invariant for the outer for loop of SelectionSort is

    (A) $a[0] \geq a[1] \geq \ldots \geq a[i-1]$, $0 \leq i \leq n-1$

    (B) $a[0] \geq a[1] \geq \ldots \geq a[i]$, $0 \leq i \leq n-1$

    (C) $a[0] \geq a[1] \geq \ldots \geq a[i-1]$, $0 \leq i \leq n-2$

    (D) $a[0] \geq a[1] \geq \ldots \geq a[i]$, $0 \leq i \leq n-2$

    (E) $a[0] \geq a[1] \geq \ldots \geq a[n-1]$, $0 \leq i \leq n-1$

22. The elements in a long list of integers are roughly sorted in decreasing order. No more than 5 percent of the elements are out of order. Which of the following is a valid reason for using an insertion sort rather than a selection sort to sort this list into decreasing order?

    I There will be fewer comparisons of elements for insertion sort.
    II There will be fewer changes of position of elements for insertion sort.
    III There will be less space required for insertion sort.

    (A) I only
    (B) II only
    (C) III only
    (D) I and II only
    (E) I, II, and III

23. The code shown sorts array a[0] ... a[n-1] in descending order.

```
void Sort(apvector <int> &a, int n)
{
    int i,j;
    for (i=0; i<n-1; i++)
        for (j=0; j<n-i-1; j++)
            if (a[j] < a[j+1])
                Swap(a[j], a[j+1]);
}
```

    This is an example of
    (A) Selection sort
    (B) Insertion sort
    (C) Mergesort
    (D) Quicksort
    (E) None of the above

24. Which of the following is a valid reason why mergesort is a better sorting algorithm than insertion sort for sorting long lists?

    I Mergesort requires less code than insertion sort.
    II Mergesort requires less storage space than insertion sort.
    III Mergesort runs faster than insertion sort.

    (A) I only
    (B) II only
    (C) III only
    (D) I and II only
    (E) II and III only

25. A large array of lowercase characters is to be searched for the pattern "pqrs." The first step in a very efficient searching algorithm is to look at characters with index

    (A) 0, 1, 2, ... until a "p" is encountered
    (B) 0, 1, 2, ... until any letter in "p" ... s" is encountered
    (C) 3, 7, 11, ... until an "s" is encountered
    (D) 3, 7, 11, ... until any letter in "p" ... "s" is encountered
    (E) 3, 7, 11, ... until any letter other than "p" ... "s" is encountered

26. `L[0]`, `L[1]`, ... , `L[9999]` is a list of 10,000 name strings. The list is to be searched to determine the location of some name `X` in the list. Which of the following preconditions is necessary for a binary search?
    - (A) There are no duplicate names in the list.
    - (B) The number of names N in the list is large.
    - (C) The list is in alphabetical order.
    - (D) Name `X` is definitely in the list.
    - (E) Name `X` occurs toward the end of the list.

27. Consider the following function:

```
int SomeFunction(const apvector <int> &a, int n, int value)
// precondition: a[0],a[1]...a[n-1] contain integers
{
    if (n == 0)
        return -1;
    else
    {
        if (a[n-1] == value)
            return n-1;
        else
            return SomeFunction(a,n-1,value);
    }
}
```

    `SomeFunction` is an example of
    - (A) Insertion sort
    - (B) Mergesort
    - (C) Selection sort
    - (D) Binary search
    - (E) Sequential search

28. The `Partition` function for quicksort partitions a list as follows: (i) A pivot element is selected from the array. (ii) The elements of the list are rearranged such that all elements to the left of the pivot are less than or equal to it; all elements to the right of the pivot are greater than or equal to it. Partitioning the array requires which of the following:
    - (A) A recursive algorithm
    - (B) A temporary array
    - (C) An external file for the array
    - (D) A swap algorithm for interchanging array elements
    - (E) A merge function for merging two sorted lists

29. Quicksort is performed on the following array:

$$45 \quad 40 \quad 77 \quad 20 \quad 65 \quad 52 \quad 90 \quad 15 \quad 95 \quad 79$$

The first element, 45, is used as the pivot. After one iteration of quicksort (i.e., after the first partitioning), which must be true?
   I 45 will be the fourth element of the array.
   II All elements to the left of 45 will be sorted.
   III All elements to the right of 45 will be greater than or equal to 45.

   (A) I only
   (B) II only
   (C) III only
   (D) I and III only
   (E) II and III only

30. Consider the following code for mergesort:

```
void MergeSort(apvector <int> &a, int first, int last)
// sorts a[first] to a[last] in increasing order
// using mergesort
{
    int mid;

    if (first != last)
    {
        mid = (first+last)/2;
        MergeSort(a, first, mid);
        MergeSort(a, mid+1, last);
        Merge(a, first, mid, last);
    }
}
```

Function MergeSort calls function Merge, which has this header:

```
void Merge(apvector <int> &a, int low, int middle, int high)
// merges a[low]...a[middle] and a[middle+1]...a[high],
// assuming both parts sorted in increasing order
```

If MergeSort is first called with the parameters MergeSort(b,0,3), how many *further* calls will there be to MergeSort before array b[0]...b[3] is sorted?
   (A) 2
   (B) 3
   (C) 4
   (D) 5
   (E) 6

Level AB Only

31. A binary search is to be performed on an array with 600 elements. In the *worst* case, which of the following best approximates the number of iterations of the algorithm?
    (A) 6
    (B) 10
    (C) 100
    (D) 300
    (E) 600

32. A worst case situation for insertion sort would be
    I   A list in correct sorted order
    II A list sorted in reverse order
    III A list in random order

    (A) I only
    (B) II only
    (C) III only
    (D) I and II only
    (E) II and III only

33. Which of the following represents a heap?

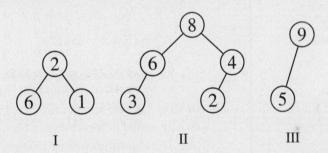

    I   II   III

    (A) I only
    (B) II only
    (C) III only
    (D) I and III only
    (E) II and III only

34. The list

    17   9   2   7   21   18   4   5

    is to be sorted into ascending order using heapsort. What is the level of the binary tree that will be formed, given that the root is at level 0?
    (A) 0
    (B) 1
    (C) 2
    (D) 3
    (E) 4

Level AB
(continued)

35. Assume array a[1]...a[7] = 6 1 5 9 8 4 7 is to be sorted using heapsort. Which of the following represents the correct sequence of swaps to be made to form the array into the original heap?

    (A) | 6 | 1 | 7 | 9 | 8 | 4 | 5 |
    |---|---|---|---|---|---|---|
    | 6 | 9 | 7 | 1 | 8 | 4 | 5 |
    | 9 | 6 | 7 | 1 | 8 | 4 | 5 |
    | 9 | 8 | 7 | 1 | 6 | 4 | 5 |

    (B) | 6 | 1 | 5 | 9 | 8 | 4 | 7 |
    |---|---|---|---|---|---|---|
    | 6 | 9 | 5 | 1 | 8 | 4 | 7 |
    | 9 | 6 | 5 | 1 | 8 | 4 | 7 |
    | 9 | 6 | 7 | 1 | 8 | 4 | 5 |

    (C) | 6 | 1 | 7 | 9 | 8 | 4 | 5 |
    |---|---|---|---|---|---|---|
    | 7 | 1 | 6 | 9 | 8 | 4 | 5 |
    | 7 | 9 | 6 | 1 | 8 | 4 | 5 |
    | 9 | 7 | 6 | 1 | 8 | 4 | 5 |
    | 9 | 8 | 6 | 1 | 7 | 4 | 5 |

    (D) | 6 | 9 | 5 | 1 | 8 | 4 | 7 |
    |---|---|---|---|---|---|---|
    | 9 | 6 | 5 | 1 | 8 | 4 | 7 |
    | 9 | 6 | 7 | 1 | 8 | 4 | 5 |
    | 9 | 8 | 7 | 1 | 6 | 4 | 5 |

    (E) None of these sequences is correct.

36. An array is to be sorted into increasing order using quicksort. If the array is initially sorted in increasing order, which of the following *must* be true?
    (A) The algorithm will be $O(n)$.
    (B) The algorithm will be $O(n \log n)$.
    (C) The algorithm will be $O(n^2)$.
    (D) The efficiency of the algorithm depends on how the pivot element is selected.
    (E) The run time will be quicker if heapsort is used instead.

37. Which represents the worst case performance of the sequential search and binary search, respectively?
    (A) $O(n^2)$, $O(n \log n)$
    (B) $O(n)$, $O(n \log n)$
    (C) $O(n)$, $O(n)$
    (D) $O(n)$, $O(\log n)$
    (E) $O(n^2)$, $O(\log n)$

38. A typical algorithm to search an ordered list of numbers has an execution time of $O(\log_2 n)$. Which of the following choices is closest to the maximum number of times that such an algorithm will execute its main comparison loop when searching an ordered list of 1 million numbers?
    (A) 6
    (B) 20
    (C) 100
    (D) 120
    (E) 1000

39. A certain algorithm sequentially examines a list of n random integers and then outputs the number of times 8 occurs in the list. Using big-O notation, this algorithm is
    (A) $O(1)$
    (B) $O(8)$
    (C) $O(n)$
    (D) $O(n^2)$
    (E) $O(\log n)$

40. Which represents the worst case performance of mergesort, quicksort, and heapsort, respectively?
    (A) $O(n \log n)$, $O(n \log n)$, $O(n \log n)$
    (B) $O(n \log n)$, $O(n^2)$, $O(n \log n)$
    (C) $O(n^2)$, $O(n^2)$, $O(n^2)$
    (D) $O(\log n)$, $O(n^2)$, $O(\log n)$
    (E) $O(2^n)$, $O(n^2)$, $O(n \log n)$

41. Consider these three tasks:
    I   A linear search of an array of n names
    II A binary search of an array of n names in alphabetical order
    III A quicksort into alphabetical order of an array of n names that are initially in random order.

    For large n, which of the following lists these tasks in order (from least to greatest) of their worst case running times?
    (A) II   I   III
    (B) I   II   III
    (C) II   III   I
    (D) III   I   II
    (E) III   II   I

42. The efficiency of a hash function depends on which of the following:
    I   The number of collisions that occur
    II The size of the data items in the list
    III The method of dealing with collisions

    (A) I only
    (B) III only
    (C) I and III only
    (D) I and II only
    (E) I, II, and III

43. The following key values are to be inserted into the hash table shown in the order given:

$$10 \quad 28 \quad 2 \quad 7 \quad 45 \quad 25 \quad 40 \quad 29$$

array index	0	1	2	3	4	5	6	7	8	9	10
key value											

The hash function is key % 11. Collisions will be resolved with the Open Addressing and Linear Probing ("hash-and-search") method. Which array slot will 29 eventually occupy?

(A) 7
(B) 8
(C) 9
(D) 10
(E) 0

44. An array contains data that was hash coded into it. How should this array be searched?

(A) A linear search should be used on the key data fields.
(B) If the array is sorted on the key fields, a binary search should be used.
(C) The C++ % operation should be applied to the key to obtain the correct array location.
(D) An exclusive-or (XOR) should be applied to the key to obtain the correct array location.
(E) The hash function and a collision resolution algorithm should be applied to the key field to find the correct location.

45. A certain hash function $h(x)$ on a key field places records with the following key fields into a hash table.

$$62 \quad 79 \quad 81 \quad 12 \quad 54 \quad 97 \quad 34$$

Collisions are handled with a rehashing function $r(x)$, which takes as an argument the result of applying $h(x)$. If the key values are entered in the order shown to produce the following table:

0	1	2	3	4	5	6	7	8	9	10	11	12	13	14	15	16	17	18	19
	81	62						34				12		54			97		79

then $h(x)$ and $r(x)$ are, respectively,

(A) key % 20, (result + 13) % 20
(B) key % 20, result % 20
(C) key % 30, (result + 14) % 20
(D) key % 20, (result + 7) % 20
(E) key % 30, (result + 7) % 30

Answer Key

1. **E**	16. **B**	31. **B**
2. **D**	17. **A**	32. **B**
3. **C**	18. **D**	33. **C**
4. **B**	19. **E**	34. **D**
5. **C**	20. **A**	35. **A**
6. **E**	21. **A**	36. **D**
7. **C**	22. **A**	37. **D**
8. **A**	23. **E**	38. **B**
9. **C**	24. **C**	39. **C**
10. **B**	25. **D**	40. **B**
11. **D**	26. **C**	41. **A**
12. **A**	27. **E**	42. **C**
13. **E**	28. **D**	43. **C**
14. **B**	29. **D**	44. **E**
15. **B**	30. **E**	45. **D**

Answers Explained

1. **(E)** The time and space requirements of sorting algorithms are affected by all three of the given factors, so all must be considered when choosing a particular sorting algorithm.

2. **(D)** Choice A doesn't make sense: the loop will be exited as soon as a value is found that does *not* equal `a[i]`. Eliminate choice B because, if value is not in the array, `a[i]` will eventually go out of bounds. You need the `i < n` part of the boolean expression to avoid this. But `i < n` must precede `value != a[i]` so that if `i < n` fails, the expression will be evaluated as false, the test will be short-circuited, and an out-of-range error will be avoided. Choice C does not avoid this error. Choice E is wrong because both parts of the expression must be true in order to continue the search.

3. **(C)** Binary search depends on the array being sorted. Sequential search has no ordering requirement. Both depend on choice A, the length of the list, while the other choices are irrelevant to both algorithms.

4. **(B)** Inserting a new element is quick and easy in this scheme—just add it to the end of the list. Computing the mean involves finding the sum of the elements and dividing by *n*, the number of elements. The execution time is the same whether the list is sorted or not. Operation II, searching, is inefficient for an unsorted list, since a sequential search must be used. If the list were sorted, the efficient binary search algorithm, which involves fewer comparisons, could be

used. In fact, if the list were sorted, even a sequential search would be more efficient than for an unsorted list if the search item were not in list: the search could stop as soon as list elements were greater than the search item.

5. **(C)** Suppose the array has 1000 elements and x is somewhere in the first 8 slots. The algorithm described will find x using no more than five comparisons. A binary search, by contrast, will chop the array in half and do a comparison six times before examining elements in the first 15 slots of the array (array size after each chop: 500, 250, 125, 62, 31, 15).

6. **(E)** The assertion states that the first element is greater than all the other elements in the array. This eliminates choices A, C, and D. Choice B is incorrect because you have no information about the relative sizes of elements `A[1]...A[N-1]`.

7. **(C)** When `key` is not in the array, `index` will eventually be large enough that `a[index]` will give an out-of-range error. In choices A and B, the algorithm will find `key` without error. Choice D won't fail if 0 is in the array. Choice E will work if `a[key]` is not out of range.

8. **(A)** The algorithm uses the fact that array `v` is sorted smallest to largest. The `while` loop terminates—which means that the search stops—as soon as `v[index] >= key`.

9. **(C)** The first pass uses the interval `a[0]...a[7]`. Since `mid` $= (0+7)/2 = 3$, `low` gets adjusted to `mid` $+1 = 4$, and the second pass uses the interval `a[4]...a[7]`.

10. **(B)** First pass: compare 27 with `a[3]`, since `low=0 high=7 mid=` $(0+7)/2 = 3$
   Second pass: compare 27 with `a[5]`, since `low=4 high=7 mid=` $(4+7)/2 = 5$
   Third pass: compare 27 with `a[6]`, since `low=6 high=7 mid=` $(6+7)/2 = 6$
   Fourth pass: compare 27 with `a[7]`, since `low=7 high=7 mid=` $(7+7)/2 = 7$
   The fifth pass doesn't happen, since `low=8`, `high=7`, and (`low <= high`) fails. Here's the general rule for finding the number of iterations when `key` is not in the list: There are eight elements in the list. Go up to the next power of 2, which is 16 in this case. $16 = 2^4$ implies four iterations of the "divide-and-compare" loop.

11. **(D)** The function returns the index of the `key` parameter, 4. Since `a[0]` contains 4, `BinSearch(a, 8, 4)` will return 0.

12. **(A)** Try 4. Here are the values for `low`, `high`, and `mid` when searching for 4:

First pass:	`low` $= 0$,	`high` $= 7$,	`mid` $= 3$
Second pass:	`low` $= 0$,	`high` $= 2$,	`mid` $= 1$

   After this pass `high` gets adjusted to `mid` -1, which is 0. Now `low` equals `high` and the test for the `while` loop fails. The function returns -1, indicating that 4 wasn't found.

13. **(E)** When the loop is exited, either `key` = `a[mid]` (and `mid` has been returned) or `key` has not been found, in which case either `a[low]` $\leq$ `key` $\leq$ `a[high]` or `key` is not in the array. The correct assertion must account for all three possibilities.

14. **(B)** Note that `low` is initialized to 0 and `high` is initialized to n-1. It would appear that $0 \leq$ `low` $\leq$ `high` $\leq$ n-1. In the algorithm, however, if `key` is not in the array, `low` and `high` cross, which means `low > high` in that instance. The correct loop invariant inequality that covers all cases is, therefore, $0 \leq$ `low` $\leq$ `high+1` $\leq$ n, which eliminates choices C, D, and E. In the algorithm, the endpoints of the new subarray to be considered are adjusted to include `a[mid+1]` (if it's the right half) or `a[mid-1]` (for the left half). This means that `key` can be at one of the endpoints. Thus, `a[low]` $\leq$ `key` $\leq$ `a[high]` is the correct assertion.

15. **(B)** Start with the second element in the array.

After first pass:	7	1	9	5	4	12
After second pass:	9	7	1	5	4	12
After third pass:	9	7	5	1	4	12

16. **(B)** An insertion sort compares `a[1]` and `a[0]`. If they are not in the correct order, `a[0]` is moved and `a[1]` is inserted in its correct position. `a[2]` is then inserted in its correct position, and `a[0]` and `a[1]` are moved if necessary, and so on. Since B has only one element out of order, it will require the fewest changes.

17. **(A)** This list is almost sorted in reverse order. This is the worst case for insertion sort, requiring the greatest number of comparisons and moves.

18. **(D)** `j >= 0` is a stopping condition that prevents an element that is larger than all those to the left of it from going off the left end of the array. If no error occurred, it means that each `a[i]` (`temp`) was less than or equal to some `a[j]` for `j >= 0` (i.e., the insertion point was greater than index 0). Omitting the `j >= 0` test will cause a run-time (out-of-range) error whenever `a[i]` (`temp`) is bigger than all elements to the left of it (i.e., the insertion point is 0).

19. **(E)** Note that i is initialized to 1, and after the final pass through the `for` loop, i equals n. Thus, $1 \leq i \leq n$, which eliminates choices A and C. Eliminate choice B since there could be duplicates in the array and `a[0]` could equal `a[1]` ....

After initialization: $i = 1$ and `a[0]` is sorted

After first pass: $i = 2$ and `a[0]` $\geq$ `a[1]`

After second pass: $i = 3$ and `a[0]` $\geq$ `a[1]` $\geq$ `a[2]`

$\vdots$

In general, after initialization and each time the `for` loop is completed, `a[0]` $\geq$ `a[1]` $\geq \ldots \geq$ `a[i-1]`.

20. **(A)**

After first pass:	109	42	−3	13	89	70	2
After second pass:	109	89	−3	13	42	70	2
After third pass:	109	89	70	13	42	−3	2

21. **(A)** i is initialized to 0, and after the final pass through the `for` loop, i equals $n - 1$. Thus, $0 \le i \le n - 1$, which eliminates choices C and D. Choice E is wrong because it implies that the whole array is sorted after each pass through the loop.

    After initialization: $i = 0$, and no elements are sorted.

    After first pass: $i = 1$, and `a[0]` is sorted.

    After second pass: $i = 2$, and `a[0]` $\ge$ `a[1]`.

    $\vdots$

    In general, after initialization and each time the `for` loop is completed, `a[0]` $\ge$ `a[1]` $\ge$ ... $\ge$ `a[i-1]`.

22. **(A)** Look at a small array that is almost sorted:

    $$10 \; 8 \; 9 \; 6 \; 2$$

    For <u>insertion sort</u> you need four passes through this array.

    The first pass compares 8 and 10—one comparison, no moves.

    The second pass compares 9 and 8, then 9 and 10. The array becomes 10 9 8 6 2—two comparisons, two moves.

    The third and fourth passes compare 6 and 8, and 2 and 6—no moves.

    In summary, there are approximately one or two comparisons per pass and no more than two moves per pass.

    For <u>selection sort</u>, there are four passes too.

    The first pass finds the biggest element in the array and swaps it into the first position.

    The array is still 10 8 9 6 2—four comparisons. There are two moves if your algorithm makes the swap in this case, otherwise no moves.

    The second pass finds the biggest element from `a[1]` to `a[4]` and swaps it into the second position: 10 9 8 6 2—three comparisons, two moves.

    For the third pass there are two comparisons, and one for the fourth. There are zero or two moves each time.

    Summary: $4 + 3 + 2 + 1$ total comparisons and a possible two moves per pass. Notice that Reason I is valid. Selection sort makes the same number of comparisons irrespective of the state of the array. Insertion sort does far fewer comparisons if the array is almost sorted. Reason II is invalid. There are roughly the same number of data movements for insertion and selection. Insertion may even have more changes, depending on how far from their insertion points the unsorted elements are. Reason III is wrong because insertion and selection sorts have the same space requirements.

23. **(E)** In the first pass through the outer `for` loop, the smallest element makes its way to the end of the array. In the second pass, the next smallest element moves to the second last slot, and so on. This is different from the sorts in choices A through D; in fact, it is a bubble sort.

24. **(C)** Reject Reason I. Mergesort requires both a `Merge` function and a `MergeSort` function—*more* code than the relatively short and simple code for insertion sort. Reject Reason II. The `Merge` algorithm uses a temporary array, which means *more* storage space than insertion sort. Reason III is correct. For long lists, the "divide-and-conquer" approach of mergesort gives it a faster run time than insertion sort.

25. **(D)** Since the search is for a four-letter sequence, the idea in this algorithm is that if you examine every fourth slot, you'll find a letter in the required sequence very quickly. When you find one of these letters, you can then examine adjacent slots to check if you have the required sequence. This method will, on average, result in fewer comparisons than the strictly sequential search algorithm in choice A. Choice B is wrong. If you encounter a "q," "r," or "s" without a "p" first, you can't have found "pqrs." Choice C is wrong because you may miss the sequence completely. Choice E doesn't make sense.

26. **(C)** The main precondition for a binary search is that the list is ordered.

27. **(E)** This algorithm is just a recursive implementation of a sequential search. It starts by testing if the last element in the array, a[n-1], is equal to value. If so, it returns the index n-1. Otherwise, it calls itself with n replaced by n-1. The net effect is that it examines a[n-1], a[n-2], ... The base case, if (n == 0), occurs when there are no elements left to examine. In this case, the function returns −1, signifying that value was not in the array.

28. **(D)** The Partition algorithm performs a series of swaps until the pivot element is swapped into its final sorted position (see Chapter 11). No temporary arrays or external files are used, nor is a recursive algorithm invoked. The Merge function is used for mergesort, not quicksort.

29. **(D)** During partitioning the array looks like this:

45	40	77	20	65	52	90	15	95	79
45	40	15	20	65	52	90	77	95	79
20	40	15	45	65	52	90	77	95	79

Note that 45, the pivot, is in its final sorted position, the fourth element in the array. All elements to the left of 45 are less than 45 but are not sorted with respect to each other. Similarly, all elements to the right of the pivot are greater than or equal to it but are unsorted.

30. (E) Here is a "box diagram" for MergeSort(b,0,3). The boldface numbers 1–6 show the order in which the MergeSort calls are made.

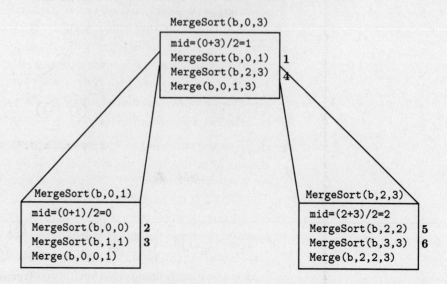

The MergeSort calls in which first == last are base case calls, which means that there will be no further function calls.

Level AB Only

31. (B) Round 600 up to the next power of 2, which is $1024 = 2^{10}$. For the worst case, the array will be split in half $\log_2 1024 = 10$ times.

32. (B) If the list is sorted in reverse order, each pass through the array will involve the maximum possible number of comparisons and the maximum possible number of element movements if an insertion sort is used.

33. (C) I violates the order property of a heap. II is not a complete binary tree.

34. (D) The elements will be inserted into the tree as shown, so the level of the tree is 3. (Remember that the top level of the tree is 0.)

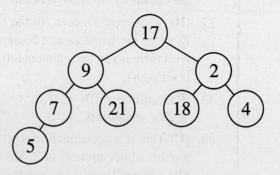

In fact, you don't need the tree or the actual elements!
The first element goes into level 0.
The next two elements go into level 1. (Total = 3)
The next four elements go into level 2. (Total = 7)
The next eight elements go into level 3. (Total = 15) . . . and so on.
Since the given array has eight elements, you need a tree with three levels.
(Note that the tree shown has not yet been formed into a heap.)

Level AB
(continued)

35. **(A)** The piece of code that forms the original heap is:

```
for (int rootIndex = n/2; rootIndex >= 1; rootIndex--)
    FixHeap(a,rootIndex,n);
```

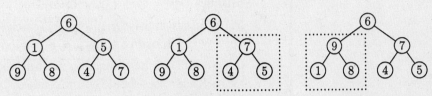

FixHeap(a,3,7)   FixHeap(a,2,7)

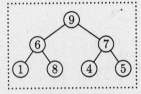

FixHeap(a,1,7)   Tree is now a heap

The sequence of swaps is:
    7 and 5
    9 and 1
    9 and 6
    8 and 6
This leads to choice A.

36. **(D)** Ideally in quicksort the pivot element should partition the array into two parts of roughly equal size. If the array is sorted and the pivot element is always the first (or last) element in the array, then one section of the array will always be empty after partitioning. This is a worst case for quicksort, $O(n^2)$. On the other hand, if the array is sorted and the pivot element is chosen near the middle of the array, quicksort will be very efficient.

37. **(D)** A sequential search, in the worst case, must examine all n elements—$O(n)$. In the worst case, a binary search will keep splitting the array in half until there is just one element left in the current subarray: $\log_2 n$ splits, which is $O(\log n)$.

38. **(B)** 1 million $= 10^6 = (10^3)^2 \approx (2^{10})^2 = 2^{20}$. Thus, there will be on the order of 20 comparisons.

39. **(C)** This is a sequential search that examines each element and counts the number of occurrences of 8. Since n comparisons are made, the algorithm is $O(n)$. Note: There is no such thing as $O(8)$.

40. **(B)** Mergesort works by breaking its array of n elements into n arrays of one element each, an $O(\log_2 n)$ process. Then it merges adjacent pairs of arrays until there is one sorted array, an $O(n)$ process. For each split of the array, the Merge function is called. Thus, mergesort is $O(n \log n)$ irrespective of the original ordering of the elements.

    The elements of heapsort are always placed in a balanced binary tree, which gives an $O(\log_2 n)$ process for fixing the heap. $n/2$ passes, each of which restores the heap, leads to an $O(n \log n)$ algorithm irrespective of the original ordering of the elements.

Quicksort partitions the array into two parts. The algorithm is $O(n \log n)$ only if the two parts of the array are roughly equal in length. In the worst case, this is not true—the pivot is the smallest or largest element in the array. The partition function, an $O(n)$ process, will then be called n times, and the algorithm becomes $O(n^2)$.

41. **(A)** A linear search is $O(n)$, a binary search $O(\log n)$, and quicksort $O(n \log n)$. For any large positive n, $\log n < n < n \log n$.

42. **(C)** An efficient hash function must have as few collisions as possible; i.e., the hash addresses should be uniformly distributed throughout the table. When there are collisions, the method of allocating a new hash address should, again, distribute these addresses uniformly throughout the table. The size of the data items is irrelevant since a hash function operates just on a *key field* of the data items.

43. **(C)** Just before 29 is inserted, the table will look like this:

array index	0	1	2	3	4	5	6	7	8	9	10
key value		45	2	25			28	7	40		10

Now 29 % 11 = 7. Slots 7 and 8 are taken, so 29 goes into slot 9.

44. **(E)** Hash coded data must always be searched with a hash function applied to the key field, followed by an algorithm that resolves any collisions.

45. **(D)** In the rehash function, result is the current hash address. Choice A works for all numbers except 34. 34 % 20 hashes to 14, which is taken by 54. (14+13) % 20 rehashes to 7, which is where 34 would go if this were the correct answer. Choice B doesn't successfully resolve collisions: 34 % 20 hashes to 14, which is already taken by 54. 14 % 20 rehashes to 14, the same slot. Recall that a rehash function of the form (result + <const>) % <number of slots> must be such that <const> and <number of slots> are relatively prime (i.e., no common factors other than 1). Otherwise, the function won't generate all the hash table slots. This eliminates choice C. Choice E produces 30 slots, but the table shown has just 20 slots. Element 81, for example, has no slot under this scheme, since 81 % 30 is 21 and `list[21]` does not exist. Choice D successfully places all the numbers in the table.

CHAPTER TWELVE

The Marine Biology Case Study

We have here other fish to fry.
—Francis Rabelais (1495–1553)

Part 1

General Description

This part simulates a fish swimming in a narrow rectangular tank. The program, aquamain.cpp, takes as input the tank size and number of steps in the simulation. The fish starts roughly in the center of the tank, and at each step of the simulation swims one foot, either left or right with equal probability. The program then outputs the number of times the fish bumps into the left or right boundary of the tank.

Use of Random Numbers

To mimic the unpredictability involved in real life events, a random number generator is used. In the case of the swimming fish, a random choice of 0 or 1 will determine whether the fish goes right or left, respectively.

The case study provides the RandGen class to produce random numbers of different types. You are expected to use this class as a "black box" (i.e., with no knowledge of the implementation of the member functions).

The RandGen Class

In general, a class can be represented by a box diagram (shaded region) in which private variables and private member functions are completely enclosed in the shaded region. Public member functions overlap the shaded region, whereas free (nonmember) functions are outside the shaded region.

The diagram at right represents the RandGen class and shows that there are two constructors and two different (overloaded) RandInt and RandReal functions.

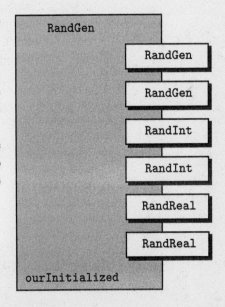

Any object constructed with the default constructor produces a different sequence of numbers every time the program is run. If a seed parameter is used, as in the second constructor, the same sequence of numbers will be produced by the same seed for each run of the program.

The function `RandInt(int max)` returns a random integer in [0 ... max) (i.e., including 0 but excluding max), whereas `RandInt(int low, int max)` returns a random integer in [low ... max] (i.e., including low and max). The function `RandReal()` returns a random `double` in [0 ... 1) (i.e., including 0 but excluding 1), whereas `RandReal(double low, double max)` returns a random `double` in [low ... max) (i.e., including low but excluding max).

Example 1

```
RandGen n;
int x = n.RandInt(4);        //x equals int 0,1,2, or 3
int y = n.RandInt(2,10);     //y equals int from 2 to 10 inclusive
double a = n.RandReal();     //a equals double from 0.0 to 1.0,
                             // including 0.0 but not 1.0
double b = n.RandReal(3.1,8.5); //b equals double from 3.1 to 8.5,
                             // including 3.1 but not 8.5
```

Example 2

```
RandGen m(123);      //RandGen object constructed with seed
for (int i=1; i<=10; i++)
    cout << m.RandInt(6) << endl;
//same sequence of 10 integers (from 0 to 5) printed for
//each run of program containing the above segment
```

The `AquaFish` Class

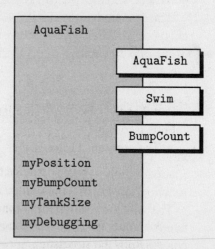

The fish in this program are objects of the `AquaFish` class. An object has both *state* and *behavior*. Its state refers to its personal attributes; its behavior, to the operations it can perform.

The state of an `AquaFish` object is contained in its private variables: `myTankSize` is initialized to be the user-entered `tankSize`. It is the number of possible fish positions in the tank. For example, if `myTankSize` is 5, picture the tank like this:

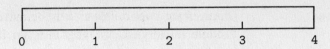

`myPosition` represents the fish's position in the tank. In the example shown in the figure, the possible values for `myPosition` are 0, 1, 2, 3, or 4. The initialization value for `myPosition` is `tankSize/2`, so the fish starts out roughly in the center of the tank. Note that when the fish gets to position 0 or 4 it "bumps" the side of the tank.

`myBumpCount` keeps track of the number of times the fish has bumped a side of the tank. In the example where `tankSize` is 5, `myBumpCount` would be incremented whenever `myPosition` is 0 or 4.

`myDebugging` is purely a tool for finding logic errors in the program. When `myDebugging` is set to true (which it is in the class constructor), the fish's position after each step will be output. If the constructor is changed so that `myDebugging` is set to false, the only output of the program will be the fish's bump count.

The behavior of an `AquaFish` object is encapsulated in the following member functions of the `AquaFish` class. The constructor needs the parameter `tankSize` because two of the private variables, `myTankSize` and `myPosition`, depend on it for initialization.

The `Swim()` function represents a single swimming move by the fish. If the fish is at an endpoint of the tank, it will automatically turn around and swim one foot in the opposite direction. Otherwise, it will move one foot to the right or left depending on the outcome of a random "flip." Note that the `Swim()` function is a modifier: `myPosition` will definitely be changed, and `myBumpCount` will be incremented if the fish bumps a side of the tank.

`BumpCount()` is an accessor that returns `myBumpCount` for the fish object.

Part 2

**General
Description**

Part 2 of the case study simulates a group of fish swimming in a small part of San Francisco Bay.

The program `fishsim.cpp` does the following:

1. Initializes and populates the fish environment from an input file `fish.dat`.
2. Displays the environment. Fish are represented as capital letters: A, B, C, ... Each cell of the grid contains no more than one fish.
3. Inputs from the user the number of steps in the simulation.
4. Runs the simulation. At each step,

    - Each fish attempts to move to an adjacent slot. There are four possible moves—north, south, east, or west. A fish may not move into an occupied spot nor may it leave the confines of the environment. A move is randomly selected from the available slots.
    - The updated environment is displayed.

Note that Part 2 of the case study has some similar features to Part 1 but that it is completely separate from it.

The Classes

Objects from seven different classes interact with each other in the fishsim program. The role and properties of each class are summarized next.

Position

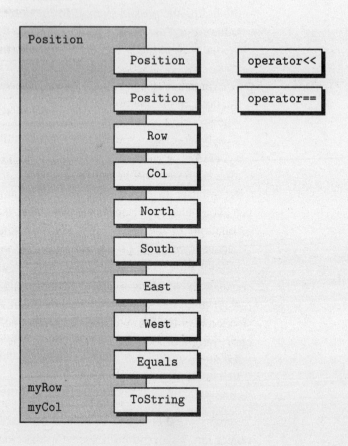

A Position object represents a two-dimensional grid position (row, column). Its only private variables are myRow and myCol. A Position representing (0, 0) can be thought of as corresponding to the top left-hand corner of an apmatrix. The default constructor initializes a Position to (−1, −1), which denotes a position not on the grid. A second constructor initializes a Position to a given row and column. Member functions North(), South(), East(), and West() each return a Position following a move of one unit in the indicated direction. Row() and Col() return the row or column number of the current Position. The function ToString() returns a Position in string form to facilitate output and debugging. The boolean function Equals() compares two positions and is used to overload the == operator. The overloaded << operator allows a Position object to be output.

Neighborhood

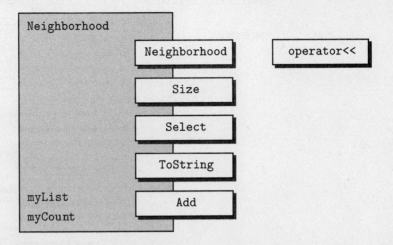

When a fish moves, it needs to know which neighboring positions are available. A `Neighborhood` object stores a list of these positions. It is implemented with `myList`, a four-element `apvector` of `Position`. The number of elements currently in the list is stored in `myCount` and returned by member function `Size()`. The `Neighborhood` constructor initializes `myList` to contain four slots and `myCount` to 0. The function `Select(index)` returns the `Position` in `myList[index]`. If there is room, `Add(pos)` stores a new `Position` at the end of the list. The function `ToString()` returns the entire neighborhood list in string form. The overloaded `<<` operator allows that list to be output.

RandGen

See the section entitled "The `RandGen` Class" in Part 1 of this chapter. A `RandGen` object returns a random number. In the `fishsim` program, it is used to randomly select an index that will determine a `Position` in the `Neighborhood` that a fish will move to.

Environment

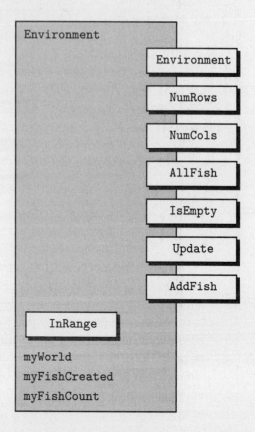

An `Environment` object models a grid of fish. It creates, maintains, and updates the grid at every stage of its evolution. Think of the `Environment` as the all-knowing god of a bounded fish world. The `Environment` also produces an up-to-date list of fish.

The `Environment` constructor initializes the environment and populates it with fish, based on information read in from an input file. The private variable `myWorld` is an `apmatrix` of `Fish` objects. The top line of the input file gives the dimensions of this matrix. Each subsequent line provides the row/column position of a single fish. This method of initialization allows easy modification of the dimensions of the grid, the size of the fish population, and the initial placements of fish: simply change the input file!

Member functions `NumRows()` and `NumCols()` return the number of rows and columns of the current `Environment`.

`AllFish()` returns an `apvector` of `Fish`, starting in the top left-hand corner and moving left to right from the top down. The private variable `myFishCount` is the number of elements in this array. It's important to understand that *every* cell in the `myWorld` matrix contains a `Fish`. A `Fish` object is either defined or undefined, depending on whether its position was read in from the input file. Think of a defined `Fish` as representing an actual fish, and an undefined `Fish` as representing an empty cell in the grid. The `AllFish()` vector is a list of *actual fish only*. The private variable `myFishCreated` provides an identification number for each actual fish. It is initialized to 0 in the constructor (before any actual fish exist) and is incremented and slapped as a unique label onto each actual fish as it is added to the environment.

AddFish(pos) places a fish at an initially empty position during construction of the environment.

IsEmpty(pos) returns true if its Position parameter is in the grid but contains no fish (i.e., an undefined Fish).

Update(oldLoc, fish) updates the environment after its Fish parameter has attempted to move. The oldLoc Position is the fish's Position before the move. If the fish moves successfully, the oldLoc position must be emptied (in other words, myWorld[old Loc.Row()][oldLoc.Col()] must be assigned an undefined Fish).

The private helper function InRange(pos) checks that its Position parameter is within the boundaries of the grid.

Fish

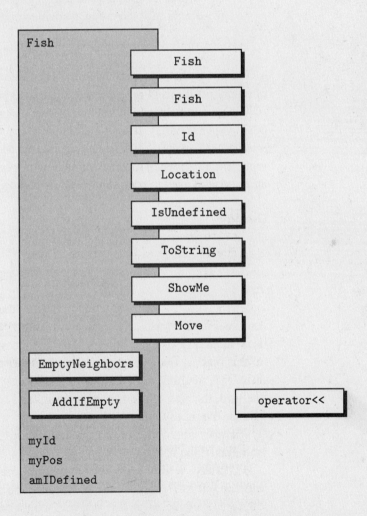

A Fish object swims in its environment. This assumes that its amIDefined variable is true. A fish whose amIDefined variable is false does not exist; it's an "empty" fish. The IsUndefined() member function distinguishes actual fish from undefined fish. The default Fish() constructor creates an undefined fish. The second constructor Fish(id, pos) assigns a unique, permanent integer ID to a fish as well as a Position. A fish keeps track of its position at all times. The member functions

Id() and Location() return the ID and current position of a fish.

ToString() returns as a string myId concatenated to myPos for a given fish. This facilitates overloading the << operator for output.

Move(env) is the member function that has a fish "swim" into an adjacent position if it can. There are four possible moves—north, south, east, or west. A fish may not move into an occupied slot nor may it leave the confines of the environment. Thus, a fish at a side boundary, for example, moves up or down or away from the boundary.

Here is how a fish moves:

- It gets a list of empty neighboring positions. If there are no empty positions, it stays put. End of move.

- If there's at least one available position, the fish

  (a) Stores its current position.
  (b) Randomly selects an available position from the list of empty positions.

- It instructs the environment to update its position.

The private helper function EmptyNeighbors(env, pos) returns a Neighborhood of empty positions in env that are adjacent to pos.

The private helper function AddIfEmpty(env, nbrs, pos) checks env to see if position pos is empty. If so, it gets added to the neighborhood of available positions.

ShowMe() makes a fish visible. It returns a character from 'A' to 'Z' that will represent a fish when the environment is displayed. If there are more than 26 fish, an asterisk is used to represent those fish whose myId field is greater than 26.

Display

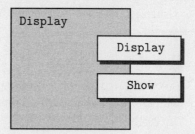

A Display object displays the entire grid of fish. The constructor readies the screen for displaying. Nothing is done for text display, which is the default implementation.

Show(env) displays the current state of env using text-based characters. The function traverses the list of actual fish provided by env.AllFish() and simultaneously traverses the grid. When there's a match between the position of a fish and a position in the grid, the current fish, fishList[fishIndex], provides the letter in 'A' to 'Z' to be printed via the ShowMe() function. If the positions don't match, a blank is printed, corresponding to an "empty" fish.

Simulation

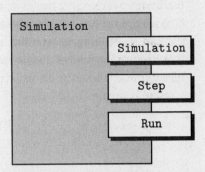

A `Simulation` object controls the simulation of fish in an environment. The constructor readies the simulation. The `Step(env)` carries out one step of the simulation in the environment. `Run(env, steps)` carries out k steps of the simulation, where k equals the `steps` parameter.

Utility Functions

The following unrelated functions are provided in `utils.h`.

`apstring IntToString(int n)`
This returns n in string form. It is used in the `ToString()` function of the `Fish` class to convert `myId` to a string.

`void Sort(apvector<Fish> & list, int numElts)`
This is provided to sort the list top-down/left-right by `Position`. This function is not used by the current version of the program. Perhaps it anticipates a different data structure for the environment, one that may require such a sort for the `fishList` vector.

`void DebugPrint(int level, const apstring & msg)`
The integer parameter `level` specifies the amount of detail desired for debugging output. The higher the level, the greater the detail. The `level` parameter can be set by modifying `utils.cpp`.

Multiple-Choice Questions on the Case Study

Questions 1 and 2 refer to the following setup: A programmer wishes to simulate an AquaFish moving in an infinitely long tank. At each step, a move will be chosen randomly from three functions: GoLeft(), GoRight(), and StayStill(). The programmer writes the following code:

```
RandGen r;
if (r.RandInt(3) == 0)
    GoLeft();
else if (r.RandInt(3) == 1)
    GoRight();
else
    StayStill();
```

1. After a large number of steps, what is the most likely finding?
   (A) The fish will perform each of GoLeft(), GoRight(), and StayStill() roughly one third of the time.
   (B) The fish will StayStill() more often than GoLeft() or GoRight().
   (C) The fish will GoLeft() more often than GoRight() or StayStill().
   (D) The fish will GoRight() more often than GoLeft() or StayStill().
   (E) The fish will never StayStill().

2. Which of the following modifications to the code will cause the fish to GoLeft(), GoRight(), or StayStill() with equal probability?
   I ```
      RandGen r;
      if (r.RandInt(3) == 0)
          GoLeft();
      else if (r.RandInt(2) == 1)
          GoRight();
      else
          StayStill();
      ```
   II ```
      RandGen r;
      int flip = r.RandInt(3);
      if (flip == 0)
          GoLeft();
      else if (flip == 1)
          GoRight();
      else
          StayStill();
      ```
   III ```
      RandGen r;
      if (r.RandInt(3) == 0)
          GoLeft();
      if (r.RandInt(3) == 1)
          GoRight();
      if (r.RandInt(3) == 2)
          StayStill();
      ```
   (A) I only
   (B) II only
   (C) III only
   (D) II and III only
   (E) I, II, and III
      ```

3. In the `fishsim` program, fish are processed in top-down, left-right order, that is, row by row and left to right in a row. Which function in the program implements this order of processing?
   - (A) `Move` in the `Fish` class
   - (B) `AddFish` in the `Fish` class
   - (C) The `Environment` class constructor
   - (D) `AllFish` in the `Environment` class
   - (E) `Add` in the `Neighborhood` class

4. What is the main advantage of having a separate `Display` class for the `fishsim` program?
   - (A) It enhances readability of the program.
   - (B) Having `cout` statements in `main()` is poor programming style.
   - (C) Changing the output from text-based characters to a graphical display requires modification of the `Display` member functions only.
   - (D) It facilitates debugging, especially the code that invokes the `fish.ShowMe()` function.
   - (E) It allows easy modification if the number of fish in the simulation has to exceed 26.

5. The `AllFish` member function of the `Environment` class returns an `apvector` `fishList` of all fish in top-down, left-right order. Consider the following test in the `for` loop of this function:

   ```
   if (!myWorld[r][c].IsUndefined())
   ```

   Which of the following replacements for this test will also achieve the correct postcondition for this function?
   - I `if (myWorld[r][c].Id() > 0)`
   - II `if (myWorld[r][c].Location().Row() != -1)`
   - III `if (!myWorld[r][c].AmIDefined)`

   - (A) I only
   - (B) II only
   - (C) III only
   - (D) I and II only
   - (E) I, II, and III

6. Which of the following tasks is *not* part of the behavior of the `Environment` class?
   - (A) Place fish in their original positions in the grid.
   - (B) Create a list of all defined fish in the grid.
   - (C) Move each fish during a step of the simulation.
   - (D) Keep track of the status of each cell in the grid.
   - (E) Maintain an up-to-date record of the state of each fish.

7. Which of the following is an advantage of creating a RandGen object with a seed parameter?

   (A) It is helpful in debugging a program that doesn't work as intended.

   (B) It ensures that each possible random number in the range of the RandGen functions is equally likely.

   (C) It provides a default sequence of random numbers for each run of the program.

   (D) It guarantees that no random number will occur more than once during a run of the program.

   (E) It guarantees that the seed will occur at least once in each run of the program.

8. Under which circumstances will a fish in the aquamain program start off in the exact center of the tank?

   (A) Whenever tankSize is even

   (B) Whenever tankSize is odd

   (C) Whenever tankSize is greater than 2

   (D) Whenever stepsPerSim is even

   (E) Whenever stepsPerSim is odd

9. Objects of several classes collaborate in the execution of moving a fish. Which class does *not* have an object that is created by a call to the Move function in the Fish class?

   (A) Environment

   (B) Simulation

   (C) Position

   (D) Neighborhood

   (E) RandGen

10. Consider adding a free function operator!= to the Position class. Where in the program is the most suitable place to test this function?

    (A) The Show function of the Display class

    (B) The Environment constructor

    (C) The Update function of the Environment class

    (D) The Equals function of the Position class

    (E) The Move function of the Fish class

11. Consider modifying the `AquaFish` class so that it is three times more likely that a fish will continue swimming in the same direction rather than turn around. It is proposed to effect this modification by changing the line

    ```
    flip = randomVals.RandInt(2);
    ```

    in the `Swim` function to

    ```
    flip = randomVals.RandInt(4);
    ```

    How will the proposed change actually affect the simulation?
    (A) The simulation will produce the same results as the original.
    (B) It is three times more likely that the fish will swim right than it will swim left, irrespective of the direction of its previous move.
    (C) It is three times more likely that the fish will swim left than it will swim right, irrespective of the direction of its previous move.
    (D) It is three times more likely that the fish will swim in the same direction as its previous move, rather than turn around.
    (E) It is three times more likely that the fish will turn around rather than swim in the same direction as its previous move.

12. Which of the following is *false* concerning fish movement in the `fishsim` program?
    (A) Every fish attempts to move during every step of the simulation.
    (B) At the end of the simulation, the environment contains the same number of fish that it started with.
    (C) When a fish moves, it goes up, down, left, or right to a cell that's adjacent to its current cell, or it stays where it is.
    (D) Random numbers are used to help determine the position that a fish will move to.
    (E) During each step of the simulation, the order in which fish move is randomly determined.

13. Which of the following is randomly determined in the `fishsim` program?
    (A) The initial positions of fish in the environment.
    (B) The position to which a fish will move, given that there is more than one available position.
    (C) The number of steps in the simulation.
    (D) The order in which the fish will move in each step of the simulation.
    (E) The characters that are used to display each fish.

14. Which is a *true* statement about the `AddFish` member function of the `Environment` class?
    (A) It is used to update the environment after a fish has moved.
    (B) The two private data members `myFishCreated` and `myFishCount` can have different values following execution of function `AddFish`.
    (C) `AddFish` is used to add a fish to the `Neighborhood` apvector.
    (D) `AddFish` performs just one task: it adds fish to the grid during the initial construction of the environment.
    (E) `AddFish` is invoked by the `AddIfEmpty` member function of the `Fish` class.

15. What is the effect of modifying the `for` loop of the `Step` member function of the `Simulation` class as follows:

```
for (k=fishList.length()-1; k>=0; k--)
{
    fishList[k].Move(env);
}
```

(A) The order in which fish move will be the same as in the original program.
(B) The order in which fish move will be left to right, top-down, namely column by column from left to right and from top to bottom in a column.
(C) The order in which fish move will be bottom-up, right to left, namely row by row from bottom to top and right to left in a row.
(D) The order in which fish move will be bottom-up, left to right, namely row by row from bottom to top and left to right in a row.
(E) The order in which fish move will be right to left, bottom-up, namely column by column from right to left and bottom to top in a column.

Answer Key

1. **B**	6. **C**	11. **C**
2. **E**	7. **A**	12. **E**
3. **D**	8. **B**	13. **B**
4. **C**	9. **B**	14. **D**
5. **D**	10. **C**	15. **C**

Answers Explained

1. **(B)** The first `if` statement will be true about one third of the time, so `GoLeft()` will happen about one third or 33% of the time. The `else-if` statement will be evaluated the other two thirds of the time. The probability that `r.RandInt(3) == 1` is 1/3. Therefore the chances of `GoRight()` are 1/3 of 2/3, which is 2/9 or 22%. Thus, `StayStill()` will occur the other 2/3 of 2/3 = 4/9 or 44% of the time.

2. **(E)** In Segment I, `r.RandInt(3) == 0` will be true about one third of the time, so `GoLeft()` will occur about one third of the time. For the other two thirds of the time, `r.RandInt(2) == 1` will be true about half the time, so `GoRight()` will occur roughly 1/2 of 2/3 = 1/3 of the time. Therefore `StayStill()` will occur the other 1/2 of 2/3 = 1/3 of the time. In Segment II, `flip` will have a value of 0, 1, or 2, each occurring with probability 1/3, which means that each of the actions will have probability 1/3. In Segment III, `r.RandInt(3)` equals 0, 1, or 2 with equal probability. Thus, each of the three actions should happen about one third of the time.

3. **(D)** `AllFish` traverses the `myWorld` matrix row by row from left to right and places each fish it encounters in a `fishList` array. The first fish found is at `fishList[0]`. The simulation code processes the fish in the same order as they occur in `fishList`.

4. **(C)** Having a separate `Display` class provides a way to separate the output from the action of the program. Changing to graphics should not interfere with the data structures and bug-free code of the program.

5. **(D)** The `fishList` vector must contain only those fish that are *actual* fish (i.e., "defined" fish). "Undefined" fish (fish that don't exist) have the following attributes: `IsUndefined()` is true; `Id()` is equal to zero; and `Location()` is a `Position` with `Row()` and `Col()` equal to -1 (`myRow` and `myCol` are initialized to -1 in the default constructor of the `Position` class). Thus, tests I and II are both legitimate substitutions for the given test. Test III doesn't work because `AmIDefined` is a private variable of the `Fish` class and cannot be accessed by functions of the `Environment` class.

6. **(C)** The `Simulation` class is responsible for moving each fish during the simulation. The `Environment` class merely records the results of those moves.

7. **(A)** Using a fixed seed means that the same sequence of random numbers will be produced during each run of the program. This is helpful in diagnosing errors.

8. **(B)** The question is trickier than it appears. Recall that if `tankSize` is `k` the tank looks like this:

Example 1: `tankSize = 4`

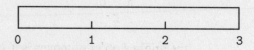

Starting position is `tankSize/2 = 4/2 = 2`. Not the center!

Example 2: `tankSize = 3`

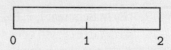

Starting position is $3/2 = 1$, in the center.

9. **(B)** The `Move` function takes an `Environment` object as parameter. A `Neighborhood` object returns a list of empty neighbors (available positions). A `RandGen` object is used to select one of these positions at random. This becomes the fish's new position. The `Update` function of the `Environment` records the move. Even though a `Simulation` object invokes the `Move` function, it is not involved in the actual move itself.

10. **(C)** A suitable place to test this function would be where two `Position` objects are compared. The `Update` function in the `Environment` class has the test

    `if (!(oldLoc == newLoc)) ...`

    To test the `operator!=` function, this could be replaced with

    `if (oldLoc != newLoc)`

11. **(C)** Notice that if `flip` is 0, the fish will swim right. If `flip` is 1, 2, or 3, the fish will swim left. This action does not take into account the direction of the previous move.

12. **(E)** The fish move in a predetermined order: row-by-row, top-to-bottom and left-to-right in each row.

13. **(B)** Choice A is incorrect because the initial positions are determined by the contents of the input file. Choice C is wrong because the number of steps is entered by the user. Choice D is wrong because the order is predetermined, top-down, left-right. Choice E is wrong because the display character for a fish depends on its ID number.

14. **(D)** Choice A is false; the environment is updated in the Update function of the Environment class by directly assigning a fish to a cell in the myWorld apmatrix. Choice B is false; myFishCount represents the number of fish so far, and myFishCreated is the ID number of the last fish created. Since both of these have initial value 0, and since no fish die in this simulation, both variables have the same value following execution of AddFish. Choice C is egregious; the apvector of the Neighborhood class contains *positions* not *fish*! Similarly, choice E is wrong; AddIfEmpty does not add a fish, it adds a position to the neighborhood.

15. **(C)** The change reverses the original order in which the fish move. If the grid looks like this:

```
B C _
A _ D
_ E _
```

the original order of moves is B, C, A, D, E. Reversing the order gives E, D, A, C, B. Notice that this is row by row, bottom-up, right to left.

Practice
Exams

Answer Sheet: Practice Exam One

1. Ⓐ Ⓑ Ⓒ Ⓓ Ⓔ
2. Ⓐ Ⓑ Ⓒ Ⓓ Ⓔ
3. Ⓐ Ⓑ Ⓒ Ⓓ Ⓔ
4. Ⓐ Ⓑ Ⓒ Ⓓ Ⓔ
5. Ⓐ Ⓑ Ⓒ Ⓓ Ⓔ
6. Ⓐ Ⓑ Ⓒ Ⓓ Ⓔ
7. Ⓐ Ⓑ Ⓒ Ⓓ Ⓔ
8. Ⓐ Ⓑ Ⓒ Ⓓ Ⓔ
9. Ⓐ Ⓑ Ⓒ Ⓓ Ⓔ
10. Ⓐ Ⓑ Ⓒ Ⓓ Ⓔ
11. Ⓐ Ⓑ Ⓒ Ⓓ Ⓔ
12. Ⓐ Ⓑ Ⓒ Ⓓ Ⓔ
13. Ⓐ Ⓑ Ⓒ Ⓓ Ⓔ
14. Ⓐ Ⓑ Ⓒ Ⓓ Ⓔ

15. Ⓐ Ⓑ Ⓒ Ⓓ Ⓔ
16. Ⓐ Ⓑ Ⓒ Ⓓ Ⓔ
17. Ⓐ Ⓑ Ⓒ Ⓓ Ⓔ
18. Ⓐ Ⓑ Ⓒ Ⓓ Ⓔ
19. Ⓐ Ⓑ Ⓒ Ⓓ Ⓔ
20. Ⓐ Ⓑ Ⓒ Ⓓ Ⓔ
21. Ⓐ Ⓑ Ⓒ Ⓓ Ⓔ
22. Ⓐ Ⓑ Ⓒ Ⓓ Ⓔ
23. Ⓐ Ⓑ Ⓒ Ⓓ Ⓔ
24. Ⓐ Ⓑ Ⓒ Ⓓ Ⓔ
25. Ⓐ Ⓑ Ⓒ Ⓓ Ⓔ
26. Ⓐ Ⓑ Ⓒ Ⓓ Ⓔ
27. Ⓐ Ⓑ Ⓒ Ⓓ Ⓔ
28. Ⓐ Ⓑ Ⓒ Ⓓ Ⓔ

29. Ⓐ Ⓑ Ⓒ Ⓓ Ⓔ
30. Ⓐ Ⓑ Ⓒ Ⓓ Ⓔ
31. Ⓐ Ⓑ Ⓒ Ⓓ Ⓔ
32. Ⓐ Ⓑ Ⓒ Ⓓ Ⓔ
33. Ⓐ Ⓑ Ⓒ Ⓓ Ⓔ
34. Ⓐ Ⓑ Ⓒ Ⓓ Ⓔ
35. Ⓐ Ⓑ Ⓒ Ⓓ Ⓔ
36. Ⓐ Ⓑ Ⓒ Ⓓ Ⓔ
37. Ⓐ Ⓑ Ⓒ Ⓓ Ⓔ
38. Ⓐ Ⓑ Ⓒ Ⓓ Ⓔ
39. Ⓐ Ⓑ Ⓒ Ⓓ Ⓔ
40. Ⓐ Ⓑ Ⓒ Ⓓ Ⓔ

Practice Exam One

COMPUTER SCIENCE A
SECTION I

Time—1 hour and 15 minutes
Number of questions—40
Percent of total grade—50

Directions: Determine the answer to each of the following questions or incomplete statements, using separate pieces of scrap paper for any necessary scratchwork. Then decide which is the best of the choices given and fill in the corresponding oval on the answer sheet. Do not spend too much time on any one problem.

Note: Assume that the standard libraries (e.g., `iostream.h`, `fstream.h`, `math.h`, etc.) and the AP C++ classes are included in any programs that use the code segments provided in individual questions. A Quick Reference to the AP C++ classes is provided.

---

1. A function is to be written to search an array for a value that is larger than a given item and return its index. The problem specification does not indicate what should be returned if there are several such values in the array. Which of the following actions would be best?
   - (A) The function should be written on the assumption that there is only one value in the array that is larger than the given item.
   - (B) The function should be written so as to return the index of every occurrence of a larger value.
   - (C) The specification should be modified to indicate what should be done if there is more than one index of larger values.
   - (D) The function should be written to output a message if more than one larger value is found.
   - (E) The function should be written to delete all subsequent larger items after a suitable index is returned.

GO ON TO THE NEXT PAGE ➤

2. Refer to the following program segment. You may assume that `a[0]...a[n-1]` is an `apvector` of integers.

```
int temp, k=0, j=n-1;
while (k < j)
{
    temp = a[k];
    a[k] = a[j];
    a[j] = temp;
    k++;
    j--;
}
```

What does this segment do?

(A) It sorts the elements of a into decreasing order.

(B) It sorts the elements of a into increasing order.

(C) It searches array a for the first occurrence of `temp`.

(D) It reverses the elements of array a.

(E) It swaps the first and last elements of a and leaves the remaining elements of the array unchanged.

3. When will function `WhatIsIt` cause a stack overflow?

```
int WhatIsIt(int x, int y)
{
    if (x > y)
        return x*y;
    else
        return WhatIsIt(x-1, y);
}
```

(A) Only when $x < y$

(B) Only when $x \leq y$

(C) Only when $x > y$

(D) For all values of x and y

(E) The function will never cause a stack overflow.

4. Refer to function Calc:

```
int Calc(int result, int x, int y)
{
    if (x > 2)
    {
        if (y < 4)
            return 3*result;
        else
            return result;
    }
    else
        return y*result;
}
```

The assignment statement

```
int N = Calc(3, 4, 5) + Calc(5, 1, 3);
```

results in N being assigned the value

(A) 8
(B) 14
(C) 18
(D) 20
(E) 24

5. The boolean expression `a[i] == max || !(max != a[i])` can be simplified to

(A) `a[i] == max`
(B) `a[i] != max`
(C) `a[i] < max || a[i] > max`
(D) `true`
(E) `false`

GO ON TO THE NEXT PAGE ➤

Questions 6 and 7 refer to the following declarations:

```
struct Address
{
    apstring street;
    apstring city;
    apstring state;
    int zipCode;
};
struct Customer
{
    apstring name;
    int IdNumber;
    apstring phone;
    Address add;
};
const int MAXCUSTOMERS = <a large integer constant>;
apvector<Customer> custList(MAXCUSTOMERS);
```

6. Given a list of customers and the ID number only of a particular customer, function Find must locate the correct Customer record and return the name of that customer.

```
apstring Find(int idNum, const apvector<Customer> & custList)
//precondition: custList contains MAXCUSTOMERS Customer records,
//              0 < MAXCUSTOMERS ≤ custList.length()
//              idNum matches the IdNumber data member of one
//              of the Customer records
//postcondition: The name of the customer whose IdNumber
//               matches idNum is returned
{
    for (int i=0; i < MAXCUSTOMERS; i++)
        if (custList[i].IdNumber == idNum)
            return custList[i].name;
}
```

A more efficient algorithm for finding the matching Customer record could be used if

(A) Customer records were in alphabetical order by name.

(B) Customer records were sorted by phone number.

(C) Customer records were sorted by IdNumber.

(D) The custList array had fewer elements.

(E) The Customer struct did not have an Address data member.

GO ON TO THE NEXT PAGE ➤

7. The company that maintains the Customer records plans to add an array data member to each Customer record to store a list of purchases for that customer. The Customer struct will be altered as follows:

```
struct Customer
{
    apstring name;
    int IdNumber;
    apstring phone;
    Address add;
    apvector<apstring> purchases;
};
```

In order to initialize the purchases apvector to contain ten slots, which of the following *must* be done?

(A) A constructor must be added to the Customer struct.

(B) An accessor member function must be added to the Customer struct.

(C) A text file of ten purchases for each Customer must be created.

(D) The list of purchases for each Customer must be entered at the keyboard.

(E) A parallel apvector of apstring must be declared in the main() function.

8. What output is produced by the following program?

```
#include <iostream.h>
void Process(int & a, int b)
{
    a *= b;
    b *= a;
}
int main()
{
    int x = 2, y = 3;
    Process(x, y);
    cout << x << y << endl;
    return 0;
}
```

(A) 318

(B) 618

(C) 218

(D) 23

(E) 63

GO ON TO THE NEXT PAGE ➤

9. Consider the following function.

```
void WhatsIt(int n)
{
    if (n > 10)
        WhatsIt(n/10);
    cout << n % 10;
}
```

What will be output as a result of the function call WhatsIt(347)?

(A) 74

(B) 47

(C) 734

(D) 743

(E) 347

10. Refer to the following function.

```
int Mystery(const apvector<int> & v)
//precondition: v is an array of nonnegative integers k
//              such that 0 ≤ k ≤ 9
{
    int value = v[0];
    for (int i=1; i < v.length(); v++)
        value = value*10 + v[i];
    return value;
}
```

Which best describes what function Mystery does?

(A) It sums the elements of v.

(B) It sums the products 10*v[0] + 10*v[1] + ... + 10*v[v.length()-1].

(C) It builds an integer of the form $d_1 d_2 d_3 \ldots d_n$, where $d_1 =$ v[0], $d_2 =$ v[1], $\ldots, d_n =$ v[v.length()-1].

(D) It builds an integer of the form $d_1 d_2 d_3 \ldots d_n$, where $d_1 =$ v[v.length()-1], $d_2 =$ v[v.length()-2], $\ldots, d_n =$ v[0].

(E) It converts the elements of v to base 10.

GO ON TO THE NEXT PAGE ➤

11. Consider the following function.

```
int FindSum(const apvector<int> & a, int n)
//precondition: a[0]...a[n-1] initialized with integers,
//               0 ≤ n ≤ a.length()
//postcondition: returns sum of elements in a.
//               returns 0 if a is empty
{
    <code>
}
```

Which of the following correctly replaces *<code>* so that the function works as intended?

```
I   int sum = 0, i = 0;
    while (i < n)
    {
        sum += a[i];
        i++;
    } return sum;

II  int sum = 0, i = 0;
    do
    {
        sum += a[i];
        i++;
    } while (i < n);
    return sum;

III if (n == 0)
        return 0;
    else if (n == 1)
        return a[0];
    else
        return a[n-1] + FindSum(a, n-1);
```

(A) I only
(B) II only
(C) III only
(D) I and II only
(E) I and III only

12. Consider two ways to code a function that prints a line of characters.

```
I void Drawline(char ch, int length)
  {
      for (int i=1; i<=length; i++)
          cout << ch;
  }

II void Drawline(char ch, int & length)
  {
      for (int i=1; i<=length; i++)
          cout << ch;
  }
```

Which of the following is true concerning the choice of headers?
(A) Both headers are equally appropriate since the function bodies are the same.
(B) Both headers are equally appropriate since length is not changed in either function body.
(C) Header I is preferable since it uses less memory space.
(D) Header I is preferable because it allows a call with an expression as an actual parameter.
(E) Header II is preferable because it avoids copying the value of length.

13. Here are three code segments, each of which is intended to set a and b to be arrays of eight dashes.

```
I apvector<char> a, b(8);
  for (int i=0; i<8; i++)
      a[i] = '-';
  b = a;

II apvector<char> a(8), b;
  for (int i=0; i<8; i++)
      a[i] = '-';
  b = a;

III apvector<char> a(8, '-');
  apvector<char> b = a;
```

Which of these segments works as intended?
(A) I only
(B) II only
(C) III only
(D) I and II only
(E) II and III only

14. A large list of numbers is to be sorted into ascending order. Which of the following is a *true* statement?
(A) If the array is initially sorted in descending order, then insertion sort will be more efficient than selection sort.
(B) The number of comparisons for selection sort is independent of the initial arrangement of elements.
(C) The number of comparisons for insertion sort is independent of the initial arrangement of elements.
(D) The number of data movements in selection sort depends on the initial arrangement of elements.
(E) The number of data movements in insertion sort is independent of the initial arrangement of elements.

GO ON TO THE NEXT PAGE ➤

15. A text file `numFile` contains an unknown number of integers, as shown:

numFile

2		27	19
13	15		
...	176		44

Assuming that there are at least k integers in `numFile`, a program to delete the kth integer but leave the file otherwise unchanged must read

(A) All numbers in the file
(B) All numbers up to and including the kth number, and no other numbers
(C) All numbers from the kth number on, but no numbers before that
(D) All numbers in the file except the kth number
(E) The kth number and no other numbers

16. Consider the following program segment:

```
//precondition: a[0]...a[n-1] is an initialized apvector of
//               integers, 0 < n ≤ a.length()
    int c = 0;
    for (int i=0; i<n; i++)
        if (a[i] > 0)
        {
            a[c] = a[i];
            c++;
        }
    n = c;
```

Which is the best postcondition for the segment?

(A) `a[0]...a[n-1]` has been stripped of all positive integers.
(B) `a[0]...a[n-1]` has been stripped of all negative integers.
(C) The number of elements in array a is less than or equal to the number of elements in array a before execution of the segment.
(D) Array a contains more elements than it did before execution of the segment.
(E) n, the number of elements in a, equals c.

17. A programmer has a file of names. She is designing a program that sends junk mail letters to everyone on the list. To make the letters sound personal and friendly, she will extract each person's first name from the name string. She plans to create a parallel file of first names only. For example,

nameFile	firstNameFile
Ms. Anjali DeSouza	Anjali
Dr. John Roufaiel	John
Mrs. Mathilda Concia	Mathilda

Here is a function intended to extract the first names from `nameFile` and write them to `firstNameFile`.

```
void GetFirstNames(ifstream & nameFile, ofstream & firstNameFile)
//precondition: nameFile is open for reading and contains a
//              list of names, one per line. Each name starts
//              with a title followed by a period. A single
//              space separates the title, first name, and
//              last name. firstNameFile is open for writing
//postcondition: Corresponding first names are written to
//               firstNameFile, one per line
{
    <code>
}
```

Which of the following replacements for `<code>` will correctly create the intended file of first names?

```
  I apstring title, firstName, lastName;
    while (nameFile >> title >> firstName >> lastName)
        firstNameFile << firstName << endl;

 II int k;
    apstring temp, firstName;
    while (getline(nameFile, name))
    {
        k=name.find(' ');
        temp = name.substr(k+1, name.length());
        k = temp.find(' ');
        firstName = temp.substr(0,k);
        firstNameFile << firstName << endl;
    }

III int firstBlank, secondBlank;
    apstring temp, firstName;
    while (getline(nameFile, name))
    {
        firstBlank = name.find(' ');
        secondBlank = name.find(' ');
        firstName = name.substr(firstBlank+1,
                        secondBlank -(firstBlank+1));
        firstNameFile << firstName << endl;
    }
```

(A) I only
(B) II only
(C) III only
(D) I and II only
(E) I and III only

GO ON TO THE NEXT PAGE ➤

18. Integers entered at the keyboard are to be processed until a special value called SENTINEL is encountered, signaling the end of the list. The SENTINEL should not be processed. Which of the following program segments are correct, assuming that function Process works as intended and that num and SENTINEL have been correctly declared?

```
I do
  {
      cin >> num;
      Process(num);
  } while (num != SENTINEL);
```

```
II cin >> num;
   while (num != SENTINEL)
   {
       Process(num);
       cin >> num;
   }
```

```
III for (cin >> num; num!=SENTINEL; cin >> num)
        Process(num);
```

(A) I only
(B) II only
(C) III only
(D) II and III only
(E) I, II, and III

19. Consider the following function.

```
int Find(const apvector<int> & list, int key)
//precondition: list is initialized with integers
//postcondition: returns index such that -1 ≤ index < list.length().
//               If index ≥ 0 is returned, then list[index] == key.
//               If -1 is returned, then key is not in list
{
    int i = 0;
    while (i < list.length() && key > list[i])
        i++;
    if (list[i] == key)
        return i;
    else
        return -1;
}
```

Under which of the following conditions will function Find *not* return the correct value?
(A) list is sorted in increasing order, and key is somewhere in list.
(B) list is sorted in decreasing order, and key is somewhere in list.
(C) key is not in list, and list is in random order.
(D) key is the first element of list, and list is in random order.
(E) key equals list[k], and list[0], list[1], ... list[k-1] are all less than key.

GO ON TO THE NEXT PAGE ➤

Questions 20–23 refer to the ElapsedTime class.

```
class ElapsedTime
{
    public:
        ElapsedTime();          //default constructor
        ElapsedTime(int h, int m, int s);   //constructor
        ElapsedTime(int N);     //constructor. N = total number of
                                // seconds of elapsed time
        void PrintTime() const; //prints elapsed time in form
                                // hh mm ss where hh=hours,
                                // mm=minutes, ss=seconds
        int ConvertToSeconds() const;  //returns number of
                                       //seconds in elapsed time
    private:
        int myHours, myMins, mySecs;   //0≤mySecs<60, 0≤myMins<60
};
```

20. Which of the following is a correct implementation for the second constructor in the ElapsedTime class?

```
    I ElapsedTime::ElapsedTime(int h, int m, int s)
        : myHours(h), myMins(m), mySecs(s) {}

   II ElapsedTime::(int h, int m, int s)
      {
          myHours(h), myMins(m), mySecs(s);
      }

  III ElapsedTime::ElapsedTime(int h, int m, int s)
      {
          myHours = h;
          myMins = m;
          mySecs = s;
      }
```

(A) I only
(B) II only
(C) III only
(D) I and III only
(E) II and III only

21. Having two different constructors with parameters is an example of
(A) Function overloading
(B) Operator overloading
(C) Parameter overloading
(D) Templated functions
(E) A copy constructor

GO ON TO THE NEXT PAGE ➤

22. Consider the implementation for the third constructor:

```
ElapsedTime::ElapsedTime(int N)
{
    <code>
}
```

Which represents a correct replacement for `<code>`?

```
 I mySecs = N;

II myHours = N/3600;
   myMins = N/60 % 60;
   mySecs = N % 60;

III mySecs = N % 60;
    N /= 60;
    myMins = N % 60;
    myHours = N/60;
```

(A) I only
(B) II only
(C) III only
(D) II and III only
(E) I, II, and III

23. A client function `TimeSum` will find the sum of two `ElapsedTime` objects:

```
ElapsedTime TimeSum(const ElapsedTime & T1,
                    const ElapsedTime & T2)
{
    <code>
}
```

Which replacements for `<code>` are correct?

```
 I int s1 = T1.ConvertToSeconds();
   int s2 = T2.ConvertToSeconds();
   ElapsedTime Temp(s1 + s2);
   return Temp;

II ElapsedTime Temp(T1 + T2);
   return Temp;

III ElapsedTime Sum;
    int totSecs = T1.mySecs + T2.mySecs;
    Sum.mySecs = totSecs % 60;
    int totMins = T1.myMins + T2.myMins + totSecs/60;
    Sum.myMins = totMins % 60;
    Sum.myHours = T1.myHours + T2.myHours + totMins/60;
    return Sum;
```

(A) I only
(B) II only
(C) III only
(D) II and III only
(E) I, II, and III

GO ON TO THE NEXT PAGE ➤

Questions 24 and 25 are based on the following code:

```
void SplitFile(ifstream & sourceFile, ofstream & posFile,
               ofstream & negFile)
//precondition: sourceFile contains one integer per line and
//              is open for reading at the beginning of the
//              file. The other two files are open for
//              writing and are initially empty
//postcondition: All nonnegative elements of sourceFile form
//               the contents of posFile, all negative
//               elements form the contents of negFile
{
    cout << "SplitFile called" << endl;
}
```

24. Which of the following statements is true about the code?
   (A) It will cause a compile-time error when processed by a standard C++ compiler.
   (B) It will cause a run-time error.
   (C) It provides an example of a driver program.
   (D) It provides an example of stub programming.
   (E) It provides an example of pseudo-code.

25. Suppose that the correct final code for function SplitFile is as follows:

```
{
    int num;
    while (sourceFile >> num)
    {
        if (num >= 0)
            posFile << num << endl;
        else
            negFile << num << endl;
    }
}
```

Assuming that the given pre- and postconditions are accurate, which of the following could be added to the postcondition without destroying its accuracy?
   I posFile and negFile are ordered numerically.
   II The elements of both posFile and negFile are, respectively, in the same order in which they appear in sourceFile.
   III The number of elements in each of posFile and negFile is less than the number of elements in sourceFile.
   (A) I only
   (B) II only
   (C) III only
   (D) II and III only
   (E) I, II, and III

GO ON TO THE NEXT PAGE ➤

26. Consider function `StringStuff`.

```
apstring StringStuff(const apstring & s1, const apstring & s2)
{
    s1 += s2;
    s2 += s1;
    return s1 + s2;
}
```

Function `StringStuff` causes a compile-time error. Why?

(A) `s1` and `s2` are not declared in the body of the function.

(B) The return type of `s1 + s2` causes a type mismatch error.

(C) The statements `s1 += s2` and `s2 += s1` illegally modify `s1` and `s2`.

(D) `apstring` parameters must always be passed by reference, not `const` reference.

(E) The `+=` operator has no meaning for `apstrings`.

27. Consider the code segment

```
if (n == 1)
    k++;
else if (n == 4)
    k += 4;
```

Suppose that the given segment is rewritten in the form

```
if (<condition>)
    <assignment statement>;
```

Given that `n` and `k` are integers and that the rewritten code performs the same task as the original code, which of the following could be used as

I *<condition>*   and   II *<assignment statement>*?

(A) I `n == 1 && n == 4`   II `k += n`

(B) I `n == 1 && n == 4`   II `k += 4`

(C) I `n == 1 || n == 4`   II `k += 4`

(D) I `n == 1 || n == 4`   II `k += n`

(E) I `n == 1 || n == 4`   II `k = n - k`

Questions 28 and 29 refer to function `Search`.

```
int Search(const apvector<int> & a, int first, int last, int key)
//precondition: a[first]...a[last] sorted in ascending order
//postcondition: returns index of key in a. If key not in a,
//               returns -1
{
    int mid;
    while (first <= last)
    {
        mid = (first + last)/2;
        if (a[mid] == key)       //found key, exit search
            return mid;
        else if (a[mid] < key)  //key to right of a[mid]
            first = mid + 1;
        else                     //key to left of a[mid]
            last = mid - 1;
    }
    return -1;                   //key not in list
}
```

28. Which assertion is true just before each execution of the `while` loop?
    (A) `a[first]` ≤ `key` ≤ `a[last]` or key is not in a
    (B) `a[first]` ≤ `key` ≤ `a[last]`
    (C) `a[first]` < `key` < `a[last]` or key is not in a
    (D) `a[first]` < `key` < `a[last]`
    (E) `key` ≤ `a[first]` or `key` ≥ `a[last]` or key is not in a

29. Consider the array `list` with values as shown:

    4, 7, 19, 25, 36, 37, 50, 100, 101, 205, 220, 271, 306, 321

    where 4 is `list[0]` and 321 is `list[13]`. Suppose that the `Search` function is called to locate the key 205. How many iterations of the `while` loop must be made in order to locate it?
    (A) 3
    (B) 4
    (C) 5
    (D) 10
    (E) 13

GO ON TO THE NEXT PAGE ➤

30. Three numbers *a*, *b*, and *c* are said to be a *Pythagorean Triple* if and only if the sum of the squares of two of the numbers equals the square of the third. A programmer writes a function IsPythTriple to test if its three parameters form a Pythagorean Triple:

```
bool IsPythTriple(double a, double b, double c)
//returns true if a² + b² = c²; otherwise returns false
{
    double d = sqrt(a*a + b*b);
    if (d == c)
        return true;
    else
        return false;
}
```

When the function was tested with known Pythagorean Triples, IsPythTriple sometimes erroneously returned false. What was the most likely cause of the error?

(A) Round-off error was caused by calculations with floating-point numbers.

(B) Type bool was not recognized by an out-of-date compiler.

(C) An overflow error was caused by entering numbers that were too large.

(D) c and d should have been cast to integers before testing for equality.

(E) Bad test data were selected.

Questions 31 and 32 are based on the following information. A simple LargeInt class will represent integers up to 100 digits long. Some of the operations that will be implemented for the class follow.

```
class LargeInt
{
    public:
        LargeInt(istream & input, int n);   //Constructor. Reads integer n from input
                                            // and converts n to LargeInt
        void Print(ostream & os) const;   //print LargeInt to os
        LargeInt & Add(const LargeInt & b);   //Is equivalent to LargeInt += b
            ...
        bool LessThan(const LargeInt & rhs) const;   //Returns true if LargeInt < rhs,
                                                     // otherwise returns false

        ...
    private:
        //Hidden!
};
```

31. Of the following pairs of functions, which should be coded and tested first to facilitate testing and debugging the other functions?

(A) The constructor and Add function

(B) The constructor and LessThan function

(C) The constructor and Print function

(D) The Print and Add functions

(E) The Print and LessThan functions

GO ON TO THE NEXT PAGE ➤

32. To simulate the loop

```
for (i=1; i<=n-1; i++)
    cout << i;
```

the following code is used, where i, One, and n are of type LargeInt.

```
LargeInt i(input, 1);
LargeInt One(input, 1);
while (i.LessThan(n))
{
    i.Print(cout);
    <statement>
}
```

Which of the following should replace <statement> to simulate the loop correctly?

(A) i.Add(n);
(B) n.Add(One);
(C) One.Add(i);
(D) i.Add(1);
(E) i.Add(One);

33. Assume that the following declarations have been made:

```
const int MAXNUM = <some positive integer>;
apvector<bool> a(MAXNUM+1);
```

Consider the following code segment:

```
int i, j;
a[0] = false;
a[1] = false;
for(i=2; i<=MAXNUM; i++)
    a[i] = true;
for(i=2; i<=MAXNUM; i++)
    for(j=1; j<=MAXNUM/i; j++)
        a[i*j] = !a[i*j];
```

For i in the range 2...MAXNUM, which of the following characterize the entries of a that will have value *true* after execution of the foregoing segment?

(A) a[i] is true for no values of i.
(B) a[i] is true for all values of i.
(C) a[i] is true for all values of i that are even.
(D) a[i] is true for all values of i that are prime.
(E) a[i] is true for all values of i that are perfect squares.

GO ON TO THE NEXT PAGE ➤

34. Given the input line abcd., where abcd is terminated by a period, what does the following function print?

```
void ProcessChars()
{
    char ch, i;
    cin >> ch;
    if (ch != '.')
    {
        for(i='a'; i<=ch; i++)
            cout << ch;
        ProcessChars();
        for(i='a'; i<=ch; i++)
            cout << ch;
    }
}
```

(A) abcdcba

(B) abbcccdddd

(C) abbcccddddddddcccbba

(D) aababcabcdabcdabcaba

(E) abbcccddddddddddddddd

GO ON TO THE NEXT PAGE ➤

35. A word game uses the following data structure to represent a related pair of strings:

```
const int MAXSTRINGLENGTH = 40;
struct stringType
{
    int start;      //0 <= start <= MAXSTRINGLENGTH
    int end;        //0 <= end <= MAXSTRINGLENGTH
};
struct stringPair
{
    apstring s;     //s.length() <= MAXSTRINGLENGTH
    stringType string1;
    stringType string2;
};
```

The `string1` and `string2` fields of `stringPair` each contain a pair of integers that are indexes of `apstring s`. A single string consists of the sequence of characters `s[start]...s[end]`. Assume that the preceding data structure is used to represent the strings "considerate" and "rate" as shown here:

s	i	n	c	o	n	s	i	d	e	r	a	t	e	l	y
	0	1	2	3	4	5	6	7	8	9	10	11	12	13	14

```
string1: 2, 12
string2: 9, 12
```

Which of the following statements is true?

    I The data structure could be altered so that it represents the pair of strings "con" and "rat" by changing just two integer values.

    II The data structure could be altered so that it represents the pair of strings "era" and "at" by changing just two integer values.

    III The data structure could be altered so that it represents the pair of strings "consideration" and "rate" by changing just three character values and one integer value.

(A) I only

(B) II only

(C) III only

(D) I and II only

(E) I and III only

Questions 36–40 involve reasoning about the code from the Marine Biology Case Study. A copy of the code is provided as part of this exam.

36. Marine biologists have observed that fish tend to swim in a preferred direction. They would like the `aquamain` program to be modified so that it is twice as likely that a fish will move to the right rather than to the left. To implement this change, which of the following will need to be modified?

    I A `RandInt` function of the `RandGen` class

    II The `Swim` function of the `AquaFish` class

    III The `main` function in `aquamain.cpp`

(A) I only

(B) II only

(C) III only

(D) I and II only

(E) I, II, and III

GO ON TO THE NEXT PAGE ➤

37. Which of the following best characterizes an object of the Neighborhood class?
    (A) A collection of no more than four fish that are adjacent to a given fish
    (B) A collection of four positions
    (C) A collection of positions that does not exceed the number of positions in the environment
    (D) An ordered collection of no more than four positions
    (E) A collection of no more than four positions

38. Suppose that the biologists studying the fish need a modification that causes the fish to be processed in left-right, top-down order, that is, column by column and top to bottom in a column. Assuming that the Display class has been correctly modified, which of the following will succeed in implementing this change?

    I Reverse the sequence of fish positions in the input file fish.dat. For example, change

2	3		2	3
0	1	to	0	0
1	2		1	2
0	0		0	1

    Note that the first line in the file gives the grid dimensions, so it is not changed.

    II Change the for loop of the Step member function in the Simulation class to be

    ```
    for (k=fishList.length()-1; k>=0; k--)
    {
        fishList[k].Move(env);
    }
    ```

    III Change the nested for loop in the AllFish() member function of the Environment class to be

    ```
    for (c=0; c<NumCols(); c++)
    {
        for (r=0; r<NumRows(); r++)
        {
            if (!myWorld[r][c].IsUndefined())
            {
                fishList[count] = myWorld[r][c];
                count++;
            }
        }
    }
    ```

    (A) I only
    (B) II only
    (C) III only
    (D) II and III only
    (E) I, II, and III

GO ON TO THE NEXT PAGE ➤

39. Which is a *false* statement about the ID number (represented by Id() or myId) of a fish?
    (A) For a given fish, this number remains constant.
    (B) If fishList[k] represents a fish, k equals its ID number. Here fishList is the apvector of fish created by the AllFish function in the Environment class.
    (C) The ID number of the last fish created by the Environment equals fishCount, the number of fish in the fishList apvector.
    (D) The function that provides a fish with its ID number is the constructor of the Environment class.
    (E) All undefined fish have an ID number of 0.

40. Consider a change to the fishsim program that outputs a tilde (~) instead of a blank to display undefined fish. This makes it look like the fish are swimming in water; for example,

    ```
    ~A~
    B~~
    DCE
    ```

    Which of the following changes will achieve this? (The changes are highlighted in bold.)

    I Modify the ShowMe function in the Fish class to be

    ```
    if (1 <= Id() && Id() <= 26)
    {
        return 'A' + (Id() - 1);
    }
    else if (!amIDefined)
        return '~';
    return '*';
    ```

    II Modify the ShowMe function in the Fish class to be

    ```
    if (1 <= Id() && Id() <= 26)
    {
        return 'A' + (Id() - 1);
    }
    return '~';
    ```

    III Modify the Show function in the Display class as follows: Replace the line

    ```
    cout << setw(WIDTH) << ' ';
    ```
    with
    ```
    cout << setw(WIDTH) << '~';
    ```

    (A) I only
    (B) II only
    (C) III only
    (D) I and III only
    (E) I, II, and III

STOP

COMPUTER SCIENCE A
SECTION II

Time—1 hour and 45 minutes
Number of questions—4
Percent of total grade—50

Directions: SHOW ALL YOUR WORK. REMEMBER THAT PROGRAM SEGMENTS ARE TO BE WRITTEN IN C++.

Note: Assume that the standard libraries (iostream.h, fstream.h, math.h, etc.) and the AP C++ classes are included in any program that uses a program segment you write. If other classes are to be included, that information will be specified in individual questions. A Quick Reference to the AP C++ classes is included in the case study insert.

---

1. Assume that information about candidates in a class election is stored using the following declarations.

```cpp
const int NUMCANDIDATES = <some appropriate integer>
struct Candidate
{
    apstring name;
    int numVotes;
    double votePercent;
};
apvector<Candidate> Clist(NUMCANDIDATES);
```

(a) Write function ComputeVotePercent as started below. ComputeVotePercent should fill in the votePercent data member for the NUMCANDIDATES records in its apvector parameter Clist. A candidate's votePercent is computed by dividing that candidate's numVotes by the total number of votes cast for all candidates, and then multiplying by 100.

Complete function ComputeVotePercent below.

```cpp
void ComputeVotePercent(apvector<Candidate> & Clist)
//precondition: Clist contains NUMCANDIDATES records,
//              0 ≤ NUMCANDIDATES ≤ Clist.length(), in which the name
//              and numVotes data members have been initialized
//postcondition: The votePercent data member in each Candidate
//               record in Clist has been calculated
```

GO ON TO THE NEXT PAGE ➤

(b) Write function IsViable as started below. A candidate is considered to be viable only if he or she received at least 10% of the vote. IsViable should return true if the Candidate parameter has a votePercent $\geq$ 10; otherwise, it should return false. Complete function IsViable below.

```
bool IsViable(const Candidate & C)
//precondition: All data members of C are initialized
//postcondition: returns true if C is viable (i.e.
//                votePercent ≥ 10), otherwise returns false
```

(c) Write function PrintViable as started below. PrintViable should print a list of names of viable candidates only, one per line, followed by that candidate's votePercent. The names should be in descending order of their votePercent. Sample output:

```
Peter Nix 42.3
David Schwager 29.7
Shawn Sorrels 15.8
```

In writing PrintViable, you may call function IsViable as specified in part (b). Assume that IsViable works as specified regardless of what you wrote in part (b). You may also assume the existence of the following function, and assume it works as specified:

```
void Swap(Candidate & C1, Candidate & C2);
//Postcondition: C1 and C2 are interchanged
```

Complete function PrintViable below.

```
void PrintViable (apvector<Candidate> & Clist)
//precondition: All data members of each record in Clist
//              are initialized. There are NUMCANDIDATES in
//              Clist, where 0 ≤ NUMCANDIDATES ≤ Clist.length()
```

2. A NumberSet, shown in the class declaration below, stores a set of integers in no particular order and contains no duplicates.

```
class NumberSet
{
    public:
        NumberSet();            //default constructor. Initializes set to empty
        int Size() const;       //returns number of integers in set
        void Insert(int num);   //adds num to set (no duplicates)
        void Remove(int num);
            //removes num from set if present, else does nothing
        int FindKth(int k) const;
            //returns kth integer in sorted increasing order, where
            // 1 ≤ k ≤ Size()
        bool Includes(int num) const;
            //returns true if set includes num, else returns false
    private:
        //private data members not shown
};
```

GO ON TO THE NEXT PAGE ➤

The public member function FindKth returns the kth integer in sorted increasing order from the set (the kth smallest number), even though the implementation of NumberSet may not be sorted. The number k ranges from 1 (first in sorted order) to N, where N is the number of integers in the set. For example, if NumberSet S stores the numbers $\{5, 15, 1, -6\}$, here are the results of calling S.FindKth(k).

k	S.FindKth(k)
1	-6
2	1
3	5
4	15

(a) Write free function CountNegatives as started below. CountNegatives returns the number of negative integers that occur in NumberSet S. In writing CountNegatives, you may call any of the member functions of the NumberSet class. Assume that the member functions work as specified. Complete function CountNegatives below.

```
int CountNegatives(const NumberSet & S)
//postcondition: returns the number of negative integers in S
```

(b) Write free function RemoveNegatives as started below. RemoveNegatives removes all negative integers from S. If there are no negative integers in S, then RemoveNegatives does nothing. In writing RemoveNegatives, you may call function CountNegatives specified in part (a). Assume that CountNegatives works as specified, regardless of what you wrote in part (a). Complete function RemoveNegatives below:

```
void RemoveNegatives(NumberSet & S)
//postcondition: NumberSet contains no negative integers, but
//               is otherwise unchanged
```

(c) Write free function CommonElements as started below. CommonElements returns the NumberSet that contains just those elements that occur in both of its NumberSet parameters. For example, if S1 stores the numbers $\{2, -3, 4\}$ and S2 stores $\{1, 3, 2, 4\}$, CommonElements(S1, S2) should return the NumberSet $\{2, 4\}$. (If you are familiar with mathematical set theory, CommonElements returns the intersection of S1 and S2.) Complete function CommonElements below.

```
NumberSet CommonElements(const NumberSet & S1, const NumberSet & S2)
//postcondition: returns the set containing the elements that
//               occur in both S1 and S2
```

3. A *color grid* is defined as a two-dimensional array whose elements are characters having values 'b' (blue), 'r' (red), 'g' (green), or 'y' (yellow). The elements are called pixels because they represent pixel locations on a computer screen. For example,

```
b  b  g  r                              y  g  r
g  r  g  r        r  r  r  r  r          b  y  g
                                        g  r  b
                                        b  b  g
```

GO ON TO THE NEXT PAGE ➤

A *connected region* for any pixel is the set of all pixels of the same color that can be reached through a direct path along horizontal or vertical moves starting at that pixel. A connected region can consist of just a single pixel or the entire color grid. For example, if the two-dimensional array is called `pixels`, the connected region for `pixels[1][0]` is as shown here for three different arrays.

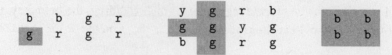

The class `Color_grid`, whose declaration is shown below, is used for storing, displaying, and changing the colors in a color grid.

```cpp
class Color_grid
{
    public:
        Color_grid(istream &infile);
            //constructor, reads color grid from infile
        void Display() const;       //displays color grid
        void PaintRegion(int row, int col, char color, char oldColor);
            //paints the connected region of its pixel parameter
            // the given color
    private:
        apmatrix<char> pixels;
};
```

(a) Write the code for the constructor that initializes a `Color_grid` as started below. The constructor reads the colors of the pixels from a file represented by the parameter `infile`. You may assume that the file is open and contains the number of rows followed by the number of columns for the grid, followed by the characters representing the colors. For example,

```
4 6
rrbgyy
brbyrr
ggrrrb
yrryrb
```

Complete the following constructor:

```cpp
Color_grid::Color_grid(istream &infile) : pixels(0,0)
//precondition: infile is open
//postcondition: pixels has been resized and initialized to the
//               color grid from the stream infile
```

GO ON TO THE NEXT PAGE ➤

(b) Write the member function PaintRegion as started below. **Note: You must write a recursive solution.** PaintRegion paints the connected region of its pixel parameter a different color specified by the color parameter. If color is the same color as the given pixel, PaintRegion does nothing. To visualize what PaintRegion does, imagine that the different colors surrounding the connected region of a given pixel form a boundary. When paint is poured onto the given pixel, the new color will fill the connected region up to (but excluding) the boundary. For example, the effect of the function call c.PaintRegion(2, 3, 'b', 'r') on the Color_grid c is shown here.

before							after					
r	r	b	g	y	y		r	r	b	g	y	y
b	r	b	y	r	r		b	r	b	y	b	b
g	g	r	r	r	b		g	g	b	b	b	b
y	r	r	y	r	b		y	b	b	y	b	b

Complete the member function PaintRegion below. **Note: Only a recursive solution will be accepted.**

```
void Color_grid::PaintRegion(int row, int col, char color, char oldColor)
//precondition: color is one of 'r', 'b', 'g', or 'y'
//              oldColor is the original color of the connected region
//postcondition: if 0 ≤ row < pixels.numrows() and 0 ≤ col < pixels.numcols(),
//               the pixels in the connected region starting at
//               pixels[row][col] are all painted color
```

4. This question involves reasoning about the code from the Marine Biology Case Study. A copy of the code is provided as part of this exam.

Consider the fish simulation in the fishsim program. Suppose that it is used to study a small population of fish in a very large grid. It then makes sense for the environment to be implemented with a data structure that uses less memory than a matrix.

Consider storing the grid of fish as an array of defined fish only. The number of elements in the array will be the number of fish created. The array will be maintained in row-major order, namely the order in which fish are processed in the current program. Thus, the elements are ordered by position, assuming a row-by-row top-down, left-right ordering if these positions were in a matrix. For example, if you picture the following grid of fish:

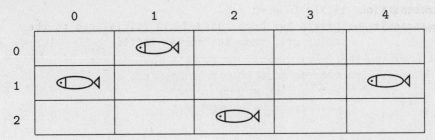

then the actual storage of the fish grid will be as follows:

myWorld

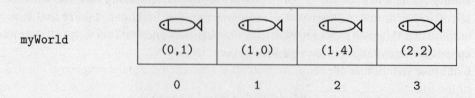

| (0,1) | (1,0) | (1,4) | (2,2) |

0   1   2   3

The following changes will be made to the private section of the Environment class. The apmatrix data member myWorld will be changed to an apvector. Two helper functions Insert and Remove will be added. Insert will take a fish and position as parameters and insert the fish into myWorld, updating myFishCount. Remove will delete from the array the fish at the given Position parameter and return that fish. It will also update myFishCount. The following declarations reflect these changes (highlighted in bold).

```
class Environment
{
    ...
    private:
        bool InRange(const Position & pos) const;
        //postcondition: returns true if pos in grid
        //               returns false otherwise
        apvector<Fish> myWorld; //grid of fish
        int myFishCreated;      //# of fish ever created
        int myFishCount;        //# fish in current environment
        void Insert(const Fish & fish, const Position & pos);
        //postcondition: fish with given pos inserted in myWorld
        //               maintaining correct order by position.
        //               myFishCount updated
        //               Does nothing if pos already occupied
        Fish Remove(const Position & pos);
        //postcondition: fish at position pos has been returned.
        //               It has been removed from myWorld.
        //               myFishCount updated
```

(a) Write a revised version of the Environment member function IsEmpty, as started below. IsEmpty should return true if its position parameter is in the grid but does not contain a fish; otherwise, it should return false.

Complete function IsEmpty.

```
bool Environment::IsEmpty(const Position & pos) const
//postcondition: returns true if pos is in grid
//               and no fish at pos
//               returns false otherwise
```

GO ON TO THE NEXT PAGE ➤

(b) Write a revised version of the Environment member function AddFish, as started below. AddFish should create a new fish at its parameter position, pos. In writing function AddFish, you may wish to call either or both of the new Environment member functions, Insert and Remove. You may assume that they work as specified. You may also assume that function IsEmpty works as specified, regardless of what you wrote in part (a).
Complete function AddFish.

```
void Environment::AddFish(const Position & pos)
//precondition: no fish already at pos, i.e. IsEmpty(pos)
//postcondition: fish created at pos
```

(c) Write a revised version of the Environment member function Update, as started below. Update should take a fish that has just moved and update its position in the environment. In writing function Update, you may wish to call one or both of the member functions Insert and Remove.
Complete function Update below.

```
void Environment::Update(const Position & oldLoc, Fish & fish)
//precondition: fish was located at oldLoc, has been updated
//postcondition: if (fish.Location() != oldLoc) then oldLoc is
//               empty; Fish fish is updated properly in this
//               environment
```

STOP

Answer Key

Section I

1. **C**	15. **A**	29. **B**
2. **D**	16. **B**	30. **A**
3. **B**	17. **D**	31. **C**
4. **C**	18. **D**	32. **E**
5. **A**	19. **B**	33. **E**
6. **C**	20. **D**	34. **C**
7. **A**	21. **A**	35. **A**
8. **E**	22. **D**	36. **B**
9. **E**	23. **A**	37. **E**
10. **C**	24. **D**	38. **C**
11. **E**	25. **B**	39. **B**
12. **D**	26. **C**	40. **C**
13. **E**	27. **D**	
14. **B**	28. **A**	

Answers Explained

Section I

1. **(C)** One of the golden rules of programming: don't start planning the program until every aspect of the specification is crystal clear. A programmer should never make unilateral decisions about ambiguities in a specification.

2. **(D)** The algorithm swaps a[0] with a[n-1], a[1] with a[n-2], and so on until the index markers j and k cross. This has the effect of reversing the elements of the array.

3. **(B)** When x ≤ y, a recursive call is made to WhatIsIt(x-1, y). If x decreases at every recursive call, there is no way to reach a successful base case. Thus, the function never terminates and eventually exhausts all available memory.

4. **(C)** Calc(3, 4, 5) passes the test if (x > 2), fails the test if (y < 4), and therefore returns result, which is 3. Calc(5, 1, 3) fails the test if (x > 2) and therefore skips right to the bottom and returns y*result, which is 15. Then 3 + 15 = 18.

5. **(A)** The expression !(max != a[i]) is equivalent to max == a[i], so the given expression is equivalent to a[i] == max || max == a[i], which is equivalent to a[i] == max.

6. **(C)** The algorithm used in function Find is a sequential search, which may have to examine all the records to find the matching one. A binary search,

which repeatedly discards a chunk of the array that does not contain the key, is more efficient. However, it can only be used if the values being examined— in this case customer `IdNumbers`—are sorted. Note that it doesn't help to have the records sorted by name or phone number since the algorithm doesn't look at these values.

7. **(A)** An `apvector` data member in a struct (or class) should be initialized with a constructor. The implementation of the constructor can be inside or outside the struct. At the very least the constructor will declare the number of slots to be created for the `purchases apvector` (see the `apvector` and `struct` section in Chapter 4).

8. **(E)** Since `a` is passed by reference, it will share memory with its actual parameter `x`. Picture the memory slots just before function `Process` is exited:

$$\begin{array}{ccc} x & y & b \\ \boxed{6} & \boxed{3} & \boxed{18} \\ a \end{array}$$

Here they are *after* the function is exited:

$$\begin{array}{cc} x & y \\ \boxed{6} & \boxed{3} \end{array}$$

9. **(E)** The function call `WhatsIt(347)` puts on the stack `cout << 7`.
The function call `WhatsIt(34)` puts on the stack `cout << 4`.
The function call `WhatsIt(3)` is a base case and writes out 3.
Now the stack is popped from the top, and the 3 that was printed is followed by 4, then 7. The result is 347.

10. **(C)** If `v` has elements 2, 3, 5, the values of `value` are

```
2                      //after initialization
2*10 + 3 = 23          //when i = 1
23*10 + 5 = 235        //when i = 2
```

11. **(E)** Segment II works in all cases except when the array is empty (i.e., n is 0). In that case, `sum` adds `a[0]`, which doesn't exist if the array has no elements.

12. **(D)** If a parameter is passed by reference, then the actual parameter must be a variable. If the parameter is passed by value, the actual parameter can be a variable, a constant, or an expression. For a simple integer parameter like `length`, passing by value allows a lot more flexibility in the function call.

13. **(E)** Segment I fails because `a` isn't resized before being assigned values. The declaration `apvector<char> a` creates an array with no slots. Contrast this with Segment II, which initializes `a` to have eight slots. The statement `b = a` will resize `b` to have the same number of slots as `a`. Segment III uses the `apvector` class constructor with the `fillValue` parameter to fill array `a` with eight dashes. Then it uses the copy constructor to initialize `b` by copying `a`.

14. **(B)** Recall that insertion sort takes each element in turn and (a) finds its insertion point and (b) moves elements to insert that element in its correct place. Thus, if the array is in reverse sorted order, the insertion point will always be at the front of the array, leading to the maximum number of comparisons and data moves—very inefficient. Thus, choices C and E are false, as is choice A.

Selection sort finds the smallest element in the array and swaps it with a[0] and then finds the smallest element in the rest of the array and swaps it with a[1], and so on. Thus, the same number of comparisons and moves will occur, irrespective of the original arrangement of elements in the array. So choice B is true, and choice D is false.

15. **(A)** Here's the algorithm that must be used. Notice that it involves reading all the numbers in numFile.

    - Open a new file for writing, outFile say.

    - For the first $k - 1$ numbers in numFile, read a number from numFile, write it to outFile.

    - Read the kth number. (Do nothing else with it. This effectively skips over it.)

    - For the rest of the numbers in numFile, read a number from numFile, write it to outFile.

    - (Rename outFile if desired.)

16. **(B)** The postcondition should be a true assertion about the major action of the segment. The segment overwrites the elements of array a with the positive elements of a. Then n is adjusted so that now the array a[0]...a[n-1] contains just positive integers. Note that even though choices C and E are correct assertions about the program segment, they are not good postconditions because they don't describe the main modification to array a (namely all negative integers have been removed).

17. **(D)** Segment I reads the three separate words of each line into three apstring variables. This will work because the title, first name, and last name are separated by whitespace. (The >> operator reads everything up to whitespace.) Segment II is clunky, but it works. First it reads the whole line into name, finds the first blank, extracts the substring following the first blank, finds the first blank in this temp string, and then extracts the first name. Note that

    ```
    temp = name.substr(k+1, name.length())
    ```

    will work even though name.length() is more characters than needed: it'll simply return all the characters up to the end of the name string, which is what is wanted. Segment III fails because

    ```
    secondBlank = name.find(' ')
    ```

    does not return the index of the second blank—it returns the index of the first blank in name. It will, therefore, have the same value as firstBlank.

18. **(D)** Segment I fails because the SENTINEL will be processed. The test comes too late. Segments II and III do a test on num before it is processed. In Segment III, the for loop has cin >> num as an initializing condition and num != SENTINEL as the test—if true, the body of the loop, Process(num), will be executed. Finally, cin >> num is the updating statement that leads to termination of the loop.

19. **(B)** It appears that this algorithm assumes as part of its precondition that list is sorted in increasing order. Without this assumption, key will generally not be found even if it's in the list. This is because the loop is exited as soon as

a value greater than `key` is encountered. Notice that choices A, C, D, and E all describe special cases where the correct index *is* returned. If `key` is not in the list, -1 will (correctly) be returned. Also, if `key` is greater than all the elements of `list` that precede it, `key` will be reached, and its correct index will be returned.

20. (**D**) Method I correctly uses an initializer list, and Method III uses correct code without an initializer list.

21. (**A**) Functions with the same name (which is true for constructors of a given class) and parameters that differ in type and/or number are called overloaded functions.

22. (**D**) Part of the class specification is that $0 \leq$ `mySecs` ≤ 60, which may be violated by Segment I.

23. (**A**) This is awkward code because the + operator is not overloaded, nor are there accessor functions (like `Hours()`, for example) that return the various attributes of an `ElapsedTime` object. Thus, the only way for a client program to add two `ElapsedTime` objects with the given functions of the class is

    • Convert each `ElapsedTime` object to seconds.

    • Add to get the sum as a number of seconds.

    • Construct a new `ElapsedTime` object using the constructor that takes a single number (seconds) as a parameter.

    By the way, don't waste time checking the algorithm for Segment III: a client function may not access the private variables of a class!

24. (**D**) The correct code for `SplitFile` still needs to be written. What is shown is a stub—temporary code that allows the rest of the code to execute when it encounters a call to `SplitFile`.

25. (**B**) Elements will be written to `posFile` and `negFile` in the order they are encountered, thus preserving the order in which they appear in `sourceFile`. Since no information is given on the ordering of numbers in `sourceFile`, you cannot assume that Statement I is true. Similarly, since you have no information of the number of negative and nonnegative numbers in `sourceFile`, you cannot assume that Statement III is true. For example, if all integers in `sourceFile` are negative, then `negFile` will have the exact same number of elements as `sourceFile`.

26. (**C**) Parameters passed by const reference have their values protected and can never be modified. Note that the += operator modifies the `lvalue` that precedes it.

27. (**D**) Notice in the original code, if `n` is 1, `k` is incremented by 1, and if `n` is 4, `k` is incremented by 4. This is equivalent to saying "if `n` is 1 or 4, `k` is incremented by `n`."

28. (**A**) The point of the binary search algorithm is that the interval containing `key` is repeatedly narrowed down by splitting it in half. For each iteration of the `while` loop, if `key` is in the list, `a[first]` $\leq$ `key` $\leq$ `a[last]`. Note that (i) the endpoints of the interval must be included, and (ii) `key` is not necessarily in the list.

29. **(B)**

	first	last	mid	list[mid]
After first iteration	0	13	6	50
After second iteration	7	13	10	220
After third iteration	7	9	8	101
After fourth iteration	9	9	9	205

30. **(A)** Since results of calculations with floating-point numbers are not always represented exactly (round-off error), direct tests for equality are not reliable. Instead of if (d == c), a test should be done to check whether the difference of d and c is within some acceptable tolerance interval (see the section on relational operators in Chapter 1).

31. **(C)** Before manipulating LargeInt objects you have to check that they've been correctly constructed, and to do that you need to output them. Therefore, the constructor and Print functions should be coded before the others.

32. **(E)** You want to simulate i++ (or i += 1). Thus, eliminate choices B and C, which don't start with i dot something. Since the ++ and += operators are not available for the LargeInt class in this question, you have to add 1 to i correctly using the Add member function. Think of i as the object and 1 as the parameter. Choice D is wrong because a LargeInt parameter must be used. Choice E does this correctly. Choice A is wrong because you're not adding n to i, you're adding 1 to i.

33. **(E)** The best way to answer a question like this is to take a small value of MAXNUM, 4 say, and see what happens to a[2], a[3], and a[4]. The first for loop sets them all to true. Here's what happens in the second for loop, as i goes from 2 to 4:

```
i=2:    j goes from 1 to 2        a[2]   a[3]   a[4]
                                   T      T      T
        j=1: Toggle a[2*1]  ⟶    [F]
        j=2: Toggle a[2*2]  ⟶                   F
i=3:    j goes from 1 to 1
        j=1: Toggle a[3*1]  ⟶           [F]
i=4:    j goes from 1 to 1
        j=1: Toggle a[4*1]  ⟶                  [T]
```

The final values are boxed. This small hand trace provides a counterexample for each of choices A–D, which leaves E as the correct answer. Note: the word "toggle" is used when there are just two possible values for a variable. To toggle it means to switch it to the other value, much like one would toggle a light switch on and off.

34. **(C)** The function reads 'a', then for i = 'a' to 'a' (namely once) prints a. When the recursive call is made, it stacks that a must be printed. Next the function reads 'b', then for i = 'a' to 'b' (namely twice) prints b. Then it stacks that bb must be printed. And so on. At the time of the base case (period read), the following has been printed:

```
abbcccddd
```

and here's what's stacked up, still to be printed:

```
dddd
ccc
bb
a
```

Popping the stack from the top and printing yields

```
abbcccddddddddcccbba
```

35. **(A)** `string1` is changed to "con" by changing 12 (its end) to 4. `string2` is changed to "rat" by changing 12 (its end) to 11. This is just two integer changes, so statement I is correct. Statement II is wrong because *four* integer changes would be needed, for the start and end of each string. Statement III is wrong because string `s` would need to be changed to "inconsideration" (three character changes), after which "rate" could not be represented since it is no longer contained in `s`.

36. **(B)** All that needs to be changed is a small piece of code in `Swim()`. The variable `flip` is changed to have three possible values. For two of them, the fish will go right. Here is the modified code:

```
    ...
else
{
    flip = randomVals.RandInt(3);
    if (flip == 0)
    {
        myPosition--;
    }
    else
    {
        myPosition++;
    }
}
```

37. **(E)** A `Neighborhood` object has a private variable `myList` that is an `apvector` of type `Position`. This vector may hold 0, 1, 2, 3, or 4 elements. Note that choice C is not incorrect, but it is not the best answer.

38. **(C)** The key is in changing the order in which fish are inserted in the `fishList` array. In Segment III, they are inserted column by column from the top row (row 0) down, which was required. Simply processing the `fishList` array in reverse order, as in Segment II, causes a bottom-up right-left processing order. Segment I doesn't work either because the pattern of movement stays the same. All that changes is the ID numbers of the fish and hence the letters that represent them.

39. **(B)** Here's a counterexample: `fishList[0]` is the first fish in the list. The ID number of the fish, however, must be greater than or equal to 1. Note that in the current version of `fishsim`, fish don't die. This is the reason that choice C is true.

40. **(C)** Modifying the `ShowMe` function doesn't work because `ShowMe` is called only if a fish is an element of `fishList` (i.e., an *actual* fish). Undefined fish are not in this list.

Section II

1. (a)
```
void ComputeVotePercent(apvector<Candidate> & Clist)
{
    int i, total = 0;
    for (i=0; i<NUMCANDIDATES; i++)
        total += Clist[i].numVotes;
    for (i=0; i<NUMCANDIDATES; i++)
        Clist[i].votePercent =
            100*Clist[i].numVotes/double(total);
}
```

(b)
```
bool IsViable(const Candidate & C)
{
    return C.votePercent >= 10;
}
```

(c)
```
void PrintViable (apvector<Candidate> & Clist)
{
    int maxPos, i, numViable = 0;
    //create list of viable candidates
    apvector<Candidate> Vlist(NUMCANDIDATES);
    for (i=0; i< NUMCANDIDATES; i++)
        if (IsViable(Clist[i]))
        {
            Vlist[numViable] = Clist[i];
            numViable++;
        }
    //sort the Vlist array in decreasing order of numVotes
    for (i=0; i<numViable-1; i++)
    {
        maxPos = i;
        for (int j=i+1; j<numViable; j++)
            if (Vlist[j].numVotes > Vlist[maxPos].numVotes)
                maxPos = j;
        Swap(Vlist[i], Vlist[maxPos]);
    }
    for (i=0; i<numViable; i++)
        cout << Vlist[i].name << " " << Vlist[i].votePercent
            << endl;
}
```

NOTE

1. In part (a), to get the correct, real-valued votePercent, you have to make sure that your percent calculation doesn't do integer division! You can achieve this either by casting the numerator or denominator to double, or by replacing 100 with 100.0.

2. In part (c), you need to create a list of viable candidates and then sort this list on the numVotes (or votePercent) field of the candidates. The sort used is selection sort, but you may use any sorting algorithm.

3. In sorting the VList array, be sure to compare just the numVotes fields; the entire record, however, must be swapped.

4. An alternative solution to part (c) is to sort the Clist array then print the viable candidates from the top of the list. This however, is inefficient if Clist is large and the number of viable candidates is small.

2. (a)
```
int CountNegatives(const NumberSet & S)
{
    int count = 0;
    while (count < S.size() && S.FindKth(count+1) < 0)
        count++;
    return count;
}
```

(b)
```
void RemoveNegatives(NumberSet & S)
{
    int N = CountNegatives(S);
    for (int i=1; i<=N; i++)
        S.Remove(S.FindKth(1));
}
```

Alternatively,

```
void RemoveNegatives(NumberSet & S)
{
    while (S.FindKth(1) < 0)
        S.Remove(S.FindKth(1));
}
```

(c)
```
NumberSet CommonElements (const NumberSet & S1,
                          const NumberSet & S2)
{
    NumberSet temp;
    int x = S1.Size();
    for (int i=1; i<=x; i++)
        if (S2.Includes(S1.FindKth(i)))
            temp.Insert(S1.FindKth(i));
    return temp;
}
```

NOTE

1. In part (a), you must check that your solution works if S is empty. For the given algorithm, count < S.Size() will fail and short circuit the test, which is desirable since S.FindKth(1) will violate the precondition of FindKth(k), namely that k cannot be greater than Size().

2. For the first solution in part (b), if your last step is

   S.Remove(S.FindKth(i))

   you get a subtle intent error. Suppose that S is initially $\{2, -4, -6\}$. After

   S.Remove(S.FindKth(1)),

   S will be $\{2, -4\}$. After

   S.Remove(S.FindKth(2)),

   S will be $\{-4\}$!! The point is that S is adjusted after each call to S.Remove. The algorithm that works is this: If N is the number of negatives, simply remove the smallest element N times. Note that the alternative solution avoids this pitfall by simply repeatedly removing the smallest element if it's negative.

3. Part (c) could also be accomplished by going through each element in S2 and checking if it's included in S1.

3. (a)
```
Color_grid::Color_grid(istream &infile) : pixels(0,0)
{
    int rows, cols, r, c;
    infile >> rows >> cols;
    pixels.resize(rows, cols);
    for (r=0; r<rows; r++)
        for (c=0; c<cols; c++)
            infile >> pixels[r][c];
}
```

(b)
```
void Color_grid::PaintRegion(int row, int col, char color,
        char oldColor)
{
    if (row >= 0 && row < pixels.numrows() && col >= 0
            && col < pixels.numcols())
        if (pixels[row][col] != color
                && pixels[row][col] == oldColor)
        {
            pixels[row][col] = color;
            PaintRegion(row+1,col,color,oldColor);
            PaintRegion(row-1,col,color,oldColor);
            PaintRegion(row,col+1,color,oldColor);
            PaintRegion(row,col-1,color,oldColor);
        }
}
```

NOTE
1. In part (a), the `pixels` matrix must be resized before reading values into it.
2. In part (b), each recursive call must test whether `row` and `col` are in the correct range for the `pixels` array; otherwise, your algorithm may sail right off the edge!
3. Don't forget to test if `color` is different from that of the starting pixel. PaintRegion does nothing if the colors are the same.
4. The color-change assignment `pixels[row][col] = color` must precede the recursive calls to avoid infinite recursion.

4. (a)
```
bool Environment::IsEmpty(const Position & pos) const
{
    if (InRange(pos))
    {
        for (int i=0; i<myFishCount; i++)
            if (myWorld[i].Location() == pos)
                return false;
    }
    return true;
}
```

```
(b) void Environment::AddFish(const Position & pos)
    {
        if (!IsEmpty(pos))
        {
            cerr << "error, attempt to create fish at nonempty:"
                << pos << endl;
            return;
        }
        myFishCreated++;
        Fish f(myFishCreated, pos);
        Insert(f, pos);
    }

(c) void Environment::Update(const Position & oldLoc,
        Fish & fish)
    {
        if (InRange(oldLoc))
        {
            Fish f = Remove(oldLoc);
            if (f.Id() != fish.Id())
            {
                cerr << "illegal fish move" << endl;
            }
            else    //place updated copy of fish in updated
                    //position
            {
                Insert(fish, fish.Location());
            }
        }
    }
```

NOTE

1. In part (a), the `myWorld` array is searched for a fish with position `pos`. If `pos` is not found, then that position has no fish in it.

2. In part (b), `myFishCount` is incremented in the `Insert` function (see the precondition) and therefore doesn't appear in `AddFish`.

3. In part (c), the fish at `oldLoc` in the array is the same fish of the parameter that just got moved. Therefore, their ID numbers must match! Notice that removing the fish from the `oldLoc` position automatically updates that position. It also provides the easiest way to access that fish's ID number.

4. In this solution `Remove` is called whether `oldLoc == newLoc` or not. Therefore, `Insert` is *always* called and the test

   ```
   if(!(oldLoc == newLoc))
   ```

   must be omitted.

Answer Sheet: Practice Exam Two

1. Ⓐ Ⓑ Ⓒ Ⓓ Ⓔ
2. Ⓐ Ⓑ Ⓒ Ⓓ Ⓔ
3. Ⓐ Ⓑ Ⓒ Ⓓ Ⓔ
4. Ⓐ Ⓑ Ⓒ Ⓓ Ⓔ
5. Ⓐ Ⓑ Ⓒ Ⓓ Ⓔ
6. Ⓐ Ⓑ Ⓒ Ⓓ Ⓔ
7. Ⓐ Ⓑ Ⓒ Ⓓ Ⓔ
8. Ⓐ Ⓑ Ⓒ Ⓓ Ⓔ
9. Ⓐ Ⓑ Ⓒ Ⓓ Ⓔ
10. Ⓐ Ⓑ Ⓒ Ⓓ Ⓔ
11. Ⓐ Ⓑ Ⓒ Ⓓ Ⓔ
12. Ⓐ Ⓑ Ⓒ Ⓓ Ⓔ
13. Ⓐ Ⓑ Ⓒ Ⓓ Ⓔ
14. Ⓐ Ⓑ Ⓒ Ⓓ Ⓔ

15. Ⓐ Ⓑ Ⓒ Ⓓ Ⓔ
16. Ⓐ Ⓑ Ⓒ Ⓓ Ⓔ
17. Ⓐ Ⓑ Ⓒ Ⓓ Ⓔ
18. Ⓐ Ⓑ Ⓒ Ⓓ Ⓔ
19. Ⓐ Ⓑ Ⓒ Ⓓ Ⓔ
20. Ⓐ Ⓑ Ⓒ Ⓓ Ⓔ
21. Ⓐ Ⓑ Ⓒ Ⓓ Ⓔ
22. Ⓐ Ⓑ Ⓒ Ⓓ Ⓔ
23. Ⓐ Ⓑ Ⓒ Ⓓ Ⓔ
24. Ⓐ Ⓑ Ⓒ Ⓓ Ⓔ
25. Ⓐ Ⓑ Ⓒ Ⓓ Ⓔ
26. Ⓐ Ⓑ Ⓒ Ⓓ Ⓔ
27. Ⓐ Ⓑ Ⓒ Ⓓ Ⓔ
28. Ⓐ Ⓑ Ⓒ Ⓓ Ⓔ

29. Ⓐ Ⓑ Ⓒ Ⓓ Ⓔ
30. Ⓐ Ⓑ Ⓒ Ⓓ Ⓔ
31. Ⓐ Ⓑ Ⓒ Ⓓ Ⓔ
32. Ⓐ Ⓑ Ⓒ Ⓓ Ⓔ
33. Ⓐ Ⓑ Ⓒ Ⓓ Ⓔ
34. Ⓐ Ⓑ Ⓒ Ⓓ Ⓔ
35. Ⓐ Ⓑ Ⓒ Ⓓ Ⓔ
36. Ⓐ Ⓑ Ⓒ Ⓓ Ⓔ
37. Ⓐ Ⓑ Ⓒ Ⓓ Ⓔ
38. Ⓐ Ⓑ Ⓒ Ⓓ Ⓔ
39. Ⓐ Ⓑ Ⓒ Ⓓ Ⓔ
40. Ⓐ Ⓑ Ⓒ Ⓓ Ⓔ

Practice Exam Two

COMPUTER SCIENCE A
SECTION I

Time—1 hour and 15 minutes
Number of questions—40
Percent of total grade—50

Directions: Determine the answer to each of the following questions or incomplete statements, using separate pieces of scrap paper for any necessary scratchwork. Then decide which is the best of the choices given and fill in the corresponding oval on the answer sheet. Do not spend too much time on any one problem.

Note: Assume that the standard libraries (e.g., `iostream.h`, `fstream.h`, `math.h`, etc.) and the AP C++ classes are included in any programs that use the code segments provided in individual questions. A Quick Reference to the AP C++ classes is provided.

---

1. The expression $20 + 21/6 * 2$ is equivalent to
   (A) $20 + 3 * 2$
   (B) $41/6 * 2$
   (C) $20 + 21/12$
   (D) $41/(6 * 2)$
   (E) $20 + (3.5 * 2)$

2. The main job of a compiler is to
   (A) Convert object code (machine language) into source code
   (B) Translate a high-level language like C++ into machine language
   (C) Link the different modules of a program into a single executable piece of code
   (D) Allocate CPU time for execution of a program
   (E) List the syntax errors in a program

GO ON TO THE NEXT PAGE ➤

Questions 3 and 4 refer to the following function.

```
int Mystery(int n)
{
    if (n == 1)
        return 3;
    else
        return 3*Mystery(n-1);
}
```

3. What value does `Mystery(4)` return?
   (A) 3
   (B) 9
   (C) 12
   (D) 27
   (E) 81

4. Which best describes what function `Mystery` does?
   (A) Multiplies n by 3
   (B) Raises 3 to the nth power
   (C) Raises n to the third power
   (D) Returns $(n)(n-1)(n-2)\ldots(1)$, namely $n!$
   (E) Finds the least common multiple of 3 and n

5. A three-digit integer is said to be a *scube* if the value of the integer equals the sum of the cubes of its digits. For example, 153 is a scube since $1^3 + 5^3 + 3^3 = 1 + 125 + 27 = 153$. However, 342 is not a scube since $3^3 + 4^3 + 2^3 = 99 \neq 342$. A programmer must write a program that lists all scubes. Assuming that she understands the problem, what should she do first?
   (A) Write input and output functions for reading and writing three-digit numbers.
   (B) Write code that breaks a three-digit number into digits.
   (C) Write a top-down design listing all operations and data structures needed in solving the problem.
   (D) Write a driver program that tests the main algorithm of the program.
   (E) Write a boolean function `IsScube` that returns true if a three-digit number is a scube, otherwise it returns false.

GO ON TO THE NEXT PAGE ➤

6. Function CharStuff deals with reading characters from a textfile. In this question, a *word* is considered to be any sequence of nonwhitespace characters.

```
void CharStuff(apstring & s, ifstream & infile)
//precondition: infile is open for reading at the beginning
//              of the file. The first line of infile
//              contains at least two words. s is an empty
//              string
{
    char ch;
    while (infile >> ch)
        s += ch;
}
```

Which of the following best describes what CharStuff does?
(A) Stores the entire first line of infile in s, including the newline character that terminates the line
(B) Stores the entire first line of infile in s, excluding the newline character that terminates the line
(C) Stores the first word of infile in s, including preceding and succeeding punctuation
(D) Stores the first word of infile in s, including preceding blanks
(E) Stores the entire contents of infile in s excluding whitespace (You may assume that s has the capacity to store the entire file.)

7. Often the most efficient computer algorithms use a divide-and-conquer approach, for example, one in which a list is repeatedly split into two pieces until a desired outcome is reached. Which of the following use a divide-and-conquer approach?
 I mergesort
 II quicksort
 III binary search

(A) I only
(B) II only
(C) III only
(D) I and III only
(E) I, II, and III

8. What will be output by this code segment?

```
for (int i=5; i>0; i--)
{
    for (int j=1; j<=i; j++)
        cout << j*j << " ";
    cout << endl;
}
```

(A) 1
     1 4
     1 4 9
     1 4 9 16
     1 4 9 16 25

(B) 1 4 9 16 25
     1 4 9 16
     1 4 9
     1 4
     1

(C) 25 16 9 4 1
     25 16 9 4
     25 16 9
     25 16
     25

(D) 25
     25 16
     25 16 9
     25 16 9 4
     25 16 9 4 1

(E) 1 4 9 16 25
     1 4 9 16 25
     1 4 9 16 25
     1 4 9 16 25
     1 4 9 16 25

GO ON TO THE NEXT PAGE ➤

9. Consider two methods of storing a set of nonnegative integers in which there are no duplicates.

Method One: Store the integers explicitly in an array in which the number of elements is known. For example, in this method, the set {6, 2, 1, 8, 9, 0} can be represented as follows:

0	1	2	3	4	5				
6	2	1	8	9	0				

6 elements

Method Two: Suppose that the range of the integers is 0 to MAX. Use a boolean array indexed from 0 to MAX. The index values represent the possible values in the set. In other words, each possible integer from 0 to MAX is represented by a different position in the array. A value of true in the array means that the corresponding integer is in the set, a value of false means that the integer is not in the set. For example, using this method the set {6, 2, 1, 8, 9, 0} would be represented as follows (T = true, F = false):

0	1	2	3	4	5	6	7	8	9	10	...	MAX
T	T	T	F	F	F	T	F	T	T	F	...	F

The following operations are to be performed on the set of integers:
   I Search for a target value in the set.
   II Print all the elements of the set.
   III Return the number of elements in the set.

Which statement is true?
(A) Operation I is more efficient if the set is stored using Method One.
(B) Operation II is more efficient if the set is stored using Method Two.
(C) Operation III is more efficient if the set is stored using Method One.
(D) Operation I is equally efficient for Methods One and Two.
(E) Operation III is equally efficient for Methods One and Two.

10. An algorithm for finding the square root of a number N involves computing successive approximations of the square root of N using the formula

$$x_{n+1} = 0.5 * (N/x_n + x_n)$$

where x_0 is an initial guess, x_n is the current approximation, and x_{n+1} is the next approximation. In a program implementing this algorithm, a programmer forgot to include a test that would check for an initial guess of zero. If the initial guess is zero, when will the error be detected?
(A) At compile time
(B) At edit time
(C) As soon as the value of N is entered
(D) During run time
(E) When an incorrect result is output

GO ON TO THE NEXT PAGE ➤

11. If a, b, and c are integers, which of the following conditions is sufficient to *guarantee* that the expression

    a < c || a < b && !(a == c)

    evaluates to true?

    (A) a < c
    (B) a < b
    (C) a > b
    (D) a == b
    (E) a == c

12. Airmail Express charges for shipping small packages by integer values of weight. The charges for a weight w in pounds are as follows:

$$0 < w \leq 2 \qquad \$4.00$$
$$2 < w \leq 5 \qquad \$8.00$$
$$5 < w \leq 20 \qquad \$15.00$$

    The company does not accept packages that weigh more than 20 pounds. Which of the following represents the best set of data (weights) to test a program that calculates shipping charges?
    (A) 2, 5, 20
    (B) 1, 4, 16
    (C) 1, 2, 3, 5, 16, 20
    (D) 1, 2, 3, 5, 16, 20, 21
    (E) All integers from 1 through 21

13. Assume that `inFile` is open for reading and contains an unknown number of integers. A programmer writes a piece of code to read the contents of `inFile` into an apvector of integers. Which of the following (inefficient) segments will work as intended?

```
 I apvector<int> a;
   i = 0;
   while(inFile >> a[i])
   {
       a.resize(i+1);
       i++;
   }
```

```
II apvector<int> a(1);
   i = 0;
   while(inFile >> a[i])
   {
       i++;
       a.resize(i);
   }
```

```
III apvector<int> a(1);
    i = 0;
    while(inFile >> a[i])
    {
        i++;
        a.resize(i+1);
    }
```

(A) None will work.
(B) I only
(C) II only
(D) III only
(E) II and III only

14. Refer to function Alter.

```
void Alter(apmatrix<int> & m, int c)
{
    for (int i=0; i<m.numrows(); i++)
        for (int j=c+1; j<m.numcols(); j++)
            m[i][j-1] = m[i][j];
}
```

If m is

```
1 3 5 7
2 4 6 8
3 5 7 9
```

then Alter(m, 1) will change m to

(A) 1 5 7 7
    2 6 8 8
    3 7 9 9

(B) 1 5 7
    2 6 8
    3 7 9

(C) 1 3 5 7
    3 5 7 9

(D) 1 3 5 7
    3 5 7 9
    3 5 7 9

(E) 1 7 7 7
    2 8 8 8
    3 9 9 9

Questions 15–17 refer to the Employee class declared below.

```
class Employee
{
    public:
        Employee();       //default constructor
        Employee(const apstring &N, int id, double HW);
        //constructor
        apstring Name() const;      //returns employee's name
        int idNum() const;          //returns employee's id number
        double HourlyWage() const; //returns employee's
                                    // hourly wage
        double IncrementWage(double amt);
        //increases hourly wage by amt
    private:
        apstring myName;
        int myIdNum;
        double myHourlyWage;
};
```

15. Which of the following correctly implements the second Employee constructor using an initializer list?

    (A)   `Employee :: Employee(const apstring &N, int id, double HW)`
```
        {
            myName = N;
            myIdNum = id;
            myHourlyWage = HW;
        }
```

    (B)   `Employee :: Employee(const apstring &N, int id, double HW)`
```
        {
            myName = N, myIdNum = id, myHourlyWage = HW;
        }
```

    (C)   `Employee :: Employee(const apstring &N, int id, double HW)`
            `: myName(N), myIdNum(id), myHourlyWage(HW) { }`

    (D)   `Employee :: Employee()`
            `: myName(N), myIdNum(id), myHourlyWage(HW) { }`

    (E)   `Employee :: Employee(const apstring &N, int id, double HW)`
            `: N(myName), id(myIdNum), HW(myHourlyWage) { }`

GO ON TO THE NEXT PAGE ➤

16. Which of the following replacements for < *code* > correctly implements the member function IncrementWage?

```
double Employee :: IncrementWage(double amt)
//returns employee's hourly wage which has been permanently
//increased by amt
{
    <code>
}
```

    I   return myHourlyWage + amt;

   II myHourlyWage += amt;
       return myHourlyWage;

  III myHourlyWage += amt;
       return HourlyWage();

(A) I only
(B) II only
(C) III only
(D) I and II only
(E) II and III only

17. A client function ComputePay will return an employee's pay based on the number of hours the employee has worked.

```
double ComputePay(const Employee & E, double hours)
//returns amount of pay for Employee based on number of hours
// worked
{
    <code>
}
```

Which replacement for < *code* > is correct?
(A) return myHourlyWage * hours;
(B) return HourlyWage() * hours;
(C) return E.HourlyWage() * hours;
(D) return E.myHourlyWage * hours;
(E) return E.HourlyWage() * E.hours;

GO ON TO THE NEXT PAGE ➤

18. Suppose `numFile` is open for reading and contains

```
5  10  15
2 6.8  18
```

The program now executes the following code segment:

```
int i, j, k;
numFile >> i >> j >> k;
cout << i << j << k;
numFile >> i >> j >> k;
cout << i << j << k;
```

What will the values of `i`, `j`, and `k` be after execution of this segment?

(A) i = 2   j = 7   k = 18
(B) i = 2   j = 6   k = 15
(C) i = 2   j = 6   k = 8
(D) i = 5   j = 10   k = 15
(E) No values are assigned because of a run-time crash.

19. This question is based on the following declarations:

```
apstring strA = "CARROT", strB = "Carrot", strC = "car";
```

Given that 'A' has ASCII value 65 and 'a' has ASCII value 97, which is true?

(A) `strA < strB && strB > strC`
(B) `strC < strB && strB < strA`
(C) `strB < strC && strB < strA`
(D) `!(strA == strB) && strB < strA`
(E) `!(strA == strB) && !(strC < strB)`

GO ON TO THE NEXT PAGE ➤

20. Consider the following two program segments. Assume that num is an integer input at the keyboard.

```
I   int newNum = 0, temp;
    while (num > 10)
    {
        temp = num % 10;
        num /= 10;
        newNum = newNum*10 + temp;
    }
    cout << newNum;

II  int newNum = 0, temp;
    do
    {
        temp = num % 10;
        num /= 10;
        newNum = newNum*10 + temp;
    } while (num > 10);
    cout << newNum;
```

Which is true?
(A) Segments I and II will produce the same output for any input value of num.
(B) Segments I and II will produce different output for any input value of num.
(C) Segments I and II will produce different output only if 0 < num < 10. All other values of num will produce the same output.
(D) Segments I and II will produce different output only if 0 < num ≤ 10 or num < 0. All other values of num will produce the same output.
(E) Segments I and II will produce different output only if 0 < num < 10 or num < 0. All other values of num will produce the same output.

Questions 21 and 22 are based on the following struct declaration.

```
struct autoPart
{
    apstring description;
    int idNum;
    double price;
};
```

21. Refer to function FindCheapest. FindCheapest examines an array of autoPart and returns the idNum of the autoPart with the lowest price whose description matches the part parameter. For example, several of the autoPart elements may have "headlight" in their description field. Different headlights will differ in both price and idNum. If the part parameter is "headlight," FindCheapest will return the idNum of the cheapest headlight.

```
int FindCheapest(const apvector<autoPart> & allParts,
        const apstring & part)
//precondition: allParts contains at least one element whose
//              description matches part
//postcondition: returns the idNum of the cheapest autoPart
//              whose description matches part
{
    double min = LARGEVALUE;   //a value larger than the price of
                               // all autoParts
    int minIndex;
    for (int i=0; i<allParts.length(); i++)
        <more code>
}
```

Which of the following replacements for <more code> will achieve the intended postcondition of the function?

```
I {                                      II {
        if (allParts[i].price < min)             if (allParts[i].description == part)
        {                                            if (allParts[i].price < min)
            min = allParts[i].price;                 {
            minIndex = i;                                min = allParts[i].price;
        }                                                minIndex = i;
    }                                                }
    return allParts[minIndex].idNum;         }
                                             return allParts[minIndex].idNum;
```

```
III {
            if (allParts[i].description == part)
                if (allParts[i].price < min)
                    min = allParts[i].price;
        }
        return allParts[min].idNum;
```

(A) I only
(B) II only
(C) III only

(D) I and II only
(E) I and III only

GO ON TO THE NEXT PAGE ➤

22. Consider the following functions:

```
template <class type>
type Min(const type & x, const type & y)
//returns the smaller of values x and y
{
    if (x < y)
        return x;
    else
        return y;
}

void Test(const autoPart & P1, const autoPart & P2)
{
    cout << Min(P1.description, P2.description) << endl;
    cout << Min(P1.idNum, P2.idNum) << endl;
    cout << Min(P1.price, P2.price) << endl;
}
```

Assuming that the `autoPart` struct is correctly declared in the program in which these functions are used, which of the following is a *true* statement concerning these functions?

(A) `Test` will fail because simple parameter values of type `int` and `double` should not be passed by `const` reference.

(B) `Test` will fail because the dot member construct cannot be used for the actual parameters in a function.

(C) `Test` will fail because the compiler cannot distinguish among the different parameter types for the three function calls to `Min`.

(D) `Test` will fail because it is meaningless to define a templated function for the data members of a struct.

(E) `Test` will work because the < (less than) operator is defined for each of the types `apstring`, `int`, and `double`.

23. What is wrong with the following recursive function?

```
double DoSomething(double x)
{
    return DoSomething(x/2);
}
```

(A) The actual parameter `x/2` does not match the formal parameter `x`.

(B) There is no termination condition (base case).

(C) The result of the recursive call `DoSomething(x/2)` must be stored in a temporary variable, which is then returned.

(D) The parameters of a recursive function must be of type `int`.

(E) In a recursive function, an object must be defined in terms of a simpler case of itself. This is not true in function `DoSomething`.

GO ON TO THE NEXT PAGE ➤

Questions 24 and 25 refer to the following function.

```
int Recur(int n)
{
    if (n == 0 || n == 1)
        return 1;
    else if (n == 3)
        return 3;
    else
        return Recur(n-1) + Recur(n-2);
}
```

24. Find the value of Recur(2).
    (A) Undefined—no value returned
    (B) 0
    (C) 1
    (D) 2
    (E) 3

25. How many times is Recur(2) called as a result of calling Recur(6)?
    (A) 2
    (B) 4
    (C) 8
    (D) 32
    (E) 64

26. A large hospital maintains a list of patients' records in no particular order. To find the record of a given patient, which represents the most efficient method that will work?
    (A) Do a sequential search on the name field of the records.
    (B) Do a binary search on the name field of the records.
    (C) Use insertion sort to sort the records alphabetically by name; then do a sequential search on the name field of the records.
    (D) Use quicksort to sort the records alphabetically by name; then do a sequential search on the name field of the records.
    (E) Use quicksort to sort the records alphabetically by name; then do a binary search on the name field of the records.

GO ON TO THE NEXT PAGE ➤

27. Refer to the following declarations and function.

```
const int NUMITEMS = <some large integer constant>;
int OddSum(const apvector<int> & v)
//precondition: v is initialized with integers. NUMITEMS is
//               the number of integers in the list.
//               0 < NUMITEMS ≤ v.length()
//postcondition: returns the sum of the odd integers in v
{
    int sum = 0, i = 0;
    do {
        if (test 1)
            sum += v[i];
        i++;
    } while (test 2);
    return sum;
}
```

Which of the following substitutions for *test 1* and *test 2* will cause OddSum to correctly return the sum of the odd integers in v?

	test 1	*test 2*
(A)	v[i] % 2 == 1	i <= NUMITEMS
(B)	v[i] % 2 == 1	i < NUMITEMS
(C)	v[i] / 2 == 1	i <= NUMITEMS
(D)	v[NUMITEMS] % 2 == 1	i < v.length()
(E)	v[NUMITEMS] / 2 == 1	i < NUMITEMS

28. Consider this program segment:

```
int a = 10, b = 1, c = 0;
do
{
    c += a*b;
    b++;
} while (b <= 5);
```

Which loop performs the same calculation as this do...while loop?

(A) for (c=1; c<=5; c++)
        c += a*b;

(B) for (b=1; b<=1; b++)
        c += a*b;

(C) for (b=5; b>1; b--)
        c += a*b;

(D) for (b=1; b<=5; b++)
        c += a*b;

(E) for (a=1; a<=5; a++)
        c += a*b;

GO ON TO THE NEXT PAGE ➤

29. Consider the design for a program that manipulates recent dates. A Date class will be written that includes the following operations:

    - Display the date. Dates must be displayed as m/d/y, for example, 6/24/1963.
    - Advance the date by *k* days. For example, the date 6/24/1963 advanced by 20 days should result in the date 7/14/1963.
    - Compare two dates. If d1 and d2 are dates, d1 < d2 if and only if d1 occurs before d2.
    - Test if a date is in a leap year. A leap year is a year divisible by 4, except for years ending in 00, which must also be divisible by 400. (Note that a leap year has 366 days.)

    A programmer is considering two different methods for storing a Date object:

    I Three integers, for the month, day, and year of a given date.
    II A single integer that represents the number of days after Jan. 1, 1900.

    Which of the following statements about methods I and II for storing dates is *false*?

    (A) Implementation code for a Display member function is simpler if Method I is used.
    (B) Implementation code for the Advance member function is simpler if Method II is used.
    (C) Code to write a LessThan member function comparing two dates is simpler if Method II is used.
    (D) Code to determine if a given date occurs in a leap year has similar complexity for Methods I and II.
    (E) If the programmer's goal is to achieve optimum run-time efficiency, choice of Method I or Method II should be determined by which operations will be performed most often on Date objects.

30. Suppose a C++ function Random(x) returns a random integer such that $0 \leq$ Random(x) $<$ x. Refer to the following program.

```cpp
void Test(int & a, int b);
{
    a = Random(a);
    b = Random(b);
}
int main()
{
    int m = 4, n = 10;
    Test(m, n);
    cout << m << n;
    return 0;
}
```

    What are the values of m and n just before the cout statement?
    (A) m and n are not predictable.
    (B) m is 4, and n is not predictable.
    (C) n is 10, and m is not predictable.
    (D) m is 4, and n is 10.
    (E) Neither m nor n is defined.

GO ON TO THE NEXT PAGE ➤

31. A car dealer needs to keep an inventory of cars on a lot that can hold at most MAXCARS cars. The model, year, and color need to be recorded for each car. Assume that the following declarations are part of the program.

```
enum Model {SUV, STATIONWAGON, SEDAN};
enum Color {RED, WHITE, BLUE, GREY, BLACK, GREEN};
```

Of the following, which is the best data structure for storing the inventory information?

(A)
```
struct Inventory
{
    Model mo;
    int year;
    Color co;
    apvector<MAXCARS> carList;
};
```

(B)
```
apvector<Model> mList(MAXCARS);
apvector<Color> cList(MAXCARS);
apvector<year> yList(MAXCARS);
```

(C)
```
Struct Inventory
{
    apvector<Model> mList;
    apvector<Color> cList;
    apvector<year> yList;
};
```

(D)
```
const int NUMMODELS;
const int NUMCOLORS;
apmatrix<year>(NUMMODELS, NUMCOLORS);
```

(E)
```
struct car
{
    Model mo;
    int year;
    Color co;
};
apvector<car> Inventory(MAXCARS);
```

32. Suppose function F(int x, double y) is of type int. Which of the following ensures that the given loop terminates?

```
do
{
    <some computation>
} while (F(x, y) != 0);
```

(A) x and y are both decreased during each iteration.
(B) x and y are both increased during each iteration.
(C) The sum of x and y is decreased during each iteration.
(D) The value of F(x, y) is decreased during each iteration.
(E) The value of the square of F(x, y) is decreased during each iteration.

GO ON TO THE NEXT PAGE ➤

33. Refer to function Mystery.

```
void Mystery(apvector<int> & a, int mid)
//precondition: a[0]...a[mid] are sorted in increasing order.
//              a[mid+1]...a[a.length()-1] are sorted in
//              increasing order
{
    apvector<int> c(a.length());
    int k, count = -1, i = 0, j = mid+1;
    while (i <= mid && j <= a.length() -1)
    {
        count++;
        if (a[i] < a[j])
        {
            c[count] = a[i];
            i++;
        }
        else
        {
            c[count] = a[j];
            j++;
        }
    }
    if (i > mid)
        for (k=j; k<a.length(); k++)
        {
            count++;
            c[count] = a[k];
        }
    else
        for (k=i; k<=mid; k++)
        {
            count++;
            c[count] = a[k];
        }
    for (k=0; k<=count; k++)
        a[k] = c[k];
}
```

What does function Mystery do?

(A) Merges two parts of array a into a single sorted array.

(B) Partitions array a into two parts using a pivot element, such that all elements a[0]...a[mid] are less than the pivot, and all elements a[mid+1]...a[a.length()-1] are greater than or equal to the pivot.

(C) Uses mergesort to sort array a into increasing order.

(D) Uses quicksort to sort array a into increasing order.

(E) Does a binary search of array a.

GO ON TO THE NEXT PAGE ➤

Questions 34 and 35 refer to function `Insert` described here. `Insert` has two string parameters and one integer parameter. `Insert` returns the string obtained by inserting the second string into the first starting at the position indicated by the integer parameter. For example, if `str1` contains `xy` and `str2` contains `cat`, then

`Insert(str1, str2, 0)`	returns	`catxy`
`Insert(str1, str2, 1)`	returns	`xcaty`
`Insert(str1, str2, 2)`	returns	`xycat`

Here is the header for function `Insert`.

```
apstring Insert(const apstring & str1, const apstring & str2, int pos);
//precondition: 0<=pos<=str1.length()
//postcondition: returns <somestring>
```

34. If $str1 = a_0a_1 \ldots a_{n-1}$ and $str2 = b_0b_1 \ldots b_{m-1}$, which of the following is a correct replacement for `<somestring>`?

   (A) $a_0a_1 \ldots a_{pos}b_0b_1 \ldots b_{m-1}a_{pos+1}a_{pos+2} \cdots a_{n-1}$
   (B) $a_0a_1 \ldots a_{pos+1}b_0b_1 \ldots b_{m-1}a_{pos+2}a_{pos+3} \cdots a_{n-1}$
   (C) $a_0a_1 \ldots a_{pos-1}b_0b_1 \ldots b_{m-1}a_{pos}a_{pos+1} \cdots a_{n-1}$
   (D) $a_0a_1 \ldots a_{n-1}b_0b_1 \ldots b_{m-1}$
   (E) $a_0a_1 \ldots a_{pos-1}b_0b_1 \ldots b_{pos-1}a_{pos}a_{pos+1} \cdots a_{n-1}$

35. Function `Insert` follows:

```
apstring Insert(const apstring & str1, const apstring & str2, int pos)
{
    apstring temp;        //temp initialized to empty string
    if (pos == 0)         //str2 inserted in front of str1
        temp = str2 + str1;
    else if (pos == str1.length())    //str2 inserted after str1
        temp = str1 + str2;
    else                  //str2 inserted in the "middle" of str1
    {
        apstring first, last;
            <more code>
        temp = first + str2 + last;
    }
    return temp;
}
```

Which of the following is a correct replacement for `<more code>`?

   (A) `first = str1.substr(0, pos);`
       `last = str1.substr(pos, str1.length()-pos);`

   (B) `first = str1.substr(0, pos-1);`
       `last = str1.substr(pos, str1.length()-pos);`

   (C) `first = str1.substr(0, pos+1);`
       `last = str1.substr(pos+1, str1.length()-pos);`

   (D) `first = str1.substr(0, pos);`
       `last = str1.substr(pos, str1.length()-pos-1);`

   (E) `first = str1.substr(1, pos);`
       `last = str1.substr(pos, str1.length()-pos-1);`

GO ON TO THE NEXT PAGE ➤

Questions 36–40 involve reasoning about the code from the Marine Biology Case Study. A copy of the code is provided as part of this exam.

36. The `aquamain` program is modified to give the fish a random starting position in the tank. Which of the following will need to be modified?

    I The constructor in the `AquaFish` class

    II The `Swim()` member function in the `AquaFish` class

    III The `main()` function in `aquamain.cpp`

    (A) I only

    (B) II only

    (C) III only

    (D) I and III only

    (E) I, II, and III

37. Consider a change to the `fishsim` program that allows a fish to move in eight possible directions: north, south, east, west, northwest, northeast, southwest, and southeast. Which of the following classes must be modified to accommodate the change?

    I `Fish` and/or `Position`

    II `Neighborhood`

    III `Environment`

    (A) I only

    (B) II only

    (C) I and II only

    (D) I and III only

    (E) I, II, and III

38. Suppose the initial configuration of fish in the environment is

    ```
    A _ B
    G D F
    E C _
    ```

    where _ denotes an empty grid space. After one step of the simulation, which of the following could be the configuration?

    (A) ```
        _ A B
        G D F
        E C _
        ```

    (B) ```
        A D B
        G _ F
        E C _
        ```

    (C) ```
        _ A B
        _ D F
        G E C
        ```

    (D) ```
        _ D B
        A _ F
        G E C
        ```

    (E) ```
        G A B
        D F _
        E _ C
        ```
        ```

39. A small modification to the `aquamain` program is required. Before any steps of the simulation, the initial position of the fish is to be output. Which is the best way to implement this change?

   (A) Change the `Swim` function of the `AquaFish` class to have as its first line
   ```
   cout << "Position = " << myPosition << endl;
   ```

   (B) Change the `Swim` function of the `AquaFish` class as follows. Move the following statement so that it's the first statement of the function:
   ```
   if (myDebugging)
   {
       cout << "***Position = " << myPosition << endl;
   }
   ```

   (C) Change the `main()` function in `aquamain` as follows: between the statement
   ```
   AquaFish fish(tankSize);
   ```
   and the `for` loop, insert the following statement:
   ```
   cout << "Position = " << myPosition << endl;
   ```

   (D) Add the following accessor function to the `AquaFish` class:
   ```
   int AquaFish::Position() const
   {
       return myPosition;
   }
   ```
   Next change the `main()` function in `aquamain` as follows: between the statement
   ```
   AquaFish fish(tankSize);
   ```
   and the `for` loop, insert the following statement:
   ```
   cout << "Position = " << fish.Position() << endl;
   ```

   (E) Add the accessor function `Position()`, as described in choice D, to the `AquaFish` class. Now change `aquamain` so that the following statement directly follows the `cin >> tankSize;` statement:
   ```
   cout << "Position = " << fish.Position() << endl;
   ```

40. Consider a decision to change the `fishsim` program so that fish can age and die. The initial age of each fish will be provided in the `fish.dat` input file on the same line as its position. Thus the format of the data will be as follows:

   ```
   rows    columns
   row-pos   col-pos    age
   row-pos   col-pos    age
         ...
   row-pos   col-pos    age
   ```

   Each time a fish moves, it will either have its age incremented by one or it will die. The probability of a particular fish dying will be correlated with its age. To implement this change, a private variable `myAge` will be added to the `Fish` class. Which of the following groups of functions needs to be modified to implement the change?

   I Constructors in the `Fish` and `Environment` classes
   II The `Move` function in the `Fish` class
   III The `Update` and `AddFish` functions in the `Environment` class

   (A) I only
   (B) II only
   (C) III only
   (D) I and II only
   (E) I, II, and III

STOP

COMPUTER SCIENCE A
SECTION II

Time—1 hour and 45 minutes
Number of questions—4
Percent of total grade—50

Directions: SHOW ALL YOUR WORK. REMEMBER THAT PROGRAM SEGMENTS ARE TO BE WRITTEN IN C++.

Note: Assume that the standard libraries (iostream.h, fstream.h, math.h, etc.) and the AP C++ classes are included in any program that uses a program segment you write. If other classes are to be included, that information will be specified in individual questions. A Quick Reference to the AP C++ classes is included in the case study insert.

---

1. This question deals with compressing lines of text in a file.
   (a) Write function CountLeadingBlanks as started below. CountLeadingBlanks should return the number of leading blanks in its string parameter s. Leading blanks are blanks at the front of a string.
   The following table illustrates the results of calling CountLeadingBlanks(s). Leading blanks are shown with the character b.

s	CountLeadingBlanks(s)
bbbThis is a test	3
bHot dog	1
No blanks here!	0

   Complete function CountLeadingBlanks.

   ```
   int CountLeadingBlanks(const apstring & s)
   //precondition: s is a nonempty string with at least one
   //              nonblank character
   //postcondition: returns number of leading blanks in s
   ```

   ```
   int CountLeadingBlanks (apstring s)
   {
       for(int i = 0; i < s.length(); i++)
           if (s[i] != ' ')
               return i;
   }
   ```

GO ON TO THE NEXT PAGE ➤

(b) Write function ReduceString as started below. ReduceString returns a string in which the leading blanks of its parameter s have been replaced with a digit representing the number of leading blanks in s.

The following table illustrates the results of calling ReduceString(s). Leading blanks are shown with the character b.

s	ReduceString(s)
bbbThis is a test	3This is a test
bHot dog	1Hot dog
No blanks here!	0No blanks here!

In writing function ReduceString you may wish to call the function CountLeadingBlanks. Assume that CountLeadingBlanks works as specified irrespective of what you wrote in part (a). Complete function ReduceString below.

```
apstring ReduceString(const apstring & s)
//precondition: s is a nonempty string with at least one
//              nonblank character
//postcondition: returns a string with the k leading blanks
//               in s replaced by a single digit whose value
//               represents k. String s remains unchanged.
//               You may assume 0 ≤ k ≤ 9
```

(c) Write function CompressFile as started below. CompressFile accesses inFile, which is a file of strings listed one per line. The function reads a string from inFile and writes it to outFile in reduced form, namely with its leading blanks replaced by a digit whose value represents the number of leading blanks. This process is repeated until all strings in inFile have been processed. The reduced strings are written consecutively to outFile with no carriage return (i.e., newline character) separating them. For example, if inFile looks like this:

```
bbbThis is a test
bHot dog
No blanks here!
    ...
```

then a call to CompressFile(inFile, outFile) will create outFile to look like this:

```
3This is a test1Hot dog0No blanks here! ...
```

In writing CompressFile, you may wish to call functions CountLeadingBlanks and ReduceString. Assume that these functions work as specified irrespective of what you wrote in parts (a) and (b).
Write CompressFile below.

```
void CompressFile(istream & inFile, ostream & outFile)
//precondition: inFile is open for reading, outFile is open for
//              writing. inFile is not empty and contains a list
//              of strings, 1 per line. Each string contains k
//              leading blanks, 0 ≤ k ≤ 9
//postcondition: Each string in inFile has been written to
//               outFile in reduced form, namely the k leading
//               blanks have been replaced with a digit whose
//               value represents k. There are no newline
//               characters separating these strings in outFile
```

GO ON TO THE NEXT PAGE ➤

2. Assume that a teacher implements a student's record using the following declarations:

```
const int MAXNUMSCORES = 20;
struct Student
{
    apstring name;
    int numScores;
    apvector<int> testScores;
    Student(ifstream &infile);        //constructor
};
```

(a) Write the code for the constructor that initializes a Student as started below. The constructor reads the name, number of scores, and a list of test scores from a file represented by the parameter infile. You may assume that the file is open and contains the student's name followed by the number of test scores on a new line. A list of test scores follows, starting on the next line. You may further assume that the number of test scores k is such that $0 \leq k \leq$ MAXNUMSCORES, and that each test score s is an integer with $0 \leq s \leq 100$. For example, the file for some student may look like this:

```
Whitman Noah
4
97 81 90
68
```

Complete constructor Student.

```
Student :: Student(ifstream & infile) : testScores(MAXNUMSCORES)
//precondition: infile is open
//postcondition: name, numScores and testScores are initialized
//               from infile. 0 < numScores ≤ MAXNUMSCORES
```

(b) Write function StudentAverage as started below. StudentAverage should find the mean of the test scores of its Student parameter. For example, if the test scores for a student are 80 and 81, StudentAverage should return 80.5 (the sum of the test scores divided by the number of scores). Complete function StudentAverage below.

```
double StudentAverage(const Student & s)
//precondition: s is appropriately initialized
//postcondition: returns the mean of the test scores for s
```

(c) Write function FillHonorsList as started below. FillHonorsList determines which students in the array list have a test score average greater than or equal to 90.0 and copies those students' records to the array honorsList. The function should also set the value of the parameter numHonors to be the number of students in the array honorsList.
In writing FillHonorsList, you may call function StudentAverage specified in part (b). Assume StudentAverage works as specified, regardless of what you wrote in part (b).
Complete function FillHonorsList below.

```
void FillHonorsList(const apvector<Student> & list, int numStuds,
    apvector<Student> & honorsList, int & numHonors)
//precondition: list contains numStuds records. 0 ≤ numStuds < list.length().
//              honorsList is initially empty and contains enough
//              slots to hold all of the honor students' records
```

GO ON TO THE NEXT PAGE ➤

3. An $n \times n$ *magic square* is a square array of n^2 distinct integers arranged such that the n numbers along any row, column, major diagonal, or minor diagonal have the same sum. We will consider only those magic squares that contain the first n^2 positive integers.

For example, here is a 3×3 magic square. It contains only the integers 1 through 9, each of which occurs exactly once. Each row, column, and diagonal sums to 15.

8	1	6
3	5	7
4	9	2

To check whether a two-dimensional array of integers is a magic square, you must check that

(i) All the rows have the same sum.

(ii) All the columns have the same sum.

(iii) Both diagonals have the same sum.

(a) Write function `CheckDiagonalSums` as started below. `CheckDiagonalSums` returns true if the sum of integers on both diagonals of its matrix parameter equals the second integer parameter; otherwise, it returns false. The first integer parameter represents the size of the matrix. For example,

```
CheckDiagonalSums(m, 3, 15)
```

would return true for the matrix shown earlier since the sum along each diagonal is 15.

8	1	6
3	5	7
4	9	2

major diagonal

8	1	6
3	5	7
4	9	2

minor diagonal

Complete function `CheckDiagonalSums` below.

```
bool CheckDiagonalSums(const apmatrix<int> & m, int size,
        int total)
//precondition: m is a size x size matrix initialized with
//               distinct positive integers from 1 to size*size
//postcondition: returns true if sum of each diagonal equals
//               total, returns false otherwise
```

GO ON TO THE NEXT PAGE ➤

(b) Write function `CreateMagicSquare` as started below. `CreateMagicSquare` will return a size ×
size `apmatrix` of integers that represents a magic square. The following algorithm achieves this
provided `size` is odd. Here is how it works when `size` is 5.

- Expand the 5 by 5 square to a 6 by 6 square by adding a border of cells along the top and the
  right edge.

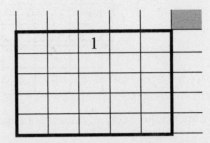

- Place 1 in the middle top cell of the original square. This cell is now occupied. All other cells
  of the matrix are considered empty except for the top right-hand corner, which is considered
  occupied. (Hint: Initialize all cells to 0 except for `m[1][size/2]` and `m[0][size]`.)
- Now place the remaining integers, 2 through 25, successively in the square as follows:
  Starting at the cell that contains 1, the general rule is to proceed diagonally upward to the
  right with successive integers. There are two exceptions to this general rule:
  (i) When a number lands in a border cell, place it inside the original square by shifting clear
      across the square, either from top to bottom or from right to left. Then continue with the
      general rule.
  (ii) If a number will land in a cell already occupied, place that number in the cell immediately
      beneath the last cell filled. Then continue with the general rule.

Thus, in the 5 by 5 example, 2 would go in the fourth cell along the top. Since this is a border cell,
it must be placed in the fourth cell of the bottom row of the original square.

			2	9	
		1	8		
	5	7			
4	6				4
10				3	10
			2	9	

Place 3 according to the general rule. When we come to 4, it falls in the third cell up along the
right border. It must therefore be placed all the way across to the left in the third cell up. Now
place 5 according to the general rule. The general rule would place 6 in the square occupied by 1.
Therefore, 6 must go in the cell directly below 5. The numbers 7 and 8 can be placed according to
the general rule. Then 9 lands in the border and must be moved to the bottom, and so on.

GO ON TO THE NEXT PAGE ➤

Here is the completed 5 × 5 magic square:

17	24	1	8	15
23	5	7	14	16
4	6	13	20	22
10	12	19	21	3
11	18	25	2	9

Notice that the matrix has been resized and no longer contains the borders used in its construction. Complete function CreateMagicSquare below.

```
apmatrix<int> CreateMagicSquare(int size)
//precondition: size ≥ 3, size odd
//postcondition: returns a size x size matrix m that represents
//               a magic square. m contains all the integers from
//               1 to size*size
```

4. This question involves reasoning about the code from the Marine Biology Case Study. A copy of the code is provided as part of this exam.

Consider the aquamain program that runs the fish-in-a-tank simulation. Biologists would like to record the number of times a fish visits each position in the tank. Recall that the positions are 0, 1, 2, ... , tankSize-1. A new private variable myNumVisits will be added to the AquaFish class:

```
apvector<int> myNumVisits;
```

myNumVisits will keep track of the number of times each position, represented by the index of the vector, is visited. For example, myNumVisits[6] will represent the number of times position 6 in the tank has been visited.

A new member function NumVisits will be added to the AquaFish class. NumVisits will return the apvector of position counts.

GO ON TO THE NEXT PAGE ➤

Here is the modified AquaFish class. Changes are in boldface.

```
class AquaFish
{
    public:
        AquaFish(int tankSize);
        void Swim();
        int BumpCount() const;
        apvector<int> NumVisits() const;
        //returns list with # of visits to each position
    private:
        int myPosition;
        int myBumpCount;
        int myTankSize;
        bool myDebugging;
        apvector<int> myNumVisits;
};
```

(a) Write the modified constructor for the AquaFish class as started below.

```
AquaFish::AquaFish(int tankSize)
```

(b) Explain how the Swim() member function should be modified to record the number of times a fish visits each position in the tank.

(c) Complete the member function NumVisits as started below.

```
apvector<int> AquaFish::NumVisits() const
//postcondition: Returns list of number of visits to each position in the tank
```

(d) Write a client function DrawHistogram as started below. DrawHistogram outputs a histogram that represents the number of times each position was visited by its AquaFish parameter. The tankSize is also provided as a parameter.

For example, suppose tankSize is 4 and the number of visits to each position is as shown below for a given fish.

Position	Number of Visits
0	2
1	6
2	4
3	1

The following output should be produced by the function call:

```
DrawHistogram(fish, tankSize);
```

```
0  **
1  ******
2  ****
3  *
```

Complete the function DrawHistogram below. You may assume that the AquaFish constructor and function NumVisits work correctly irrespective of what you wrote in parts (a) and (c).

```
void DrawHistogram(AquaFish fish, int tankSize)
//precondition: fish and tankSize defined
```

STOP

Answer Key

1. **A**	15. **C**	29. **D**
2. **B**	16. **E**	30. **C**
3. **E**	17. **C**	31. **E**
4. **B**	18. **B**	32. **E**
5. **C**	19. **E**	33. **A**
6. **E**	20. **E**	34. **C**
7. **E**	21. **B**	35. **A**
8. **B**	22. **E**	36. **A**
9. **C**	23. **B**	37. **C**
10. **D**	24. **D**	38. **E**
11. **A**	25. **A**	39. **D**
12. **D**	26. **A**	40. **E**
13. **D**	27. **B**	
14. **A**	28. **D**	

Answers Explained

Section I

1. **(A)** The operators / and * have equal precedence and both have higher precedence than +. Thus, 21/6 * 2 must be evaluated first from left to right. 21/6 evaluates to 3 (integer division), and so the given expression is equivalent to 20 + 3 * 2. (The next steps in evaluating would be 20 + 6 = 26.)

2. **(B)** A compiler is a piece of software that translates your program into machine language (i.e., instructions that the machine can execute). Without it, the computer cannot understand high-level languages like C++, Pascal, and Java.

3. **(E)**

$$
\begin{aligned}
\text{Mystery}(4) &= 3 * \text{Mystery}(3) \\
&= 3 * 3 * \text{Mystery}(2) \\
&= 3 * 3 * 3 * \text{Mystery}(1) \\
&= 3 * 3 * 3 * 3 \\
&= 81
\end{aligned}
$$

4. **(B)** Look at the solution to the previous question. Notice that 3 gets multiplied by itself n times (i.e., 3 gets raised to the nth power).

5. **(C)** Before writing any code, a programmer must have an overall plan that includes all functions that will be needed. Since this plan is almost always dependent on the data structure used, the data structure must also be chosen before actual code is written. For example, in this problem, the programmer can sequentially examine all three-digit integers from 100 to 999, or she can have nested loops:

```
for (i=1; i<=9; i++)
    for (j=0; j<=9; j++)
        for (k=0; k<=9; k++)
            ...
```

The choice directly affects the program's overall code.

6. **(E)** The >> operator does not read whitespace, including blanks and newline characters. Thus, all nonblank characters of infile will be read, one at a time, into ch. The while loop will terminate when the end of the file is reached.

7. **(E)** Mergesort repeatedly splits an array of *n* elements in half until there are *n* arrays containing one element each. Now adjacent arrays are successively merged until there is a single merged, sorted array. Quicksort repeatedly partitions the array such that all elements to the left of a pivot element are less than the pivot and all elements to the right of the pivot are greater than or equal to the pivot. This algorithm very quickly leads to a sorted array. A binary search repeatedly splits an array into two, narrowing the region that may contain the key being searched for.

8. **(B)** This code translates into

> for five rows (starting at i = 5 and decreasing i)
> print the first i perfect squares
> go to a new line

Thus, in the first line the first five perfect squares will be printed. In the second line the first four perfect squares will be printed, and so on down to i = 1, with just one perfect square being printed.

9. **(C)** To return the number of elements in the set for Method One requires no more than returning the number of elements in the array. For Method Two, however, the number of cells that contain true must be counted, which requires a test for each of the MAX values. Note that searching for a target value in the set is more efficient for Method Two. For example, to test whether 2 is in the set, simply check if a[2] == true. In Method One, a sequential search must be done, which is less efficient. To print all the elements in Method One, simply loop over the known number of elements and print. Method Two is less efficient because the whole array must be examined: each cell must be tested for true before printing.

10. **(D)** Division by zero gives a run-time error. The program will crash.

11. **(A)** Note the order of precedence for the expressions involved: (1) parentheses, (2) !, (3) <, (4) ==, (5) &&, (6) ||. This means that a < c, a < b, and !(a == b) will all be evaluated before || and && are considered. The given expression then boils down to value1 || (value2 && value3), since && has higher precedence than ||. Notice that if value1 is true, the whole expression is true since true || any evaluates to true. Thus, a < c will guarantee that the expression evaluates to true. None of the other conditions will guarantee an outcome of true. For example, suppose a < b (choice B). If a == c, then the whole expression will be false because you get F || F.

12. **(D)** Test data should always include a value from each range in addition to all boundary values. The given program should also handle the case in which a weight over 20 pounds is entered. Note that choice E contains redundant data

and so is wasteful. There is no new information gained in testing both 3 and 4 pounds, for example.

13. **(D)** The point of this question is that array a must contain an available slot for reading in the current a[i]. Segment I fails on the very first inFile >> a[i]: there's no slot for a[0]. Segment II fails on the second inFile >> a[i]. After a[0] is read in, a should be resized to 2, but it's resized to 1, the current value of i. Segment III does the resizing correctly, creating an additional slot before reading in the next integer.

14. **(A)** Function Alter shifts all the columns, starting at column c+1, one column to the left. Also, it does it in a way that overwrites column c. Here are the replacements for the function call Alter(m, 1):

```
m[0][1] = m[0][2]
m[0][2] = m[0][3]
m[1][1] = m[1][2]
m[1][2] = m[1][3]
m[2][1] = m[2][2]
m[2][2] = m[2][3]
```

15. **(C)** In an initializer list, the parameter list for the function is followed by a colon and then a list of the private data members, each of which is assigned, in parentheses, the corresponding parameter value. Note that choice A is an alternative (correct) implementation of the constructor. It does not, however, use an initializer list as was required.

16. **(E)** The point of this question is that myHourlyWage must be *permanently* incremented, which segments II and III both do. Even though segment I returns the same value as segments II and III, the increase will be lost when the function is exited. Note that since IncrementWage is a member function, it can access a private variable (myHourlyWage) as well as another member function (HourlyWage()).

17. **(C)** ComputePay is a client function and, therefore, cannot access the private variables of the class. This eliminates choices A and D. The member function HourlyWage() must be accessed with the dot member construct; thus, choice B is wrong, and choice C is correct. Choice E is way off base—hours is not part of the Employee class, so E.hours is meaningless.

18. **(B)** The integers 5, 10, and 15 will successfully be read into i, j, and k, respectively. Then 2 will be stored in i. The decimal point in 6.8 is inappropriate for type int, and so the >> operator will stop reading when it gets to the point. Here's what happens: 6 will be stored in j, and the numFile stream will go into a failed state. k will retain its current value of 15, and all future statements in the program that refer to numFile will be ignored until numFile is cleared.

19. **(E)** Strings are compared for equality by doing a character-by-character comparison starting with the leftmost character of each string. Thus, strA < strB since 'A' < 'a' ('A' comes before 'a' in the ASCII table). This eliminates choices B, C, and D. Eliminate choice A since strB < strC because 'C' < 'c'.

20. **(E)** The do...while loop will always execute at least once. Thus, if 0 < num < 10, segment II will output num (try it!), and segment I will output 0 since

the loop will never be executed. Notice that exceptions occur when num is 0 or 10. The nature of the algorithm causes 0 to be output for either segment. When num is negative, the while loop in segment I won't execute, producing output of 0. The loop in segment II will be executed once, producing output different from 0. All positive integers greater than 10 will produce the same output with both segments.

21. **(B)** Segment II correctly keeps track of the index of the current element with the minimum price. If this is not done, the idNum that must be returned will be lost. Thus, segment III is incorrect. min cannot be used as an index because it's a value of type double. Segment I is incorrect because it doesn't check that part matches allParts[i].description. Thus, it simply finds the autoPart with the lowest price, which is not what was required.

22. **(E)** Choice A is false because it's *desirable* to pass the value parameters of a templated function by const reference, to avoid copying large objects. The size of type is unknown. Choices B and D are false. As long as the two parameters for a Min function call are of the same type and that type has a < operator defined (so that function Min makes sense), the data members of a struct can be used as parameters. Thus, by extension, the dot member construct can be used. Choice C is the most diabolical of the false statements. The whole point of a templated function is that the compiler *will* distinguish between the different parameter types, provided that the different parameters are correctly declared in the program.

23. **(B)** If there is no base case in a recursive function, then the function will run until it exhausts the computer's memory.

24. **(D)**

$$Recur(2) = Recur(1) + Recur(0) \quad \text{(both base cases)}$$
$$= 1 + 1$$
$$= 2$$

25. **(A)** Here are the calls that are made. Base cases are underlined.

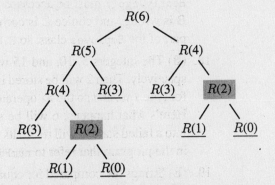

26. **(A)** Since the records are not sorted, the quickest way to find a given name is to start at the beginning of the list and sequentially search for that name. Choices C, D, and E will all work, but it's inefficient to sort and then search because all sorting algorithms take longer than simply inspecting each element. Choice B won't work: a binary search can only be used for a sorted list.

27. **(B)** The array being examined is v[0], v[1], ... , v[NUMITEMS-1]. Thus, the array must be processed while i < NUMITEMS (test 2). The test i <= NUMITEMS will cause v[NUMITEMS] to be looked at, which is out of range. Test 1 checks if v[i] is odd: is the remainder when v[i] is divided by 2 equal to 1 (i.e., is v[i] % 2 ==1)?

28. **(D)** Here's what the do...while loop does:

```
b = 1:   c = 0 + 10 = 10
b = 2:   c = 10 + 20 = 30
b = 3:   c = 30 + 30 = 60
b = 4:   c = 60 + 40 = 100
b = 5:   c = 100 + 50 = 150
```

Executing the loop in choice D gives the identical sequence of steps, leading to a value of 150 for c. None of the other choices give this answer.

29. **(D)** If Method I is used, testing for a leap year requires no more than checking if the year integer is divisible by 4. Additionally, if the year ends in 00, it must be tested for divisibility by 400. That's it. Method II requires subtracting multiples of 365 from the number of days representing the date and keeping track of when it is necessary to subtract 366 (a leap year has 366 days). Whether you do this by brute force or by getting the number of multiples of 365 in the number of days and then correcting that multiple for the number of leap years, the algorithm is considerably more complicated than for Method I.

30. **(C)** Since a is passed by reference, it will share memory with m, the actual parameter. Since b is passed by value, it will have its own memory slot. When Test(m, n) is invoked, the memory slots can be thought of like this:

```
    m        n
  ┌───┐    ┌────┐   ┌────┐
  │ 4 │    │ 10 │   │ 10 │
  └───┘    └────┘   └────┘
    a                 b
```

The statement a = Random(a) will change the value in m's slot randomly, whereas b = Random(b) will leave n unchanged. When the function is exited, the memory slots look like this:

```
    m        n
  ┌───┐    ┌────┐
  │ ? │    │ 10 │
  └───┘    └────┘
```

31. **(E)** The best data structure to keep track of all the cars is an array of car records where each record (i.e., car struct) stores information about a particular car. The array should have MAXCARS slots.

32. **(E)** The loop body has to ensure that the value of F(x, y) eventually reaches 0. None of the choices A, B, or C will necessarily do that. Choice D looks promising until you realize that decreasing the value of F(x, y) can cause it to become negative without ever hitting zero. The square of F(x, y), however, will never be negative, and so it will eventually reach zero if it's decreased on each iteration.

33. **(A)** An example of array a could be

```
2  6  8  1  3  4  5  10  12
```

In this case mid equals 2: a[0]...a[2] are sorted and a[3]...a[8] are sorted. The algorithm merges the two parts into

$$1\ 2\ 3\ 4\ 5\ 6\ 8\ 10\ 12$$

(Note: This merge function is needed whenever mergesort is used to sort an array.)

34. **(C)** Suppose, for example, str1 is "strawberry" and str2 is "cat."
Insert(str1, str2, 5) will return the following pieces, concatenated:

$$\text{straw} + \text{cat} + \text{berry}$$
$$= a_0a_1a_2a_3a_4 + b_0b_1b_2 + a_5a_6a_7a_8a_9$$
$$= a_0a_1a_2a_3a_4b_0b_1b_2a_5a_6a_7a_8a_9$$

35. **(A)** Recall that s.substr(k, m) (member function of apstring) returns a substring of s starting at position k and containing m characters. Again consider the example in which str1 = "strawberry" and str2 = "cat" and the function call is Insert(str1, str2, 5). The string str1 must be split into two parts, first and last. The string str2 will be inserted between them. Since str2 is inserted starting at position 5 (the 'b'), first = "straw," namely the substring of str1 starting at 0 and containing 5 characters. Similarly, if pos were 6, you'd need 6 characters. So

```
first = str1.substr(0, pos);
```

Notice that last, the second substring of str1, must start at the index for 'b', which is pos, the index at which str2 was inserted. The number of characters in this second substring is (length of str1 − the pos characters already removed). So

```
last = str1.substr(pos, str1.length()-pos);
```

Note: If the second parameter in the preceding substr function call is larger than str1.length()-pos, it won't matter. The substring will contain the remainder of str1 as required. If, however, that second parameter is less than str1.length()-pos, some characters will be lost. Thus, choices D and E can be eliminated immediately.

36. **(A)** Note that myPosition is initialized to tankSize/2 in the AquaFish constructor. The Swim and main functions are both independent of the starting position of the fish.

37. **(C)** The Position class will need four additional Position functions:

NorthWest()	NorthEast()
SouthWest()	SouthEast()

The Fish class will need four additional calls to AddIfEmpty in its EmptyNeighbors function—the new positions must now be considered for addition to the neighborhood of available positions. The constructor in the Neighborhood class must be changed to include eight possible slots for myList. The duties of the Environment are not affected by the additional positions. Note that you can avoid modifying the Position class if EmptyNeighbors includes calls like AddIfEmpty(env, nbrs, pos.North().East());.

38. **(E)** Remember, the fish move row by row from top to bottom and left to right. Thus, for the given configuration, the fish will move in the sequence A, B, G, D, F, E, C. A fish *must* move if there's at least one empty adjacent spot. If there are no empty adjacent spots the fish doesn't move. Here is the only possible sequence of moves for the given configuration:

```
        _ A B              G A B              G A B
   (1)  G D F         (2)  _ D F         (3)  D _ F
        E C _              E C _              E C _


        G A B              G A B
   (4)  D F _    OR   D _ _
        E C _              E C F


        G A B              G A B
   (5)  D F _    OR   D C _
        E _ C              E _ F
```

39. **(D)** Eliminate choices A and B since it's incorrect to modify the Swim function: the initial position should be output *once* at the start of the program. Subsequent positions are output only if myDebugging is true. Choice C is wrong because myPosition is a private variable that cannot be used in a client program. Choice E is wrong because fish.Position() is meaningless if invoked before fish has been defined.

40. **(E)** I. Both constructors need to initialize the age of fish as they are created. II. The age of a fish should be incremented when a fish moves. III. The Update function must be modified to deal with the case when a fish dies; and AddFish uses the Fish constructor, which must be modified to include an age parameter.

Section II

1. (a)
```
int CountLeadingBlanks(const apstring & s)
{
    int count = 0;
    while(s[count] == ' ')
        count++;
    return count;
}
```

(b)
```
apstring ReduceString(const apstring & s)
{
    int k = CountLeadingBlanks(s);
    char value = k + '0';
    apstring temp = value + s.substr(k,s.length()-k);
    return temp;
}
```

(c)
```
void CompressFile(istream & inFile, ostream & outFile)
{
    apstring line;
    while (getline(inFile, line))
        outFile << ReduceString(line);
}
```

NOTE
1. In part (b), the integer k must be converted to the character 'k' before being concatenated to the rest of the string.
2. In part (b), if there are k blanks, the substring you want starts at position k. The length of the substring is just the original string length minus the number of leading blanks.
3. In part (c), getline stores the entire line of text in line except for the newline character, which is discarded. Thus, the reduced string, ReduceString(line), will contain no newline character as required by the postcondition.

2. (a)
```
Student :: Student(ifstream & infile)
        : testScores(MAXNUMSCORES)
{
    getline(infile, name);
    infile >> numScores;
    for (int i=0; i<numScores; i++)
        infile >> testScores[i];
}
```

(b)
```
double StudentAverage(const Student & s)
{
    double total = 0;
    for (int i=0; i<s.numScores; i++)
        total += s.testScores[i];
    return total/s.numScores;
}
```

(c)
```
void FillHonorsList(const apvector<Student> & list, int
numStuds, apvector<Student> & honorsList, int & numHonors)
{
    int j = 0;
    for (int k=0; k < numStuds; k++)
        if (StudentAverage(list[k]) >= 90.0)
        {
            honorsList[j] = list[k]
            j++;
        }
    numHonors = j;
}
```

NOTE
1. In part (a), getline is used to read a string, and the extractor operator >> is used to read the numerical data. The operator >> will skip over whitespace, including carriage returns.
2. In part (b), you don't need to test for division by zero since it is part of the precondition of the Student constructor that numScores > 0.
3. In part (b), if total is of type int, you must cast either total or s.numScores to double to ensure that real (vs. integer) division is used to calculate the average.

3. (a)
```
bool CheckDiagonalSums(const apmatrix<int> & m, int size,
     int total)
{
    int majorSum = 0, minorSum = 0;
    for (int i=0; i<size; i++)
    {
        majorSum += m[i][i];
        minorSum += m[i][size-i-1];
    }
    if (majorSum != total || minorSum != total)
        return false;
    else
        return true;
}
```

(b)
```
apmatrix<int> CreateMagicSquare(int size)
{
    apmatrix<int> m(size+1, size+1, 0);
    m[1][size/2] = 1;
    m[0][size] = -999;
    int numSquares = size*size;
    int row = 1, col = size/2;     //starting position
    for (int val=2; val <=numSquares; val++)
    {
        if (m[row-1][col+1] != 0) //cell occupied
            row++;
        else                         //cell not occupied
        {
            row--;
            col++;
            if (row == 0)        //outside square (on top)
                row = size;
            else if (col == size) //outside (right side)
                col = 0;
        }
        m[row][col] = val;
    }
    for (int i=1; i<=size; i++)
        m[i-1] = m[i];              //overwrite top border
    m.resize(size,size);       //remove right side border
    return m;
}
```

NOTE
1. In part (a), the line
    ```
    minorSum += m[i][size-i-1];
    ```
   can be replaced by
    ```
    minorSum += m[size-i-1][i];
    ```
2. In part (a), the if...else and return statements can be replaced by the single statement
    ```
    return majorSum == total && minorSum == total
    ```
3. In part (b), a for loop can be used since precisely size*size integers will be placed.
4. After filling the magic square, the borders must be eliminated and the matrix resized. We use the fact that m is an apvector of rows

and replace `m[0]` with `m[1]`, `m[1]` with `m[2]`, and so on. Resizing the matrix automatically cuts off the border on the right-hand side.

4. (a) ```
    AquaFish::AquaFish(int tankSize)
         : myPosition(tankSize/2),
           myTankSize(tankSize),
           myBumpCount(0),
           myDebugging(true),
           myNumVisits(tankSize, 0)
         {}
    ```

    (b) The function of `Swim` is to place the fish in a new position. When `myPosition` has been updated, add this statement:
    ```
    myNumVisits[myPosition]++;
    ```

    (c) ```
    apvector<int> AquaFish::NumVisits() const
    {
        return myNumVisits;
    }
    ```

    (d) ```
    void DrawHistogram(AquaFish fish, int tankSize)
    {
        apvector<int> posCounts = fish.NumVisits();
        for (int i=0; i<tankSize; i++)
        {
            cout << i << " ";
            for (int j=1; j<=posCounts[i]; j++)
                cout << '*';
            cout << endl;
        }
    }
    ```

NOTE

1.  In part (a), the number of elements in `myNumVisits` must equal the number of positions in the tank, which is given by `tankSize`. Each element in `myNumVisits` represents a count and should be initialized to 0. The `fillValue` feature of the `apvector` class gives an easy way to do this in the constructor.

2.  In part (d), the outer `for` loop gives the number of lines in the histogram, namely a line for each position. The number of asterisks in line `i` is the value of `posCounts[i]`.
    ```

Answer Sheet: Practice Exam Three

1. Ⓐ Ⓑ Ⓒ Ⓓ Ⓔ
2. Ⓐ Ⓑ Ⓒ Ⓓ Ⓔ
3. Ⓐ Ⓑ Ⓒ Ⓓ Ⓔ
4. Ⓐ Ⓑ Ⓒ Ⓓ Ⓔ
5. Ⓐ Ⓑ Ⓒ Ⓓ Ⓔ
6. Ⓐ Ⓑ Ⓒ Ⓓ Ⓔ
7. Ⓐ Ⓑ Ⓒ Ⓓ Ⓔ
8. Ⓐ Ⓑ Ⓒ Ⓓ Ⓔ
9. Ⓐ Ⓑ Ⓒ Ⓓ Ⓔ
10. Ⓐ Ⓑ Ⓒ Ⓓ Ⓔ
11. Ⓐ Ⓑ Ⓒ Ⓓ Ⓔ
12. Ⓐ Ⓑ Ⓒ Ⓓ Ⓔ
13. Ⓐ Ⓑ Ⓒ Ⓓ Ⓔ
14. Ⓐ Ⓑ Ⓒ Ⓓ Ⓔ

15. Ⓐ Ⓑ Ⓒ Ⓓ Ⓔ
16. Ⓐ Ⓑ Ⓒ Ⓓ Ⓔ
17. Ⓐ Ⓑ Ⓒ Ⓓ Ⓔ
18. Ⓐ Ⓑ Ⓒ Ⓓ Ⓔ
19. Ⓐ Ⓑ Ⓒ Ⓓ Ⓔ
20. Ⓐ Ⓑ Ⓒ Ⓓ Ⓔ
21. Ⓐ Ⓑ Ⓒ Ⓓ Ⓔ
22. Ⓐ Ⓑ Ⓒ Ⓓ Ⓔ
23. Ⓐ Ⓑ Ⓒ Ⓓ Ⓔ
24. Ⓐ Ⓑ Ⓒ Ⓓ Ⓔ
25. Ⓐ Ⓑ Ⓒ Ⓓ Ⓔ
26. Ⓐ Ⓑ Ⓒ Ⓓ Ⓔ
27. Ⓐ Ⓑ Ⓒ Ⓓ Ⓔ
28. Ⓐ Ⓑ Ⓒ Ⓓ Ⓔ

29. Ⓐ Ⓑ Ⓒ Ⓓ Ⓔ
30. Ⓐ Ⓑ Ⓒ Ⓓ Ⓔ
31. Ⓐ Ⓑ Ⓒ Ⓓ Ⓔ
32. Ⓐ Ⓑ Ⓒ Ⓓ Ⓔ
33. Ⓐ Ⓑ Ⓒ Ⓓ Ⓔ
34. Ⓐ Ⓑ Ⓒ Ⓓ Ⓔ
35. Ⓐ Ⓑ Ⓒ Ⓓ Ⓔ
36. Ⓐ Ⓑ Ⓒ Ⓓ Ⓔ
37. Ⓐ Ⓑ Ⓒ Ⓓ Ⓔ
38. Ⓐ Ⓑ Ⓒ Ⓓ Ⓔ
39. Ⓐ Ⓑ Ⓒ Ⓓ Ⓔ
40. Ⓐ Ⓑ Ⓒ Ⓓ Ⓔ

Practice Exam Three

COMPUTER SCIENCE AB
SECTION I

Time—1 hour and 15 minutes
Number of questions—40
Percent of total grade—50

Directions: Determine the answer to each of the following questions or incomplete statements, using separate pieces of scrap paper for any necessary scratchwork. Then decide which is the best of the choices given and fill in the corresponding oval on the answer sheet. Do not spend too much time on any one problem.

Note: Assume that the standard libraries (e.g., `iostream.h`, `fstream.h`, `math.h`, etc.) and the AP C++ classes are included in any programs that use the code segments provided in individual questions. A Quick Reference to the AP C++ classes is provided.

---

1. The AllMart Catalog Company has a system of storing customers' orders that allows for (i) very efficient insertion of new orders; (ii) very efficient retrieval of any particular order. Which of the following data structures is the best choice for storing customer orders?
   - (A) A stack
   - (B) A queue
   - (C) A priority queue
   - (D) A hash table
   - (E) A binary search tree ordered alphabetically by customer name

2. An arbitrary binary tree with n nodes is searched for a particular value. Which of the following best describes the run time in the worst case?
   - (A) $O(1)$
   - (B) $O(n)$
   - (C) $O(n^2)$
   - (D) $O(\log n)$
   - (E) $O(n \log n)$

GO ON TO THE NEXT PAGE ➤

Level A also

3. Consider the following class declaration:

```
class C
{
    public:
        ...
    private:
        int v1;
        double v2;
};
```

In order for a client program to be able to have the declaration

```
C c_object(value1, value2);
```

what kind of member function must exist in class C? Here value1 is type int and value2 is type double.

(A) A copy constructor
(B) A default constructor
(C) A constructor with parameters
(D) An accessor that returns the values of the two private variables of C
(E) A function to overload the assignment operator

4. Assume that A is an apvector of n integers and that A[k] > A[k-1] for all k such that 0 < k < n. Which of the following is a valid conclusion?

I The array is sorted in descending order.
II There are no duplicates in the array.
III A[n-1] holds the largest value in the array.

(A) I only
(B) II only
(C) III only
(D) I and II only
(E) II and III only

Level A also

Questions 5 and 6 refer to the following function:

```
int Result(int n)
//precondition: n ≥ 0
{
    if (n == 0)
        return 1;
    else
        return n*Result(n-1);
}
```

5. What does Result(5) return?
    (A) 120
    (B) 60
    (C) 20
    (D) 5
    (E) 1

6. Which of the following iterative algorithms could be used to replace the body of function Result such that an equivalent value is returned for any valid input value n?

```
 I  int prod = 1, i = 1;
    while (i <= n)
    {
        ++i;
        prod *= i;
    }
    return prod;

II  int prod = 1;
    for (int i=1; i<=n; i++)
        prod *= i;
    return prod;

III int prod = 1, i = 1;
    do
    {
        ++i;
        prod *= i;
    } while (i != n);
    return prod;
```

   (A) None
   (B) I only
   (C) II only
   (D) I and II only
   (E) I, II, and III

7. Refer to the following code segment:

```
int N;
cin >> N;
for (int i=N; i>=1; i/=2)
{
    Process(i);
}
```

Given that `Process(i)` has a run time of $O(1)$, what is the run time of the algorithm shown?

(A) $O(1)$

(B) $O(N)$

(C) $O(N^2)$

(D) $O(N/2)$

(E) $O(\log N)$

Level A also

8. A program to print a calendar includes the following code:

```
for (int month=1; month<=12; month++)
{
    PrintHeading(month, year);
    PrintDays(month, year);
}
```

The `PrintDays` function includes the following code:

```
PrintSpaces(month, year);
for (int day=1; day<=NumDaysIn(month, year); day++)
{
    cout << " " << day;
    if (EndOfWeek(day, month, year))
        cout << endl;
}
```

When the program is run, every week on the calendar printed has eight days. Which of the following functions is most likely to contain the bug?

(A) `PrintHeading`

(B) `PrintDays`

(C) `PrintSpaces`

(D) `NumDaysIn`

(E) `EndOfWeek`

9. A large sorted array containing about 30,000 elements is to be searched for a value `key` using an iterative binary search algorithm. Assuming that `key` is in the array, which of the following is closest to the smallest number of iterations that will guarantee that `key` is found? Note: $10^3 \approx 2^{10}$.

(A) 15

(B) 30

(C) 100

(D) 300

(E) 3000

GO ON TO THE NEXT PAGE ➤

10. Refer to function SearchAndStack:

```
void SearchAndStack(const apvector <int> & v,
    apstack & s, int value)
//precondition: v[0]...v[v.length()-1] initialized with integers.
//              stack s is empty. value may or may not be in v.
{
    for (int i=0; i<v.length(); i++)
    {
        if (v[i] > value % 2)
            s.push(v[i]);
        else if (v[i] < value % 2)
            s.pop();
        else
            break;
    }
}
```

Suppose v initially contains 2 9 -1 6 -6 -5 0 10, and SearchAndStack(v,s,4) is invoked. Which of the following will be true after execution of the function?

(A) The stack will be empty.
(B) The stack will contain three elements with s.top() equal to 6.
(C) The stack will contain two elements with s.top() equal to 9.
(D) The stack will contain two elements with s.top() equal to 10.
(E) A run-time error will have occurred.

Level A also

11. Which of the following will evaluate to true only if boolean expressions A, B, and C are all false?

(A) (!A && !(B && !C))
(B) (!A || !B || !C)
(C) (!(A || B || C))
(D) (!(A && B && C))
(E) (!A || !(B || !C))

GO ON TO THE NEXT PAGE ➤

Level A also

12. The following code fragment is performed on an array of N elements, a[0] ... a[N-1]:

```
int k, j, hold;
for (k=0; k<N-1; k++)
{
    hold = a[k+1];
    for (j=k; j>=0; j--)
        if (a[j] >= hold)
        {
            int temp = a[j];
            a[j] = hold;
            a[j+1] = temp;
        }
}
```

This fragment is

(A) A selection sort
(B) An insertion sort
(C) A partition-exchange sort
(D) A merge algorithm
(E) A sequential search

13. N integers are to be inserted into the *leaves* of a full binary tree. The final value of level in the following code segment gives the *lowest level* of tree needed to store all N elements in its leaves. Which replacement for *<boolean expression>* leads to the correct value of level? Note: Start counting levels at the root, which is level 0.

```
int level = 0;
while (<boolean expression>)
    level++;
```

(A) N < pow(2, level)
(B) N >= pow(2, level) && N < pow(2, level+1)
(C) N > pow(2, level)
(D) N > pow(2, level+1)
(E) N >= pow(2, level)

GO ON TO THE NEXT PAGE ➤

Use the following declarations for questions 14 and 15:

```
struct treeNode
{
    int data;
    treeNode *left;      //pointer to left child
    treeNode *right;     //pointer to right child
    treeNode *parent;    //pointer to parent
    treeNode(int d, treeNode *L, treeNode *R, treeNode *P)
        : data(d), left(L), right(R), parent(P) {}
};
treeNode *root; //pointer to root of tree
treeNode *last; //pointer to leftmost leaf
treeNode *p;
```

Assume that a nonempty, complete binary tree is filled with data up to and including the node pointed to by last and that last points to a left child, as shown.

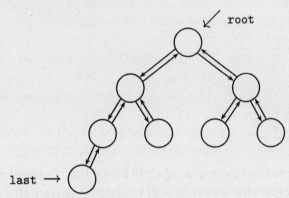

14. Suppose a new node is to be attached to the tree "next to" the node pointed to by last. What is the address of the new node's potential parent?

(A) last->parent->parent->right

(B) last

(C) last->right->parent

(D) last->parent

(E) last->parent->parent

15. Which of the following will correctly attach a new node with integer value num "next to" the node that last points to.

(A) last->parent->right = new treeNode(num,NULL,NULL, last->parent);

(B) last->parent=new treeNode(num,NULL,NULL,last->parent);

(C) last->parent->right = new treeNode(num,NULL,NULL, last->parent->right);

(D) last = new treeNode(num,NULL,NULL,last->parent);

(E) last = new treeNode(num,NULL,NULL,last->parent->right);

GO ON TO THE NEXT PAGE ➤

16. A large club has a membership list of *n* names and phone numbers stored in a text file in random order, as shown:

```
RABKIN ARI 694-8176
HUBBARD JUDITH  583-2199
GOLD JONAH 394-5142
    . . .
```

The text file is edited by hand to add new members to the end of the list and to delete members who leave the club.

A programmer is to write a program that accesses the text file and prints a list of names/phone numbers in alphabetical order. Three methods are considered:

  I Read each line of the file into a string and insert it into a binary search tree. Print the list with an inorder traversal of the tree.

  II Read the lines of the file into an array of strings. Sort the array with a selection sort. Print the list.

  III Read each line of the file into a string and insert it into its correct sorted position in a linear linked list of strings. Thus, the list remains sorted after each insertion. Print the list.

Which is a *false* statement?

(A) Each of methods I, II, and III, if implemented correctly, will work.

(B) Method III, on average, has $O(n)$ run time.

(C) If the names in the text file are approximately in alphabetical order, methods I, II, and III will have the same big-O run times.

(D) If the names in the text file are randomly ordered, method I has the fastest run time.

(E) The part of the algorithm that prints the list of names is $O(n)$ in each of the three methods.

Level A also

17. Refer to the following program segment:

```
apstring st;
getline(cin, st);
int k = st.find(' ');
apstring sub = st.substr(k+1, st.length());
for (int i=sub.length()-1; i>=0; i--)
    cout << sub[i];
```

If the input is John Mulcahy, where the first and last names are separated by a single blank, what will be output?

(A) yhacluM nhoJ

(B) Mulcahy

(C) yhacluM

(D) yhacluM followed by a blank

(E) An out-of-range error will occur

Level A also

Questions 18 and 19 refer to function Foo.

```
int Foo(int n)
{
    if (n % 2 == 0)
        return 0;
    else if (n < 10)
        return 1;
    else
        return Foo(n-1) + Foo(n-2);
}
```

18. What will be returned by `Foo(21) + Foo(14)`?

(A) 21
(B) 14
(C) 6
(D) 2
(E) 1

19. If Foo were rewritten nonrecursively in the most efficient way possible, but always returning the same results as before, the worst case run time of the revised Foo would be

(A) $O(2^n)$
(B) $O(n)$
(C) $O(n \log n)$
(D) $O(\log n)$
(E) $O(1)$

Level A also

Questions 20–23 refer to the following class definition:

```
class Rectangle
{
    public:
        Rectangle();
        Rectangle(int topL_x, int topL_y, int botR_x, int botR_y);
        int Perimeter() const;
        int Area() const;
        Rectangle & Alter(int newTopL_x, int newTopL_y,
            int newBotR_x, int newBotR_y);  //changes coords
                                            //of current rectangle
    private:
        int myTopLeft_x;  //x-coord of top left corner
        int myTopLeft_y;  //y-coord of top left corner
        int myBotRight_x; //x-coord of bottom right corner
        int myBotRight_y; //y-coord of bottom right corner
        bool CheckRect() const;
        //returns true if rectangle valid, false otherwise
        //rectangle is valid iff "top" y-coord > "bottom"
        //y-coord and "right" x-coord > "left" x-coord
};
```

20. Which of the following is a *false* statement about the `Rectangle` class?

    (A) There are two constructors.
    (B) There is no copy constructor.
    (C) There are three accessor functions.
    (D) The implementation of `Alter()` will require use of the keyword `this`.
    (E) The `CheckRect()` function will allow clients of the class to check the validity of any given rectangle.

21. The constructor with parameters will be implemented as follows:

    ```
    Rectangle :: Rectangle(int topL_x, int topL_y, int botR_x,
                  int botR_y) : <initializer list> {}
    ```

    Which of the following represents correct code for `<initializer list>`?

    (A) `topL_x(myTopLeft_x), topL_y(myTopLeft_y),`
    `        botR_x(myBotRight_x), botR_y(myBotRight_y)`

    (B) `myTopLeft_x(topL_x), myTopLeft_y(topL_y),`
    `        myBotRight_x(botR_x), myBotRight_y(botR_y)`

    (C) `myTopLeft_x(),myTopLeft_y(),myBotRight_x(),myBotRight_y()`

    (D) `topL_x(),topL_y(),botR_x(),botR_y()`

    (E) `{`
    `        myTopLeft_x = topL_x;`
    `        myTopLeft_y = topL_y;`
    `        myBotRight_x = botR_x;`
    `        myBotRight_y = botR_y;`
    `    }`

GO ON TO THE NEXT PAGE ➤

Level A also

22. A client program of the Rectangle class contains the following function:

```
bool IsSquare(const Rectangle & rect)
//returns true if rect is a square, false otherwise
//precondition: rect is a valid rectangle
{
    return ((myBotRight_x - myTopLeft_x) ==
            (myTopLeft_y - myBotRight_y));
}
```

This code is incorrect. Why?

(A) The return statement is mathematically incorrect. It should be
```
return (abs(myBotRight_x - myTopLeft_x) ==
            abs(myTopLeft_y - myBotRight_y));
```

(B) The return statement is mathematically incorrect. It should be
```
return ((myTopLeft_x - myBotRight_x) ==
            (myTopLeft_y - myBotRight_y));
```

(C) The condition is insufficient: all four sides of the rectangle must be tested for equality.

(D) The Rectangle parameter should be passed by value.

(E) The variables myTopLeft_x, myTopLeft_y, myBotRight_x, and myBotRight_y cannot be used in a client program.

23. A member function to overload the *= operator is added to the Rectangle class. Here is its implementation:

```
Rectangle & Rectangle :: operator*=(int factor)
//scales up a rectangle by multiplying each corner coordinate
// by factor
{
    <implementation code>
}
```

Which of the following is a correct replacement for <implementation code>?

(A)
```
if (this != factor)
{
    myTopLeft_x *= factor;
    myTopLeft_y *= factor;
    myBotRight_x *= factor;
    myBotRight_y *= factor;
    return *this;
}
```

(B)
```
Rectangle rec;
rec *= factor;
return rec;
```

(C)
```
myTopLeft_x *= factor;
myTopLeft_y *= factor;
myBotRight_x *= factor;
myBotRight_y *= factor;
return this;
```

(D)
```
myTopLeft_x *= factor;
myTopLeft_y *= factor;
myBotRight_x *= factor;
myBotRight_y *= factor;
return *this;
```

(E)
```
Rectangle rec;
rec.myTopLeft_x *= factor;
rec.myTopLeft_y *= factor;
rec.myBotRight_x *= factor;
rec.myBotRight_y *= factor;
return *this;
```

24. What is the prefix form of the expression $2/3 - 4 * 5 + 6$?
   (A) $+ - / 2\ 3 * 4\ 5\ 6$
   (B) $+ * - / 2\ 3\ 4\ 5\ 6$
   (C) $+ - *2/3\ 4\ 5\ 6$
   (D) $2\ 3/4\ 5 * -6+$
   (E) $2\ 3/4 - 5 * 6+$

GO ON TO THE NEXT PAGE ➤

Level A also

25. Student names and ID numbers are to be read from the file `nameFile` shown:

```
Perl Greta
2194
Majumdar Aveek
3785
Sorrells Shawn
6868
    . . .
```

This data should then be output to the screen as follows:

```
Perl Greta 2194
Majumdar Aveek 3785
Sorrells Shawn 6868
    . . .
```

The following code segment assumes that `nameFile` is open for reading and that `NUMSTUDENTS` is a valid positive integer.

```
apstring name, str;
int idNum;
for (int i=1; i<=NUMSTUDENTS; i++)
{
    <code>
    cout << name << " " << idNum << endl;
}
```

Which of the following replacements for `<code>` will lead to the desired output?

(A) `getline(nameFile, name);`
    `nameFile >> idNum;`
    `getline(nameFile, str);`

(B) `getline(nameFile, name);`
    `nameFile >> idNum;`

(C) `nameFile >> name;`
    `nameFile >> idNum;`

(D) `getline(nameFile, name);`
    `getline(nameFile, idNum);`

(E) `nameFile >> name;`
    `getline(nameFile, idNum);`

Level A also

26. Consider the following function:

```
void Sketch(int x1, int y1, int x2, int y2, int n)
{
    int xm, ym;
    if (n <= 0)
        DrawLine(x1, y1, x2, y2);
    else
    {
        xm = (x1+x2+y1-y2)/2;
        ym = (y1+y2+x2-x1)/2;
        Sketch(x1,y1,xm,ym,n-1);
        Sketch(xm,ym,x2,y2,n-1);
    }
}
```

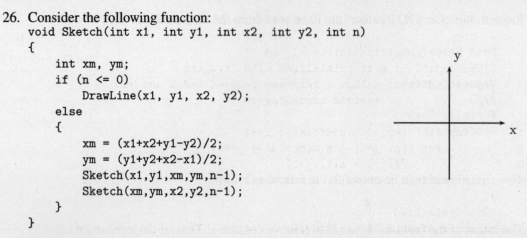

Assume that the screen looks like a Cartesian coordinate system with the origin at the center, and that Drawline connects (x1,y1) to (x2,y2). Assume also that x1, y1, x2, and y2 are never too large or too small to cause errors. Which picture best represents the sketch drawn by the function call

```
Sketch(a, 0, -a, 0, 2)
```

where a is a positive integer?

(A)

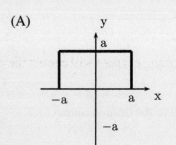

(B)

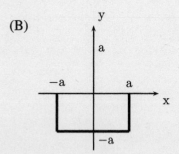

(C)

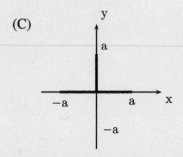

(D)

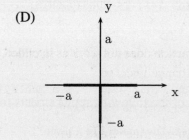

(E)

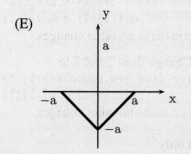

Level A also

27. Refer to function `Alter` below (the lines are numbered for reference):

```
void Alter(apmatrix <int> & m, int c)
//precondition: m is initialized with integers
//postcondition: column c has been removed and m has been
//                resized accordingly
{
1     for (int i=0; i<m.numrows(); i++)
2         for (int j=c; j<m.numcols(); j++)
3             m[i][j] = m[i][j+1];
4     m.resize(m.numrows(), m.numcols()-1);
}
```

The intent of the function `Alter` is to remove column c. Thus, if the input matrix is

$$
\begin{matrix}
2 & 6 & 8 & 9 \\
1 & 5 & 4 & 3 \\
0 & 7 & 3 & 2
\end{matrix}
$$

the function call `Alter(m,1)` should change m to

$$
\begin{matrix}
2 & 8 & 9 \\
1 & 4 & 3 \\
0 & 3 & 2
\end{matrix}
$$

The function does not work as intended. Which of the following changes will correct the problem?

I Change line 2 to
```
for (int j=c; j < m.numcols()-1; j++)
```
and make no other changes.

II Change lines 2 and 3 to
```
for (int j=c+1; j<m.numcols(); j++)
        m[i][j-1] = m[i][j];
```
and make no other changes.

III Change lines 2 and 3 to
```
for (int j=m.numcols()-1; j>c; j--)
        m[i][j-1] = m[i][j];
```
and make no other changes.

(A) I only
(B) II only
(C) III only
(D) I and II only
(E) I, II, and III

GO ON TO THE NEXT PAGE ➤

28. A list of numbers in unknown order is inserted into a binary search tree. Which of the following is true?
    (A) If the tree produced is reasonably balanced, the run time to create the tree is $O(\log n)$.
    (B) If the tree is balanced, the run time to search for a given element is $O(n \log n)$.
    (C) The worst case run time to insert a new element into the tree is $O(n^2)$.
    (D) A postorder traversal of the tree will produce the elements in ascending order.
    (E) The run time to print out the elements sorted in ascending order is $O(n)$.

Questions 29 and 30 refer to the following templated class:

```
template <class T>
class Container
{
 public:
    const T & ReadValue() const; //returns myValue
    void StoreValue(const T &x); //sets myValue equal to x

 private:
    T myValue;
};
//Implementation
template <class T>
const T & Container<T>::ReadValue() const
{
    return myValue;
}
template <class T>
void Container<T>::StoreValue(const T &x)
{
    myValue = x;
}
```

29. Here is a client program that uses this class. You may assume that all the relevant files have been linked to it.

```
int main()
{
    Container C;
    C.StoreValue(7);
    cout << "Container contents are "
        << C.ReadValue() << '\n';
    return 0;
}
```

This code is incorrect. Why?
    (A) The copy constructor for type T is not defined.
    (B) The line template <class T> does not appear in main().
    (C) Type T does not have a default constructor.
    (D) The declaration of C does not include an actual type parameter.
    (E) ReadValue() may not be accessed by a client program.

30. Refer to the client program. Which of the following changes would make it work?

    (A) Replace `Container C` with `Container<T> C`.

    (B) Replace `Container C` with `Container<int> C`.

    (C) Replace `Container C` with
```
template <class T>
Container C;
```

    (D) Replace `C.StoreValue(7)` with
```
Container<int> C.StoreValue(7)
```

    (E) Replace `C.StoreValue(7)` with
```
C<int>.StoreValue(7)
```

31. Assume that linear linked lists are implemented as follows:

```
struct node
{
    int info;
    node *next;
};
```

Refer to function `Mystery`.

```
node *Mystery(node *list)
{
    node *p;
    if (list == NULL)
        return NULL;
    else
    {
        p = new node;
        p->info = list->info;
        p->next = Mystery(list->next);
        return p;
    }
}
```

What does function `Mystery` do?
    (A) It creates an exact copy of the linear linked list pointed to by `list` and returns a pointer to this newly created list.
    (B) It creates a copy in reverse order of the linear linked list pointed to by `list` and returns a pointer to this newly created list.
    (C) It reverses the pointers of the linear linked list pointed to by `list` and returns a pointer to the original list, which is now in reverse order.
    (D) The net effect of the function is that the original list remains unchanged and a pointer is returned to the original list.
    (E) It causes a run-time error by attempting to dereference a null pointer.

GO ON TO THE NEXT PAGE ➤

For questions 32 and 33 assume that trees are implemented with the following declaration:

```
struct node
{
    int data;
    node *left, *right;
    node(int d, node *l, node *r);
};
node :: node(int d, node *l, node *r)    //constructor
    : data(d), left(l), right(r) {}
```

32. Consider the function PrintStuff:

```
void PrintStuff(node *tree)
//precondition: tree points to the root of a binary tree
{
    if (tree != NULL)
    {
        if (tree->left != NULL)
            cout << tree->left->data << endl;
        PrintStuff(tree->left);
        PrintStuff(tree->right);
    }
}
```

Which best describes what function PrintStuff does?
(A) Prints every number in tree except the number in the root node
(B) Prints every number in tree
(C) Prints the number in the left child of every node in tree
(D) Prints every number in the left subtree of tree
(E) Prints the number in the root node as well as every number in the left subtree of tree

GO ON TO THE NEXT PAGE ➤

33. Refer to function Mtree:

```
node *Mtree(node *T)
//returns a pointer to a newly created tree
{
    node *temp;
    if (T == NULL)
        return NULL;
    else
    {
        temp = new node(T->data, Mtree(T->right),
                Mtree(T->left));
        return temp;
    }
}
```

Suppose p = Mtree(T) is invoked for the tree shown.

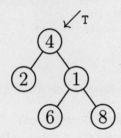

Which of the following trees will be created?

(A)

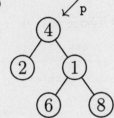

(B)

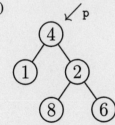

(C)

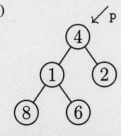

(D)

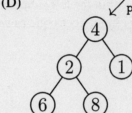

(E)

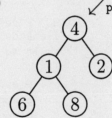

34. Assume that circular linked lists are implemented using this declaration:

```
struct listNode
{
    int info;
    listNode *next;
};
```

Consider function SplitList:

```
void SplitList(listNode * & q, listNode *p)
//precondition: p points to a nonempty circular linked list containing an even
//              number of nodes.
//postcondition: circular linked list p has been split into two disjoint circular
//              linked lists each containing exactly half the number of nodes of
//              the original list. p and q point to these lists.
//Note: The choice of which nodes to include in which list is arbitrary. The only
// requirement is that half the nodes of the original list go into the new
// list q; the other half remain in p.
{
    <code>
}
```

Which of the following replacements for <code> will implement the SplitList function so that its postcondition is satisfied?

```
I  listNode *temp = p;                    II listNode *p_end =p, *q_end = p;
   q = p;                                     int count = 0;
   do                                         do
   {                                          {
       q = q->next;                               q_end = q_end->next;
       temp = temp->next->next;                   count++;
   } while (temp != p);                       } while (q_end->next != p);
   temp = temp->next;                         for (int i=1; i<=count/2; i++)
   p->next = q->next;                             p_end = p_end->next;
   q->next = temp;                            q = p_end->next;
                                              p_end->next = p;
                                              q_end->next = q;
```

```
III q = p->next;
    listNode *p_end =p, *q_end = q;
    while (q_end->next != p)
    {
        p_end->next = q_end->next;
        p_end = p_end->next;
        q_end->next = p_end->next;
        q_end = q_end->next;
    }
    q_end->next = q;
    p_end->next = p;
```

(A) I only

(B) II only

(C) III only

(D) I and III only

(E) I, II, and III

35. Refer to function `Match` below:

```
bool Match(const apvector<int> & v, const apvector<int> & w,
    int N, int M)
//returns true if there is an integer k that occurs in both
// arrays. Otherwise returns false.
//precondition: v[0]..v[N-1] and w[0]..w[M-1] initialized,
// with v[0] < v[1] < .. < v[N-1] and w[0] < w[1] < .. < w[M-1]
{
    int vIndex = 0, wIndex = 0;
    while (vIndex < N && wIndex < M)
    {
        if (v[vIndex] == w[wIndex])
            return true;
        else if (v[vIndex] < w[wIndex])
            vIndex++;
        else
            wIndex++;
    }
    return false;
}
```

Assuming that the function has not been exited, which assertion is true at the end of every execution of the `while` loop?

(A) `v[0] .. v[vIndex-1]` and `w[0] .. w[wIndex-1]` contain no common value,
   `vIndex ≤ N` and `wIndex ≤ M`.

(B) `v[0] .. v[vIndex]` and `w[0] .. w[wIndex-1]` contain no common value,
   `vIndex ≤ N` and `wIndex ≤ M`.

(C) `v[0] .. v[vIndex-1]` and `w[0] .. w[wIndex-1]` contain no common value,
   `vIndex ≤ N-1` and `wIndex ≤ M-1`.

(D) `v[0] .. v[vIndex]` and `w[0] .. w[wIndex]` contain no common value,
   `vIndex ≤ N-1` and `wIndex ≤ M-1`.

(E) `v[0] .. v[N-1]` and `w[0] .. w[M-1]` contain no common value,
   `vIndex ≤ N-1` and `wIndex ≤ M-1`.

Questions 36–40 involve reasoning about the code from the **Marine Biology Case Study**. A copy of the code is provided as part of this exam.

Level A also

36. When the `aquamain` program is run, the position of the fish is output after each swimming move. To disable this feature, which of the following should be modified?

   I   The constructor of the `AquaFish` class
   II The `Swim` member function of the `AquaFish` class
   III The aquamain program

   (A) I only
   (B) II only
   (C) III only
   (D) I and II only
   (E) I, II, and III

Level A also

37. Assume that the following constructor has been added to the AquaFish class:

```
AquaFish::AquaFish(int tankSize, bool dbug)
: myPosition(tankSize/2), myTankSize(tankSize),
  myBumpCount(0), myDebugging(dbug) {}
```

Now suppose that aquamain is to be modified so that debugging statements are output only if the number of steps in the simulation is fewer than 10. Thus, for example, if there are 20 steps in the simulation, there will be *no* debugging statements. Which of the following modifications to aquamain will correctly achieve this?

    I Replace the statement

```
AquaFish fish(tankSize);
```

    with

```
bool dBug = (stepsPerSim < 10);
AquaFish fish(tankSize, dBug);
```

    II Replace the statement

```
AquaFish fish(tankSize);
```

    with

```
if (stepsPerSim < 10)
    AquaFish fish(tankSize, true);
else
    AquaFish fish(tankSize, false);
```

    III Remove the statement

```
AquaFish fish(tankSize);
```

    and replace the for loop with

```
bool dBug = false;
AquaFish fish(tankSize, dBug);
for (step=0; step<stepsPerSim; step++)
{
    fish.Swim();
    if (step < 10)
        dBug = true;
}
```

(A) I only

(B) II only

(C) III only

(D) I and II only

(E) I, II, and III

GO ON TO THE NEXT PAGE ➤

Level A also

38. A person running the fishsim program suspects, but is not sure, that the order of moving fish has been changed. Consider the following configuration of fish:

```
C B
A _
```

After two complete steps of the simulation, the configuration is

```
_ C
A B
```

What was the order of moving fish?
(A) Row by row, top-down, left to right
(B) Row by row, top-down, right to left
(C) Column by column, left to right, top-down
(D) Column by column, left to right, bottom-up
(E) Column by column, right to left, top-down

39. Suppose that the implementation of the Neighborhood class is changed to store a collection of positions in a linear linked list rather than an apvector. Which of the following classes will need to be changed?

   I Fish
  II Environment
 III Position

(A) None
(B) I only
(C) II only
(D) III only
(E) I, II, and III

GO ON TO THE NEXT PAGE ➤

Level A also

40. Consider a new member function `FishAt` in the `Environment` class. It takes a grid position as a parameter and returns the fish occupying that position:

```
Fish Environment::FishAt(const Position & pos)
```

An attempt is made to change the implementation of the `Show` function in the `Display` class. Instead of using a list of fish, each grid position in the environment will be examined using `FishAt`, and the fish at that position will be displayed. Consider the following implementation of `Show` (some lines have been numbered for reference).

```
         void Display::Show(const Environment & env)
         //postcondition: state of environment written as text
         //                to cout
         {
             const int WIDTH = 1;    //for each fish
             int r, c;
line 1:      Fish tempFish;
line 2:      Position p;
line 3:      for (r=0; r<env.NumRows(); r++)
line 4:      {
line 5:          for (c=0; c<env.NumCols(); c++)
line 6:          {
line 7:              tempFish = env.FishAt(r,c);
line 8:              cout << setw(WIDTH) << tempFish.ShowMe();
line 9:          }
line 10:         cout << endl;
             }
         }
```

The new implementation does not work as intended. Which of the following changes are required to make this implementation work correctly?

I Replace line 3 with
```
for (r=0; r<p.Row(); r++)
```
and replace line 5 with
```
for (c=0; c<p.Col(); c++)
```

II Remove line 2 and replace line 7 with
```
tempFish = env.FishAt(Position(r,c));
```

III Replace line 8 with
```
if (tempFish.IsUndefined())
{
    cout << setw(WIDTH) << ' ';
}
else
{
    cout << setw(WIDTH) << tempFish.ShowMe();
}
```

(A) I only
(B) II only
(C) III only
(D) II and III only
(E) I, II, and III

STOP

COMPUTER SCIENCE AB
SECTION II

Time—1 hour and 45 minutes
Number of questions—4
Percent of total grade—50

Directions: SHOW ALL YOUR WORK. REMEMBER THAT PROGRAM SEGMENTS ARE TO BE WRITTEN IN C++.

Note: Assume that the standard libraries (`iostream.h`, `fstream.h`, `math.h`, etc.) and the AP C++ classes are included in any program that uses a program segment you write. If other classes are to be included, that information will be specified in individual questions. A Quick Reference to the AP C++ classes is included in the case study insert.

Level A also

1. Consider the problem of storing and displaying information about seat availability for a theater performance. Available seats can be represented as a two-dimensional array of integers where each element in the array represents a seat in the theater. A value of 0 indicates that the seat is available, and a value of 1 indicates that the seat is taken. We consider only theaters in which every row has the same number of seats, as in the following example:

	0	1	2	3	4	5	6	7	8	9	10	11	12	13	14
0	0	0	0	0	0	1	0	0	0	0	0	1	1	0	0
1	0	0	1	1	1	0	1	1	0	0	0	0	1	1	1
2	1	1	1	1	1	1	1	1	1	1	1	1	1	1	1
3	0	0	0	0	1	1	1	0	0	0	1	1	1	1	0
4	0	0	1	0	0	1	0	0	1	1	0	0	0	0	0

This theater has 5 rows and 15 seats in each row. All the seats in row 2 are taken, but all of the seats in row 4 are available except for seats 2, 5, 8, and 9.

GO ON TO THE NEXT PAGE ➤

Level A also

The class `Theater`, whose declaration is shown here, is used to keep track of the seats for a given theater performance.

```
class Theater
{
    public:
    Theater(istream & infile);        //constructor
    void PrintAvailable();
    void Find_n_Together(int n);
        ...                           //other public member functions
    private:
        apmatrix <int> mySeats;
        int myNumRows;
        int mySeatsPerRow;
};
```

(a) Write the code for the constructor that initializes the theater by completing the code started below. The constructor reads the state of the seats for a given performance from a file represented by `infile`. You may assume that the file is open and contains the number of rows followed by the number of seats per row followed by the seat values separated by spaces. For example, the theater shown in the diagram would be stored in `infile` like this:

```
5 15
0 0 0 0 0 1 0 0 0 0 0 1 1 0 0
0 0 1 1 1 0 1 1 0 0 0 0 1 1 1
1 1 1 1 1 1 1 1 1 1 1 1 1 1 1
0 0 0 0 1 1 1 0 0 0 1 1 1 1 0
0 0 1 0 0 1 0 0 1 1 0 0 0 0 0
```

Complete the constructor below:

```
Theater :: Theater(istream & infile) : mySeats(0,0)
//precondition: infile is open
//postcondition: myNumRows and mySeatsPerRow have been read from
//               infile. mySeats has been resized and initialized
//               to the seat values from the infile stream
```

GO ON TO THE NEXT PAGE ➤

Level A also

(b) Write the public member function PrintAvailable whose header is given below. The output of PrintAvailable for the case of the theater diagram should be formatted roughly as shown below, with information about each row on a separate line. Assume that the list of available seats for any row will fit on a single line.

```
Row     Available Seats
 0       0 1 2 3 4 6 7 8 9 10 13 14
 1       0 1 5 8 9 10 11
 2      None available
 3       0 1 2 3 7 8 9 14
 4       0 1 3 4 6 7 10 11 12 13 14
```

```
void Theater::PrintAvailable()
//precondition: mySeats[i][j] has value 0 if and only if
//              the corresponding seat is available.
//              0 ≤ i < myNumRows, 0 ≤ j < mySeatsPerRow
//postcondition: available seats in each row are printed to
//              the screen. "None available" is printed for any
//              row with no available seats
```

(c) Write the public member function Find_n_Together whose header is given below. The integer parameter n of the function specifies how many adjacent seats are required. These seats *must* be in the same row. The function finds *just one set* of n seats together (consecutive seat numbers). It prints the information to the screen, with the seats listed in increasing order. More than one set of valid output is therefore possible. If n adjacent seats are not available, the function should print "Not available". For example, the function call Find_n_Together(5) for the theater diagram could produce either

```
Row 0    Seats 0 1 2 3 4
```

or

```
Row 4    Seats 10 11 12 13 14
```

The function call Find_n_Together(8) should produce the output

```
Not available
```

Complete the member function Find_n_Together below.

```
void Theater::Find_n_Together(int n)
//precondition: mySeats[i][j] has value 0 if and only if the
//              corresponding seat is available. 0 ≤ i < myNumRows,
//              0 ≤ j < mySeatsPerRow, n ≥ 2
//postcondition: Exactly one set of n seats together in the same
//              row is printed to the screen. If no row contains
//              n seats together, "Not available" is printed
```

GO ON TO THE NEXT PAGE ➤

2. Consider implementing a queue as a circular singly linked list, with one external pointer that points to the rear of the queue. For example, the circular linked list shown here represents the queue of integers 3, 7, 4, 8, with 3 at the front and 8 at the rear.

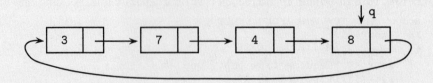

Here is part of the declaration for a Queue class that uses the implementation described.

```
template <class itemType>
class Queue
{
    public:
        //constructors, destructor
            ...
        //assignment
            ...
        //accessors
        bool isEmpty() const;    //returns true if queue empty,
            ...                  // false otherwise
        //modifiers
        void enqueue(const itemType & item);    //insert item at rear
        void dequeue(itemType & item);  //remove front element
                                        // and store in item
        void MakeEmpty();        //make the queue empty
    private:
        int mySize;
        struct queueNode
        {
            itemType info;
            queueNode *next;
            queueNode() : next(NULL) {}
            queueNode(const itemType & item, queueNode *n=NULL)
                : info(item), next(n) {}
        };
        queueNode *myBack;
            ...
};
```

GO ON TO THE NEXT PAGE ➤

(a) Complete the body of the member function `dequeue`, which is started below:

```
template <class itemType>
void Queue <itemType> :: dequeue(itemType & item)
//precondition: queue is e1,e2,...,en with n ≥ 1
//postcondition: queue is e2,e3,...,en and item = e1
{
    if (isEmpty())
    {
        cerr << "dequeue from empty queue" << endl;
        exit(1);
    }
}
```

(b) Write the body of the member function `enqueue` whose header is given below:

```
template <class itemType>
void Queue <itemType> :: enqueue(const itemType & item)
//precondition: queue is e1,e2,...,en with n ≥ 0
//postcondition: queue is e1,e2,...,en,item
```

(c) Discuss the running times of the algorithms used in parts (a) and (b), using big-O notation. Give a brief explanation of your answer for each part.

3. Consider designing a simple line-oriented text editor. The text editor maintains a current line pointer and pointers to the first and last lines of the text. Each line of text is stored as a string. The text itself is stored as a linear doubly linked list of lines. The operations supported by the text editor are described in the following `TextEditor` class.

```
class TextEditor
{
    public:
        TextEditor();                       //default constructor
        ~TextEditor();                      //destructor
        TextEditor(istream & inFile);       //constructor. Lines of text
                                            // read in from inFile
        void Next();        //move current line pointer to next line
                            // Precondition: current pointer not equal to bottomPtr
        void Previous();    //move current line pointer to previous line
                            // Precondition: current pointer not equal to topPtr
        void Top();     //move current line pointer to first line
        void Bottom();  //move current line pointer to last line
        void Insert(const apstring & line); //insert line after
                    // the line pointed to by current line pointer
        void PrintLine(ostream & output);   //print line pointed to by
                    // current line pointer to output. Leave current
                    // line pointer still pointing to that line
        bool AtEnd();       //true if current line pointer points to
                            // last line, otherwise false

    private:
        struct LineNode
        {
            apstring line;
            LineNode *prevLine;
            LineNode *nextLine;
            LineNode(const apstring & L, LineNode *P, LineNode *N)
              : line(L), prevLine(P), nextLine(N) {}    //constructor
        };
        LineNode *current, *topPtr, *bottomPtr;
};
```

GO ON TO THE NEXT PAGE ➤

(a) Write the code for the member function `Insert` as started below. `Insert` should insert its parameter `line` after the line pointed to by the current pointer.

For example, if this is the state of the text editor `T`,

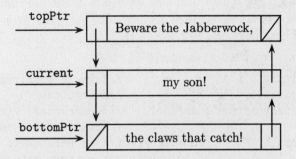

the function call

```
T.Insert("The jaws that bite,");
```

should result in

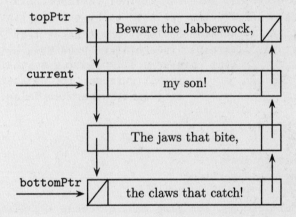

Complete function `Insert`:

```
void TextEditor::Insert(const apstring & line)
//precondition: current is not null
//postcondition: line inserted following line pointed to
//               by currrent
//               bottomPtr adjusted if necessary
```

GO ON TO THE NEXT PAGE ➤

(b) Write the code for the constructor that initializes a text editor, as started below. The constructor reads lines of text from inFile. You may assume that inFile is open and contains at least one line of text. Note that the postcondition specifies that current is initialized to the top line of text.

In writing the constructor, you may wish to call function Insert specified in part (a). You may assume Insert works as specified, regardless of what you wrote in part (a).

Complete the constructor below:

```
TextEditor::TextEditor(istream & inFile)
//precondition: inFile is open for reading with at least one
//              line of text
//postcondition: lines of inFile inserted into TextEditor.
//               topPtr and current point to first line,
//               bottomPtr points to last line
```

(c) A client function PrintAlternate prints every second line of text to output, starting with the first line and proceeding to the end of the text. You may assume that all member functions of the TextEditor class work as specified.

Write function PrintAlternate as started below:

```
void PrintAlternate(TextEditor & T, ostream & output)
//precondition: T contains at least one line of text
//postcondition: Alternate lines of text have been printed to
//               output, starting with the first line
```

GO ON TO THE NEXT PAGE ➤

4. This question involves reasoning about the code from the Marine Biology Case Study. A copy of the code is provided as part of this exam.

The grid of fish in the fishsim simulation is currently stored as an apmatrix. An alternative way of storing this grid is in a binary search tree. The tree will contain defined fish only and will be ordered by position, where positions are compared as follows: If P_1 and P_2 are Position objects, where P_1 represents (x_1, y_1) and P_2 represents (x_2, y_2), then $P_1 < P_2$ if either $x_1 < x_2$ or $x_1 = x_2$ and $y_1 < y_2$. For example, $(2, 6) < (4, 1)$ and $(3, 4) < (3, 5)$.

If the Fish elements in the binary search tree are in order from smallest position to largest, the order obtained is the same as that in which fish are currently processed in the fishsim program. For example, if the grid of fish in the original program were obtained from fish.dat as follows, you could picture this setup (the first row of numbers gives the dimensions of the apmatrix grid):

```
fish.dat
4    6
2    0
1    2
0    3
2    3
1    5
3    4
```

	0	1	2	3	4	5
0				🐟		
1			🐟			🐟
2	🐟			🐟		
3					🐟	

The corresponding binary search tree would be

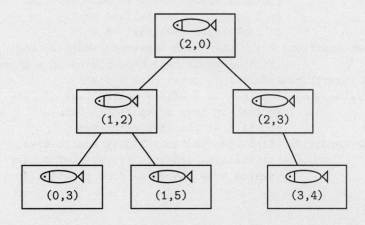

You may assume that the following free function has been defined for the Position class to overload the < (less than) operator and that it works as specified.

```
bool operator<(const Position & P1, const Position & P2)
//returns true if P1 < P2; otherwise returns false
```

To implement the fish grid as a binary search tree, the following changes will be made to the private section of the Environment class. The apmatrix data member will be replaced by a TreeNode struct and a pointer to a TreeNode. Two helper functions Inorder and Insert will be added. Inorder will take a tree pointer, an apvector, and an integer index as parameters. The integer parameter index is the initialized index of the apvector. Function Inorder will perform an inorder traversal of the tree, placing the tree elements in the apvector as it goes. Insert will take a tree pointer and Fish object as parameters and will insert the fish into the binary search tree in the correct position.

The following declarations reflect these changes (highlighted in bold).

```
class Environment
{
        ...
    private:
        bool InRange(const Position & pos) const;
        //postcondition: returns true if pos in grid
        //               returns false otherwise
        struct TreeNode
        {
            Fish data;
            TreeNode *left;
            TreeNode *right;
            TreeNode(Fish D, TreeNode *L, TreeNode *R)  //constructor
                : data(D), left(L), right(R) {}
        };
        TreeNode *myWorld;
        int myFishCreated;      //# fish ever created
        int myFishCount;        //# fish in current environment
        //private helper functions
        void Inorder(TreeNode *T, apvector<Fish> &v, int & index) const;
        //precondition: binary tree T contains fish. vector v
        //              contains enough slots to hold all fish
        //              in T. index is initialized to 0.
        //              It represents the index of v
        //postcondition: tree T has been traversed inorder, and
        //               Fish elements have been placed in v inorder
        void Insert(TreeNode * & T, const Fish & fish);
        //precondition: T points to a binary search tree of Fish.
        //              No fish in tree occupies the same
        //              position as the fish parameter
        //postcondition: fish inserted into binary search tree,
        //               maintaining ordering property of binary
        //               search tree, based on fish position in grid
};
```

GO ON TO THE NEXT PAGE ➤

(a) Write the implementation of the helper function `Inorder` as started here.

```
void Environment::Inorder(TreeNode *T, apvector<Fish> &v, int & index) const
//precondition: binary tree T contains fish. apvector v
//            contains enough slots to hold all fish
//            in T. index is initialized to 0.
//            It represents the index of v
//postcondition: tree T has been traversed inorder, and
//              Fish elements have been placed in v inorder
```

(b) Write the implementation of the helper function `Insert` as started here.

```
void Environment::Insert(TreeNode * & T, const Fish & fish)
//precondition: T points to a binary search tree of Fish.
//            No fish in tree occupies the same
//            position as the fish parameter
//postcondition: fish inserted into binary search tree,
//              maintaining ordering property of binary
//              search tree based on fish position in grid
```

In writing parts (c) and (d), you may wish to call one or both of the new `Environment` member functions `Inorder` and `Insert`. You may assume that they work as specified, regardless of what you wrote in parts (a) and (b). You may also use any of the `Environment` member functions—assume that they have been modified for the binary search tree data structure and work as specified.

(c) Write a revised version of the `Environment` member function `AddFish`, as started below. `AddFish` should create a new fish at its parameter position, `pos`.

   Complete function `Addfish` below.

```
void Environment::AddFish(const Position & pos)
//precondition: No fish already at pos, i.e. IsEmpty(pos) is true
//postcondition: fish created at pos
```

(d) Write a revised version of the `Environment` member function `AllFish`, as started below. `AllFish` should return an `apvector` of `Fish` in the order in which they will be processed, namely ordered by position from smallest to largest.

   Complete function `AllFish` below.

```
apvector<Fish> Environment::AllFish() const
//postcondition: returned apvector (call it fishList) contains
//            all fish in top-down, left-right order:
//            top-left fish in fishList[0], bottom-right
//            fish in fishList[fishList.length()-1].
//            Number of fish in environment is fishList.length()
```

STOP

Answer Key

1. **D**	15. **A**	29. **D**
2. **B**	16. **B**	30. **B**
3. **C**	17. **C**	31. **A**
4. **E**	18. **E**	32. **C**
5. **A**	19. **E**	33. **C**
6. **D**	20. **E**	34. **E**
7. **E**	21. **B**	35. **A**
8. **E**	22. **E**	36. **A**
9. **A**	23. **D**	37. **A**
10. **A**	24. **A**	38. **B**
11. **C**	25. **A**	39. **A**
12. **B**	26. **B**	40. **D**
13. **C**	27. **D**	
14. **D**	28. **E**	

Answers Explained

Section I

1. **(D)** A good hash table in which the customer orders are uniformly distributed throughout the table can allow for $O(1)$ insertion and retrieval of any particular customer order.

2. **(B)** If the tree is arbitrary (i.e., has no ordering property), then all n nodes must be examined in the worst case, so the algorithm is $O(n)$.

3. **(C)** The class object shown is being constructed with two values, which means that there must be a constructor in the class definition that creates an object with two parameters. For example,

```
C :: C(int intVal, double dVal)
    : v1(intVal), v2(dVal) {}
```

4. **(E)** According to the given assertion, A[n-1]>A[n-2]> ... >A[0]. This means that the array is sorted in *ascending* order, there are no duplicates (> means "strictly greater than"), and A[n-1] is the largest value in the array.

5. **(A)** Result(n) finds $n!$. Explicitly,

$$
\begin{aligned}
\text{Result}(5) &= 5 * \text{Result}(4) \\
&= 5 * 4 * \text{Result}(3) \\
&= \cdots \\
&= 5 * 4 * 3 * 2 * 1 * \text{Result}(0) \\
&= 5 * 4 * 3 * 2 * 1 * 1 \\
&= 120
\end{aligned}
$$

6. **(D)** Segment III fails when $n = 0$ or 1. In each of these cases, i is incremented to 2, and the incorrect value 2 is returned.

7. **(E)** The for loop is executed $\log_2 N$ times (i.e., the number of times that i, which is initialized to N, is divided by 2 until it reaches 1).

8. **(E)** Notice that PrintHeading, PrintDays, PrintSpaces, and NumDaysIn all depend on the month and year only. This suggests that the culprit is the boolean EndOfWeek function. What is probably happening is that after printing seven days, EndOfWeek remains false and only becomes true after the eighth day is printed.

9. **(A)** $30,000 = 1000 \times 30 \approx 2^{10} \times 2^5 = 2^{15}$. Since a successful binary search in the worst case requires $\log_2 n$ iterations, 15 iterations will guarantee that key is found. (Note that $30,000 < 2^{10} \times 2^5 = 32,768$.)

10. **(A)** Since value 4 is even, value % 2 is 0. Array v is examined sequentially. Each time a positive element is encountered, it is pushed onto the stack. Each time a negative element is encountered, the stack is popped. If 0 is encountered, the loop is exited. Thus, the following sequence of actions will occur: push 2, push 9, pop, push 6, pop, pop, exit loop. Three pushes and three pops leave the stack empty.

11. **(C)** In order for !(A || B || C) to be true, (A || B || C) must evaluate to false. This will happen only if A, B, and C are *all* false. Choice A evaluates to true when A and B are false and C is true. In choice B, if any *one* of A, B, or C is false, the boolean expression evaluates to true. In choice D, if any one of A, B, or C is false, the boolean expression evaluates to true since we have !(false). All that's required for choice E to evaluate to true is for A to be false. Since true || (any) evaluates to true, both B and C can be either true or false.

12. **(B)** Elements from a[1] to a[N-1] take turns to be hold. When hold = a[1], a[1] is compared to a[0] and swapped downward if a[1] < a[0]. When hold = a[2], comparisons are made with a[1] and a[0], and a[2] is swapped downward if necessary. The array is being sorted in ascending order. In each pass through the outer for loop, the correct insertion point for the hold element is found. This is an insertion sort.

13. **(C)**   If $N = 1$, the required level is 0
    If $N = 2$, the required level is 1
    If $N = 3$ or 4, the required level is 2
    If $N = 5$–8, the required level is 3
    ...

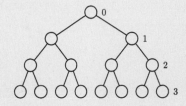

Test each of choices A–E with $N = 4$, where the desired answer is 2. Choice C works. Choices A and B fail the test on the first try and return level = 0. Choice D fails on the second try, leaving level = 1. Choice E executes the while loop one time too many, giving level a value of 3 when 2 will suffice. The conditions of the problem specify that the lowest possible level should be found.

14. **(D)** The new node will have the same parent node as the node that last points to, namely last->parent.

15. **(A)** The third pointer field in the constructor must be the address of the new node's parent, namely `last->parent`. This eliminates choices C and E. The new node will be the right child of `last->parent`. Thus, the left side of the assignment must be `last->parent->right`, which eliminates choices B and D.

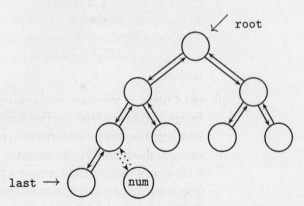

16. **(B)** Method III is $O(n^2)$: For each element in the text file, its insertion point in the linear linked list must be found. For one element, this would be $O(n)$. For n elements, it is $O(n^2)$. Choice A is true: an inorder traversal of a binary search tree accesses the values in ascending order, which is alphabetical order if the elements are strings. Choice C is true: approximately ordered elements lead to an unbalanced binary search tree (worst case). Number of comparisons to form the tree is $1 + 2 + \cdots + (n-2) + (n-1) = n(n-1)/2$, which is $O(n^2)$. Selection sort is $O(n^2)$ irrespective of the order of the elements. Choice D is true: random order of the elements generally leads to a balanced binary search tree. Creation of the tree is then $O(n \log n)$, which is faster than the $O(n^2)$ run times of methods II and III. Choice E is true: traversal of a linear linked list and printing elements of an array are both $O(n)$. An inorder traversal of a binary search tree visits each node once, which is $O(n)$.

17. **(C)** The string `John Mulcahy` will be read into `st`. Then `k` will get the value 4, since the blank is in position 4 of `st`. The function call `st.substr(k+1,st.length())` is equivalent to `st.substr(5,12)`. Thus, `sub` will get the substring of `st` starting at position 5 (the M) and extending through 12 characters. Since this goes off the end of the string `st`, `sub` will have value `Mulcahy` with no blanks at either end. The `for` loop prints this out backwards.

18. **(E)** Note that only odd values of n lead to a recursive call. Foo(14) is a base case and returns 0. Foo(9) is a base case and returns 1.

$$
\begin{aligned}
\text{Foo}(21) &= \text{Foo}(20) + \text{Foo}(19) \\
&= 0 + \text{Foo}(18) + \text{Foo}(17) \\
&= 0 + 0 + \text{Foo}(16) + \text{Foo}(15) \\
&= \cdots \\
&= 0 + \cdots + 0 + \text{Foo}(10) + \text{Foo}(9) \\
&= 0 + \cdots + 0 + 0 + 1 \\
&= 1
\end{aligned}
$$

19. **(E)** Any odd parameter, whether greater than or less than 10, will return 1. Any even parameter will return 0. The run time is independent of n and is, therefore, $O(1)$. Here is the revised body of Foo:

```
{
    if (n % 2 == 0)
        return 0;
    else
        return 1;
}
```

20. **(E)** Clients of the class may not use CheckRect since it is a private member function. It can only be used by member functions of the class. Choice A is correct: constructors have no return type. The first constructor is the default constructor, the second is a constructor with two parameters. Choice B is correct: a copy constructor would require a parameter of type Rectangle to be copied. The constant member functions Area(), Perimeter(), and CheckRect() are the accessor functions. This means they will access the private variables of a Rectangle object without altering them. Thus, choice C is correct. Choice D is also correct: a Rectangle object will be changed. The updated object must then be returned with the statement return *this.

21. **(B)** The private variables myTopLeft_x, myTopLeft_y, myBotRight_x, and myBotRight_y must be assigned the parameter values given in the parameter list. Only choices B and E do this. Choice E is incorrect because it's not using an initializer list for the assignments.

22. **(E)** A client program may not access private variables of a class. The return statement as given is mathematically correct: if two adjacent sides of a rectangle have the same length, the rectangle is a square. Also, since the rectangle is valid, the subtraction operations given in the function will produce positive lengths.

23. **(D)** Each private variable must be multiplied by factor according to the specification of the function. The changed object must be returned with the statement return *this. Thus, eliminate choices B and C. The if (this != factor) test in choice A is meaningless—for one thing, factor is not a Rectangle object, and the keyword this refers only to objects of the class. The dot member construct is being used incorrectly in choice E. If a Rectangle object is being modified in a member function, the private variables should be accessed directly. The declaration Rectangle rec is incorrect in this context, since it's the *current* Rectangle object that must be modified, not a newly created one.

24. **(A)** The given expression is in infix form. To convert to prefix form, change the highest precedence operations to prefix first:

$$
\begin{aligned}
&\quad 2/3 - 4 * 5 + 6 \\
&= \ (/2\ 3 - *4\ 5) + 6 \\
&= \ (-/2\ 3 * 4\ 5) + 6 \\
&= \ + - /2\ 3 * 4\ 5\ 6
\end{aligned}
$$

25. **(A)** The statement getline(nameFile,name) reads the entire line of text into the name string and throws away the carriage return. The statement nameFile >> idNum reads the number into idNum but leaves the carriage return. This means that another getline statement, namely getline(nameFile,str), is needed to read the empty string into str and throw away the carriage return. The reason the code in choice B doesn't work is that getline(nameFile,name), when executed the second time through the loop, will read an empty string into name. Choices C and E are wrong because the >> operator will read only as far as the first whitespace. Thus, name will contain the last name only. Choice D is incorrect because the statement getline(nameFile,idNum) reads idNum into a string, not an integer, which is the type of idNum.

26. **(B)** Here is the "box diagram" for the recursive function calls, showing the order of execution of statements. Notice that the circled statements are the base case calls, the only statements that actually draw a line.

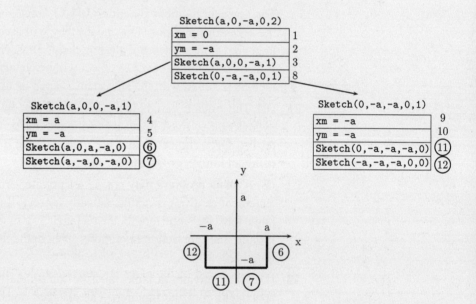

27. **(D)** The problem in the function as given is that it will produce an out-of-range error. For the matrix in the example m.numcols() is 4. The function call Alter(m,1) gives c a value of 1. Thus, in the inner for loop j goes from 1 to 3. When j is 3, the line m[i][j] = m[i][j+1] becomes m[i][3] = m[i][4]. Since columns go from 0 to 3, m[i][4] is out of range. The changes in segments I and II both fix this problem. In each case the correct replacements are made for each row i: m[i][1] = m[i][2] and m[i][2] = m[i][3]. Segment III makes the following incorrect replacements as j goes from 3 to 2: m[i][2] = m[i][3] and m[i][1] = m[i][2]. This will cause both columns 1 and 2 to be overwritten. Before resizing, m will be

$$
\begin{array}{cccc}
2 & 9 & 9 & 9 \\
1 & 3 & 3 & 3 \\
0 & 2 & 2 & 2
\end{array}
$$

This does not achieve the intended postcondition of the function.

28. **(E)** An inorder traversal of the tree will produce the elements in ascending order. Whether the tree is balanced or not, each of the n nodes will be visited once during the traversal, which is $O(n)$. Choice A is incorrect: *each* of the n elements may require a $\log_2 n$ search to find its slot, so creating the tree is $O(n \log n)$. Choice B is incorrect: to find a single element in a balanced tree requires no more than one comparison on each of $\log_2 n$ levels. This is $O(\log n)$. Choice C is incorrect: even if the tree is completely unbalanced and consists of one long linked list (worst case), there will be no more than n comparisons to insert one element. This is $O(n)$. Choice D is incorrect. A postorder traversal for the binary search tree shown below produces 1, 7, 6, which is not in ascending order. In a binary search tree, the order property causes the leftmost elements to be the smallest and the rightmost the largest. Thus, an *inorder* traversal will produce the elements sorted in ascending order.

29. **(D)** A templated class cannot be used in a program until it has been declared (instantiated) with an actual type. For example,

```
int main()
{
    Container<int> C;
    ...
```

Note that the program cannot be compiled if type T has not been replaced by some type, either built-in or user-defined.

30. **(B)** The name of the class is `Container<T>`. The T must be replaced by an actual type in the `main()` function that uses it. This eliminates choices A and C. Choices D and E do not correct the incorrect line `Container C`, and then they go on to use incorrect syntax.

31. **(A)** If `Mystery(list)` is invoked for the following linear linked list:

the function will create three new nodes whose pointer connections are pending:

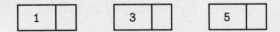

In the function call that creates the last node (containing 5), the statement `p->next = Mystery(list->next)` involves a base case, resulting in

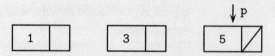

Now each of the previous function calls can be completed, resulting in the following sequence of pointer connections:

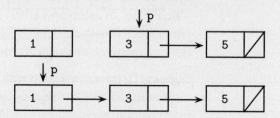

After the execution of the first recursive call has been completed, the final pointer value returned points to the first node of a linear linked list that is identical to the original list.

32. **(C)** The `cout << tree->left->data ...` statement indicates that the data in the root node is not printed. This eliminates choices B and E. Notice that there's no `NULL` test on `tree->right`, nor is there any `cout << tree->right->data` statement. This means that no right children are ever printed, which certainly eliminates choice A. It also eliminates choice D, since nodes in the left subtree of `tree` do contain right children.

33. **(C)** The function creates a tree that is a mirror image of its parameter. Note the order of the parameters in the node constructor: `(data,left,right)`. In the function definition the order is `(T->data,MTree(T->right),MTree(T->left))`. Matching up parameters means that the right subtree of `T` becomes the left connection of the new tree, and the left subtree of `T` becomes the right connection.

34. **(E)** All three work! Segment I traverses the list by moving pointer `temp` two nodes for each move that pointer `q` makes. This puts `temp` in its original place when `q` is exactly halfway around the list. For an initial list of the form

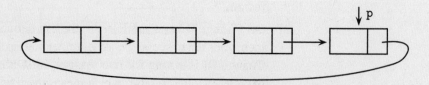

here's a picture of the final position of the pointers:

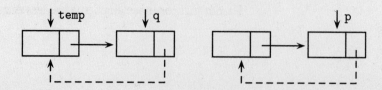

Segment II traverses the list with q_end and counts the number of nodes, leaving count with a value one less than the total number of nodes. Next, using the count, p_end is positioned at the end of what will be list p. Finally, q_end is positioned at what will be the end of list q. Here is the final pointer arrangement:

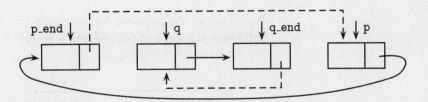

Segment III traverses the list with pointers p_end and q_end, creating the new disjoint lists during traversal by linking alternate nodes as they go. Here is the final position of pointers:

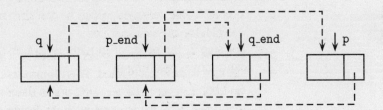

35. (A) Notice that either vIndex or wIndex is incremented at the end of the loop. This means that, when the loop is exited, the current values of v[vIndex] and w[wIndex] have not been compared. Therefore, you can only make an assertion for values v[0]..v[vIndex-1] and w[0]..w[wIndex-1]. Also, notice that if there is no common value in the arrays, the exiting condition for the while loop will be that the end of one of the arrays has been reached, namely vIndex equals N or wIndex equals M.

36. (A) The boolean private variable myDebugging determines whether the fish's position will be output after every move: if true, yes it will; if false, no it won't. Initializing myDebugging to false in the constructor will, therefore, disable this feature.

37. (A) Change II has a subtle error: the fish defined in the if . . . else statement goes out of scope (becomes undefined) as soon as the statement is exited! Change III is wrong for two reasons. First, fish is defined with the second parameter equal to false, which means there will be no debugging during the simulation loop irrespective of the value of stepsPerSim. Second, the specification for the change calls for debugging only if stepsPerSim is fewer than 10, not just for those steps that are less than 10.

38. **(B)** Suppose that the order were top-down, left to right, the original order in the fishsim program. Then the order of moving fish in step 1 of the simulation would be C, B, A. Each fish must move if it can. C can't move, B moves down, A can't move. The resulting configuration after step 1 is, therefore,

```
C _
A B
```

For step 2, the order of moving fish will be C, A, B. C moves right, A moves up, and B moves left, resulting in

```
A C
B _
```

Thus, the user was correct; the order *has* been changed.

For choice B—top-down, right to left—the order of moving for step 1 is B, C, A. B moves down, C moves right, and A moves up, resulting in

```
A C
_ B
```

For step 2, the order of moving is C, A, B. C can't move, B moves left, and A can't move, resulting in

```
_ C
A B
```

39. **(A)** Changing the internal representation of a Neighborhood object will change the implementation of the Neighborhood member functions but not the interface between the Neighborhood class and the other classes of the program.

40. **(D)** Change I doesn't make sense. The grid in the Environment is being examined, so lines 3 and 5 are correct. Change II is valid: FishAt takes a Position parameter, and that position (namely row r and column c) must be constructed using a constructor from the Position class. For Change III, the ShowMe function displays only fish that are defined. Therefore, it's necessary to test for undefined fish that are then displayed with a blank.

Section II

1. (a)
```
Theater :: Theater(istream & infile)
             : mySeats(0,0)
{
        infile >> myNumRows >> mySeatsPerRow;
        mySeats.resize(myNumRows, mySeatsPerRow);
        for (int r=0; r<myNumRows; r++)
            for (int s=0; s<mySeatsPerRow; s++)
                infile >> mySeats[r][s];
}
```

(b)
```
void PrintAvailable()
{
        cout << "Row    Available Seats" << endl << endl;
        for (int row=0; row< myNumRows; row++)
        {
            cout << " " << row << "    ";
            int count = 0;
            for (int seat=0; seat< mySeatsPerRow; seat++)
                if (mySeats[row][seat] == 0)
                {
                    count++;
                    cout << seat << " ";
                }
            if (count == 0)
                cout << "None available";
            cout << endl;
        }
}
```

(c)
```
void Find_n_Together(int n)
{
        for (int r=0; r<myNumRows; r++)
        {
            int seat = 0;
            while (seat <= mySeatsPerRow - n)
            {
                int count = 0;
                while (count < n && mySeats[r][seat] == 0)
                {
                    seat++;
                    count++;
                }
                if (count == n) //found n adjacent seats
                {
                    cout << "Row " << r << " Seats ";
                    for (int i=count; i>=1; i--)
                        cout << seat - i;
                    cout << endl;
                    return;
                }
                seat++;
            }
        }
        cout << "Not available" << endl;
}
```

NOTE

1. In part (a), the `mySeats` matrix must be resized before elements can be read into it.

2. In part (c), if the seat number is greater than `mySeatsPerRow-n`, you can no longer find n seats together in that row. This is the reason for the test in the first `while` loop

```
while (seat <= mySeatsPerRow - n)
```

If instead you test whether `seat < mySeatsPerRow`, you have to be careful not to go out of range in the test

```
while (count < n && mySeats[r][seat] == 0)
```

The value of `seat` can go too high if you are not careful. *Somewhere* in the algorithm you have to test for not being too close to the end of a row.

2. (a)
```
template <class itemType>
void Queue <itemType> :: dequeue(itemType & item)
{
    if (isEmpty())
    {
        cerr << "dequeue from empty queue" << endl;
        exit(1);
    }
    item = myBack->next->info;
    queueNode *p = myBack->next;
    myBack->next = p->next;
    if (p == myBack)     //just 1 element in original queue
        myBack == NULL;
    delete p;
    mySize--;
}
```

(b)
```
template <class itemType>
void Queue <itemType> :: enqueue(const itemType & item)
{
    if (isEmpty())
    {
        myBack = new queueNode(item, NULL);
        myBack->next = myBack;
    }
    else        //add item to rear
    {
        myBack->next = new queueNode(item, myBack->next);
        myBack = myBack->next;
    }
    mysize++;
}
```

(c) Both algorithms are $O(1)$ since the number of operations involved is independent of N, the number of elements in the queue.

NOTE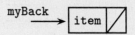

1. In the code for enqueue, after the `if (isEmpty())` test, a single statement

   `myBack = new queueNode(item, myBack);`

   won't work as intended because the right-hand side is evaluated first. The current value of `myBack` is NULL, and the statement will do the following:

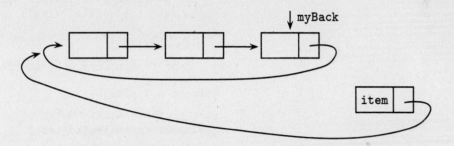

   To maintain the queue as a circular linked list, you need the statement `myBack->next = myBack;`

2. The `else` segment of enqueue can be achieved with the single statement

   `myBack = myBack->next = new queueNode(item, myBack->next);`

   Because the execution occurs from right to left, this statement will do the following:

   - Create a new node with `item` that points to the current `myBack->next`.

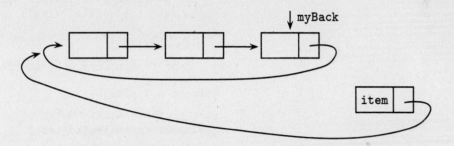

   - Assign the current `myBack->next` to point to the new node.

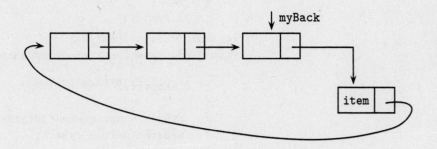

   - Reassign `myBack` to point to the new node.

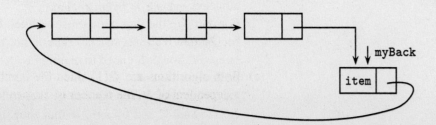

3. (a)
```
void TextEditor::Insert(const apstring & line)
{
    LineNode *newLine =
            new LineNode(line, current, current->nextLine);
    if (current != bottomPtr)
    {
        current->nextLine->prevLine = newLine;
        current->nextLine = newLine;
    }
    else
    {
        current->nextLine = newLine;
        bottomPtr = newLine;
    }
}
```

(b)
```
TextEditor::TextEditor(istream & inFile)
{
    apstring line;
    getline(inFile, line);
    bottomPtr = current = topPtr =
        new LineNode(line, NULL, NULL);
    while (getline(inFile, line))
    {
        Insert(line);
        current = current->nextLine;
    }
    current = topPtr;
}
```

(c)
```
void PrintAlternate(TextEditor & T, ostream & output)
{
    T.Top();
    T.PrintLine(output);
    while (!T.AtEnd())
    {
        T.Next();
        if (!T.AtEnd())
        {
            T.Next();
            T.PrintLine(output);
        }
    }
}
```

NOTE

1. There are two cases for part (a), current either points to the last line or it doesn't. If it does, there's no prevLine field to be adjusted for a node that will follow the new node. The bottomPtr, however, must be adjusted.

2. For part (b), the first node must be filled first because the precondition for Insert requires that current is not null. Don't forget to reassign current! You don't need to reassign bottomPtr: that will automatically be done in Insert.

3. Part (c) is tricky! You have to be sure to have the right combination of calls to Next() and AtEnd() so that your algorithm handles odd and even numbers of lines, as well as one and two lines.

4. (a)
```
void Environment::Inorder(TreeNode *T, apvector<Fish> & v,
    int & index) const
{
    if (T != NULL)
    {
        Inorder(T->left, v, index);
        v[index] = T->data;
        index++;
        Inorder(T->right, v, index);
    }
}
```

(b)
```
void Environment::Insert(TreeNode * & T, const Fish & fish)
{
    TreeNode *p, *q;
    if (T == NULL)
        T = new TreeNode(fish, NULL, NULL);
    else        //find insertion point
    {
        q = T;
        while (q != NULL)
        {
            p = q;
            if (fish.Location() < p->data.Location())
                q = p->left;
            else
                q = p->right;
        }
        if (fish.Location() < p->data.Location())
            p->left = new TreeNode(fish, NULL, NULL);
        else
            p->right = new TreeNode(fish, NULL, NULL);
    }
}
```

Alternatively, here is a recursive solution:

```
void Environment::Insert(TreeNode * & T, const Fish & fish)
{
    if (T == NULL)
        T = new TreeNode(fish, NULL, NULL);
    else
        if (fish.Location() < T->data.Location())
            Insert(T->left, fish);
        else
            Insert(T->right, fish);
}
```

(c) Note: Changes from original are highlighted in bold.

```
void Environment::AddFish(const Position & pos)
{
    if (!IsEmpty(pos))
    {
        cerr << "error, attempt to create fish at nonempty:"
            << pos << endl;
        return;
    }
    myFishCreated++;
    Fish fish(myFishCreated, pos);
    Insert(myWorld, fish);
    myFishCount++;
}
```

(d)
```
apvector<Fish> Environment::AllFish() const
{
    apvector<Fish> fishList(myFishCount);
    int count = 0;
    apstring s = "";
    Inorder(myWorld, fishList, count);
    for (int k=0; k< myFishCount; k++)
    {
        s += fishList[k].Location().ToString() + " ";
    }
    DebugPrint(5, "fish vector = " + s);
    return fishList;
}
```

NOTE

1. No resizing is necessary in part (a)—it's part of the precondition that v has enough slots for all the elements.

2. In part (a), index must be passed as a parameter because it needs to be initialized *outside* of the recursive function. Otherwise, it will be set back to zero for each recursive call—a disaster! Also, it must be passed by reference if it is used in the for loop that follows the Inorder call (you don't want to lose its final value). Note that it is OK to use myFishCount rather than count in the for loop since it represents the number of fish that were in the binary search tree.

3. In part (d), the inorder traversal of the binary search tree returns the elements sorted from smallest to largest, by position, which was required.

Answer Sheet: Practice Exam Four

1. Ⓐ Ⓑ Ⓒ Ⓓ Ⓔ
2. Ⓐ Ⓑ Ⓒ Ⓓ Ⓔ
3. Ⓐ Ⓑ Ⓒ Ⓓ Ⓔ
4. Ⓐ Ⓑ Ⓒ Ⓓ Ⓔ
5. Ⓐ Ⓑ Ⓒ Ⓓ Ⓔ
6. Ⓐ Ⓑ Ⓒ Ⓓ Ⓔ
7. Ⓐ Ⓑ Ⓒ Ⓓ Ⓔ
8. Ⓐ Ⓑ Ⓒ Ⓓ Ⓔ
9. Ⓐ Ⓑ Ⓒ Ⓓ Ⓔ
10. Ⓐ Ⓑ Ⓒ Ⓓ Ⓔ
11. Ⓐ Ⓑ Ⓒ Ⓓ Ⓔ
12. Ⓐ Ⓑ Ⓒ Ⓓ Ⓔ
13. Ⓐ Ⓑ Ⓒ Ⓓ Ⓔ
14. Ⓐ Ⓑ Ⓒ Ⓓ Ⓔ

15. Ⓐ Ⓑ Ⓒ Ⓓ Ⓔ
16. Ⓐ Ⓑ Ⓒ Ⓓ Ⓔ
17. Ⓐ Ⓑ Ⓒ Ⓓ Ⓔ
18. Ⓐ Ⓑ Ⓒ Ⓓ Ⓔ
19. Ⓐ Ⓑ Ⓒ Ⓓ Ⓔ
20. Ⓐ Ⓑ Ⓒ Ⓓ Ⓔ
21. Ⓐ Ⓑ Ⓒ Ⓓ Ⓔ
22. Ⓐ Ⓑ Ⓒ Ⓓ Ⓔ
23. Ⓐ Ⓑ Ⓒ Ⓓ Ⓔ
24. Ⓐ Ⓑ Ⓒ Ⓓ Ⓔ
25. Ⓐ Ⓑ Ⓒ Ⓓ Ⓔ
26. Ⓐ Ⓑ Ⓒ Ⓓ Ⓔ
27. Ⓐ Ⓑ Ⓒ Ⓓ Ⓔ
28. Ⓐ Ⓑ Ⓒ Ⓓ Ⓔ

29. Ⓐ Ⓑ Ⓒ Ⓓ Ⓔ
30. Ⓐ Ⓑ Ⓒ Ⓓ Ⓔ
31. Ⓐ Ⓑ Ⓒ Ⓓ Ⓔ
32. Ⓐ Ⓑ Ⓒ Ⓓ Ⓔ
33. Ⓐ Ⓑ Ⓒ Ⓓ Ⓔ
34. Ⓐ Ⓑ Ⓒ Ⓓ Ⓔ
35. Ⓐ Ⓑ Ⓒ Ⓓ Ⓔ
36. Ⓐ Ⓑ Ⓒ Ⓓ Ⓔ
37. Ⓐ Ⓑ Ⓒ Ⓓ Ⓔ
38. Ⓐ Ⓑ Ⓒ Ⓓ Ⓔ
39. Ⓐ Ⓑ Ⓒ Ⓓ Ⓔ
40. Ⓐ Ⓑ Ⓒ Ⓓ Ⓔ

Practice Exam Four

COMPUTER SCIENCE AB
SECTION I

Time—1 hour and 15 minutes
Number of questions—40
Percent of total grade—50

Directions: Determine the answer to each of the following questions or incomplete statements, using separate pieces of scrap paper for any necessary scratchwork. Then decide which is the best of the choices given and fill in the corresponding oval on the answer sheet. Do not spend too much time on any one problem.

Note: Assume that the standard libraries (e.g., `iostream.h`, `fstream.h`, `math.h`, etc.) and the AP C++ classes are included in any programs that use the code segments provided in individual questions. A Quick Reference to the AP C++ classes is provided.

Questions 1 and 2 refer to the following program:

An animal guessing game program is being designed to enable the computer to learn about animals. A user will think of an animal and, after a sequence of yes/no questions, the computer will try to guess the user's animal. If it guesses wrong, the computer will ask the user to name the animal and provide a distinguishing characteristic. Assuming that the program works correctly, if any subsequent user thinks of that animal, the computer should guess what it is.

A typical exchange between the computer (C) and the user (U) may be:

    C: Does it have antlers?
    U: No.
    C: Does it bark?
    U: Yes.
    C: Is it a dog?
    U: No.
    C: I give up! Tell me your animal.
    U: A seal.
    C: What should I have asked to distinguish a dog from a seal?
    U: Does it have flippers?

GO ON TO THE NEXT PAGE ➤

Any subsequent user who thinks of a seal should have a dialog like the following with the computer:

C: Does it have antlers?

U: No.

C: Does it bark?

U: Yes.

C: Does it have flippers?

U: Yes.

C: Is it a seal?

U: Yes.

C: Yay! I won.

When the user quits, the computer's previous knowledge about animals plus the newly acquired information is saved in a file, to be read in when the program is run again.

1. Assuming that the programmer understands all the requirements of the specification for the animal program, what should he/she do next?
   (A) Design the user interface for the program.
   (B) Create a short file of simple animals to seed the computer's knowledge base.
   (C) Get the file input/output routines to work.
   (D) Write a Help file for the user that precisely describes the rules of the game.
   (E) List the operations and data structures that will be needed for the entire program.

2. The file of information that is read in at the start of the program and saved at the end consists of animal guesses and questions about animals, one per line. For example,

   Does it have antlers?
   Is it a deer?
   Does it bark?
   Does it have flippers?
   Is it a seal?
   Is it a dog?
   Is it a pig?
   . . .

   When the program is run, the line strings are read into a data structure, which is then modified as new guesses and characteristics questions are inserted. Which of the following is the best data structure?
   (A) A linear linked list
   (B) A doubly linked list
   (C) A binary tree
   (D) A hash table
   (E) Two parallel arrays, one with guesses and the other with characteristics questions

GO ON TO THE NEXT PAGE ➤

Level A also

3. What output will be produced by the following program. Ignore spacing.

```
#include <iostream.h>
void WhatsIt(int &p, int q)
{
    cout << p << q << endl;
    p +=q;
    q += p;
    cout << p << q << endl;
}
int main()
{
    int a = 5, b = 2;
    WhatsIt(a, b);
    cout << a << b << endl;
    return 0;
}
```

(A) 5 2
     7 9
     7 2

(B) 5 2
     7 9
     5 2

(C) 5 2
     7 9
     7 9

(D) 5 2
     7 7
     7 2

(E) 5 2
     7 7
     5 2

GO ON TO THE NEXT PAGE ➤

For questions 4 and 5, assume that the following type declaration has been made:

```
struct ListNode
{
    int data;
    ListNode *next;
    ListNode(int D, ListNode *N) : data(D), next(N) {}
};
```

The header of a function InsertZero follows:

```
void InsertZero(ListNode *current)
//precondition: current points to a node in a linear linked
//              list. current is not NULL
//postcondition: the node following the node that current
//              points to contains 0
```

Examples:

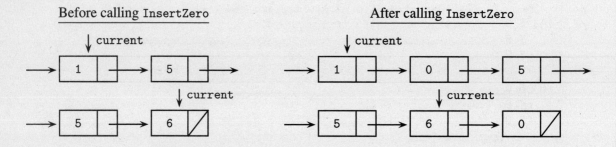

Before calling InsertZero   After calling InsertZero

4. Which of the following could be used as the body of InsertZero such that its postcondition is satisfied?

    I `current->next = new ListNode(0, current->next);`

    II `ListNode *p = new ListNode(0, current->next);`
       `current->next = p;`

    III `ListNode *p = new ListNode;`
        `p->next = current->next;`
        `current->next->data = 0;`
        `current->next = p;`

(A) I only
(B) II only
(C) III only
(D) I and II only
(E) I, II, and III

5. A function PadList, whose code is given below, is to insert a zero between each pair of existing nodes in its parameter, List, a linked list of integers. For example, if the list is initially

PadList(List) should result in

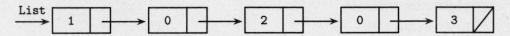

If there are fewer than two nodes in the list, then the list should remain unchanged.

```
void PadList(ListNode *List)
//precondition: List points to a linear linked list of
//              integers representing the sequence
//              a1,a2,...,an, n ≥ 0
//postcondition: List points to the linear linked list
//               representing a1,0,a2,0,...,0,an. The list
//               remains unchanged if 0 ≤ n < 2
{
    if (List != NULL)
    {
        ListNode *temp = List;
        while (temp->next != NULL)
        {
            InsertZero(temp);
            temp = temp->next;
        }
    }
}
```

Assuming that the precondition for PadList is satisfied, for which lists will PadList work correctly?

(A) For all linear linked lists
(B) For no linear linked lists
(C) Only for empty lists
(D) Only for lists that contain exactly one node
(E) Only for lists that contain fewer than two nodes

GO ON TO THE NEXT PAGE ➤

6. A large charity organization maintains a data base of its donors. For each donor, the following information is stored: name, address, phone number, amount and date of most recent contribution, and total contributed so far. Two methods for organizing and modifying the data are considered:

   I A one-dimensional array of donor structs maintained in alphabetical order by name.

   II A hash table of donor structs implemented using an array of linked lists. The hash address for any given donor struct will be determined by a hash function that uniformly distributes donors throughout the table.

Which of the following is false?
(A) Methods I and II have roughly the same memory efficiency.
(B) Insertion of a new donor is more time efficient using method II.
(C) Modifying an existing donor's record is more time efficient using method II.
(D) Printing out a mailing list in alphabetical order is more time efficient using method I.
(E) Printing out a list of donors in decreasing order of total amount contributed has a more efficient run time using method I.

7. Consider the following declarations:

```
struct donor
{
    apstring name;
    double contribution;
    double totalContr;
}
apvector <donor> donorList;
```

Which of the following statements about initializing donorList is true?
(A) A constructor must be added to the donor struct before donorList can be initialized.
(B) The donorList apvector must be resized before being assigned values.
(C) The default constructor for apvector must be modified to allow an apvector of structs.
(D) A constructor must be added to apstring to allow it to be initialized as part of a struct.
(E) Suppose dataFile is open for reading and contains line-by-line data to match the fields given in the struct. Assuming that NUMDONORS is a known integer constant and donorList contains NUMDONORS elements, the following code will successfully initialize donorList:

```
for (int i=0; i<NUMDONORS; i++)
{
    getline(dataFile, donorList[i].name);
    dataFile >> donorList[i].contribution;
    dataFile >> donorList[i].totalContr;
}
```

GO ON TO THE NEXT PAGE ➤

8. Inorder and postorder traversals yield the same output for which of the following trees?

(A)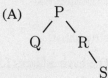

(B)

(C)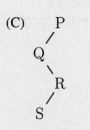

(D)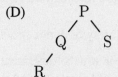

(E)

9. A program includes the following declaration:

```
struct node
{
    int value;
    node *left;
    node *right;
};
```

Function Search returns true if key is found but false otherwise.

```
bool Search(node *ptr, int key)
{
    if (ptr == NULL)
        return false;
    if (key == ptr->value)
        return true;
    else
        return (Search(ptr->left,key) ||
            Search(ptr->right,key));
}
```

Assuming that the programmer is competent, function Search is best characterized as performing a search in

(A) An unordered linear linked list
(B) An unordered doubly linked list
(C) An ordered doubly linked list
(D) An unordered binary tree
(E) A binary search tree

GO ON TO THE NEXT PAGE ➤

10. Worst case run time is $O(n^2)$ for which of the following sorting algorithms?

    I Mergesort

    II Heapsort

    III Quicksort

  (A) I only

  (B) II only

  (C) III only

  (D) I, II, and III

  (E) None

Level A also

11. Consider the following declarations:

```
struct Vertex
{
    int x; //x-coordinate of vertex
    int y; //y-coordinate of vertex
    int z; //z-coordinate of vertex
};

struct Polyhedron    //a 3-dimensional solid with polygon faces
{
    int nFaces;      //number of faces in polyhedron
    apvector <Vertex> vertices;
};

apvector <Polyhedron> figures;   //array of polyhedron figures
```

Which of the following lists the number of faces for each polyhedron figure?

```
(A) for (int i = 0; i < figures.length(); i++)
        cout << figures[i].nFaces << endl;

(B) for (int i = 0; i < vertices.length(); i++)
        cout << figures[i].nFaces << endl;

(C) for (int i = 0; i < nFaces; i++)
        cout << figures[i].nFaces << endl;

(D) for (int i = 0; i < figures.length(); i++)
        cout << vertices[i].nFaces << endl;

(E) for (int i = 0; i < Polyhedron.length(); i++)
        cout << figures[i].nFaces << endl;
```

GO ON TO THE NEXT PAGE ➤

12. Consider the following function max:

```
template<class T>
T max (const T &a, const T &b)
//returns max of a and b
{
    if (a < b)
        return b;
    return a;
}
```

Which of the following is a *false* statement about function max?
(A) The function will not work if the parameters are passed by value instead of by const reference.
(B) The function will work if T is int or char.
(C) The function will work if T is apstring.
(D) If T is a class type, the function will work only if the < (less than) operator has been overloaded for that class.
(E) The return type for the function is a value of type T.

Level A also

13. The boolean expression value > min || !(min < value) can be simplified to
    (A) true
    (B) false
    (C) min != value
    (D) min == value
    (E) value < min && ! (min < value)

14. Which of the following is a valid reason for implementing a stack or queue with a linear linked list rather than an apvector?

    I The stack and queue operations tend to be faster with pointers.

    II If the stack or queue elements are large objects, then copying these objects when resizing the array can significantly slow down the insertion operations.

    III When inserting new elements, the apvector implementation may have expensive space requirements when the array is doubled during resizing.

    (A) I only
    (B) II only
    (C) III only
    (D) II and III only
    (E) I, II, and III

GO ON TO THE NEXT PAGE ➤

15. A program is to be written that simulates and keeps track of the random motion of a point whose position is represented by coordinates (x, y). It starts at $(0, 0)$ at time $= 0$. It is to move randomly a large, but unknown, number of times. A record of its (x, y) positions must be kept so as to be able to re-create any part of its path starting from a given previously recorded (x, y) position. The program is to print the point's (x, y) movements, forward or backward in time, from the given (x, y) position. You may assume that no point is visited more than once. Which of the following is the best data structure for the task?

(A) A one-dimensional array of structs, where each struct holds a pair of coordinates

(B) A two-dimensional array of integers in which the array indexes represent the position visited by the point and each integer cell of the array is a counter that keeps track of the number of moves to that position.

(C) A circular doubly linked list in which each node holds a pair of coordinates

(D) A stack of structs in which each struct holds a pair of coordinates

(E) A queue of structs in which each struct holds a pair of coordinates

16. What is the (a) minimum and (b) maximum number of nodes in a complete binary tree of level n?

(A) (a) 2^n (b) 2^{n+1}

(B) (a) 2^n (b) $2^{n+1} - 1$

(C) (a) 2^{n-1} (b) $2^n - 1$

(D) (a) $2^{n+1} - 1$ (b) $2^{n+1} - 1$

(E) (a) $2^n - 1$ (b) $2^n - 1$

GO ON TO THE NEXT PAGE ➤

17. Assume that doubly linked lists are implemented as follows:

```
struct ListNode
{
    char info;
    ListNode *next, *back;
};
```

Refer to functions Test and Print:

```
void Test(ListNode *p)
{
    p = p->back;
    p->info = 'c';
}
void Print(ListNode *list)
//precondition: list points to a circular doubly linked list
//postcondition: the contents of a single node have been
//               printed
{
    Test(list);
    cout << list->next->back->back->info;
}
```

If function Print is applied to the circular doubly linked list shown, what will be output?

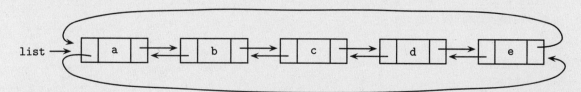

Note that arrows pointing to the right correspond to next and those to the left correspond to back.

(A) a

(B) b

(C) c

(D) d

(E) e

18. The binary tree shown is traversed preorder. During the traversal, each element, when accessed, is pushed onto an initially empty stack s of char. What output is produced when the following code is executed? You may assume the existence of the usual stack operations.

```
char ch;
while (!s.isEmpty())
{
    s.pop(ch);
    cout << ch;
}
```

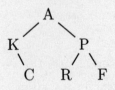

(A) AKCPRF

(B) CKRFPA

(C) FPRACK

(D) APFRKC

(E) FRPCKA

19. Suppose that a queue of integers has been implemented supporting the usual queue operations enqueue, dequeue, and isEmpty. Consider the following code segment (q is a queue):

```
int time, value, limit;
do
{
    time = 0;
    q.dequeue(value);
    do
    {
        value--;
        time++;
    } while (value != 0 && time < limit);
    if (value > 0)
        q.enqueue(value);
} while (!q.isEmpty());
```

Suppose that initially the values in the queue are 1, 10, 8, 5, 12 (1 is at the front of the queue, 12 is at the back). Which of the following is the least value of limit that would ensure that the total number of dequeue operations is 6 or less?

(A) 3

(B) 5

(C) 6

(D) 7

(E) 10

GO ON TO THE NEXT PAGE ➤

For questions 20 and 21 assume that linked lists are implemented as follows:

```
struct node
{
    int info;
    node *next;
    node(int inf, node*N);
};
node :: node(int inf, node *N) : info(inf), next(N) {}
```

Consider a function that finds the insertion point for any given value in a linear linked list that is sorted in increasing order:

```
node *FindInsertionPoint(node *list, int value)
//precondition: list points to ordered linear linked list
//              e1,e2,...,en where e1 ≤ e2 ≤ ... ≤ en
//postcondition: returns a pointer to the node that will precede
//              value if value is inserted in the list.
//              Returns NULL if list is empty or if value < e1
```

Examples:

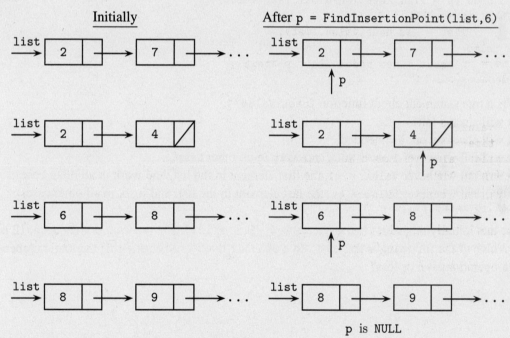

Here is the implementation of function FindInsertionPoint:

```
{
    if (list == NULL || value < list->info)
        return NULL;
    else
    {
        node *q = list;
        while (q->next != NULL && q->next->info < value)
            q = q->next;
        return q;
    }
}
```

GO ON TO THE NEXT PAGE ➤

20. Which of the following assertions is true following the final execution of the while loop?
    (A) `q->next == NULL || q->next->info >= value`
    (B) `q == NULL || q->info < value`
    (C) `q->next == NULL && q->next->info >= value`
    (D) `q->next == NULL || q->info < value`
    (E) Each of the following could be true:

    ```
    q == NULL
    q->next == NULL
    q->info <= value
    ```

21. Function `InsertValue`, defined here, calls the function `FindInsertionPoint` described earlier:

    ```
    void InsertValue(node *& list, int value)
    //precondition: list points to ordered linear linked list
    //              e1,e2,...,en where e1 ≤ e2 ≤ ... ≤ en
    //postcondition: value has been inserted into its correct
    //              position, i.e. list now points to
    //              e1,...,en,e(n+1) where e1 ≤ ... ≤ en ≤ e(n+1)
    {
            node *p = FindInsertionPoint(list, value);
            if (p == NULL)
                list = new node(value,list);
            else
                p->next = new node(value, p->next);
    }
    ```

    Which is a true statement about function `InsertValue`?
    (A) It will always fail.
    (B) It will always work as intended.
    (C) It will fail whenever `list` is `NULL` and work in all other cases.
    (D) It will fail whenever `value` ≤ e1, the first element in the list, and work in all other cases.
    (E) It will fail whenever `value` > en, the last element in the list, and work in all other cases.

GO ON TO THE NEXT PAGE ➤

Level A also

Questions 22–24 refer to the Sentence class below. Note: A *word* is a string of consecutive nonblank (and nonwhitespace) characters. For example, the sentence

"Hello there!" she said.

consists of the four words

```
      "Hello     there!"     she     said.
class Sentence
{
    public:
        Sentence();          //default constructor
        Sentence(istream &inFile);      //constructor. Reads
                                        //sentence from inFile
        Sentence(const Sentence &rhs);  //copy constructor
        int NumWords() const;   //returns number of words in sentence
        Sentence & RemoveBlanks();     //postcondition: mySentence
                        //contains no blanks. myNumWords=1
        Sentence & StripPunctuation();  //postcondition: mySentence
                //contains no punctuation. myNumWords unchanged
        Sentence & LowerCase();  //postcondition: all letters in
                //mySentence lowercase. myNumWords unchanged
        Sentence & ReverseWords();  //postcondition: words in
            //mySentence in reverse order. myNumWords unchanged
            //e.g. if mySentence is "Dave Gilbert is smart." it
            //becomes "smart. is Gilbert Dave"
        bool Equal(const Sentence &rhs) const;  //returns true
                        //if sentence == rhs, false otherwise
        void Print(ostream &os) const;  //prints sentence
    private:
        apstring mySentence;
        int myNumWords;
};
```

Level A also

22. Consider the implementation of the second Sentence constructor:

```
Sentence :: Sentence(istream &inFile)
//precondition: inFile open for reading. Sentence contained
//              in a single line of inFile, terminated by
//              newline character '\n' directly following
//              last word. Words of sentence separated by a
//              single space
{
    const char BLANK = ' ';
    getline(inFile, mySentence);
    <code to initialize myNumWords>
}
```

Which of the following is a correct replacement for *<code to initialize myNumWords>*?

```
  I apstring temp(mySentence);
    myNumWords = 1;
    int k = temp.find(BLANK);
    while (k != npos)         //note: npos has value -1
    {
        myNumWords++;
        k = temp.find(BLANK);
    }
```

```
 II apstring temp(mySentence);
    myNumWords = 1;
    int k = temp.find(BLANK);
    while (k != npos)
    {
        myNumWords++;
        temp = temp.substr(k+1, temp.length()-(k+1));
        k = temp.find(BLANK);
    }
```

```
III myNumWords = 1;
    for (int i=0; i<mySentence.length(); i++)
        if (mySentence[i] == BLANK)
            myNumWords++;
```

(A) I only
(B) II only
(C) III only
(D) I and III only
(E) II and III only

GO ON TO THE NEXT PAGE ➤

23. The implementation of the `Equal` member function follows:

```
bool Sentence :: Equal(const Sentence &rhs) const
//returns true if sentence == rhs, false otherwise
{
        return <code>
}
```

Which is a correct replacement for `<code>`?

(A) `mySentence == rhs.mySentence;`

(B) `*this == rhs.mySentence;`

(C) `myNumWords == rhs.myNumWords;`

(D) `lhs.mySentence == rhs.mySentence;`

(E) `*this == rhs.*this;`

Level A also

24. A palindrome is a sentence, word, or phrase that reads the same from left to right and right to left. Some examples:

> noon
>
> Able was I ere I saw Elba.
>
> Rise to vote, sir!

Notice that capital letters, blanks, and punctuation are ignored in determining whether a string is a palindrome. A client function `isPalindrome` tests whether its `Sentence` parameter is a palindrome:

```
bool isPalindrome(const Sentence &s)
//returns true if s is a palindrome, false otherwise
{
    Sentence temp(s);
    temp = temp.LowerCase();
    temp = temp.StripPunctuation();
    temp = temp.RemoveBlanks();
    Sentence rev = temp.ReverseWords();
    return temp.Equal(rev);
}
```

Which of the following is a true statement?

(A) `isPalindrome` will return the correct boolean value for all parameters `s`.

(B) `isPalindrome` will return the correct boolean value for no parameters `s`.

(C) `isPalindrome` will return `true` for all parameters `s`.

(D) `isPalindrome` will return `false` for all parameters `s`.

(E) If the statements `temp = temp.LowerCase();` and `Sentence rev = temp.ReverseWords();` are interchanged, `isPalindrome` will work as intended for all parameters `s`.

GO ON TO THE NEXT PAGE ➤

Questions 25–27 are based on the following procedure, which copies items from an array A containing N distinct numbers into a binary search tree T and then prints the elements.

Procedure:

Step 1: Initialize T to be empty.

Step 2: Insert A[0], A[1],..., A[N-1] into T using a standard algorithm for insertion of item A[i] into T.

Step 3: Print the elements stored in T, using an inorder traversal.

Assume that the insert operation used in Step 2 does no balancing of T.

25. Which of the following best characterizes the output produced in Step 3 of the above procedure?
    (A) The items are printed in the original order in which they appear in array A.
    (B) The items are printed in sorted order, from smallest to largest.
    (C) The items are printed in sorted order, from largest to smallest.
    (D) The items are printed in the reverse of the order in which they appear in array A.
    (E) The items are printed in random order.

26. Which best describes the best case running time of the procedure?
    (A) $O(1)$
    (B) $O(N)$
    (C) $O(\log N)$
    (D) $O(N \log N)$
    (E) $O(N^2)$

27. The procedure is most likely to exhibit its best case running time when the numbers are stored in array A in which of the following ways?

    I   Ascending order

    II Descending order

    III Alternating positive and negative numbers

    (A) I only
    (B) II only
    (C) III only
    (D) I and II only
    (E) Best case can *never* be achieved with any of choices I, II, or III

GO ON TO THE NEXT PAGE ➤

28. Refer to function Mystery below. You may assume that function Swap correctly interchanges the values of its two integer parameters.

```
void Mystery(apvector<int> & v, int n)
{
    int i, m;
    if (n == 1)
        return;
    else
    {
        for (m=0, i=1; i<n; i++)
            if (v[m] < v[i])
                m = i;
        Swap(v[n-1], v[m]);
        Mystery(v, n-1);
    }
}
```

What does function Mystery do?

(A) Sequentially searches v[0]...v[n-1] for v[m], the largest element in the array
(B) Sorts v[0]...v[n-1] in descending order
(C) Sorts v[0]...v[n-1] in ascending order
(D) Merges v[0]...v[m] with v[m+1]...v[n-1]
(E) Partitions array v such that v[0]...v[m-1] are less than v[m] and v[m+1]...v[n-1] are greater than or equal to v[m]

29. Which of the following syntactically correct boolean expressions will never cause a run-time error?

```
(A) a[i] < max        //a of type apvector<int>
(B) p->info < max     //p a pointer of type SomeNodeType *
(C) x == y            //x, y of type double
(D) i/j < max         //i, j of type int
(E) k % m == 0        //k, m of type int
```

30. Resizing an apvector involves copying all elements into a new, larger vector. Consider the following pseudo-code algorithm for reading n integers into an apvector from a file:

- Start with an apvector called list of size 1
- Each time an integer is read in
    if (count of elements so far == list.length())
        resize list to 2 * count

This algorithm is

(A) $O(n)$
(B) $O(n^2)$
(C) $O(\log n)$
(D) $O(n \log n)$
(E) $O(2^n)$

31. Function `BinSearch`, whose code is given here, implements a binary search using recursion.

```
int BinSearch(const apvector<int> & a, int first, int last,
        int key)
//precondition: a[first]...a[last] sorted in ascending order
//              key is target to be searched for
//postcondition: returns position of key in a. If key not in
//               a, returns -1
{
        if (first > last)
            return -1;
        else
        {
            int mid = (first+last)/2;
            if (a[mid] == key)
                return mid;
            else if (key < a[mid])
                return BinSearch(a, first, mid - 1, key);
            else
                return BinSearch(a, mid+1, last, key);
        }
}
```

What is the (I) run-time efficiency and (II) space efficiency of this algorithm? (Ignore storage required for the original array.)

(A) I $O(\log n)$ II $O(n)$
(B) I $O(2^n)$ II $O(n)$
(C) I $O(2^n)$ II $O(\log n)$
(D) I $O(\log n)$ II $O(\log n)$
(E) I $O(n \log n)$ II $O(n)$

Level A also

32. Consider the following `while` loop:

```
i = 1;
while (i <= max && a[i] != 0)
    i++;
```

Which of the following assertions is true every time the loop is exited?

(A) $i \leq max$
(B) $a[j] = 0$ for all $j < i$
(C) $a[j] \neq 0$ for all $j \geq i$
(D) $a[j] \neq 0$ for all j such that $0 \leq j < i$
(E) $a[j] \neq 0$ for all j such that $0 \leq j \leq i$

Level A also

33. Which is true of the following boolean expression, given that x is a variable of type double?

$$3.0 == x * (3.0/x)$$

(A) It will always evaluate to true.
(B) It will always evaluate to false.
(C) It will evaluate to false only when x is zero.
(D) It will evaluate to false only when x is very large or very close to zero.
(E) It may evaluate to false for some values of x.

GO ON TO THE NEXT PAGE ➤

34. Assume that linked lists are implemented as follows:

```
struct node
{
    int data;
    node *next;
};
```

Consider the function ListStuff below:

```
void ListStuff(node * & list)
//precondition: list points to a linear linked list of
//              integers that is sorted in increasing order
{
    node *temp;
    if (list != NULL)
        if (list->next != NULL)
            if (list->data == list->next->data)
            {
                temp = list;
                list = list->next;
                delete (temp);
                ListStuff(list);
            }
            else
                ListStuff(list->next);
}
```

Suppose ListStuff(head) is invoked for the following linked list:

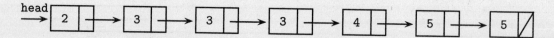

What will the list contain after execution?

(A) The list will be empty.

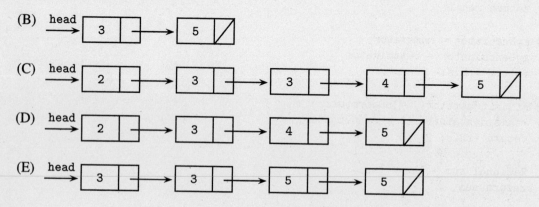

(B) head

(C) head

(D) head

(E) head

35. Here is the declaration for a rational number class:

```
class Rational
{
    public:
        //constructors
        Rational();
        Rational(int numerator, int denominator);
        Rational(const Rational & r);
        //accessors
        int numerator() const;
        int denominator() const;
        //assignment
        const Rational & operator=(const Rational & rhs);
    private:
        //data members
        int myNumerator, myDenominator;
        //helper function
        void reduce();
};
```

Free (nonmember) functions are implemented to perform arithmetic operations on rational numbers. For example, here is the implementation of the operator+() function:

```
Rational operator+(const Rational & lhs, const Rational & rhs)
{
    int numerator = lhs.numerator()*rhs.denominator() +
                    rhs.numerator()*lhs.denominator();
    int denominator = lhs.denominator()*rhs.denominator();
        <code>
}
```

Which of the following replacements for <code> correctly completes the function?

(A) `return numerator/denominator;`

(B) `Rational result(numerator, denominator);`
    `return result;`

(C) `myNumerator = numerator;`
    `myDenominator = denominator;`
    `return *this;`

(D) `*this.numerator() = numerator;`
    `*this.denominator() = denominator;`
    `return *this;`

(E) `Rational sum = lhs + rhs;`
    `return sum;`

GO ON TO THE NEXT PAGE ➤

Questions 36–40 involve reasoning about the code from the Marine Biology Case Study. A copy of the code is provided as part of this exam.

36. Consider a decision to change the implementation of the fishList array to a linear linked list of Fish instead of an apvector of Fish. Which of the following groups of classes will require modification?

    I Environment
   II Fish, Neighborhood
  III Display, Simulation

  (A) I only
  (B) II only
  (C) III only
  (D) I and III only
  (E) I, II, and III

Level A also

Questions 37 and 38 refer to the following change in the fishsim program. When it is the turn of fish F1 to move, that fish will definitely move to one of the four slots adjacent to it—north, south, east, or west. If the randomly selected position is occupied by another fish, F2, the moving fish will "eat" fish F2. In other words, F1 will replace F2 in that slot. Thus, F2 will disappear, and the collection of fish will contain one fewer element.

37. Which member function will *not* need to be modified to implement this change?
  (A) The Add function in the Neighborhood class
  (B) The EmptyNeighbors function in the Fish class
  (C) The AddIfEmpty function in the Fish class
  (D) The Update function in the Environment class
  (E) The Show function in the Display class

38. Refer to the change described earlier. Which is a *false* statement?
  (A) No changes need to be made in the Position class.
  (B) No changes need to be made in the Simulation class.
  (C) The sixth line of the Move function in the Fish class should be changed to
        `myPos = nbrs.Select(randomVals.RandInt(4));`
  (D) In the Update function of the Environment class, the test
        `if (!oldLoc == newLoc)`
    can be omitted.
  (E) In the Update function of the Environment class, the statement
        `myWorld[newLoc.Row()][newLoc.Col()] = fish;`
    must be changed.

GO ON TO THE NEXT PAGE ➤

39. Suppose the `fishsim` program is run with N fish and M steps in the simulation. The run-time efficiency will be

(A) $O(N + M)$

(B) $O(NM)$

(C) $O(N)$

(D) $O(M)$

(E) $O(N^M)$

Level A also

40. Consider the following two alternatives for moving a fish:

   I In the current implementation, the responsibility for moving a fish lies in the Fish class.

   II An alternative implementation is to create a new member function `MoveFish` in the `Environment` class that takes a fish as a parameter.

Which of the following is *false*?

(A) If implementation II were used, it would no longer be necessary for a fish to keep track of its own position.

(B) If implementation II were used, the `Update` function in the `Environment` class would no longer be necessary.

(C) If implementation II were used, the `Neighborhood` class would not need to be modified.

(D) Modifying the program to change the state of a fish each time it moves would be simpler using implementation II.

(E) If implementation II were used, the `EmptyNeighbors` and `AddIfEmpty` member functions in the `Fish` class would no longer be needed in this class.

STOP

COMPUTER SCIENCE AB
SECTION II

Time—1 hour and 45 minutes
Number of questions—4
Percent of total grade—50

Directions: SHOW ALL YOUR WORK. REMEMBER THAT PROGRAM SEGMENTS ARE TO BE WRITTEN IN C++.

Note: Assume that the standard libraries (`iostream.h`, `fstream.h`, `math.h`, etc.) and the AP C++ classes are included in any program that uses a program segment you write. If other classes are to be included, that information will be specified in individual questions. A Quick Reference to the AP C++ classes is included in the case study insert.

---

1. This question involves the implementation of a `Set` data structure. In preparation, consider the definition of a sorted collection.

   A *sorted collection* is a list of elements of the same type maintained in increasing sorted order, together with a record of the number of elements in the list. When elements are inserted into or deleted from the list, the ordering property must be preserved, and the number of elements in the list must be updated.

   Here is the declaration for class `SortedCollection`:

```
template <class T>
class SortedCollection
{
    public:
        //constructors
        SortedCollection();
        SortedCollection(const SortedCollection<T> & sc);
        //member functions
        int ListLength() const;      //current list length
        int index_of(const T & item) const; //returns
                //position of first occurrence of item,
                //-1 if not in list
        void Insert(const T & item);    //insert item into list
        SortedCollection<T>& operator=(const SortedCollection<T> & sc);
                        //overload assignment
        T DeleteFirst();      //deletes first element of
                            // nonempty collection
    private:
    //some data structure to implement a list and its length
};
```

GO ON TO THE NEXT PAGE ➤

A *set* is a collection of elements of the same type in no particular order. The elements in a set are unique—there are no duplicates. One way of implementing a set is with a sorted collection. This will provide an efficient way to access the elements when implementing the set operations. This implementation will be hidden from clients of the Set class, which cannot assume that the elements are in sorted order.

The declaration for class Set follows:

```
const int MAXSETSIZE = 200;
template <class T>
class Set
{
    public:
        Set();  //default constructor, initializes set to empty
        Set(const Set<T> & s);   //copy constructor
        bool isEmpty() const;     //true if set empty, else false
        int SetSize() const;      //returns number of elements in set
        bool includes(const T & item);  //true if item in set,
                                        // otherwise false
        void Add(const T & item);       //add item to set
        void Remove(const T & item);     //remove item from set.
                          //does nothing if item not in set
        Set<T> operator+(const Set<T> &s); //return union of
                                           // this set and s
        Set<T> operator*(const Set<T> &s); //return intersection
                                           // of this set and s
        Set<T> & operator=(const Set<T> &s);  //assignment
    private:
        SortedCollection<T> myElements;
};
```

(a) Write the implementation of the isEmpty member function for the Set class as started below:

```
template <class T>
bool Set<T>::isEmpty() const
//postcondition: returns true if set is empty;
//                otherwise returns false
```

(b) Write the implementation of the includes member function for the Set class as started below:

```
template <class T>
bool Set<T>::includes(const T & item) const
//precondition: the current Set object is initialized
//postcondition: returns true if item is in Set;
//                otherwise returns false
```

GO ON TO THE NEXT PAGE ➤

(c) Write the implementation of the `operator*` member function for the `Set` class as started below. This function returns a set that is the intersection of the current `Set` object and the `Set` parameter. The intersection of two sets `s1` and `s2` is a set that contains the elements that are in both `s1` and `s2`. For example, if `s1` is the set {6, 1, 9} and `s2` is {1, 5, 9, 4}, the intersection will be {1, 9}. Thus, the result of `Set s3 = s1 * s2` will be to store 1 and 9 in `s3`.

In writing `operator*`, you may assume that the member functions of the `SortedCollection` and `Set` classes work as specified.

Complete function `operator*` below:

```
template <class T>
Set<T> Set<T>::operator*(const Set<T> & s)
//precondition: current Set object and s are initialized
//postcondition: returns the intersection of the two sets.
//               Both s and the current set remain unchanged
```

2. Consider designing a data structure to represent the schedule of a teacher in the Math Department of a large high school. The information to be stored for each teacher is as follows:

(i) The teacher's name.

(ii) A linked list of math courses. For each course, the course name and the number of the period it is taught are stored. The linked list is ordered by class period.

The following declarations satisfy these requirements. The first declaration is for a node in the linked list of courses, and the second is for an individual teacher.

```
struct Course
{
    apstring courseName;
    int period;      //periods 1, 2, ..., 9
    Course *next;
    //constructor:
    Course(const apstring & cN, int P, Course *nxt)
        : courseName(cN), period(P), next(nxt) {}
};

struct Teacher
{
    apstring tchrName;  //name of teacher
    Course *courseList;
    Teacher();           //default constructor
    Teacher(const apstring & tName);    //constructor
};
```

GO ON TO THE NEXT PAGE ➤

For example, shown below are two variables of type Teacher. Notice that each list is ordered by class period.

Teacher1

    tchrName: K Seifert

Teacher2

    tchrName: L Thompson

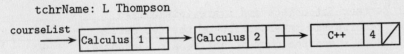

(a) Write function InsertCourse, as started below. This function adds a course with the given name and period to the given teacher's course list. For example, after the call,

        InsertCourse("Trig", 3, Teacher2);

variable Teacher2 would be as shown below:

Teacher2

    tchrName: L Thompson

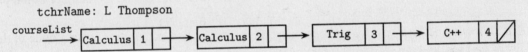

Complete function InsertCourse:

```
void InsertCourse(const apstring & cName, int per, Teacher someTeacher)
//precondition: someTeacher contains zero or more courses sorted by period.
//              per does not appear in someTeacher's list,
//              and per is an integer from 1 through 9
//postcondition: an additional course with the given name and
//               period per has been added to someTeacher, in the
//               correct sorted position by period
```

(b) Write function TeachesThisPeriod as started below. This function returns true if someTeacher has a class in the specified period, false otherwise. For example, the call

        TeachesThisPeriod(Teacher1, 7);

returns false since Teacher1 does not have a class in period 7, while

        TeachesThisPeriod(Teacher2, 1);

returns true since Teacher2 has a class during period 1.

    Complete function TeachesThisPeriod below:

```
bool TeachesThisPeriod(const Teacher & someTeacher, int per)
//precondition: per is an integer from 1 through 9
//postcondition: returns true if someTeacher has a class during
//               the specified period, false otherwise
```

GO ON TO THE NEXT PAGE ➤

(c) Write function `PrintHeaviestPeriods` as started below. This function has an array of `Teacher` as a parameter. It determines which of the periods from 1 through 9 has the heaviest usage. If there is a tie, multiple periods are printed, one period per line.

For example, if `teachers` is the array shown below, then `PrintHeaviestPeriods(teachers)` would print

    2
    3

since these periods have the most classes taught during them, namely three classes each.

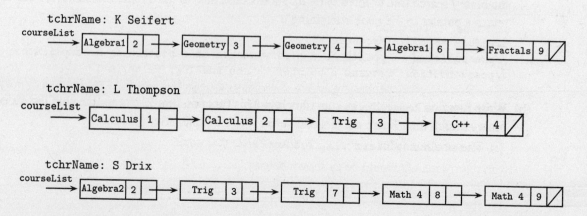

In writing `PrintHeaviestPeriods` you may call function `TeachesThisPeriod` specified in part (b). Assume `TeachesThisPeriod` works as specified, regardless of what you wrote in part (b).

Complete function `PrintHeaviestPeriods` below:

```
void PrintHeaviestPeriods(const apvector<Teacher> & teacherList)
//precondition: teacherList contains teacherList.length() teachers
//postcondition: prints the period number or numbers (1 - 9) that
//               have the heaviest usage, one per line
```

3. Consider a binary search tree of integers in which no integer appears more than once. For example,

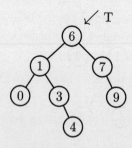

GO ON TO THE NEXT PAGE ➤

Assume that the tree is implemented using the following declaration:

```
struct TreeNode
{
    int info;
    TreeNode *left;
    TreeNode *right;
};
```

(a) Write function `FindMin` as started below. This function returns a pointer to the smallest value in the binary search tree pointed to by its parameter. Thus, in the tree pictured above, `FindMin` would return a pointer to the node containing 0.

```
TreeNode *FindMin(TreeNode *T)
//precondition: T points to a binary search tree containing no duplicates
//postcondition: returns a pointer to the smallest value in T
```

(b) Write function `RemoveMin` as started below. This function should remove the smallest value from a binary search tree. There are just two cases:

(i) The smallest value is a leaf. Then just delete that node.

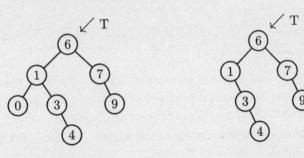

Before deletion   After deletion

(ii) The smallest value has a right subtree only. Adjust a pointer of the smallest value's parent to bypass the to-be-deleted node.

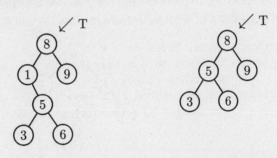

Before deletion   After deletion

In writing `RemoveMin`, you may call function `FindMin` as specified in part (a). Assume that `FindMin` works as specified, regardless of what you wrote in part (a).

GO ON TO THE NEXT PAGE ➤

Complete function `RemoveMin` below:

```
void RemoveMin(TreeNode * & T)
//precondition: T points to a binary search tree with no
//              duplicate values
//postcondition: smallest value removed from tree
```

(c) Consider the problem of deleting any given value from a binary search tree. Here is an algorithm that achieves this while maintaining the ordering property of the binary search tree.

   If the value is in the tree:

   • If the node to be deleted is a leaf, delete it.

   • If the node to be deleted has just one child, adjust the pointer of that node's parent to bypass the to-be-deleted node.

   • If the node to be deleted has two children (call it node k), replace its `info` field with the smallest value in its right subtree (call it node m) and delete node m instead.

   For example, delete the value 1 from the tree shown.

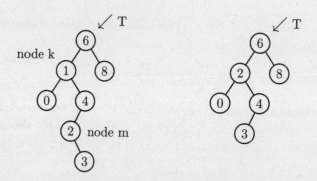

Before deletion   After deletion

Write function `Remove` as started below. In writing `Remove` you may call functions `FindMin` and `RemoveMin` as specified in parts (a) and (b). Assume that functions `FindMin` and `RemoveMin` work as specified regardless of what you wrote in parts (a) and (b).

```
void Remove(int value, TreeNode * & T)
//precondition: T points to a binary search tree with no
//              duplicate values
//postcondition: value removed from tree T. Tree remains
//              unchanged if value is not in the tree.
```

4. This question involves reasoning about the code from the Marine Biology Case Study. A copy of the code is provided as part of this exam.

In the existing Marine Biology Case Study, the `Neighborhood` class is implemented with an `apvector` of `Position` and a count of positions in the neighborhood. Consider modifying the `Neighborhood` class so that the list of positions is implemented as a linear linked list. Assume the following declaration is added to the implementation file `nbrhood.cpp` to restrict the length of the list to a maximum of four elements.

GO ON TO THE NEXT PAGE ➤

```
const int MAXLISTLENGTH = 4;
```

The following declarations in the private part of the Neighborhood class reflect the change of data structure.

```
class Neighborhood
{
    public:
        ...
    private:
        struct ListNode
        {
            Position posInfo;
            ListNode *next;
            ListNode(Position P, ListNode *N)    //constructor
                : posInfo(P), next(N) {}
        };
        ListNode *myList;
        int myCount;
};
```

(a) Write a revised version of the Neighborhood constructor as started below. The constructor should have as a postcondition that Size() == 0.

```
Neighborhood::Neighborhood()
```

(b) Write a revised version of the Neighborhood member function Select as started below. The count parameter indicates which position in the neighborhood list should be returned. If count is 0, Select should return the first element. In general, if count is k, Select should return the $(k + 1)$th position in the list, where $0 \le k <$ MAXLISTLENGTH.
     Complete function Select.

```
Position Neighborhood::Select(int count) const
//precondition: 0 ≤ count < Size()
//postcondition: returns the (count+1)th Position in Neighborhood
```

(c) Write a revised version of the Neighborhood member function ToString() as started below.

```
apstring Neighborhood::ToString() const
//postcondition: returns a string version of Positions in Neighborhood
```

(d) Write a revised version of the Neighborhood member function Add as started below. Function Add should add position pos to the neighborhood. Since there is no preferred ordering of positions in the neighborhood, pos should be added to the front of the linked list—this is the most efficient algorithm.

```
void Neighborhood::Add(const Position & pos)
//precondition: there is room in the neighborhood
//postcondition: pos added to Neighborhood at front of list
```

STOP

Answer Key

Section I

1. **E**	15. **C**	29. **C**
2. **C**	16. **B**	30. **A**
3. **A**	17. **C**	31. **D**
4. **D**	18. **E**	32. **D**
5. **E**	19. **E**	33. **E**
6. **E**	20. **A**	34. **D**
7. **B**	21. **B**	35. **B**
8. **B**	22. **E**	36. **D**
9. **D**	23. **A**	37. **E**
10. **C**	24. **C**	38. **E**
11. **A**	25. **B**	39. **B**
12. **A**	26. **D**	40. **D**
13. **A**	27. **C**	
14. **D**	28. **C**	

Answers Explained

Section I

1. **(E)** The programmer must have an overall plan before writing any code. This includes a top-down design listing all the main operations, plus decisions about the data structures involved in the program.

2. **(C)** Any program that creates a path based on a sequence of two-way decisions is a good candidate for using a binary tree.

3. **(A)** p is passed by reference and will, therefore, share memory with its actual parameter a. Parameter q is passed by value, so a copy of b will be placed in q. Just before exiting function Whatsit, the memory slots can be pictured like this:

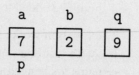

When the function is exited, q is erased, and the line

```
cout << a << b << endl;
```

will produce 7   2.

4. **(D)** Segments I and II both correctly use the constructor for the `ListNode` struct. Segment III is wrong, not because it doesn't use the constructor, but because it places zero in the wrong node. For example,

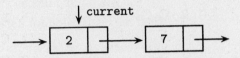

will become

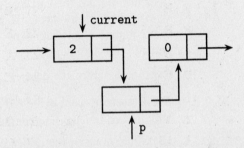

If the last two statements of Segment III are interchanged, the algorithm, though awkward, will be correct.

5. **(E)** The problem with the code is in the last line; change it to

```
temp = temp->next->next;
```

and the function will work as intended for all cases. As it is, `temp` doesn't advance far enough, and you have an infinite `while` loop that produces an endless stream of zeros:

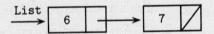

becomes

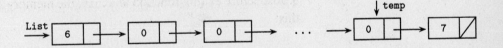

The function works for an empty list because nothing is done. It works for a list with just one node because the `while` test fails immediately and the list remains unchanged.

6. **(E)** To print a list of donors in order of total contributions requires the same three steps for each method:

  (1) insert all donor structs into a temporary array;
  (2) sort the array with respect to total contributions;
  (3) print the elements.

Note that simply sorting the existing array in method I is not a good idea; the array will then need to be "sorted back" into alphabetical order. Choices B and C are true: insertion and searching in a good hash table are both $O(1)$, whereas in a sorted array searching for a given donor or insertion point is $O(\log n)$ (assuming that an efficient method like binary search is used).

7. **(B)** If the declaration for `donorList` had been

```
apvector<donor> donorList(NUMDONORS);
```

then no resizing would be necessary. As given, `donorList` is an empty array that must be resized before receiving values. Note that the reason choice E fails is that `getline` and `>>` are used for the same stream. The operator `>>` does not discard the carriage return at the end of a line, so the next `getline` will read an empty string. Remember that `getline` reads all characters until it encounters a newline, `'\n'`. Then it discards `'\n'`. To fix the problem, one can add the statement

```
getline(dataFile, dummy);
```

as the last statement in the `for` loop. This will read the empty string into `dummy` and discard the newline character.

8. **(B)** Since none of the nodes has a right subtree, the recursive left-root-right of the inorder traversal becomes left-root. Similarly, the left-right-root of a postorder traversal becomes left-root. In either case, the traversal yields S, R, Q, then P.

9. **(D)** The algorithm is a recursive tree search. The left and right subtrees are both searched for `key`, which implies that the tree is not ordered. If the tree were ordered (i.e., a binary search tree), the code following the `else` would be

```
if (key < ptr->value)
    return Search(ptr->left);
else
    return Search(ptr->right);
```

10. **(C)** Mergesort recursively divides the array into two pieces of roughly the same size until there are n arrays of length 1. This is $O(\log n)$. Then adjacent sorted arrays are recursively merged to form a single sorted array. Thus, the algorithm is $O(n \log n)$, irrespective of the initial ordering of array elements. Heapsort creates a balanced binary tree irrespective of the ordering of the array elements, which leads to an $O(n \log n)$ algorithm in best and worst cases. Quicksort recursively partitions the array into two pieces such that elements in the left piece are less than or equal to a pivot element, whereas those in the right piece are greater than or equal to the pivot. In the worst case, the pivot element repeatedly splits the array into pieces of length 1 and $n - 1$, respectively. In this case, there will be n splits, each using an $O(n)$ partitioning algorithm. Thus, the final run time becomes $O(n^2)$. An example where this could happen is a sorted array in which one of the end elements is repeatedly chosen as the pivot.

11. **(A)** `figures[i]` is a Polyhedron. The number of faces for `figures[i]` is `figures[i].nFaces`. This eliminates choice D. The code should loop over all the elements of the `figures` array (i.e., the loop variable `i` should start at 0 and end at `figures.length()-1`). This eliminates choices B, C, and E, which are all syntactically invalid.

12. **(A)** Passing the parameters by value causes copies to be made, which is often inefficient. But the function will still work.

13. **(A)** The given expression is equivalent to `min < value || !(min < value)` which is always true: one of `a` or `!a` is always true.

14. **(D)** Reason I: The main advantage of the array-based implementation is speed. The operations are fast and don't have the overhead of creating and destroying nodes that the linear linked list uses. Thus, reason I is not a valid reason for using a linear linked list. Reason II: Note that doubling the array and copying elements for N insertions is in the *worst* case $O(\log_2 N)$ for a given insertion. Thus, the time cost of recopying elements is small if `itemType` is simple. It becomes significant, however, if `itemType` is large. Thus, reason II is valid. Reason III is valid. A disadvantage of the vector implementation is that, at the time the array is doubled, memory is needed to store both the old and new (double-sized) array. This can be very space-expensive if `itemType` is a large object.

    In general, the array implementation is preferable for small items. The linear linked list implementation is preferable for large items if space is scarce or items are so large that the time cost of array doubling becomes significant.

15. **(C)** A circular doubly linked list works well for this program because of the ability to traverse forward and backward from any given node. Note that a stack provides easy backtracking from the current top element but does not allow for convenient access to any other specified position or for easy forward traversal. Similarly, a queue allows easy forward traversal from the front position but is awkward for backtracking and random access of elements in the "middle" of the queue. Choice A seems reasonable for both forward and backward traversal. The number of moves, however, is large and unknown, which makes a dynamic data structure preferable. Choice B doesn't satisfy the requirements of the program at all. It also has the problem of representing real-number coordinates (x, y) with the indexes of the array; the indexes must be integers.

16. **(B)** A complete binary tree is either full (i.e., every leaf is on the same level and every nonleaf node has two children) or full to the next to last level, with leaves in the highest level as far left as possible. Test the numbers with a tree of level 2, say.

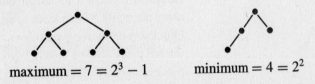

$$\text{maximum} = 7 = 2^3 - 1 \qquad \text{minimum} = 4 = 2^2$$

17. **(C)** This question is about passing a pointer parameter by value. When function `Test` is exited, its pointer parameter `list` has the same address value as it had before execution, namely it points to a. Notice, however, that passing a pointer by value does not protect the *contents* of the linked list. As a result of function `Test`, this list contains

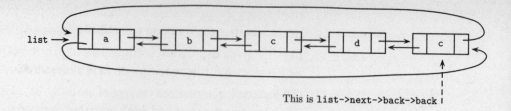

This is `list->next->back->back`

18. **(E)** A preorder traversal pushes the elements onto s in the following order: A, K, C, P, R, F.

    The elements will be popped and printed in reverse order, namely F, R, P, C, K, A.

19. **(E)** Note that `dequeue` occurs until q is empty. You want to `dequeue` a minimum number of times, which means that you want to avoid `enqueue`. This means that you want the stopping condition for the inner `do...while` loop to be `value == 0`, not `time == limit` (since `value > 0` will lead to more `enqueue` operations). Thus, `limit` should be made as large as possible.

20. **(A)** Here is a counterexample for each of choices B through E. Choice B: The algorithm is constructed so that q is never `NULL`. Also `q->info` could *equal* `value`, which makes the entire assertion false. Choice C: `q->next` is not necessarily `NULL` (see the first example following the postcondition of `FindInsertionPoint`). Choice D: `q->next` is not necessarily `NULL`, and `q->info` could equal `value`. Choice E is invalid since q can never equal `NULL`.

21. **(B)** If the line

    ```
    node *p = FindInsertionPoint(list, value);
    ```

    returns `NULL`, you have two possible cases:

    (1) `list` was `NULL`, and you need to insert `value` into an originally empty list. The statement

    ```
    list = new node(value, list);
    ```

    creates the node

    since `list` is `NULL`, and then reassigns `list` to point to it, as required:

    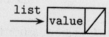

    (2) `value` was less than the first element in the list, and you need to insert `value` as the first node of this list. For example, to insert 6 into

    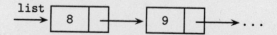

the statement

```
list = new node(value, list);
```

evaluates the right-hand side first, to create this setup:

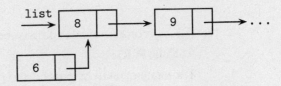

Then list is reassigned, leading to the correct postcondition:

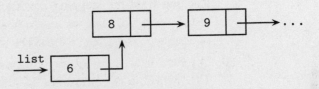

If

```
node *p = FindInsertionPoint(list, value);
```

does not return NULL, the new value must be inserted either in the middle or at the end of the list. The statement

```
p->next = new node(value, p->next);
```

takes care of both cases. As an example of inserting in the middle, consider inserting 6 in

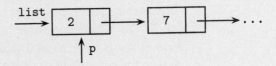

The algorithm is

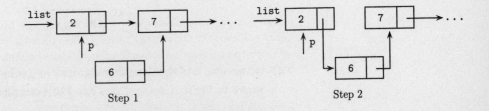

Step 1   Step 2

As an example of inserting at the end, consider inserting 6 in

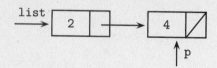

The algorithm is

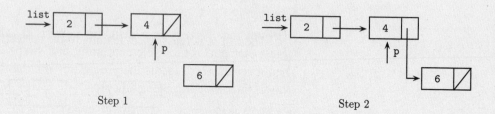

Step 1   Step 2

22. (**E**) For every occurrence of BLANK in mySentence, myNumWords must be incremented. If there is at least one BLANK in mySentence, segment I will have
an infinite loop, since k = temp.find(BLANK) will find the index of the first
BLANK and k will never equal npos. Recall that the apstring member function
find returns npos if its char or apstring parameter does not occur in the
current string. Segment II locates *all* the BLANKs in mySentence by replacing
temp with the substring that consists of the piece of mySentence directly following the most recently located BLANK. Segment III examines each character
in mySentence and increments myNumWords whenever a BLANK is found.

23. (**A**) Note that choice A is a sufficient condition for equality: myNumWords will
automatically equal rhs.myNumWords if their sentence strings are identical.
Choice C is *not* a sufficient condition for equality even though the syntax is
correct. Choice B is wrong because *this refers to the entire current object,
whereas rhs.mySentence refers to just one attribute of rhs. Choice D is wrong
because lhs is understood but not explicitly defined. Choice E is wrong because *this is never used to refer to a parameter of a member function; it
refers to the current object of the function.

24. (**C**) The problem with this function is that there is no statement or piece of code
that will reverse the *characters* of the sentence. Suppose that the parameter is
Nachos cause heartburn. (which is not a palindrome).

```
temp = temp.LowerCase();  → nachos cause heartburn.
temp = temp.StripPunctuation();  → nachos cause heartburn
temp = temp.RemoveBlanks();  → nachoscauseheartburn
Sentence rev = temp.ReverseWords();  → rev=nachoscauseheartburn
                               (only one word, so no reversing to do) return
temp.equal(rev);  → will always return true
```

25. (**B**) An inorder traversal of a binary search tree produces the elements in sorted
increasing order. (Recall that the leftmost leaf of the binary search tree is the
smallest element in the tree and that this is the first element visited.)

26. **(D)** The best case run time occurs when the binary search tree produced is balanced. This means that for each of the N items in A no more than $\log_2 N$ comparisons will need to be made to find its insertion point. Thus, the run time is $O(N \log N)$. Printing the elements is $O(N)$, which is less than $O(N \log N)$. Thus, the overall run time is $O(N \log N)$.

27. **(C)** Any kind of sorted array leads to worst case behavior for insertion into a binary search tree. The tree obtained is completely unbalanced, with a long chain of left links or right links. Run time of insertion becomes $O(N^2)$ (see the section on creating a binary search tree in Chapter 10). Choice III is thus the most likely of the three choices to lead to a balanced tree and best case behavior.

28. **(C)** Function Mystery is a recursive version of selection sort. It finds the largest element in the n-element array and swaps it with the last element. Then it recursively repeats the procedure with the first $n-1$ elements. The array is thus sorted in ascending order.

29. **(C)** The expression x == y may give the wrong answer because of round-off error in calculating with and storing real numbers, but it cannot cause a run-time error. Each of the other choices has the potential for a run-time error. For choice A, a[i] may be out of range. For choice B, p->info may dereference a null pointer. For choice D, i/j may cause a division by zero, as can k % m in choice E.

30. **(A)** For the given algorithm, copying of elements is done only when necessary. Each time a copy is made, the sum of all copies so far is roughly double the length of the copy to be made at that stage. Since the final list to be copied is at most of length n, the total number of copies is at most $2n$, which is $O(n)$. For example, try this with $n = 8$:

   - Before final copy is made, list length $= 4$
   - Total number of copies so far is $1 + 2 + 4 = 7 \approx (2)(4)$
   - After final copy is made, total number of copies is $1 + 2 + 4 + 8 = 15$, which is less than 16, which is $2n$. (See Chapter 4, Question 17.)

31. **(D)** Recall that the run-time efficiency of the iterative version of this algorithm is $O(\log n)$. Even though the two recursive calls in the recursive version suggest that this version may have exponential run time, note that for each split of the array at most *one* recursive call is made. Thus, in the worst case, the number of recursive calls depends solely on the number of times the array must be split before there is just one element remaining to be examined (i.e., $\log_2 n$ times).

    Note that, for each recursive call, memory must be allocated for the local variables in that call. Since there may be $\log_2 n$ recursive calls (worst case), the space requirements are $O(\log n)$. By contrast, the iterative version of binary search does not require additional space.

32. **(D)** Note that, after each iteration of the loop, a[0], a[1], ... a[i-1] are all nonzero. Since i is incremented at the end of the loop, we cannot make an assertion about a[i]. So reject choices C and E, which include j equal to i. Choice A is wrong because i could be greater than max on the final exit from the loop. Choice B cannot be correct because if a[j] were equal to 0 for any value of j the test would fail and the loop would not be executed.

33. **(E)** Although the given expression is always algebraically true for nonzero x, the expression may evaluate to false. This could occur because of round-off error in performing the division and multiplication operations. Whether the right-hand side of the expression evaluates to exactly 3.0 depends on the value of x. Note that if x is zero, the expression will not be evaluated because of a run-time crash.

34. **(D)** This function recursively eliminates duplicates from the list. Note that if the first recursive call is made with list->next as parameter instead of list, duplicate values that occur more than twice will remain as duplicates in the list.

35. **(B)** The purpose of this function is to create a rational number that is the result of adding its two Rational parameters. The first two statements in the implementation find the numerator and denominator of the sum. These must then be used to construct the Rational number that will be returned by the function. Choice B correctly does this, using the appropriate constructor of the Rational class. *The only way for a non-member function to create a class object is with one of the constructors.* This requirement eliminates all the other answer choices. Note that *this should be used only in the implementation of member functions, which immediately eliminates choices C and D.

36. **(D)** The Environment class creates the fishList in its AllFish function. The Show and Step functions in the Display and Simulation classes, respectively, are the only functions that use this list.

37. **(E)** The Show function gets a list of current fish and displays each fish in the list. The fact that some fish have disappeared from the scene doesn't alter this process in any way. At least one change must be made in each of the other choices.

38. **(E)** This statement replaces the (old) fish in newLoc with the parameter fish, which was required. Note that the "eaten" fish automatically gets overwritten by the moving fish of the function's parameter (if there was in fact an actual, defined fish there). Choices A and B are correct since the action of these classes is not affected in any way by the described change. Choice C is correct—since there are exactly four slots, a range of four random integers is required to select one. Choice D is correct because that test will always be true: the fish was required to move!

39. **(B)** For each step in the simulation, all N fish move (or attempt to move). Processing each fish takes a number of operations independent of N or M (i.e., $O(1)$). Since there are M steps the algorithm is $O(NM)$.

40. **(D)** Implementation I allows direct access to the private variables of a fish during the Move function. In extended versions of the program, one could imagine fish possibly aging, dying, reproducing, and so on during a Move. If this function were in the Environment class, it would be difficult to change the attributes of a fish. Thus, choice D is false.

    Note that if the Environment class controlled the movement of fish, the myWorlds grid could be automatically updated during the move. As it is in the current implementation, a fish needs to keep track of where it moved so that it can pass the information to the environment in the Update function. Thus, choices A and B are both true. Choice C is true—the Neighborhood object could be used in the same way for Implementation II as for Implementation I. Choice E is true because `EmptyNeighbors` and `AddIfEmpty` are used only to assist in the `Move`.

Section II

1. (a)
```
template <class T>
bool Set<T> :: isEmpty()
{
    return myElements.ListLength() == 0;
}
```

(b)
```
template <class T>
bool Set<T> :: includes(const T & item) const
{
    return myElements.index_of(item) != -1;
}
```

(c)
```
template <class T>
Set<T> Set<T> :: operator*(const Set<T> & s)
{
    Set<T> temp(s);         //make copy of parameter s
    Set<T> intersection;    //intersection initially empty
    T element;
    for (int i=1; i<=s.SetSize(); i++)
    {
        element = temp.myElements.DeleteFirst();
        if (includes(element)) //if element in current set
            intersection.Add(element);
    }
    return intersection;
}
```

Alternatively,
```
template <class T>
Set<T> Set<T> :: operator*(const Set<T> & s)
{
    Set<T> temp(*this);  //make copy of current set object
    Set<T> intersection; //intersection initially empty
    T element;
    for (int i=1; i<SetSize(); i++)
    {
        element = temp.myElements.DeleteFirst();
        if (s.includes(element))
            intersection.Add(element);
    }
    return intersection;
}
```

NOTE

1. To access any of the Set member functions, use the Set variable name and the dot construct. For example, for the Set parameter S in part (c),

   ```
   s.includes(element);
   ```

   If the current Set object accesses a Set member function, don't use the dot construct, just the function name. For example, in the first version of part (c),

   ```
   if(includes(element))
   ```

   tests whether element is in the current Set object.

2. To access the SortedCollection member functions, use the private data member of the Set class, myElements, together with the dot construct. For example,

   ```
   temp.myElements.DeleteFirst()
   ```

3. The return statement in part (a) could have been

   ```
   return SetSize() == 0;
   ```

   since SetSize() is a member function of the Set class and the set being tested is the current object. When myElements is used, the ListLength() function is a SortedCollection member function.

4. In part (b) myElements *must* be used since index_of is a member function of the SortedCollection class, not the Set class.

5. To examine each element of one of the sets, you must repeatedly use the DeleteFirst() member function of the SortedCollection class.

6. In part (c), repeated use of DeleteFirst() alters the set whose elements are being examined. This is the reason for first copying one of the sets into temp. The current object should not be changed, nor should the const reference parameter.

7. The first version of part (c) makes a copy of the parameter in temp, strips off each element of temp, and checks to see if that element is in the current set. The second version copies the current set object into temp and checks to see if each element of temp is in the parameter set s.

8. For part (c), you should not use the Remove function of the Set class because the elements of the current set are unknown. Remove should be used only if its parameter is a known item of the set.

2. (a)
```
void InsertCourse(const apstring & cName, int per,
        Teacher someTeacher)
{
    Course *q = someTeacher.courseList;
    if (q == NULL || per < q->period)
        someTeacher.courseList = new Course(cName, per, q);
    else        //find insertion point
    {
        while (q->next != NULL && per > q->next->period)
            q = q->next;
        q->next = new Course(cName, per, q->next);
    }
}
```

(b)
```
bool TeachesThisPeriod(const Teacher & someTeacher, int per)
{
    Course *q = someTeacher.courseList;
    while (q != NULL && q->period != per)
        q = q->next;
    return q != NULL;
}
```

(c)
```
void PrintHeaviestPeriods(const apvector<Teacher>
        & teacherList)
{
    apvector<int> perCount(10,0);
    for (int k=0; k<teacherList.length(); k++)
        for (int p=1; p<=9; p++)
            if (TeachesThisPeriod(teacherList[k], p))
                perCount[p]++;
    //now find highest usage count in perCount array
    int max = perCount[1];
    for (int p=2; p<=9; p++)
        if (max < perCount[p])
            max = perCount[p];
    //print each period that has highest usage count
    for (int p=1; p<=9; p++)
        if (max == perCount[p])
            cout << p << endl;
}
```

NOTE

1. In part (a), the first test checks whether the new node must be inserted at the front of the list. If the `q == NULL` part is true, the whole boolean expression will be true and the test will be short-circuited. This is important: if q is NULL, `q->period` will cause a run-time error.
2. The `else` segment in part (a) must not allow q to go too far—if it does you will not be able to connect the list to the new node. This is the reason for testing `q->next` rather than q.
3. In part (b), q will eventually become NULL if and only if the given period per is not in someTeacher's course list. In this case, false must be returned.

4. In part (b), beware of the statement

```
return q->period != per;
```

If q is NULL, it will cause a run-time error.

5. In part (c), perCount[1] is the number of courses taught in period 1, perCount[2] is the number of courses taught in period 2, and so on. perCount[0] is not used—this is why the array has ten slots.

6. Notice that the fillvalue parameter of the apvector class constructor is used to initialize all the counts to 0.

3. (a)
```
TreeNode *FindMin(TreeNode *T)
{
    if (T != NULL)
        while(T->left != NULL)
            T = T->left;
    return T;
}
```

(b)
```
void RemoveMin(TreeNode * & T)
//iterative solution
{
    if (T != NULL)
    {
        TreeNode *temp = FindMin(T);
        if (T == temp)  //smallest value is in root node
            T = T->right;
        else
        {
            TreeNode *q = T;
            while (q->left != temp)
                q = q->left;
            q->left = temp->right;
        }
        delete temp;
    }
}
```

Alternatively,

```
void RemoveMin(TreeNode * & T)
//recursive solution
{
    if (T != NULL)
    {
        if (T->left != NULL)
            RemoveMin(T->left);
        else
        {
            TreeNode *temp = T;
            T = T->right;
            delete temp;
        }
    }
}
```

```
(c) void Remove(int value, TreeNode * & T)
    {
        if (T != NULL)
        {
            if (value < T->info)
                Remove(value, T->left);
            else if (value > T->info)
                Remove(value, T->right);
            else        //T points to node that must be removed
            {
                TreeNode *temp;
                if (T->left != NULL && T->right != NULL)
                //2 children
                {
                    temp = FindMin(T->right);
                    T->info = temp->info;
                    RemoveMin(T->right);
                }
                else        //1 or 0 children
                {
                    temp = T;
                    if (T->left != NULL)
                        T = T->left;
                    else
                        T = T->right;
                    delete temp;
                }
            }
        }
    }
```

NOTE

1. In part (a), the binary search tree ordering property guarantees that the smallest value will be in the leftmost node.
2. In part (b), don't forget to take care of the case where the smallest value is in the root.
3. In part (b), the iterative algorithm needs to have a pointer to the parent of the node to be deleted. This allows the pointer connections to be made that will bypass the node to be deleted. In the recursive algorithm, it may appear that the tree becomes disconnected. Not true! Since T is passed by reference, the recursion stack keeps track of the parent pointers.
4. In part (c), you are given the algorithm—just follow it!

4. Changes are highlighted in bold.

(a)
```
Neighborhood::Neighborhood()
    : myList(NULL), myCount(0) {}
```

(b)
```
Position Neighborhood::Select(int count) const
{
    ListNode *p = myList;
    for (int k=0; k<count; k++)
        p = p->next;
    return p->posInfo;
}
```

(c)
```
apstring Neighborhood::ToString() const
{
    apstring s = "Neighborhood: ";
    ListNode *p = myList;
    int k;
    for (k=0; k<myCount; k++)
    {
        s += p->posInfo.ToString() + " ";
        p = p->next;
    }
    return s;
}
```

(d)
```
void Neighborhood::Add(const Position & pos)
{
    if (myCount < MAXLISTLENGTH)
    {
        DebugPrint(5, "Adding" + pos.ToString) +
            "to neighborhood.");
        myList = new ListNode(pos, myList);
        myCount++;
    }
    else
    {
        DebugPrint(5, "Neighborhood had no room for "
                + pos.ToString());
    }
}
```

NOTE   In part (b), the parameter is the random integer used to select a position. It was determined in the Move function of the Fish class. When the Neighborhood data structure is an apvector, this random integer is simply used as the index of the vector. For a linear linked list data structure, it's more complicated—the parameter becomes the number of moves for a temporary pointer in the linked list before returning the position in the current node.

APPENDIX A
Glossary of Useful Computer Terms

I hate definitions.
—*Benjamin Disraeli,* Vivian Grey *(1826)*

Bit: From "binary digit." Smallest unit of computer memory, taking on only two values, 0 or 1.

Byte: Eight bits. Similarly, megabyte (Mb, 10^6 bytes) and gigabyte (Gb, 10^9 bytes).

Cache: A small amount of "fast" memory for the storage of data. Typically, the most recently accessed data from disk storage or "slow" memory is saved in the main memory cache to save time if it's retrieved again.

Compiler: A program that translates source code into object code (machine language).

CPU: The central processing unit (computer's brain). It controls the interpretation and execution of instructions. It consists of the arithmetic/logic unit, the control unit, and some memory, usually called "on-board memory" or cache memory. Physically, the CPU consists of millions of microscopic transistors on a chip.

Debugger: A program that helps find errors by tracing the values of variables in a program.

Firmware: Programs that are embedded in ROM, for example, the instructions that control basic arithmetic operations.

GUI: Graphical user interface.

Hardware: The physical components of computers. These are the ones you can touch, for example, the keyboard, monitor, printer, CPU chip.

Hertz (Hz): One cycle per second. It refers to the speed of the computer's internal clock and gives a measure of the CPU speed. Similarly, Megahertz (MHz, 10^6 Hz) and Gigahertz (GHz, 10^9 Hz).

Hexadecimal number system: Base 16.

High-level language: A human-readable programming language that enables instructions that require many machine steps to be coded concisely, for example, C++, Pascal, BASIC, FORTRAN.

Linker: A program that links together the different modules of a program into a single executable program after they have been compiled into object code.

Low-level language: Assembly language. This is a human-readable version of machine language, where each machine instruction is coded as one statement. It is translated into machine language by a program called an assembler. Each different kind of CPU has its own assembly language.

Mainframe computer: A large computer, typically used by large institutions, such as government agencies and big businesses.

Microcomputer: Personal computer.

Minicomputer: Small mainframe.

Modem: A device that connects a computer to a phone line or TV cable.

Network: Several computers linked together so that they can communicate with each other and share resources.

Object code: Machine language. Produced by compiling source code.

Operating system: A program that controls access to and manipulation of the various files and programs on the computer such as DOS, Windows, and UNIX.

Primary memory: RAM. This gets erased when you turn off your computer.

RAM: Random Access Memory. This stores the current program and the software to run it.

ROM: Read Only Memory. This is permanent and nonerasable. It contains, for example, programs that boot up the operating system and check various components of the hardware. In particular, ROM contains the BIOS (Basic Input Output System)— a program that handles low-level communication with the keyboard, disk drives, and so on.

Secondary memory: Hard drive, disk, magnetic tapes, CD-ROM, and so on.

Software: Computer programs written in some computer language and executed on the hardware after conversion to machine language. If you can install it on your hard drive, it's software (e.g., programs, spreadsheets, word processors).

Source code: A program in a high-level language like C++, Pascal, or FORTRAN.

Transistor: Microscopic semiconductor device that can serve as an on-off switch.

Workstation: Desktop computer that is faster and more powerful than a microcomputer.

APPENDIX B
The ASCII Table

0	NUL (null)	32	SPACE	64	@	96	`
1	SOH (start of heading)	33	!	65	A	97	a
2	STX (start of text)	34	"	66	B	98	b
3	ETX (end of text)	35	#	67	C	99	c
4	EOT (end of transmission)	36	$	68	D	100	d
5	ENQ (enquiry)	37	%	69	E	101	e
6	ACK (acknowledge)	38	&	70	F	102	f
7	BEL (bell)	39	'	71	G	103	g
8	BS (backspace)	40	(	72	H	104	h
9	TAB (horizontal tab)	41	)	73	I	105	i
10	LF (line feed)	42	*	74	J	106	j
11	VT (vertical tab)	43	+	75	K	107	k
12	FF (form feed)	44	,	76	L	108	l
13	CR (carriage return)	45	−	77	M	109	m
14	SO (shift out)	46	.	78	N	110	n
15	SI (shift in)	47	/	79	O	111	o
16	DLE (data link escape)	48	0	80	P	112	p
17	DC1 (device control 1)	49	1	81	Q	113	q
18	DC2 (device control 2)	50	2	82	R	114	r
19	DC3 (device control 3)	51	3	83	S	115	s
20	DC4 (device control 4)	52	4	84	T	116	t
21	NAK (negative acknowledge)	53	5	85	U	117	u
22	SYN (synchronous idle)	54	6	86	V	118	v
23	ETB (end of trans. block)	55	7	87	W	119	w
24	CAN (cancel)	56	8	88	X	120	x
25	EM (end of medium)	57	9	89	Y	121	y
26	SUB (substitute)	58	:	90	Z	122	z
27	ESC (escape)	59	;	91	[	123	{
28	FS (file separator)	60	<	92	\	124		
29	GS (group separator)	61	=	93	]	125	}
30	RS (record separator)	62	>	94	^	126	~
31	US (unit separator)	63	?	95	_	127	DEL

APPENDIX C

Pointer Implementation of Stacks and Queues

apLLstack.h

```cpp
#ifndef _APLLSTACK_H
#define _APLLSTACK_H

// ********************************************************************
// File apLLstack.h
// APCS stack class  Pointer implementation
// ********************************************************************

template <class itemType>
class apLLstack
{
  public:

  // constructors/destructor

    apLLstack( );                               // construct empty stack
    apLLstack( const apLLstack & s );           // copy constructor
    ~apLLstack( );                              // destructor

  // assignment

    const apLLstack & operator = ( const apLLstack & rhs );

  // accessors

    const itemType & top( ) const; // return top element (NO pop)
    bool   isEmpty( )        const; // return true if empty, else false
    int    length( )        const; // return number of elements in stack

  // modifiers

    void push( const itemType & item );   // push item onto top of stack
    void pop( );                          // pop top element
    void pop( itemType & item );   // pop top element and return in item
    void makeEmpty( );            // make stack empty (no elements)
```

```
    private:
        int size;
        struct stackNode  // Nodes for storage of stack elements
        {
                itemType info;
                stackNode *next;
                stackNode():next(NULL) {}
                stackNode(const itemType &item, stackNode * n = NULL)
                                :info(item), next(n) {}
        };
        stackNode * stackPtr; // External pointer to stack

      void copy(stackNode * &newList, stackNode * oldList);
      // copies oldList into newList
};
  //
********************************************************************
  //
  // Specifications for stack functions
  //
  // Any violation of a function's precondition will result in an error
  // message followed by a call to abort.
  //
  //
  // constructors/destructor
  //
  //  apLLstack( )
  //    postcondition: the stack is empty
  //
  //  apLLstack( const apLLstack & s )
  //    postcondition: stack is a copy of s
  //
  //  ~apLLstack( )
  //    postcondition: stack is destroyed
  //
  // assignment
  //
  //  const apLLstack & operator = ( const apLLstack & rhs )
  //    postcondition: normal assignment via copying has been performed
  //
  // accessors
  //
  //  const itemType & top( ) const
  //    precondition: stack is [e1, e2, ..., en] with n >= 1
  //    postcondition: returns en
  //
  //  bool isEmpty( ) const
  //     postcondition: returns true if stack is empty, false otherwise
```

```
//
//  int length( ) const
//      postcondition: returns # of elements currently in stack
//
// modifiers
//
//  void push( const itemType & item )
//      precondition: stack is [e1, e2, ..., en] with  n >= 0
//      postcondition: stack is [e1, e2, ..., en, item]
//
//  void pop( )
//      precondition: stack is [e1, e2, ..., en] with n >= 1
//      postcondition: stack is [e1, e2, ..., e(n-1)]
//
//
//  void pop(itemType & item )
//      precondition: stack is [e1,e2, ..., en] with n >= 1
//      postcondition: stack is [e1,e2, ..., e(n-1)] and item == en
//
//  void makeEmpty( )
//      postcondition:  stack is empty
//
//  Examples of variable definition
//
//    apLLstack<int> istack;       // creates empty stack of integers
//    apLLstack<double> dstack;    // creates empty stack of doubles
//

#include "apLLstack.cpp"

#endif
```

apLLstack.cpp

```cpp
// *****************************************************************
//  File apLLstack.cpp
//  APCS stack class  IMPLEMENTATION
//
//  stack implemented using a linear linked list
// *****************************************************************

#include "apLLstack.h"
#include <stdlib.h>

template <class itemType>
apLLstack<itemType>::apLLstack( )
  : size(0), stackPtr(NULL)
// postcondition: the stack is empty
{}

template <class itemType>
apLLstack<itemType>::apLLstack(const apLLstack<itemType> & s)
// postcondition: stack is a copy of s
{
  size = s.size;
  copy(stackPtr, s.stackPtr);
}

template <class itemType>
apLLstack<itemType>::~apLLstack()
// postcondition: stack is destroyed
{
  makeEmpty();
}

template <class itemType>
const apLLstack<itemType> &
apLLstack<itemType>::operator = (const apLLstack<itemType> & rhs)
// postcondition: normal assignment via copying has been performed
{
  if (this != &rhs)
  {
    makeEmpty();
    size = rhs.size;
    copy(stackPtr, rhs.stackPtr);
  }
  return *this;
}

template <class itemType>
```

```
bool
apLLstack<itemType>::isEmpty() const
// postcondition: returns true if stack is empty, false otherwise
{
  return stackPtr == NULL;
}


template <class itemType>
int
apLLstack<itemType>::length() const
// postcondition: returns # of elements currently in stack
{
  return size;
}


template <class itemType>
void
apLLstack<itemType>::push(const itemType & item)
// precondition: stack is [e1, e2, ..., en] with  n >= 0
// postcondition: stack is [e1, e2, ...,  en, item]
{
    stackPtr = new stackNode(item, stackPtr);
    size++;
}


template <class itemType>
void
apLLstack<itemType>::pop()
// precondition: stack is [e1,e2,..., en] with n >= 1
// postcondition: stack is [e1,e2,..., e(n-1)]
{
  if (isEmpty())
  {
    cerr << "error, popping an empty stack" << endl;
    abort();
  }
  stackNode * p = stackPtr;
  stackPtr = stackPtr->next;
  delete p;
  size--;
}


template <class itemType>
void
apLLstack<itemType>::pop(itemType & item)
// precondition: stack is [e1,e2,..., en] with n >= 1
// postcondition: stack is [e1,e2,..., e(n-1)] and item == en
{
```

```
  if (isEmpty())
  {
    cerr << "error, popping an empty stack" << endl;
    abort();
  }
  item = stackPtr->info;
  stackNode * p = stackPtr;
  stackPtr = stackPtr->next;
  delete p;
  size--;
}


template <class itemType>
const itemType &
apLLstack<itemType>::top() const
// precondition: stack is [e1, e2, ..., en] with n >= 1
// postcondition: returns en
{
  if (isEmpty())
  {
    cerr << "error, accessing top of an empty stack" << endl;
    abort();
  }
  return stackPtr->info;
}


template <class itemType>
void
apLLstack<itemType>::makeEmpty()
// postcondition:  stack is empty
{
  stackNode * curr = stackPtr;
  while (stackPtr != NULL)
  {
    stackPtr = stackPtr->next;
    delete curr;
    curr = stackPtr;
  }
  size = 0;
}


template <class itemType>
void apLLstack<itemType>::copy(stackNode * & newList,
                               stackNode * oldList)
// precondition:  newList is empty
// postcondition: newList points to list that is identical to oldList
{
  if (oldList == NULL)
```

```
    newList = NULL;
  else
  {
    newList = new stackNode(oldList->info, NULL);
    stackNode *temp = oldList->next;
    stackNode *curr = newList;
    while(temp != NULL)
    {
      curr->next = new stackNode(temp->info, NULL);
      curr = curr->next;
      temp = temp->next;
    }
  }
}
```

apLLqueue.h

```
#ifndef _APLLQUEUE_H
#define _APLLQUEUE_H
// *******************************************************************
// File apLLqueue.h
// APCS queue class. Implemented with a linear linked list.
// *******************************************************************

template <class itemType>
class apLLqueue
{
  public:
  // constructors/destructor

    apLLqueue( );                             // construct empty queue
    apLLqueue( const apLLqueue & q );         // copy constructor
    ~apLLqueue( );                            // destructor

  // assignment

    const apLLqueue & operator = ( const apLLqueue & rhs );

  // accessors

    const itemType & front( )   const;      // return front (no dequeue)
    bool        isEmpty( ) const;  // return true if empty else false
    int         length( )  const;  // return number of elements in queue
```

```
// modifiers

    void enqueue( const itemType & item );   // insert item (at rear)
    void dequeue( );                          // remove first element
    void dequeue( itemType & item );          // combine front and dequeue
    void makeEmpty( );                        // make queue empty

  private:
    int mySize;              // # of elements currently in queue
    struct queueNode         // Nodes for storage of queue elements
    {
      itemType info;
      queueNode * next;
      queueNode():next(NULL) {}
      queueNode(const itemType & item, queueNode * n = NULL)
      :info(item), next(n) {}
    };
    queueNode * myFront;     // External pointer to front of queue
    queueNode * myBack;      // External pointer to rear of queue

    void copy(queueNode * &newFront,
              queueNode * &newBack, queueNode * oldFront);
    // newFront points to list that is identical to oldFront
    // and newBack points to last node of newFront list
};

// ******************************************************************
// Specifications for queue functions
//
// Any violation of a function's precondition will result in an error
// message followed by a call to abort.
//
// constructors/destructor
//
//  apLLqueue( )
//     postcondition: the queue is empty
//
//  apLLqueue( const apLLqueue & q )
//     postcondition: queue is a copy of q
//
//  ~apLLqueue( )
//     postcondition: queue is destroyed
//
// assignment
//
//  const apLLqueue & operator = ( const apLLqueue & rhs )
//     postcondition: normal assignment via copying has been performed
//
```

```
// accessors
//
//  const itemType & front( ) const
//     precondition: queue is [e1, e2, ..., en] with n >= 1
//     postcondition: returns e1
//
//  bool isEmpty( ) const
//     postcondition: returns true if queue is empty, false otherwise
//
//  int length( ) const
//     precondition: queue is [e1, e2, ..., en] with n >= 0
//     postcondition:  returns n
//
// modifiers:
//
//  void enqueue( const itemType & item )
//     precondition: queue is [e1, e2, ..., en] with n >= 0
//     postcondition: queue is [e1, e2, ..., en, item]
//
//  void dequeue( )
//     precondition: queue is [e1, e2, ..., en] with n >= 1
//     postcondition: queue is [e2, ..., en]
//
//  void dequeue( itemType & item )
//     precondition: queue is [e1, e2, ..., en] with n >= 1
//     postcondition:  queue is [e2, ..., en] and item == e1
//
//  void makeEmpty( )
//     postcondition: queue is empty
//
// Examples for use:
//
//    apLLqueue<int> iqueue;           // creates empty queue of integers
//    apLLqueue<double> dqueue         // creates empty queue of doubles

#include "apLLqueue.cpp"

#endif
```

apLLqueue.cpp

```cpp
// *********************************************************************
//  File apLLqueue.cpp
//  APCS queue class using linked lists.    IMPLEMENTATION
// *********************************************************************

#include "apLLqueue.h"
#include <stdlib.h>

template <class itemType>
apLLqueue<itemType>::apLLqueue()
    : mySize(0),
      myFront(NULL),
      myBack(NULL)
// postcondition: the queue is empty
{
}


template <class itemType>
apLLqueue<itemType>::apLLqueue(const apLLqueue<itemType> & q)
:  mySize(q.mySize)
// postcondition: queue is a copy of q
{
  copy(myFront, myBack, q.myFront);
}


template <class itemType>
apLLqueue<itemType>::~apLLqueue()
// postcondition: queue is destroyed
{
  makeEmpty();
}


template <class itemType>
const apLLqueue<itemType> &
apLLqueue<itemType>::operator = (const apLLqueue<itemType> & rhs)
// postcondition: normal assignment via copying has been performed
{
  if( this != &rhs)
  {
    makeEmpty();
    mySize = rhs.mySize;
    copy(myFront, myBack, rhs.myFront);
  }
  return *this;
}
```

```
template <class itemType>
const itemType &
apLLqueue<itemType>::front() const
// precondition: queue is [e1, e2, ..., en] with n >= 1
// postcondition: returns e1
{
  return myFront->info;
}


template <class itemType>
bool
apLLqueue<itemType>::isEmpty() const
// postcondition: returns true if queue is empty, false otherwise
{
  return myFront == NULL;
}


template <class itemType>
int
apLLqueue<itemType>::length() const
// precondition: queue is [e1, e2, ..., en] with n >= 0
// postcondition:  returns n
{
  return mySize;
}



template <class itemType>
void
apLLqueue<itemType>::enqueue(const itemType & item)
// precondition: queue is [e1, e2, ..., en] with n >= 0
// postcondition: queue is [e1, e2, ..., en, item]
{
  if (isEmpty())
  {
    mySize++;
    myBack = myFront = new queueNode(item, NULL);
  }
  else                      // add element at back of queue
  {
    myBack = myBack->next = new queueNode(item, NULL);
    mySize++;
  }
}


template <class itemType>
void
apLLqueue<itemType>::dequeue()
```

```
// precondition: queue is [e1, e2, ..., en] with n >= 1
// postconditions:  queue is [e2, ..., en] and item == e1
{
  if (isEmpty())
  {
    cerr << "dequeue from empty queue" << endl;
    abort();
  }
  queueNode *p = myFront;
  myFront = myFront->next;
  delete p;
  if (myFront == NULL)  //there was just 1 element in queue
      myBack = NULL;

  mySize--;              // one fewer element
}


template <class itemType>
void
apLLqueue<itemType>::dequeue(itemType & item)
// precondition: queue is [e1, e2, ..., en] with n >= 1
// postcondition:  queue is [e2, ..., en] and item == e1
{
  if (isEmpty())
  {
    cerr << "dequeue from empty queue" << endl;
    abort();
  }
  item = myFront->info;
  queueNode * p = myFront;
  myFront = myFront->next;
  delete p;
  if (myFront == NULL)  //there was just 1 element in queue
      myBack = NULL;

  mySize--;                        // one fewer element
}

template <class itemType>
void
apLLqueue<itemType>::makeEmpty()
// postcondition: queue is empty
{
  queueNode * curr = myFront;
  while(myFront != NULL){
    myFront = myFront->next;
    delete curr;
```

```
    curr = myFront;
  }
  myBack = NULL;
  mySize = 0;
}


template <class itemType>
void apLLqueue<itemType>::copy(queueNode * &newFront,
                          queueNode * &newBack, queueNode * oldFront)

// postcondition: newFront points to list that is identical to oldFront
// and newBack points to last node of newFront list
{
  if (oldFront == NULL)
    newFront = newBack = NULL;
  else
  {
    newFront = new queueNode(oldFront->info, NULL);
    queueNode *temp = oldFront->next;
    queueNode *curr = newFront;
    while(temp!= NULL)
    {
      curr->next = new queueNode(temp->info, NULL);
      curr = curr->next;
      temp = temp->next;
    }
    newBack = curr;
  }
}
```

Index

THERE'S ONLY ONE PLACE TO TURN FOR TOP SCORES...

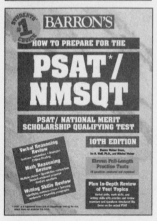

SAT I
How to Prepare for SAT I, 21st Ed., *$14.95, Canada $21.00*
Math Workbook for SAT I, 2nd Ed., *$13.95, Canada $19.50*
Verbal Workbook, SAT I, 10th Ed., *$12.95, Canada $17.95*
Pass Key to SAT I, 4th Ed., *$8.95, Canada $12.50*

Hot Words for SAT I
$8.95, Canada $12.50

Advanced Placement Examinations in:
Biology, 6th Ed., *$14.95, Canada $21.00*
Calculus, 7th Ed., *$16.95, Canada $23.95*
Chemistry, 2nd Ed., *$16.95, Canada $23.95*
Computer Science, *$14.95, Canada $21.00*
English, 7th Ed., *$14.95, Canada $21.00*
European History, 2nd Ed., *$14.95 Canada $21.00*
French, (Book & Cassettes), *$24.95, Canada $32.50*
Macroeconomics/Microeconomics, *$14.95, Canada $21.00*
Physics B, 2nd Ed., *$14.95, Canada $19.95*
Physics C, *$16.95, Canada $23.95*
Psychology, *$16.95, Canada $23.95*
Spanish, 3rd, (Book & CDs), *$24.95, Canada $34.95*
Statistics, *$14.95, Canada $21.00*
United States Government & Politics, 2rd, *$16.95, Canada $23.95*
United States History, 6th Ed., *$14.95, Canada $21.00*
World History, *$16.95, Canada $23.95*

PSAT/NMSQT (Preliminary Scholastic Aptitude Test/National Merit Scholarship Qualifying Test)
How to Prepare for the PSAT/NMSQT, 10th Ed., *$13.95, Canada $18.95*
Pass Key to the PSAT/NMSQT, *$7.95, Canada $10.50*

ACT (American College Testing Program Assessment)
How to Prepare for the ACT, 12th Ed., *$14.95, Canada $21.00*
Pass Key to the ACT, 4th Ed., *$8.95, Canada $12.50*

SAT II (Subject Tests) in:
American History and Social Studies, 10th Ed., *$14.95, Canada $21.00*
Biology, 13th Ed., *$14.95, Canada $21.00*
Chemistry, 7th Ed., *$14.95, Canada $21.00*
French, 7th Ed., (Book & CD), *$19.95, Canada $27.95*
Literature, 2nd Ed., *$13.95, Canada $19.50*
Mathematics IC, 8th Ed., *$13.95, Canada $19.50*
Mathematics IIC, 6th Ed., *$13.95, Canada $19.50*
Physics, 7th Ed., *$14.95, Canada $19.95*
Spanish, 9th Ed., (Book & CD), *$19.95, Canada $27.95*
World History, 2nd Ed., *$14.95, Canada $21.00*
Writing, 3rd Ed., *$13.95, Canada $19.50*

CLEP (College Level Exam Programs)
How to Prepare for the College Level Exam
Program, 8th Ed., (CLEP) *$14.95, Canada $19.95*

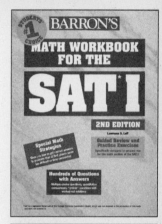

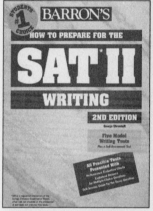

COMPUTER STUDY PROGRAMS AVAILABLE!

* **SAT I Book with Safari CD-ROM, $29.95, Canada $41.95**
* **SAT I Safari, CD-ROM, $24.95, Canada $32.50**
* **ACT Book w/CD-ROM, $29.95, Canada $41.95**

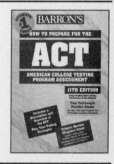

BARRON'S EDUCATIONAL SERIES, INC.
250 Wireless Boulevard
Hauppauge, NY 11788
In Canada: Georgetown Book Warehouse
34 Armstrong Avenue
Georgetown, Ontario L7G 4R9
www.barronseduc.com

Prices subject to change without notice. Books may be
purchased at your local bookstore, or by mail from Barron's.
Enclose check or money order for total amount plus sales tax
where applicable and 18% for postage and handling (minimum
charge $5.95). All books are paperback editions.

(#4) R 3/02

CHOOSING A COLLEGE

For every question you have,
Barron's guides have the right answers.

BARRON'S COLLEGE GUIDES
AMERICA'S #1 RESOURCE FOR EDUCATION PLANNING.

PROFILES OF AMERICAN COLLEGES, 25th Edition, w/CD-ROM

Compiled and Edited by the College Division of Barron's Educational Series, Inc. Today's number one college guide comes with computer software to help with forms and applications. Book includes profiles plus Barron's INDEX OF COLLEGE MAJORS! Vital information on majors, admissions, tuition, and more. *$26.95, Can. $37.95 (0-7641-7436-3)*

BARRON'S GUIDE TO THE MOST COMPETITIVE COLLEGES

Barron's latest and most innovative college guide describes and examines America's top 50 schools. What makes this guide unique is its special "insider" information about each school including commentaries on faculty, and more. *$16.95, Can. $23.95 (0-7641-1272-4)*

COMPACT GUIDE TO COLLEGES
Revised 13th Edition

A concise, fact-filled volume that presents all the essential facts about 400 of America's best-known, most popular schools. Admissions requirements, student body, faculty, campus environment, academic programs, and so much more are highlighted. *$9.95, Can. $13.95 (0-7641-1785-8)*

PROFILES OF AMERICAN COLLEGES REGIONAL EDITION: THE NORTHEAST, Revised 15th Edition

Comprehensive data specifically for students interested in schools in Connecticut, Delaware, D.C., Maine, Maryland, Massachusetts, New Hampshire, New Jersey, New York, Pennsylvania, Rhode Island, or Vermont. *$16.95, Can. $23.95 (0-7641-1786-6)*

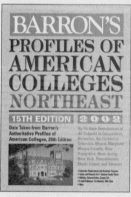

BARRON'S BEST BUYS IN COLLEGE EDUCATION, 7th Edition

Solorzano
Here are detailed descriptions—with tuitions and fees listed—of 300 of the finest colleges and universities in America judged on a value-for-your-dollar basis. *$18.95, Can. $26.50 (0-7641-2018-2)*

COMPLETE COLLEGE FINANCING GUIDE, 4th Edition

Dennis
This newly updated practical source book tells students and parents how, when, and where to apply for scholarships, grants, low-interest loans, and other financial aid. *$14.95, Can. $19.95 (0-8120-9523-5)*

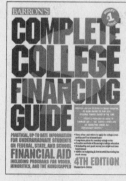

BARRON'S EDUCATIONAL SERIES, INC.
250 Wireless Blvd., Hauppauge, NY 11788
In Canada: Georgetown Book Warehouse
34 Armstrong Ave., Georgetown, Ont. L7G 4R9
$ = U.S. Dollars   Can.$ = Canadian Dollars

Prices subject to change without notice. Books may be purchased at your bookstore, or by mail from Barron's. Enclose check or money order for total amount plus 18% for postage and handling (minimum charge of $5.95). New York State residents add sales tax to total. All books are paperback editions.
Visit us at www.barronseduc.com

(#8) R 3/02

Success on Advanced Placement Tests Starts with Help from Barron's

Each May, thousands of college-bound students take one or more Advanced Placement Exams to earn college credits—and for many years, they've looked to Barron's, the leader in Advanced Placement test preparation. You can get Barron's user-friendly manuals for eleven different AP subjects. That includes two—in French and Spanish—that come with audiocassettes to improve your listening comprehension skills. Every Barron's AP manual gives you—

- • **Diagnostic tests**
- • **Extensive subject review**
- • **Full-length model AP exams**
- • **Study help and test-taking advice**

Model exams are designed to reflect the actual AP exams in question types, subject matter, length, and degree of difficulty. All questions come with answers and explanations. All books are paperback.

AP: Biology, 6th Ed.
0-7641-1375-5, 430 pp., $14.95, Can$21.00

AP: Calculus, 7th Ed.
0-7641-1790-4, 624 pp., $16.95, Can$23.95

AP: Chemistry, 2nd Ed.
0-7641-0474-8, 672 pp., $14.95, Can$19.95

AP: Computer Science
0-7641-0546-9, 600 pp., $14.95, Can$21.00

AP: English, 7th Ed.
0-7641-1230-9, 464 pp., $14.95, Can$21.00

AP: European History, 2nd Ed.
0-7641-0458-6, 240 pp., $13.95, Can$19.50

AP: French with Two Cassettes, 2nd Ed.
0-7641-7159-3, 450 pp.,
cassettes 90-min. each, $24.95, Can$32.50

AP: Macroeconomics/ Microeconomics
0-7641-1164-7, 496 pp., $14.95, Can$21.00

AP: Physics B, 2nd Ed.
0-7641-0475-6, 460 pp., $14.95, Can$19.95

AP: Physics C
0-7641-1802-1, 500 pp., $16.95, Can$23.95

AP: Psychology
0-7641-0959-6, 320 pp., $14.95, Can$21.00

AP: Spanish with Three CDs, 3rd Ed.
0-7641-7397-9, 480 pp., cassettes 90-min. each, $24.95, Can$34.95

AP: Statistics, 2nd Ed.
0-7641-1091-8, 432 pp., $14.95, Can$21.00

AP: U.S. Government and Politics, 3rd Ed.
0-7641-1651-7, 512 pp., $16.95, Can$23.95

AP: U.S. History, 6th Ed.
0-7641-1157-4, 336 pp., $14.95, Can$21.00

AP: World History
0-7641-1816-1, 512 pp., $16.95, Can$23.95

All prices are in U.S. and Canadian dollars and subject to change without notice. Order from your bookstore—or directly from Barron's by adding 18% for shipping and handling (minimum charge $5.95). New York State residents add sales tax to total after shipping and handling.

Barron's Educational Series, Inc.
250 Wireless Blvd.
Hauppauge, NY 11788
Call toll-free: 1-800-645-3476
Order by fax: 1-631-434-3217

Visit our website at:
www.barronseduc.com

In Canada:
Georgetown Book Warehouse
34 Armstrong Ave.
Georgetown, Ontario L7G 4R9
Canadian orders: 1-800-247-7160
Order by fax: 1-800-887-1594

(#93) R3/02